Issues and Approaches
in the
Psychological Therapies

Issues and Approaches in the Psychological Therapies

Edited by

D. Bannister

Head of the Psychology Department,
Bexley Hospital, Kent

JOHN WILEY & SONS

London · New York · Sydney · Toronto

Library of Congress Cataloging in Publication Data:

Bannister, Donald.
Issues and approaches in the psychological therapies.

1. Psychotherapy. I. Title. [DNLM: 1. Psychotherapy. WM420 B2193i]

RC480.B25   616.8'914   74–6996
ISBN 0 471 04740 6

Text set in 11/12pt. Photon Times,
printed by photolithography,
and bound in Great Britain at The Pitman Press, Bath

CONTRIBUTORS

D. BANNISTER
: *MRC External Scientific Staff, Bexley Hospital, Kent.*

P. T. BROWN
: *Staff Clinical Psychologist, Frederick Chusid & Co., London; Partners, Norris, Norris and Brown. Formerly Principal Clinical Psychologist, Central Hospital, Warwick.*

SIDNEY CROWN
: *Consultant Psychiatrist, The London Hospital.*

ALBERT ELLIS
: *Executive Director, Institute for Advanced Study in Rational Psychotherapy, New York, USA.*

CHRIS. KIERNAN
: *Senior Lecturer in Child Development, Thomas Coram Research Unit, University of London Institute of Education.*

A. W. LANDFIELD
: *Professor of Psychology, University of Nebraska, Nebraska, USA.*

GRAHAME LEMAN
: *Independent Management Consultant and writer.*

JOHN R. LICKORISH
: *Principal Psychologist, Institute of Family Psychiatry, Ipswich, Suffolk.*

ANDRÉE LIDDELL
: *Principal Lecturer, Department of Psychology, NE London Polytechnic.*

DAVID H. MALAN
: *Consultant Psychiatrist, Tavistock Clinic, London.*

VICTOR MEYER
: *Reader in Psychology, Academic Department of Psychiatry, Middlesex Hospital, London.*

JOSEPH F. RYCHLAK
: *Professor of Psychology, Purdue University, Indiana, USA.*

JAMES S. SIMKIN
: *Clinical Psychologist, Big Sur, California, USA.*

DAVID J. SMAIL
: *Principal Psychologist, Nottingham Area Psychological Services.*

DOROTHY STOCK WHITAKER
: *Professor of Social Work, University of York.*

ACKNOWLEDGEMENTS

THE editor gratefully acknowledges the assistance of the following publishers who have granted permission for the reproduction of extracted material quoted in the text, sources being given in the References at the end of each chapter:

Chandler Publishing Company, New York.
Harper & Row Publishers Inc., New York.
Houghton Mifflin Company, Boston.
Jason Aronson, Inc., New York.
Science & Behavior Books, Inc., Palo Alto, California.

PREFACE

This is essentially a summarizing book—the contributors have been asked to cover vast areas in small compass.

Under 'Issues' are three chapters dealing with the kinds of question which face every psychotherapist whatever his background or method. Thus the first three chapters are addressed to classic questions such as 'What is wrong with the client?' and 'What kind of situation exists between me (the therapist) and the client?' and 'What general social role am I undertaking when I act as a therapist?'. The authors of the later 'Approaches' section have been asked to bear these questions in mind in setting out their particular methods. The reader is invited to judge how far particular approaches surmounts or are impaled upon the various intellectual *cheveaux de frise* raised in the 'Issues' section.

The first three chapters of the 'Approaches' section deal with particular contexts for psychotherapeutic ventures—therapeutic communities, groups and the family—and demonstrate how particular strategies are developed to deal with what are essentially social situations.

Then come three chapters dealing with highly defined approaches to psychotherapy (personal construct theory psychotherapy, Gestalt psychotherapy and rational–emotive psychotherapy). These are followed by two chapters each on very broad lines of attack in the field—those stemming from psychoanalytic theory and from behavioural psychology. The final chapter sets out a particular approach as an answer to the problems raised by the very idea of a behavioural psychotherapy.

The authors were chosen for their commitment and enthusiasm, as well as for their knowledge and experience. It may be that any approach in psychotherapy which cannot arouse personal and professional passion will, by that token, fail.

The essential aim of the book is to enable you (in the hallowed words of the exam question) to *compare and contrast* varying arguments which are being conducted in the field of psychotherapy. Mayhap the book will provide just enough detail for you to react both to major values in the field and to particulars of method.

INTRODUCTION

The general attitude of psychologists towards psychotherapy can fairly be described as neurotic. It seems an ambivalent compound of hostility, carefully cultivated ignorance and excessive reverence. Consider three examples of the kind of confusion psychologists have manifested in relation to the theory and the practice of psychotherapy.

Some 22 years ago, on the basis of a muddled assembly of actuarial statistics, it was proposed that psychotherapy has no effect. Astonishingly enough, this proposition was seriously entertained and much debated. To this day it is bandied about like some precious piece of folk wisdom. Yet the proposition might well have been dismissed at the outset if its logic as a *general psychological statement* had been examined. Instead, it was treated as a statement of the specific kind 'aspirin does (or does not) cure headache'. Psychotherapy, whatever its style, is a form of human interaction and, however formalized, what is generally true of human interaction must be true of psychotherapy. Therefore, to argue that psychotherapy 'has no effect' is to argue that human interaction, your enmities, your love affairs, your long dialogue with your Uncle Fred, have no effect. No one seriously entertains the second proposition, but the first is still being solemnly considered. The seriousness with which it is treated is significantly seen in the recent analysis of outcome in psychotherapy in Bergin and Garfield (*Psychotherapy and Behaviour Change*, Wiley, 1971). Bergin very cogently reexamines the data on outcome of psychotherapy from early Freudian studies onwards, and by carefully analysing the effects of varying definitions of 'cure', checking for differences in statistical methods and recalculating 'spontaneous remission' rates he concludes that psychotherapy, in general, gives an improvement rate of 65 per cent, against a spontaneous improvement rate of 30 per cent. After this admirable and exhaustive analysis of data and this conclusion, he rushes to '*impose caution on any tendency to conclude that therapy studies reveal strong positive findings*'. There is surely no field, other than psychotherapy, where an intelligent writer would feel it necessary to lean over quite so far backwards.

The second example of the neurosis of psychologists where psychotherapy is concerned is the chronic 'phobia of psychotherapy' manifested by academic psychologists. The psychotherapeutic situation is clearly unusually rich as a source of information and as a representative model for psychology in general. Clients come forward, often with unusual honesty, and strive to present and explain the nature of their experience. If the therapist is even halfway competent they are listened to carefully over a considerable period of time, and between the two and in relation to the outside world many intriguing experiments are conducted. The client comes from a cultural context so that a consideration of 'social' implications is undertaken. The joint venture between therapist and client or between therapist and group is itself a model of 'relationship' posing ethical and reflexivity issues of a fascinating kind. The undertaking often extends over a long time line, so that process and change have a reasonable chance to be made manifest. In short, the therapeutic venture is an ideal situation for psychological study in the kinds of question it raises, the concerns it illuminates and the observations it provides. Yet for decades academic psychologists have laboriously pursued the antics of the woodlouse and the navigational problems of the rat; they have tried to use the short-term, impersonal, mini-situation experiment as their primary mode of investigation; in pursuit of arbitrarily segmented behaviours they have endured and inflicted boredom and irrelevance on a vast scale. They have given virtually no consideration to the venture of psychotherapy as such.

The third manifestation of a curious stance towards psychotherapy is apparent amongst many who are directly involved in its practice. The psychotherapeutic venture is clearly so much part of living as she is spoke, so complex, fast-flowing and interactive that to say one has, in some fundamental sense, understood, mastered or 'worked out' psychotherapy is to say that one has solved the basic problems of psychology and understood the nature of man. Few are bold enough to make the latter statement, but many imply the former claim. Thus many practising particular psychotherapeutic approaches, ranging from that of the behaviour therapist through to Gestalt work, show a tendency to opt solely for highly specific and detailed procedures, as if we could have the kind of understanding and confidence which warranted that degree of precision in method. This is in no way to argue for some kind of liquorice-allsorts eclecticism in psychotherapy—there is everything to be said for consistently pursuing an approach to see where it leads and what it means. Yet if the practitioner, like, say, some psychoanalysts, pursues an approach convinced that not just the broad approach but the concrete detail of his activities is exclusively right, then clearly his clients are failing to teach him anything of the multitude of possibilities that exist where human experience and relationships are concerned. We do but speculate, and while we can have the courage and optimism of the pioneer we are not entitled to the confidence of the technical expert.

It signifies that the three examples of *psychotherapeutica nervosa* that have been chosen can be seen as deriving on the one hand from science worship and on the other from the pervasive medical model.

The 'psychotherapy has no effect argument' rests partly on an implicit acceptance of the medical model, whereby there are thought to be known ailments which known specifics either do or do not cure. Equally, science is equated with 'precise measurement', and usably precise measurement of 'cure' is thought to have been achieved.

Academic ignoring of psychotherapy is explicitly or implicitly justified by assuming that it belongs to medicine and not to a science of psychology as conventionally conceived.

The reduction of psychotherapy to particular sets of concrete procedures is both an attempt to mimic the specificity of the medical pill, potion or surgery and an attempt to achieve an 'operational definition' such as would grace a 'scientific experiment'.

And yet.

In spite of the tendency of psychologists either to evade or become overobsessed with psychological therapies, involvement in the field has already contributed more to inventiveness in psychology than any other single venture undertaken in the past three decades. While ranging from the highly arguable to the manifestly absurd, the whole series of developments since the 1940s, centred around Rogers and client-centred work, Ellis and rational–emotive psychotherapy, personal construct theory and Kellyan psychotherapy, Gestalt therapy, behavioural therapies and the explosion of techniques in group work and in the humanistic approaches, have contributed enormously to the creation of new ideas, questions, concerns, methods and argument in psychology. And if there was anything that psychology seemed to need after the descent in the 1940s into Hull (better we had gone to Hell or Halifax), originality and inventiveness was that thing.

This book is designed to convey a sense of that inventiveness. It is manifestly incomplete. Yet an array of enthusiasts arguing from a range of psychological assumptions towards issues of method, problem, change and social context may convey something of the purpose of involvement in psychotherapy. That purpose—as I see it—is to maintain an intransigent dialogue with our own tendency to become glib and professional; to make make us open to our clients so that we are continually challenged and overthrown; to make psychology as an intellectual endeavour recognize its own grandiose nature and thereby prevent it settling for something trivial; to encourage experiment—not the simple accumulating of 5 per cent significance levels for storage in the journals, but risky, personal experiment of a kind which actually changes people and nourishes psychological understanding.

D. BANNISTER

May, 1974

CONTENTS

xiii

ISSUES

1

THE COMPLAINT: A CONFRONTATION OF PERSONAL URGENCY AND PROFESSIONAL CONSTRUCTION

A. W. Landfield

> *Man is the only animal that laughs and weeps; for he is the only animal that is struck with the difference between what things are what they ought to be*—WILLIAM HAZLITT

The Complaint

Complaints may be defined as feelings of personal distress which are generated by the capacity of the human being to differentiate between his experience of what is or seems to be and his alternative experience of what could be, should be or must be. This capacity to differentiate and to experience alternative viewpoints directs our attention to man's fundamentally dialectical nature, a quality of human feeling and thought that encourages the cry of distress as well as man's foremost creative effort. Paradoxically, it is possible that the same dialectical process which leads man to his most debilitating experience may also be utilized in resolving his distress. Psychotherapy may be viewed as one way in which man attempts to confront the dialectic of pain with a more hopeful dialectic of new directions in feeling, thought and behaviour.

Since distress may be experienced in relation to either physically defined or psychologically construed causes, there is a tendency to speak of psychological complaints and physical or medical complaints. Although at some levels of discourse this differentiation can be useful, and it will be employed in this chapter, it is important to note that complaints, even as they relate to organic or bodily pathology, can be defined as psychological phenomena. The attribution of a physical cause to an experience or the employment of a physical treatment in relation to it does not deny the importance of also describing the experience psychologically. Experience, no matter what objective cause is attributed to it, remains a personal and psychological construction for the human being. Moreover, a personal construction of stressful experience is the starting point for the psychological complaint which eventually

3

4

may be externalized, exhibited or shared in some form with a friend, casual acquaintance, physician or psychotherapist.

The psychological complaint, conceptualized within a professional setting, begins with a person who shares an experience of distress in such a manner that it implies that either he is seeking help for himself or that he is seeking help for someone else. In the event that he is seeking help for someone else, the clinician has a number of options available to him. First of all, he may encourage the complaining person to consider help for himself. Secondly, he may briefly discuss with this person ways in which he could interact more constructively with the other person. Then again, he may suggest ways in which the person might be encouraged to seek treatment. Of course, the clinician might try reassuring the complaining person by stating that he is worrying overly much about a problem that may not be that serious. Finally, the clinician may refer his client to another professional person, a lawyer, physician, policeman or psychotherapist.

In the following chapter, many illustrations and observations will be given which highlight the varied interpretive frameworks which clinicians and their clients may bring to the complaint. Hopefully, the reader may draw inferences from these clinical vignettes and brief discussion which will suggest ways in which the clinician and his client may understand and interact with one another differently and more constructively.

Categorization of People with Complaints

Ecology

Complaints may be ordered along dimensions of ecology. Using Sarbin's (1970) terminology, complaints can be referred to one or more of the following categories: self-maintenance, social, normative or transcendental. Sarbin defines *self-maintenance ecology* by an ability to discriminate between hostile and benign persons and objects. *Social ecology* refers to locating oneself within the role system of the community. Questions such as 'Who am I?' and 'Who are you?' are most appropriate for defining one's place within the social role system. However, questions such as 'How well am I doing?' point to the *normative ecology*. *Transcendental ecology*, in contrast to self-maintenance ecology, relates to the question 'What am I in relation to ... God, the universe, mankind, justice, departed ancestors ...?' (p. 94).

Reflection suggests that many present complaints can be assigned to these categories, although multiple designations seem necessary in many instances. This multiple assignment of a complaint poses no problem for the clinician unless he prefers a system in which the individual is forced into one pigeonhole from which he cannot escape.

Perhaps the most interesting aspect of this ecological categorizing is the way in which Sarbin then relates it to various forms of psychotherapy and community treatment. He states:

the targets of behavior therapists are the discriminative habits of persons who mislocate themselves in the self-maintenance ecology; the targets of psychodynamically oriented therapists are the cognitive constructions of persons who mislocate themselves in the normative ecology; the targets of humanist–existential therapists are the abstractions of persons who mislocate themselves in relation to the transcendental ecology; and the targets of the community psychologist are the social identities of persons who mislocate themselves in the social (or role) ecology (p. 112).

Although Sarbin's system may not prove optimally useful as a way of ordering and treating complaints, he has clearly recognized that a system of personality and problem classification should lead to inferences about the individual's fundamental dilemmas and suggest guidelines for their resolution. In these respects, i.e. problem and treatment centredness, Sarbin's classification system may be sharply contrasted with the Psychiatric Nomenclature, a primitive non-theoretical form of classification which emphasizes gross behaviour and lacks explanatory power. Although this latter system has been criticized as (1) unreliable, (2) superficial, (3) illogical, (4) non-theoretical, (5) non-explanatory, (6) static, (7) stereotypic, (8) culturally biased, (9) anti-therapeutic and (10) useless except for purposes of actuarial head-counting, psychiatrists, psychologists and social workers continue to use it. Because many professionals react to complaints by diagnosing according to this system, the next section will highlight the nature of this nomenclature and, hopefully, may shed some light on why clinicians continue to use it.

Psychiatric Nomenclature Diagnosis

How does formal psychiatric labelling, for example, schizo-affective, dissociative, inadequate, schizoid, depressive, dysocial, habit reactions, etc., relate to how people function as individuals with their particular complaints and life histories? Does a nomenclature of mental disease and deviancy suggest ways of interacting beneficially with the individual patient?

That the medical model of illness is not appropriate for describing the complaints and problems of personally and socially maladjusted people was emphasized by Klineberg (1940) over 30 years ago, when he provided strong evidence for the following assumptions: (1) behaviours considered abnormal vary from culture to culture; (2) situations precipitating mental disturbance vary from culture to culture; (3) the degree to which behaviour is declared maladjustive varies from culture to culture; and (4) there are fads and fashions in the ways maladjustments and complaints are expressed. Thomas Szasz (1960) takes a similar position when he states that the myth of mental illness should be replaced by 'problems in living' which are associated with personal, moral and legal norms.

In a recent article entitled 'On being sane in insane places', Rosenhan (1973) reported how eight pseudopatients were placed in 12 different mental hospitals located in five different states (USA). These hospitals represented a cross-section of American institutions. The experiment began with a compaint telephoned to the hospital by the pseudopatient. The complaint was that of hearing voices, unclear and unfamiliar. The voices produced such distinct words as 'empty', hollow' and 'thud'. It was as if the patient were saying, 'My life is empty and hollow'. The pseudopatient did not refer to his complaint after he was placed on the psychiatric ward. Moreover, except for using a pseudonym and in some instance changing his vocation, the pseudopatient faithfully reported the details of his life. Although the pseudopatient made a public show of being sane, he was never detected. Eventually, each pseudopatient was discharged with the diagnosis of 'schizophrenia in remission'. Rosenhan concluded from this study that medical diagnosis of abnormality coloured how all of the person's behaviour was interpreted. In no instance did the healthy circumstances of the pseudopatient's life effect a lessening in the seriousness of the diagnosis. As for the pseudopatient's life in the institution, Rosenhan emphasized the powerlessness of the patient. He commented that 'depersonalization reached such proportions that pseudopatients had the sense that they were invisible' (p. 256).

Rosenhan's study of pseudopatients raises serious questions about the meaning of diagnosis as it is applied within the walls of the mental hospital and reaffirms the doubts which many psychotherapists and social scientists hold about the constructiveness of the Psychiatric Nomenclature. The results of this research also reaffirm my belief that gross labelling of patients will continue until social scientists produce a system of classification which is demonstrably relevant to understanding how people create and resolve their personal and social complaints.

One may ask why the clinician persists in using a nomenclature which provides limited meaning and tends to stereotype people in ways which may contribute to their feelings of depersonalization? Although no simple answer can be given to this question, it is hypothesized that the nomenclature may help him organize experience in a manner which supports his feeling of certainty and security. The works of Kelly (1955), Kuhn (1962), Singer (1966) and Gibson (1970) support the idea that man organizes, simplifies and seeks continuity in his life. That the nomenclature could provide structure, simplicity and even a sense of continuity for the experiencing psychologist or psychiatrist seems evident.

If it is true that the mental health worker searches for his professional security within dependable or consistent organizational structures, it seems equally true that the definitions of these structures may vary. One dimension along which we may plot these structures can be identified by *products* at the one extreme and *processes* at the other, products being used in relation to conceptions of man's stable, unchanging nature and processes being used in relation to conceptions of man's development and creativeness.

The distinction which may be drawn between descriptions used within the Psychiatric Nomenclature and descriptions used within theories of personality and learning illustrates this dimension of product and process. Inferences made within the Psychiatric Nomenclature may be viewed as forms of static description which grossly oversimplify the behaviour of the individual. To state that a patient is schizophrenic reveals very little about him as a person, suggests a stable entity and may also suggest the presence of behaviours that have not been observed in the person. Moreover, the label of schizophrenia sometimes is used to explain behaviour in a most curious way. If a diagnostician is asked why a particular patient is suspicious, he may respond that the patient is suspicious *because* he is a paranoid. If you ask him to explain the nature of the paranoid he may talk about suspiciousness. Of course, not all diagnosticians are this naive about the nature of scientific explanation. Nevertheless, there are diagnosticians who apparently feel that they possess important explanatory knowledge when they can properly assign lables to patients.

In contrast to this diagnosis by Psychiatric Nomenclature are evaluations made within theories of personality and learning. These alternative evaluations may describe the individual's rich and complex nature, indicate ways and contexts in which he may have developed and suggest strategies for his treatment. Theories of personality and learning seem most useful to those who are interested in psychological process and change. The nomenclature seems most helpful to those who are concerned with the product of diagnosis.

Although products and processes may refer to different aspects of man's nature, it is conceivable that one man's product could be another man's process. This point may be illustrated by considering the case of Paul, a 16-year-old black boy, who was officially diagnosed as a criminal psychopath. During an initial diagnostic staffing, Paul was questioned about his involvements in auto theft and drug 'pushing'. He also was given the opportunity to talk about his activities in the hospital. In the latter context, he produced a thick notebook in which he had written an autobiography of his life, a document which he continually updated. Following this interview, staff discussion focused on Paul's emotional instability, long criminal history and the impossibility of rehabilitation. These conclusions, reached quickly and with finality, were questioned by one person who admitted that he was curious about Paul's literary efforts. He was intrigued by the idea that an uneducated black boy should make such an effort to find order, meaning and a sense of personal identity through writing about his life and suggested that psychotherapeutic intervention might be appropriate in his case. Granted, it was a long shot, but it might be interesting. These comments astonished the other staff members. How could a professional be so naive, absurd and impractical? After all, this boy was black, uneducated, a criminal, unstable and a liar. He was a criminal psychopath.

Presumably, the other staff members were correct about Paul. Nevertheless, the manner in which they confronted their colleague's position was disconcerting. There was no possibility of a dialectic where different viewpoints are actively encouraged. In this context, one which is not atypical of many clinical settings, what hope can there be for a patient if hospital personnel remain closed to alternative ideas? Without the dialectic, patients are the prisoners of closed professional minds. In this instance, these staff members were closed to alternative ideas about Paul. They perceived him only in relation to his 'bad' and unchanging nature. He was a *finished product* and they seemed secure in this knowledge.

Perhaps the current status of the medical model, as understood by social scientists, is best summarized by Levine (1974), who states '. . . the terms "crime", "mental illness", "social deviance", and "political dissent" are not scientifically useful and . . . they are becoming increasingly confused, so that scientific progress has stalled and . . . much social and human injustice has taken place' (p. 1).

Personality Evaluation

Diagnostic effort can create more problems than it resolves. In the previous section, preoccupation with the taxonomy of problem behaviour was criticized as being non-theoretical, anti-therapeutic, culturally biased and even dehumanizing. Although the usefulness of the diagnosis may be questioned in relation to evaluation by the Psychiatric Nomenclature, can we then assume that all forms of evaluation are inappropriate?

Rogers (1951), representing the negative pole of the dialectic on evaluation, discounts the importance of any pre-therapy evaluation and even views it as countertherapeutic. He comments that prescriptive treatment tends to be superficial and places the clinician in a godlike role. Beginning with the idea that psychological cause is best defined in relation to the client's perception, Rogers understands the client as coming to know himself and his relationships with others. The role of the therapist then is to provide conditions of warmth, acceptance and reflective understanding which will enable his client to achieve a new and more constructive view of himself. In this Rogerian setting, diagnosis would be conceptualized in relation to the emerging new ideas, insights and feelings which a client shares with his therapist. This understanding of diagnosis contrasts with formal evaluation which, for Rogers, tends to remove responsibility from the client when he most needs independently to struggle with the problems of his existence. Rogers strongly contends that maturity cannot be attained by following blindly the authoritarian prescriptions of other people. He clearly states his viewpoint in the following quotation.

> In order for behavior to change, a change in perception must be experienced. Intellectual knowledge cannot substitute for this. It is this proposition which has perhaps cast the most doubt upon the usefulness of psychological diagnosis. If the therapist knew, with an assurance surpassing any he could have on the basis of present diagnostic tools, exactly what had brought about the present psychological maladjustment, it is doubtful that he could make effective use of this knowledge. Telling the client would most assuredly not help. Directing the client's attention to certain areas is perhaps as likely to arouse resistance as to bring nondefensive consideration of these areas. It seems reasonable to hypothesize that the client will explore the areas of conflict as rapidly as he is able to bear the pain, and that he will experience a change in perception as rapidly as that experience can be tolerated by the self (p. 222).

Although Rogers may have taken an extreme position on 'independence training' for his client, experienced therapists of many varieties do recognize that provided insights and rote-learned roles may not be optimally helpful to their clients. When insight is personally meaningful and contextually relevant; when learned roles are thoughtfully experienced; then, and only then, does therapy become most constructive for the client. Therapists, even as they may question Rogers' extreme stand against diagnosis and evaluation, can appreciate the significance of his arguments. Even as they evaluate their clients in formal ways, they can remain open to the issues that Rogers has raised.

The contrasting position to that of Rogers is forcefully stated by Strupp (1971).

> Client-centered therapy shows a cavalier disregard for the problem of diagnosis. It is un-

deniable that prospective patients suffer from a wide variety of psychological disorders ranging from mild disturbances to severe problems in living. Often there are psychosomatic symptoms which require both psychotherapy and medical management; in the case of schizophrenia, in addition to the psychological aspects of the disorder, there may be biochemical imbalances and genetic factors which complicate the situation. In short, the patient's genetic and constitutional makeup as well as his life history are important determinants of his current difficulties, and all may play an important part in arriving at a meaningful prognosis. To assert, as client-centered therapists do, that diagnosis is evaluative and judgmental is a half-truth which is contradicted by the foregoing considerations. To be sure, diagnostic procedures often serve to pin a label on a patient which may at the same time communicate society's censure of deviant behaviour. However, the, the above factors must be weighted before accepting a patient for psychotherapy (p. 48).*

Just as Roger's counterdiagnostic stance can be appreciated, in some measure, by experienced therapists, Strupp's firm diagnostic position also can be seen as having merit. Undoubtedly, certain complaints are best construed within a model of physical pathology. Moreover, it can be argued that accurate information about homicidal or suicidal potential in one's client would serve a useful therapeutic purpose. Such foreknowledge would mean that the therapist could arrange more frequent meetings with his client, work a bit harder at being optimally supportive and wise and make certain that a colleague was available to see his client in the therapist's absence.

Evaluation in Contrast

The typical psychotherapist does evaluate his client's complaint in relation to a dimension of severity. He also constructs hypotheses about the nature of his client's problem, hypotheses which, hopefully, will have implications for how the therapist may best relate to and assist his client. As the therapist tries to interact helpfully with his client, he may focus on two interesting 'diagnostic' questions. First, what are the client's strengths? Second, how can the client's weaknesses be reformulated into strengths and constructive characteristics? Now clinicians addicted to the traditional diagnostic model for assessing mental illness will not enjoy the challenge of such questions, since it is easier to describe pathology than to state what is right about a person. Mitchell and Berenson (1970) allude to this pathology bias when they observe that therapists who are high facilitators are more likely to emphasize their clients' strengths or resources, whereas low facilitators tend to focus more on their clients' weaknesses or limitations.

At this point, a few suggestions are in order about how one might reformulate weaknesses into strengths. For example, rigidity could be translated into steadfast purpose. Immaturity might be reinterpreted as aggressive exploration. Hostility could be related to involvement. Anxiety and guilt could be seen as aspects of value. Rationalization allows one to step back from a problem rather than being overwhelmed by it. Great certainty can be viewed as a factor in belief and strong motive. Exhibitionism, reconstrued as one's desire to feel important, might be

---

* From *Psychotherapy and the Modification of Abnormal Behaviour* by H. Strupp. Copyright 1971 by McGraw-Hill Book Company. Used with permission of McGraw-Hill Book Company.

observed in areas other than the sexual. Finally, confusion may be construed as the breaking down of old structures in preparation for new growth (Dabrowski, 1966). It is hypothesized that the clinician who is adept at transposing the negative into the positive will be most effective as a therapist.

Problems in Defining, Elaborating and Working with the Complaint

Ascertaining the nature of the complaint can be a most difficult task. The complaint as initially presented may be peripheral, fragmentary or even fraudulent. The complaint also may suggest that the client is very unsure about what is troubling him. His complaint, as he initially states and elaborates it, sometimes is most unusual and exceedingly complex. As we try to understand more about how defining the complaint can be a most difficult task, a number of issues will be considered. First of all, we shall focus on the interpretive frameworks of both the client and his therapist. In this instance, interpretive frameworks will be described in terms of expectancies and uncertainties. Then several general factors will be abstracted which may account for restrictions on client–therapist communication. In this regard, research will be cited which points to the influence of therapy structuring and value congruency within the therapy dyad. Finally, the variety and complexity of the complaint will be considered in relation to psychotherapy clients whose complaints seem confusing, fragmented, one-sided, unusual, frustrating, symbolic, constricted, dishonest, manipulating, physical and irresponsible.

Client Expectancies and Uncertainties

The person seeking assistance from a psychotherapist feels anxious and upset in relation to his problem. He also experiences other kinds of anxieties, those which are related to his anticipations and uncertainties about the nature of the therapist, the treatment and what will happen when he relates the details of his complaint. It is the latter kind of anxiety which may complicate the task of defining the nature of the complaint at the first interview.

Although persons who have previously experienced the therapy encounter and those who are overwhelmed with the urgency of their dilemmas may talk more freely about their complaints, most persons seeking help from a professional therapist for the first time, even those who are more sophisticated in their understandings of treatment procedures, are concerned about how they will feel about talking to a particular therapist and how he will react to their problems. The following comments are commonly heard by psychotherapists: 'I know you will think I'm just a kook, but . . .'; 'I realize that you must have heard this problem a hundred times . . .'; 'Maybe I shouldn't be here. Other people are able to solve their problems'; 'Well, here goes'; 'I guess I've talked too much'; 'You must think of me as a terrible person'; 'I feel very silly now that I have told you'; 'I guess you are trained to react that way'; 'Do you want me to come back?'; 'Tell me something about yourself, doctor!'.

Focusing now on more specific problems of expectancy, it is not uncommon for a client to expect that his problem will be minimized by the clinician. After all, friends and relatives have told him many times that he ought to quit complaining so much. Thus, in the context of this expectancy, he may exhibit a 'worthy' complaint by exaggerating his situation and his feelings about it. He may even fabricate a complaint. Experienced therapists expect that complaints sometimes will be exaggerated. They also expect that some improved clients, at the point of termination, will revive old complaints which have been 'laid to rest'.

The fear that one will be stigmatized by seeking professional counsel is another expectancy affecting when and how a complaint will be stated. Moreover, it is a fear which the professional may overlook because he is accustomed to the idea of pathology. In spite of the efforts of mental health organizations, there is evidence that having an emotional problem tends to lessen one's status in the eyes of other people (Farina *et al.*, 1966; 1968). It seems reasonable that a society which defines the good life as personal achievement and an ability independently to cope with the problems of one's life would not reward the complaints of the maladjusted.

Another expectancy which could markedly affect, positively or negatively, the elaboration of a complaint is the client's anticipation that the clinician will be a kindly, understanding and helpful sort of person. Hopefully, this expectancy will be validated by the clinician. However, if this positive anticipation of therapy is challenged by a detached professional who quizzes and confronts him diagnostically, the client may become sullen and uncooperative. When the clinician becomes patronizing in relation to his client's sullenness and the client feels that he is being treated like a child, the interview assuredly will deteriorate quickly. The clinician, failing to comprehend the nature of his relationship with his client, may focus on the client's uncooperative attitude, which later is recorded as an 'objective' trait, one which is associated with mental disease.

In contrast to the previous expectancy is the client's anticipation that the professional will assume a disinterested or even rejecting attitude. Such an expectancy would severely reduce possibilities for a constructive communication between a client and his therapist. Sometimes this expectancy may be construed by the therapist as an aspect of his client's problem, a dissatisfaction with people which is 'acted out' directly in relation to his therapist. Although an expectancy of rejection is more frequently encountered in state hospital situations where treatment is forced on the patient and where life values of lower-class patients are in sharp contrast to those held by the professional, it is a problem with which the private therapist also must contend. Being misunderstood is a common complaint among those who suffer from personal and social maladjustments.

Finally, there is the client who expects his therapist to assume full responsibility for his cure. This type of client tends to be impatient, demanding and hypocritical at the one extreme and passive at the other. In the passive role, the client may quietly and steadfastly share his feelings of complete helplessness. In the aggressive role, the client may demand that the therapist ask him questions or insist that he should be told exactly how to behave, although reserving for himself the right not to follow any prescription. He may also be most unwilling to elaborate the context of his well-formulated complaint. Then again, he may insist that he can be cured only if the therapist changes certain people who are thwarting or frustrating him. In response to such expectancies, the therapist may point out that he and his client have joint responsibility to work on the client's problem. Furthermore, without denying the influence of other people, the therapist may encourage his client to consider how his own attitudes and behaviour may influence the ways in which others treat him. In certain instances, the therapist may try to influence both his client and those whom his client complains about by playing the role of family therapist or community consultant. Sometimes the clinician may threaten his client with treatment termination if he continues to insist that his therapist assume all the responsibility.

A psychotherapist who wishes to convince people that each person must bear some responsibility for his problems as well as his cure works against heavy odds. His underprivileged patients learn early that life has limitations. They also learn that treatment for them is largely custodial and medical. His more privileged clients do learn that professionals will talk with them about their problems. However, they also learn from pamphlets circulated by associations for mental health that an emotional problem is sickness (Beisser, 1965) for which the person often is not responsible. A corollary to this type of logic suggests that if one is not responsible for one's problem, then one assuredly cannot be held responsible for one's own cure. To further complicate the therapist's task of encouraging his clients to assume more responsibility for their lives, the 'body' theorists attribute the cause of behaviour to genetics and spleen, while the 'environmentalists' attribute cause to external circumstances. The psychotherapist, not wishing to be caught up in the expectancies of environmental laws or organic truths, may resort to theories about how man actively experiences his world, a position that neither denies the realities of one's culture nor the impact of organic structure.

Therapist Expectancies and Uncertainties

Just as client expectations influence how complaints are stated, therapist expectations also affect the ways in which complaints are initially presented and elaborated. Beginning with the therapist's preferred theory or model of man, a client's behaviour will be guided to some degree by the therapist's theoretically based questions and the differential interest he shows in relation to certain of his client's statements. If the therapist has strong preconceived ideas about the nature of his client's complaint and how his client should respond, he may seek only those kinds of information which validate his preconceived notions about the complaint. If his client fails to provide him with validational support, he may become upset. It is conceivable that a therapist might comunicate this anxiety to the client by accusing him of being defensive or uncooperative, a strategy which often retards the client's elaboration of *his* complaint.

The experienced therapist, more tolerant of ambiguity, may also feel uneasy about his therapy role since he realizes that many facets of the initial interview cannot be quickly or easily comprehended. It is not uncommon for an experienced therapist to leave a first interview with some feelings of perplexity, that there are many loose ends that he does not understand, loose ends which include the 'not so 'remote' possibility that he will experience difficulties in understanding and communicating with his client.

Occasionally, we find a therapist who feels quite secure in relation to any client or patient. Perhaps he is an 'activity-secure' therapist who does not attend to the relationship between himself and his client. This type of therapist defines his role as the 'doing' of therapy. In this role context, any difficulties experienced in the first interview can be attributed to the client. After all, the client is the one who has the problem. In contrast to the 'activity-secure' therapist is the one whose generalized therapy role has emerged through being sensitive and responsive to the ongoing interpersonal process; a therapist whose 'doing' role is integrated with an emphatic understanding of how his client feels and thinks.

The therapist who can integrate 'feeling with his client' and 'doing for his client' is likely to continue in his role of psychotherapist. The therapist who develops his therapy style with little interpersonal awareness may depart from the therapy enterprise and employ his energies in more rigorous and scientific ways. He may even specialize in psychological diagnosis.

Factors Restricting Communication

Several factors pertaining to how man orders his experience may be abstracted which can adversely influence the ease with which a client converses with his therapist in the initial sessions of treatment. These factors include: (1) the client's expectancies about the nature of treatment and his role in the process which are incongruent with the expectancies of his therapist; (Stone *et al.*, 1964; Levitt, 1966); (2) the therapist's expectancies about the nature of treatment and his role in the process which are incongruent with the expectancies of his client; (3) a high level of interpersonal risk associated with self-disclosure; (4) a high degree of incongruency between client and therapist in the content of their attitudes, social language or values; and (5) an ambiguity or lack of direction in the treatment of clients who need the security of greater structure.

Doster (1971; 1972), analysing the influence of treatment ambiguity in a series of studies on self-disclosure, states that the least productive of the therapist orientations is that which provides only minimal information to the interviewee about the purpose and direction of the interaction. Moreover, even as the interviewees show remarkable persistence under the ambiguous condition, their revelations tend to be superficial, vague and loosely related. In contrast, interviewees reach higher levels of self-disclosure when they are offered detailed information about roles, structure and processes of exploration. Stone *et al.* (1964) recommend using pre-treatment role induction procedures which facilitate the patient's understanding of therapy and what is expected of him and his therapist.

Landfield (1971), pursuing the idea that premature termination in psychotherapy is related to a lack of congruency in the content of the client–therapist personal construct systems, provides evidence that (1) premature termination in therapy occurs frequently, even in a setting where clients and their therapists share common cultural background, and (2) premature termination occurs less frequently in those

14

client–therapist pairs in which there is more similarity in the content of their personal constructs. Keith–Spiegel and Spiegel (1967), in their study of an in-patient population, show that the professionals are regarded as most helpful to the more highly educated patients, whereas the aides and fellow patients are regarded as most helpful to the less educated patients. Welkowitz *et al.* (1967) report that patients who are rated most improved by their therapists in two psychoanalytic training centres are more similar to their therapists in values than those patients rated least improved. A study of friendship formation recently completed by Duck and Spencer (1972) provides evidence for the hypothesis that after the initial stages of acquaintanceship, the relationship between an individual's personal constructs and his friendships is one of mutual influence. Although this study does not focus on psychotherapy, it can be argued that studies relating 'liking' to measures of congruency do have implications for the development of working relationships in psychotherapy.

Strupp and Bergin (1969) allude to an interesting problem raised by E. S. Bordin (p. 36). If client–therapist similarity is high, it may mean that the client is not very maladjusted; conversely, it may mean that the therapist is too disturbed to be of much help to his client. This interesting dilemma is resolvable by taking a more analytical approach to similarity. One solution proposed by Landfield (1971) is to differentiate between the content of personal constructs and the ways in which personal construct dimensions are organized.

Kelly's position that some commonality in personal construct systems is important in establishing social relationships, together with the idea that a difference in construct organization at the beginning of psychotherapy may be a critical component of *methodological stimulation,* suggested that a congruence in the content of personal constructs may provide a shared context within which communication processes may develop. Conversely, an incongruence in the way personal construct dimensions are organized may facilitate the emergence of new ideas, particularly if one of the social participants is seeking assistance and guidance from the other member of the dyad (p. 22).*

Strupp and Bergin (1969) suggest another solution which may have promise, but it is one which does not encompass the interesting idea of the hierarchical nature of man's thinking and behaving suggested above.

Perhaps a concept of therapist–patient pairing would be more appropriate. Research might then focus on which specific therapist characteristics are more often related to positive outcome with regard to specific client characteristics. Thus, for example, it might be found that clients who score low on a dominance scale, show the highest probability of improvement with a therapist who scores at a moderate level on the same scale but a lower probability of improvement with therapists who score high and low (p. 36).

Craig (1972) concludes his summary of the literature on client–therapist congruency by stating:

From the theoretical and empirical work reviewed here, it may be concluded that there are important similarities and dissimilarities in client–therapist characteristics which do affect the quality of the psychotherapy relationship and its outcome and that, even given

* A. W. Landfield, *Personal Construct Systems in Psychotherapy,* © 1971 by Rand McNally and Company, Chicago, p. 22. Reprinted by permission of Rand McNally College Publishing Company.

the best techniques and the highest quality of therapists available, success is still crucially dependent on what client gets what therapist (p. 85).

Craig's review suggests that efforts to match the patient to the therapist may be more useful and ultimately rewarding than attempts to define the 'good' patient bearing his proper complaint or the 'good' therapist carrying his sign of Everyman. I suspect that there are few optimally 'good' therapists or optimally 'good' patients; however, there may be many therapists who can behave constructively in relation to certain patients, and there may be many patients who can behave constructively in relation to certain therapists.

Complexity and Variety of Complaints

To the uninitiated, the statement that the psychotherapist reduces complaints may seem quite simple and straightforward. For the experienced therapist, even the process of defining the complaint can be a most perplexing and difficult task. For example, how does one conceptualize the verbalizations of Ann, a young woman who states that she has a problem, is unsure of its nature, feels that she does *not* have a problem, and definitely needs help? Ann may be construed as confused. However, Ann does not complain about feeling confused. Can we then say that her problem of confusion is so profound that she is unable to state it? In other words, is she so confused that she does not have a stable base from which to judge her confusion? Well, maybe not. Certainly, Ann's therapist experienced confusion as he listened to the unfolding of her life history. In no way could he relate what she was telling him to a serious problem of maladjustment. Finally, at the sixth interview he shared *his* feelings of desperation. 'Ann, I have listened to a detailed account of your life for five interviews and frankly I do not understand how you have a problem. You seem sure of your values and of the direction you want for your life. Is there something else you wish to tell me?' At this point, Ann commented that she had waited six interviews for his evaluation. Although she had hoped he would say this, she was willing to face other possibilities. She then pointed out for the first time that other people had criticized her because she was different. Although she was comfortable with herself, she respected the opinions of others and wanted to be open to their viewpoints. Now that her own assessment of herself was consensually validated, there was no reason to continue in therapy.

In retrospect, the therapist realized that Ann's complaint was a question: 'Am I really that different from others and should I be concerned about it?'. She had then conducted her experiment with life in the office of the therapist. Ann posed a question which she did not share with the therapist, established an hypothesis that she was 'really alright' and hoped that he, a person whom she respected, would provide the validating evidence. Although her problem was not that serious, at least to an outsider, she was concerned about herself. Follow-up information about Ann indicates that she did not continue her search for professional validation.

In contrast to Ann's less serious but, nonetheless, interesting 'complaint', a client named Joe expressed his complaint in the following manner:

I don't know. It seems like I'm pressure, built up over a period of time. It's come to a point, you know, points, where ... I don't think this was the most serious time. ... It's not tangible; it's just a something, push, pushing me. E-mea ... It's not, eh, it's not an outward forced like any, you know, keeps on shoving ya. An it just turns into mistakes.

Now Joe is a very confused person. His complaint is feeling pushed by something he cannot clarify. Only in bits and pieces can the therapist begin to understand much about his complaint. Joe's ability to state his complaint clearly would be seen as a therapeutic gain. If Joe is confused, other people certainly will be confused about Joe. Undoubtedly, some of them may complain about him. 'Can't you help Joe make a bit more sense? He really makes me nervous. And he scares me a little. Is he crazy? Maybe you can make him into the person I used to know, the person with whom I feel more comfortable?' In other words, help Joe and help me with my complaint about Joe.

That the complaint of one person may be only a partial account of a problem is well illustrated by the complaints given by a mother and her daughter:

> Doctor, my daughter is associating with a group of delinquents. We have tried to talk with her but she refuses to listen. Will you see her?

> Doctor, my parents are driving me right up the wall. It is really bad, I mean bad, so bad that it makes me physically sick. Just because I have some friends who dress and act a little different, they think I'm on hard drugs and doing all kinds of ridiculous things. The way they are restricting me—I might as well be ten years old.

In this case, the parents asked the therapist to change their daughter, i.e. convince her that she was keeping bad company. The daughter wanted the therapist to change the attitudes of her parents, i.e. convince them that she was dependable and deserving of greater freedom. Now whose complaint has greater validity and whose complaint do we reduce? The therapist chose to work with the family as a group. Rather than trying to decide which family member had the legitimate complaint or which member of the family really was crazy, he focused instead on the troubling interactions between them.

The interpersonal nature of complaints is again illustrated by the following statements which were made by a complaining wife.

> Doctor, my husband is impossible to live with. He doesn't want to talk with me and he flies into fits of rage. I don't know what to do with him. I don't sleep well anymore and my migraine is worse. I wish you could see him. Maybe you could talk him into coming here. He really does need help! He had a physical examination just a week ago and the physician said he was in good health. If his health is good, he must have a mental problem of some kind. I'm terribly upset about him.

Captured in these examples is the paradoxical nature of many complaints encountered by psychotherapists. The complaining person feels that the other person has the problem. However, the complaining person also has a problem in relationship to the other one. In response to the complaint about another person, the therapist may do little more than sympathize with the complaining person. Then again, he may suggest practical steps in regard to how one might interact differently with this person or how one might go about making a referral. Not infrequently, it is the person who complains about the other person who finally refers himself for treatment.

Satir (1967), recognizing the interpersonal nature of the complaint, has developed a group therapy in which she works conjointly with all members of a family. This community treatment seems to have originated in the context of her reconstruction of the nature of the complaint. She states:

> The germ of my particular theory and practice grew out of a new appraisal of the meaning of relatives' calls to me about the 'patient' I was seeing. These calls were ostensibly in the form of complaints about the patient, or about my handling, or reports about things they thought I should know about. In traditional psychotherapeutic practice, I had been taught to view any attempt by a relative to communicate with the therapist as a particularly dangerous obstacle to the treatment relationship. As I began to try to understand the meaning of these calls, I saw that there were at least two messages conveyed in them; one about the pain or trouble that the relative observed in the patient, and one about the pain and trouble in himself.
>
> The next step was to see that the call not only contained an offer of help to the patient, but also a request for help for the relative. . . . From this point of view, we can begin to stop seeing relatives' activities only as dangers, and look at them as forces for growth and indicators of the power of interactional transactions (p. ix).

Satir's redirection of therapeutic effort towards finding ways of affecting systems of interpersonal communication is an exciting trend. However, her position should not be judged simply by the usefulness of her particular methods. Rather, one should appreciate Satir's insightfulness about the interpersonal nature of complaints, i.e. her *understanding* that an individual's emotional problem can be defined by interacting systems of meaning and interpretation and that a serious complaint about someone else has broader implications than that of 'detecting' the one who *really* is mentally ill. Certainly, the crux of many emotional problems can be understood best through an analysis of the ways in which two or more persons understand one another and the implications these ways of understanding have for processes of interaction between or among them.

That the elaboration of complaints may be unusual is well illustrated by the following case. Steve, a 21-year-old professional baseball player, complained about pains in his right shoulder which had affected his batting average the previous season. His physician suggested that he talk with a psychotherapist since there was no physical basis for his problem. In therapy, Steve seemed most anxious to talk about his family relationships and his ambivalence about being in college. He described his parents as hard-working, uneducated people for whom he had great respect. His father and grandfather, skilled builders of small boats, were assigned such characteristics as honest, unassuming, practical and down-to-earth. After eight interviews, Steve said that he was feeling better and terminated therapy. A year later, Steve's name was mentioned in a conversation about baseball. His batting average had improved and he was having a good season. Someone also commented that his decision to withdraw from the university would not be appreciated by his upper-class, professional and famous parents. The therapist, at first, could not believe that Steve had constructed an anti-history, one which supported his decision to withdraw from school. Then he realized that even as Steve was talking in contrast, he was meaningfully confronting his problems of value. The importance of conversations in contrast can be appreciated fully by dialecticians and personal construct psychologists (Landfield, 1972).

In the next illustration, the therapist was confronted with a girl's refusal to state her complaint. Carmen, a 17-year-old girl, was brought to a university clinic by the Dean of Women. The complaint as stated by the Dean focused on Carmen's refusal to attend classes, avoidance of other girls in the dormitory and an unwillingness to talk with anyone—even her roommate. She remained in her room except for eating one meal each day. Carmen, rather than explicitly stating her complaints, was exhibiting her dissatisfactions through her withdrawn, uncooperative and mute behaviour. The clinician assigned to her elicited only her name during the first 'interview', several yes and no answers on the following morning, a few statements during the third contact and a statement of the complaint at the fourth session. Briefly, Carmen became acutely upset when her roommate asked her to visit her home over the weekend. If Carmen had accepted this invitation, she would have had to reciprocate. To have done so would have been out of the question since Carmen's parents lived in a shack along a railroad siding. The shack was built on stilts and there was no inside plumbing. When her roommate extended the invitation, one which Carmen would have liked to accept, it reminded Carmen of the 'fact' that she could not make friends among her middle-class associates. In this context of thinking, Carmen became upset, depressed and angry about her life situation.

That phobic complaints cannot be fitted into the same mould is illustrated by two clients, Mrs G and Max W. Mrs G complained about her intense fear of dogs. This very real fear and avoidance of dogs was transformed into a fear of a husband whom she sometimes loathed, a feeling which she could not admit at the beginning of therapy. In this instance, it seemed constructive to understand her fear of dogs as a symbol of the underlying family problem. Mrs G's treatment may be contrasted with that of Max. Max feared 'shots' to such an extent that five men held him whenever his physician administered antibiotics to him intravenously. Although the origin of Max's problem seemed intimately related to the relationship with his physician father, his fear did not subside when he became aware of the relationship between his fear and the aggressive behaviour of his father. In this instance, a specific desensitization procedure proved most effective.

A complex type of complaint which therapists may wish to avoid is one with a hidden agenda. The problem of the hidden agenda is nicely illustrated by Helen, a 40-year-old woman who was seen by a private therapist. Helen presented her problem as chronic anxiety and a general dissatisfaction with her life situation. After four months of treatment, the therapist received a letter from an insurance company which stated that his client was claiming that her nervous condition resulted from an automobile accident which occurred two months before entering treatment. This request for information from the insurance company surprised the therapist since his client had never mentioned the accident. Moreover, the therapist could not perceive any relation between her complaints and the alleged accident. When the therapist stated that he was unable to take a position on her claim, Helen terminated her treatment and refused to pay for the clinical service she had received.

Another complaint with a hidden agenda is associated with dependency. Certain clients are not really concerned about resolving their stated complaints. Their complaints are simply 'tickets for admission' to a dependency relationship. Psychotherapy for them is *the* solution and they must maintain the therapist's interest in their problems. Even as the therapist may be clever about manipulating the transference relationship, his resourceful client presents him with a glittering array of challenging problems, a deep appreciation of the therapist's skill and regular payments on his bill for treatment.

The hidden agenda of dependency is illustrated by Clara, who emphasized the fact that she had selected her therapist only after a most careful investigation of his training and theoretical position. She had particularly selected him because his procedures would be most different from those used by two other psychotherapists whom she had seen for a period of seven years. Her first therapist had died of natural causes after four years. Her second therapist committed suicide after three. Now she was ready for her third encounter. Her complaint, suicidal ideation and depression, was elaborated in great detail. Her responses on the Thematic Apperception Test and Rorschach were appropriately most complex and bizarre. Her mission was a prolonged treatment. In therapy, she immensely enjoyed an active dialectic with her therapist. When she seemed to improve, the therapist would receive a letter and an artistic drawing which described her feelings of depression and helplessness. Some letters and drawings were quite sensual and seductive. When the dialogue of therapy slowed, she could be counted on to come up with a most unusual and interesting new problem or a dramatic extension of an old one. Therapy was most enjoyable for both the client and her therapist.

To further complicate the work of the therapist, he also must be attuned to whether or not the complaint has a physical rather than a psychological origin. Consider the case of Mary, who was advised by her physician to talk with a psychotherapist. Mary's complaint was chronic exhaustion for which her physician could not find a physical basis. The psychotherapist, after eight hours of unenlightening conversation, discovered quite by accident that Mary's mother regularly depended on dexadrine. Not only did mother thrive on this medication but she had also suggested that Mary try it whenever she was overly tired. Mary's therapist asked her to return to the physician when he learned that she was taking several pills each day. The process of withdrawing Mary from an overuse of dexadrine was immediately begun and several months later Mary reported that she was feeling much better.

Judging Change in the Complaint

As I have stated previously, the definition and elaboration of a complaint is not a simple task. Likewise, the assessment of change in the complaint is also difficult and for many reasons. We shall mention two of them. First of all, the psychoanalysts, in particular, have pointed out that a symptom or complaint may be changed without altering the underlying problem. In such a case, the disappearance of one complaint may herald the onset of a new one. To have reduced the complaint, in this instance, does not imply that the client has been successfully treated. Since the issue of 'chasing symptoms or complaints' has not been resolved (Montgomery and

20

Crowder, 1972), the psychotherapist should remain alert to the broader implications of complaint reduction.

Another interesting issue relates to *when* one judges that a complaint has been resolved. In this regard, the following statements are enlightening. They were given by a female client several years after therapy termination.

> ... I think it takes me quite a while to get any perspective ... ., in November everything literally tumbled together for me. ... Throughout this year I've been thinking about our talks and experiences I had in the group. Once I played a word game with myself similar to the one we played using realist, idealist, true and false. It was fun and enlightening. ... I've read Fromm's *Chains of Illusion* and Storr's *Aggression* and seen myself as another person. Really, I am another person. I'm not scared of being with men. I can't believe I ever was. I remember how panicstricken I was in group therapy when one of the guys reached out and held my hand. Held my hand! That's really fantastic. ... Sometimes I get scared of what people are thinking of me but that doesn't happen often. My stomach hardly ever acts up now. I don't plan what I'm going to say or how I'm going to say it. I disagree with the people at work. I even tell them to shut up and go to hell—I'm not mad though and they don't get mad either. ... I want to have meaningful relationships and not play roles. I realize now that I used to play roles. I see people around behaving just like I did and I have a real feeling of salvation. I'm not so confused or concerned about myself. That's peace, I think. ... At first I needed just one person—you—sort of a reassurance of worth. Then I got to know ... who were nearer my age but still had the attitude you had and I found out I didn't have to change.

The Ideal Complainer

The literature generally supports the hypothesis that the ideal client for psychotherapy is one who (1) is not too 'sick', (2) volunteers for treatment, (3) is well educated, (4) talks fluently and (5) is capable of thoughtful reflection. Strupp (1971), in reviewing studies on openness to therapeutic influences, notes that therapy is facilitated by the client's willingness to express feelings, accept responsibility for problems, attend to internal events and perceive disorder in psychological instead of medical terms. These criteria for the ideal client suggest that the psychotherapist will work effectively with persons who are most like himself and who also are not severely maladjusted.

If the complaining person is well educated and financially secure, he may actively seek advice from the professional counsellor or psychotherapist. However, if the complaining person is uneducated and classifiable either as underprivileged or working class, he probably will not seek help from the professional psychotherapist. Psychotherapy for the underprivileged person usually is provided in the context of the state mental hospital, and then only on a limited basis.

Supporting evidence for class bias in the selection of candidates for psychotherapy is provided by Hollingshead and Redlich (1958) in their classical study of differential treatment of psychiatric patients. These investigators found that lower-class patients receiving the label of psychotic were more likely to receive a physical and manipulative form of treatment, whereas middle- and upper-class patients, more often labelled neurotic, were viewed as persons with problems which might be talked about in the context of psychotherapy. Now one might conclude that class bias in the use of psychotherapy is just a matter of an inability to pay for treatment, or possibly an inability of the lower-class or working-class person to talk about feelings and to reflect on his own nature. Although these constructions seem plausible, it may be fruitful to also consider the hypothesis that differences in life experience may adversely affect the ease with which a therapist and his client may converse with one another. A middle- or upper middle-class psychotherapist may simply find it easier to talk with someone from his own background, a client who employs a similar social language and with whom he shares similar values.

It may be comforting to the professional if he can state that lower- or working-class patients do not have the proper characteristics for a psychotherapeutic interaction. This type of reasoning then allows him to focus on the few persons with whom he can talk most easily. Alternatively, he may employ techniques of treatment which do not require him to know much about his patient. It seems reasonable to assume that most psychotherapists, at one time or another, have chosen one of these two defensive ploys when they have become most confused or frustrated in relationship to their patients, when their own self-doubts have intensified and when the psychological puzzles which they enjoy resolving become enlarged paradoxes which defy solution.

Hope for the Underprivileged

It seems apparent that the underprivileged person will not seek help from the private psychotherapist and the private therapist will not seek his clientele from the non-paying segment of the community. Consequently, the lower-class person's most direct access to treatment and a respite from the onerous realities of his life (Braginsky *et al.*, 1969) is the state mental hospital.

When the underprivileged person arrives at the mental hospital, the chances are excellent that he will be labelled schizophrenic, a construction which implies that he may be untreatable and will be an unlikely candidate for psychotherapy. If the schizophrenic construction does not place him in a most unprivileged position with respect to treatment, his lower-class status will constrict the treatment alternatives which are available for him. Assuming that differences in social language, values and personal 'sophistication' separate the therapist from his lower-class patient, how can psychotherapy be used with him? Obviously, psychotherapy requires verbal communication between therapist and client.

Two solutions to the communication gap are found in Cartwright's (1968) review of psychotherapy. First of all, behaviour modification techniques can be used more extensively. Secondly, untrained personnel and volunteers may be most helpful in the treatment of deeply disturbed patients. In regard to this second point, Cartwright underscores a research by Poser (1966) as the most influential research of that year. Poser studied 340 male schizophrenic patients who were placed in 34 groups of 10. Six of these groups were used as untreated controls and the remaining 28 groups were assigned randomly to trained and untrained therapists. Trained therapists were defined as highly experienced psychiatrists and social workers. Untrained therapists were identified as college girl volunteers. The therapy groups, which were equated on pre-therapy status, met five times each week for a period of

22

five months. Effective therapy as measured by test score change showed that the untrained therapists were more effective than the trained and experienced therapists. Both types of therapy groups were superior to the untreated controls. Now, if these results are generalizable, it does indeed raise a serious question about the inflexibility of the average institutional psychotherapists—the limitations of his style, language and assumptions about the nature of problem behaviour.

If we consider the behaviour modifier and the untrained volunteer therapist as being superior to the average professional who is employed in state mental hospitals, can we explain this hypothesized superiority within the same theoretical model? My answer is yes. It may be possible to explain the superiority of both kinds of therapists by turning to Hunt's (1961) conception of 'noise in the communications system', a disruption of interpersonal communication which is produced by differing therapist–patient language codes. Within a communications model, it may be argued that both the untrained volunteer and the behaviour modifier produce less noise in the system. Both tend to approach the patient in simpler, more individualized ways which may be less confusing for both therapist and patient. Perhaps one can say that the behaviour modifier and the untrained therapist are more relevant. The former does focus on the behaviour of the individual patient. The latter, without sophistication in and knowledge of esoteric and complex theories, or nomenclatures of insanity which tend to stereotype patients, may listen more carefully to the individual patient. Hopefully, in this listening process the untrained volunteer may learn something about how the patient feels and thinks and how this internal perspective may relate to his behaviour.

If Poser's study of untrained volunteers has validity and if females are more socially complex and sensitive (Landfield, 1971, p. 131), the superiority of the unsophisticated female therapist may lie in her greater attention to the inner experience of each patient. That the professional also should attend to this inner experience is strongly emphasized by Kaplan (1964) in a volume dedicated to understanding more about how the seriously disturbed patient views his world.

> But if the vital center of the process of getting well is the acquiescence to the psychiatrist's view of things, the center of the process of getting and being sick is the patient's framework. From the point of view of the sickness, the subjective perspective, distorted though it may be is the more relevant one . . . if our concern is with understanding the illness, what is required is an empathy and even sympathy with it which contrasts sharply with the psychiatrist's aim of destroying it and changing it into something else. In other words, some kind of appreciation of the 'value' of the illness seems indicated (p. viii).

Symptoms and Complaints

Although the clinician may describe his client in relation to symptoms, a symptom may be understood as a complaint. First of all, certain symptomatic descriptions may simply point to the clinician's acknowledgement of his client's complaint, for example, he complains about his nervousness and anxiety. Then again, symptomatic description may define the clinician's observations of his client's unsatisfactory behaviour, for example, he seems evasive and suspicious. In the latter instance, the symptom may be interpreted as the clinician's complaint.

A clinician who focuses more on his own complaint or accepts the client's initial statement as *the* complaint may perceive his task as the direct elimination of these first presented symptoms. If he asks the client to elaborate on his feelings and experiences, this elaboration is done within a tightly circumscribed framework. In this regard, Wright (1970) comments:

> A symptom may be regarded as a part of a person's experience of himself which he has singled out and circumscribed as in some way incongruous with the rest of his experience of himself. It is normally something experienced as issuing from his person, but incongruous with his view of himself (his self'). On account of the incongruity with the 'self', it tends to be regarded as not-self, and is offered by the person as that which requires treatment (removal). . . .
>
> Faced with such a manoeuvre on the part of a patient, a therapist has two main moves open to him. . . . If the patient is understood to be saying 'Here is a piece of my experience whose meaning is incompatible with my system of personal meanings—please take it away', the first possibility is for the therapist to attempt to do just this. He accepts the patient's rejection of certain meanings, and joins with him in regarding the symptom as isolated and meaningless. He then places this isolated fragment within some theoretical system of his own, accounting for it, giving it a meaning, within his own frame of reference as sign of illness (nosological psychiatrist) or as learned, maladaptive habit (learning theorist). His second possible attitude towards the patient might be expressed thus: 'I can see that you want to be rid of this experience which seems to you so incompatible with the whole fabric of your life, but let us first look much more closely at what it is you are trying to get rid of. Let us explore the meanings which you are trying to reject' (pp. 222–3).

Wright's polarization of therapist choice highlights a fundamental dilemma in the treatment of people with emotional and behavioural problems. Obviously, as scientists, we wish to point to hard, objective evidence regarding our client's problem. On the other hand, it is the client's own life and experiences with which we are confronted. The phenomenologist, recognizing the importance of human experiencing, attunes himself to the thoughts and feelings of his client. The learning specialist, concerned with exactness, truth and the development of a science, may focus on that which can be most readily defined—his client's initially expressed complaint and external behaviour. These two positions, one represented by the phenomenologist and the other by the learning specialist, both have merit. Yet neither position is satisfactory if we wish to appreciate the human being in full stature.

The Complaint as a Criterion of Improvement

Kelly (1955) stated that the goal of psychotherapy is to alleviate the person's complaints about himself and others as well as the complaints of others about him. The implication of this statement is clear. Insight, personality reorganization, behavioural change and reconstruing one's life are important only to the extent that such changes reduce the complaint, and, at the same time, do not contribute to the development of new complaints. Many changes may be reported by a psychotherapist; however, only to the extent that these changes are relevant to the complaint can one speak of the efficacy of psychotherapy. Not only should psy-

24

chotherapy reduce complaints, at the moment, within the person's current living situation, but psychotherapy should also have implications for a continuing or stable reduction of complaints outside the therapy office or hospital ward. Furthermore, if a person is prone to having complaints or being complained about, psychotherapy should prepare him for coping with and reducing his complaints without professional assistance. It is a questionable treatment that requires or encourages the person to become dependent on a continuing therapy assistance or drug medication.

In Conclusion

Whatever the ecology of the complaint may initially seem to be or whatever the appropriate treatment may initially seem to be, each of us, as psychotherapists, should proceed most thoughtfully as we seek elaboration and reduction of the complaint, ensuring for ourselves again and again that our construction of the complaint appropriately represents the client's problem and also leads systematically to our form of treatment. Moreover, our treatment should take into account the client's individuality as a person—his feelings, values and expectations. Likewise, we must recognize that the personal feelings, values and expectations which we, as psychotherapists, bring with us to the therapy setting assuredly will influence how our client elaborates his complaint and responds to our treatment. Finally, in the role of investigator, we should remember that most people discover or create ways of reducing their complaints to manageable levels without psychiatric assistance. How ordinary people reduce their complaints without professional assistance should be studied more carefully and from their viewpoints.

References

Beisser, A. R. (1965), 'The paradox of public belief and psychotherapy', *Psychotherapy: Theory, Research, and Practice,* **2,** 92.
Braginsky, B. M., Braginsky, D. D., and Ring, K. (1969), *Methods of Madness,* Holt, Rinehart and Winston, New York.
Cartwright, R. D. (1968), 'Psychotherapeutic processes', in P. R. Farnsworth (Ed.), *Annual Review of Psychology,* Annual Reviews, Palo Alto, California.
Craig, W. R. (1972), 'The effects of cognitive similarity between client and therapist upon the quality and outcome of the psychotherapy relationship', Unpublished PhD Thesis, University of Missouri.
Dabrowski, K. (1966), 'The theory of positive disintegration', *International Journal of Psychiatry,* **2,** 229.
Doster, J. A. (1972), 'Effects of instructions, modeling, and role rehearsal on interview verbal behaviour', *Journal of Consulting and Clinical Psychology,* **39,** 202.
Dorster, J. A., and Strickland, B. R. (1971), 'Disclosing of verbal material as a function of information requested, information about the interviewer, and interviewee differences', *Journal of Consulting and Clinical Psychology,* **37,** 187.
Duck, S. W., and Spencer, C. (1972), 'Personal constructs and friendship formation', *Journal of Personality and Social Psychology,* **23,** 40.
Farina, A., Allen, J. G., and Saul, B. B. (1968), 'The role of the stigmatized person in affecting social relationships', *Journal of Personality,* **36,** 169.

Farina, A., Holland, C. H., and Ring, K. (1966). 'Role of stigma and set in interpersonal interaction', *Journal of Abnormal Psychology*, **71**, 421.

Gibson, E. J. (1970). 'The ontogeny of reading', *The American Psychologist*, **25**, 136.

Hollingshead, A. B., and Redlich, F. (1958). *Social Class and Mental Illness: A community Study*, Wiley, New York.

Hunt, R. G. (1961). 'Conceptual congruity among psychiatric patients and staff', *Psychological Reports*, **9**, 53.

Kaplan, B. (1964). *The Inner World of Mental Illness*, Harper & Row, New York.

Keith-Spiegel, P., and Spiegel, D. (1967). 'Perceived helpfulness of others as a function of compatible intelligence levels', *Journal of Counseling Psychology*, **14**, 61.

Kelly, G. A. (1955). *The Psychology of Personal Constructs*, Norton, New York.

Klineberg, O. (1940). *Social Psychology*, Holt, New York.

Kuhn, T. (1962). *The Structure of Scientific Revolutions*, University of Chicago Press, Chicago.

Landfield, A. W. (1971). *Personal Construct Systems in Psychotherapy*, Rand McNally, Chicago.

Landfield, A. W. (1972). 'Contrast: The embedded figure', Symposium paper given at the American Psychological Association meeting in Hawaii.

Levine, D. (1974). 'Crime, mental illness, and political dissent', in J. Tapp (Ed.), *Issues of Law and Justice for Legal Socialization*, SPSSI sponsored volume.

Levitt, E. E. (1966). 'Psychotherapy research and the expectation–reality discrepancy', *Psychotherapy: Theory, Research, and Practice*, **3**, 163.

Mitchell, K. M., and Berenson, B. G. (1970). 'Differential use of confrontation by high and low facilititative therapists'. *Journal of Nervous and Mental Disease*, **15**, 303.

Montgomery, G. T., and Crowder, J. E. (1972). 'The symptom substitution hypothesis and the evidence', *Psychotherapy: Theory, Research, and Practice*, **9**, 98.

Poser, E. (1966). 'The effect of therapeutic training on group therapeutic outcome', *Journal of Consulting Psychology*, **30**, 283.

Rogers, C. R. (1951). *Client-centered Therapy*, Houghton Mifflin, Boston.

Rosen, D. L. (1973). 'On being sane in insane places', *Science*, **179**, 250.

Sarbin, T. R. (1970). 'A role-theory perspective for community psychology: The structure of social identity', in D. Adelson and D. Kalis (Eds.), *Community Psychology and Mental Health*, Chandler, New York.

Satir, V. (1967). 'Conjoint family therapy', *Science & Behavior Books*, Palo Alto, California.

Singer, J. E. (1966). 'Motivation for consistency', in S. Feldman (Ed.), *Cognitive Consistency: Motivational Antecedents and Behavioral Consequences*, Academic Press, New York, London.

Stone, A. R., Frank, J. D., Hoehn-Saric, R., Imber, S. D., and Nash, E. H. (1964). 'Some situational factors associated with response to psychotherapy', *American Journal of Orthopsychiatry*, **34**, 682.

Strupp, H. (1971). *Psychotherapy and the Modification of Abnormal Behaviour*, McGraw-Hill, New York.

Strupp, H. H., and Bergin, A. E. (1969). 'Some empirical and conceptual bases for coordinated research in psychotherapy: A critical review of issues, trends, and evidence', *International Journal of Psychiatry*, **7**, 18.

Szasz, T. S. (1960). 'The myth of mental illness', *American Psychologist*, **15**, 113.

Welkowitz, J., Cohen, J., and Ortmeyer, D. (1967). 'Value system similarity: Investigation of patient-therapist dyads', *Journal of Consulting Psychology*, **31**, 48.

Wright, K. J. T. (1970). 'Exploring the uniqueness of common complaints', *British Journal of Medical Psychology*, **43**, 221.

2

DIALECTICAL VERSUS DEMONSTRATIVE CONCEPTIONS OF MENTAL ILLNESS AND ITS CURE

Joseph F. Rychlak

It is fashionable today to speak of the metatheoretical assumptions made by a proponent of some school of thought in psychotherapy. We probably owe this current recognition of the immense importance which our theoretical premises have on the subsequent development of our thought to the highly popular work of Kuhn (1970) on the nature of scientific revolutions. Of course, in speaking of accepted or revolutionary paradigms Kuhn is referring to what might be called the formal and conscious elaboration of a particular schema to the problems of science. Philosophers of science and indeed philosophers of all types across history have spent a good portion of their time in elucidation of the informal and unconscious premises, assumptions or world views held to by thinkers who unknowingly fed these meanings into some area of knowledge as if they were discovering things to be as they actually presumed them to be from the outset. These subtle factors are even more difficult to circumscribe than the normal paradigms, since they are never-ending in their abstractness and therefore sift through our grasp to influence us even as we strive to name their presumptive influence.

In the present chapter we propose to name one such historically important dimension of contrast along which theories of behaviour may be seen to vary. After circumscribing its meaning we shall then show how the very nature of 'mental' illness and its cure varies depending upon which end of the dimension one embraces.

The Meanings of Dialectical versus Demonstrative

These terms are taken from Greek philosphy. The concept of a dialectic in nature is as old as philosophical thought, and it was Aristotle (1952, p. 143) who named the demonstrative conceptualization in human reason. For a thorough consideration of these terms the reader is referred elsewhere (Rychlak, 1968; Ch. IX; 1970a; 1973a).

The term *dialectic* carries the signification and connotation of opposition, reversal, taking either side of an arbitrary point in argument, twisting a premise into its observe, and so forth. It also bears the meaning of a uniting of such opposites (thesis–antithesis) into a 'synthesis', which might be thought of as a struck bargain or compromise as well as the taking of the best from both sides into a single resolution. The essential feature of a dialectical formulation is the presumption of a bipolarity in meaning, so that in a true sense it is possible to say that at some point all meanings share a *common* expression—as a sort of dimensional tying together by way of opposition. Greek philosophy referred to this as the 'one' among the 'many' and *vice versa* (Rychlak, 1968, pp. 395–7). In a curious way flatly opposite meanings are identical, so that to know 'left' is to know 'right', 'up' defines 'down' and 'sweet' teaches us the meaning of 'sour'.

Dialectical formulations have always been intrinsically related to dynamic accounts, for even when we have a resolution of opposition into a synthesis there remains that tension of contrasting meanings to threaten the delicate balance. Theories of change which take their motive power from conflict are likely to be dialectical in conceptualization. In the ancient world an example is the theory of four elements (earth, air, fire and water) proposed by Empedocles. He viewed these elements as constantly stirred and altered by the opposites of 'love and strife'. A more recent conflict theory having declared dialectical meanings is the class-conflict formulations of Marxian communism, borrowed in turn from the cultural conflict theories of the Hegelian dialectic.

This dynamic feature of dialectic carries over to the interpersonal, as in the so-called Socratic method, in which a series of questions posed by the teacher were framed to stimulate an open exchange of viewpoints between the participants. The very heart of this method was to be openness and seeking of truth no matter where this exchange would take the participants. If the student selected point A to contend, Socrates contended not-A; if the student chose not-A, Socrates held to A. It was all the same to Socrates, for he did not think of himself as having 'knowledge' to 'communicate' from his head to the student's head. He and the student were two of the 'many' intelligences which summated to the 'one' clear truth, and by way of dialectical examination they could come to know that truth. Two men could talk and learn so long as they retained a free and open dialectical exchange. Beginning in admitted error, they could come to know truth, since error is merely the other side of truth (both of which constitute the totality of human knowledge). To use a dialectical frame of questioning in order to direct or manipulate a student's thought in some *predetermined* direction was to practise sophistry (a pejorative reference based on the fact that the Sophists actually did do this).

It was Aristotle who first rallied against the 'armchair' features of the dialectical method, where two men talked and talked, often kidding themselves into believing that they were coming to know truth when in fact they were simply perpetuating opinion at best and downright error in all likelihood. Aristotle was our first 'toughminded' thinker, for he rejected the view that one could begin in error and come to know truth. Unfounded premises can only lead to unfounded conclusions. Aristotle did not deny that man *could* reason dialectically. In fact, he admitted that when under attack concerning our major premises in any theoretical or factual argument we all must resort to a dialectical defence—since in the realm of pure possibility there is no clear 'proof' to settle a question one way or the other. Kuhn's (1970) analysis of science is nothing less than a modern extension of this insight.

Even in science, one can only prove what one looks for, and what one looks for is never dictated by the 'facts' but by the possibility of facts flowing from one's *arbitrarily* selected conception (paradigm).

In order to propound more legitimate theories of nature, Aristotle called for a *demonstrative* method of reasoning and study. Whereas dialecticians base their premises on mere opinion (the 'possible'), the demonstrative reasoner relies only upon 'primary and true' meanings to initiate a course of thought. Aristotle had various rules for what constituted a primary and true premise, but the essential idea was that of a *unipolarity* in meaningful denotation. This unipolarity is best seen in Aristotle's 'laws of contradiction', where it is argued that 'A is not not-A'. Such opposites have no intrinsic unity, and one cannot take an arbitrary stand in relation to premises which are primary and true. For example, the tautology 'All bachelors are unmarried males' is unipolar and not open to challenge. Another primary and true premise would be any empirical 'fact', as an operational definition of what is truly the case in reality. Aristotle was the father of biology precisely because he wished to turn our attention away from dialectical discussion to the empirically discernible facts of existence.

This demonstrative conception fostered a world view having 'points' or 'circumscribed givens' of independent existence, attachable to be sure, but also clearly distinct from other such points of meaningful reference. It is this unipolarity of demonstrative formulations which most attracts our interest as counterpoint to the dialectical formulation. We have an historical bifurcation here which was to play an inestimable role in the way in which human behaviour was to be construed. In the rise of natural science, beginning from roughly the turn of the seventeenth century (see Rychlak, 1968, pp. 110–28), it has been the demonstrative view of the world which has taken hold. When today we speak of natural laws in operation throughout the universe these have not only been proved to 'exist' by way of an experimental method based upon demonstrative logic, but literally conceptualized from the outset in terms of such a uniform directedness in the singularity of a cause–effect sequence. Such laws may collate and summate in mathematical fashion, the total of which may be thought of as a 'field' of force or whatever. But they never summate to that totality of the 'one' which the dialectical formulations held to implicitly. The nature of change has been redefined, from a kind of organized play of connected opposition to the uniform push over time of consequents by antecedents—neither of which need be intrinsically related. The dynamic interchange of opposites bringing equal influence to bear on one another has given way to the determinate importance of the antecedent, which ever calls the shot over the consequent. Separateness, distinctiveness as to role unequivocalness as to meaning—these are the hallmarks of the demonstrative conception.

Mental Illness and our Historic Bifurcation

Psychoanalytical Tradition

Modern conceptions of psychotherapy begin with the word of Freud, who was faced with the time-hounoured demonstrative 'medical model' in accounting for mental illness. This model held that some given substrate influence uniformly accounted for why it was that behavioural abnormality arose, as due possibly to anomalies in the genetic structure, or to some identifiable toxin introduced into the bloodstream of a perfectly sound body. To think of the sick individual as in any way responsible for his illness—even unconsciously—was likely to be viewed by medical men of Freud's time as a throwback to the anthropomorphic accounts of medieval theology.

Thus, by this point in history the use of teleological explanations of the world had been subjugated to what Aristotle had termed the material and efficient causes. Whereas Aristotle (1952, pp. 276–7) in his physics had theorized that leaves exist for the sake of providing shade on trees and therefore nature is a cause that operates for a purpose (i.e. a final cause), Sir Francis Bacon subsequently carried on a vigorous attack against what he took to be such ineffable characterizations (Bacon, 1952, p. 44). Bacon did accept teleological description for the arts and ethics, but he helped fix the current sanction in natural science to explain things *only* in substantial (material cause) and impetus (efficient cause) terminology. This is the source of reductionism, since to explain events on the basis of plans or designs (formal cause) 'for the same of which' (final cause) intentions or purposes might be projected was considered *insufficient* explanation. One must ever search for the underlying factors 'causing' (efficiently, materially) the plans and the seeming intentions themselves!

Rather than viewing his patients as material objects under the *unidirectional* push of purposeless forces, Freud conceptualized the human predicament from the introspective slant and conceived of neurotic individuals as caught between the pincers of conflicting intentions. It is rarely appreciated that in what seems to be his very first solo theoretical effort Freud (1966a) accounted for the hysterias in terms of 'antithetical ideas' and 'counter-wills' as casual agents. This paper appeared even before the Breuer and Freud (1955) 'preliminary communication' on hysteria, which took up the more generally known theory of abreaction and catharsis. Freud was eventually to speak of the conflicting *wishes* (rather than antithetical ideas) which the neurotic experienced, so that in *every* instance a neurotic symptom is symbolic of two wishes: the repressed wish and the repressing wish. A wish is most certainly *not* something factual or 'primary and true'. It is a mere possibility. Yet people—Freud was to find—can become mentally ill as a result of such chimerical yearnings. Freud thus described an early case in which an unmarried woman's hysterical vomiting symptom was due to an unconscious (repressed) wish to be pregnant—even from an imaginary lover?—while *also* becoming emaciated and undesirable sexually in response to the moral indignation (repressing wish) this woman felt for her lustful sexual fantasies (Freud, 1954, p. 273). The demonstrative law of contradiction was contravened in mind, something which Freud (1953, p. 61) loved to point out.

There were great pressures on Freud to remain within a classical medical model of illness. His beloved teacher, Ernst Brücke, was a confirmed advocate of natural science reductionism, calling for every explanation to be framed in terms of *forces* (efficient causes) acting upon physical *atoms* (material causes) (see Jones, 1953, p. 41). Freud's first collaborator, Joseph Breuer (1955, p. 216), held that the hysterias were due to an inherited physical tendency (hypnoid state) to 'split' experience into unconscious realms entirely by accident and without purpose. Freud's personal correspondent and friend, Wilhelm Fliess (Freud, 1954), contended to the last hours of their friendly relationship that Freud was a 'though reader' and that mental illness was in reality due to malfunction in those 'periodic cycles' of physiological functioning (blood flow, life rhythm, etc.) which guide the lives of both men and women. Fliess once prompted Freud to begin work on a completely demonstrative *Project for a Scientific Psychology* (in late 1895), one which was to be built on two fundamental conceptions: *motion* (efficient cause) and *material particles* (material cause) (Freud, 1966b, p. 295). Within a few months Freud was again completely out of touch with this line of explanation, and even though he made a fitful start or two again subsequently under Fliess's prompting, he never completed the *Project* and in later years tried to have it destroyed unpublished (see Rychlak, 1968, pp. 171–80, for a complete account of this incident).

Even though his demonstrative efforts in the *Project* were unsuccessful, Freud did bring into his theories a quasi-physical formulation in the libido theory. This, of course, came in relatively late in the decade of the 1890s, and really did not play a major role in his thought until after the turn of the century. An energy, whether mental or physical, is most assuredly an efficient cause conception—well suited to the unipolarity of a demonstrative account. Energies are directionless, carrying the movement of activity this or that way depending upon the sum total of a force field (physics) or the pressures of weather systems (meterology). Such energies function essentially according to a 'constancy' or a 'conservation of energy' principle. That is, energic pressure is expended in the direction of least resistance, so that force will be uniformly distributed throughout a closed system. Though Brücke greatly favoured this principle of explanation and Breuer and Freud used it in their preliminary communication, a careful reading of Freud will reveal that he was *never* drawn to this type of explanation to account for human motivation.

There is a certain irony in the fact that a man who began his conceptualizations of mental illness entirely at the level of intentional analysis (conflicting ideas, wishes, etc.), and who on more than one occasion challenged Fliess to suggest how they might in some way explain neurosis physiologically or organically (Freud, 1954, pp. 169 and 265), was to end up as apostle for instinctive drives and mental energies. It is easy to document that, from the very beginning, Freud's use of mental energy transcended the meaning of efficient causality and reached for the meanings of formal–final causation or 'teleology' (Rychlak, 1968, Ch. X). There would be nothing uniquely Freudian in viewing mental energies as forces which propel the organism when they rise and cease this propulsion as they fall off in volume or level by way of a constancy principle. The blind hedonism of a 'rat psychologist' makes use of such demonstrative concepts, and we do not think of these theories as in any way like those of Freud.

What then *is* peculiar to Freud's mental energies? The fact that in his theoretical formulations *drive power* always issued from a dialectical ploy, of wishes oriented for some goal and then rephrased in energy after the teleological implications were clear. It was not merely the instinctual drive or its (efficient cause) 'energy' which provided the dynamics of motion, but the energy as stimulated and then opposed by another, oppositional (antithetical) 'energy' which called for a resolution or synthesis in sympton formation, dream manufacture and related personality dynamics such as projection, sublimation or whatever. Energies which run to their uniform, demonstrative expenditure in physics are never manipulated with 'strategies' (formal causes) 'for the sake of which' (final causes) one side of the mind (id) makes itself known through devious parapraxes (slips of the tongue) despite the vigilance of an opposing side of mind (ego, superego). In the Freudian unconscious there *is* trickery and deceit, ploy and counterploy, until one's head is sent spinning trying to keep up with the dialectical machinations supposedly going on. Each therapy client is a marvel of intricate detail and fascinating motivation.

Moreover, the psyche (which amounts to saying 'a system of ideas') could remove the charges of energy which had been affixed (cathected) to certain goals (objects) 'at will'. It is therefore not surprising to find in the unfolding theory that just as ideas are never lost to mind (out of consciousness is *not* out of mind), libidinal 'energies' are never dissipated or used up! What physical energy functions in this way? It is obvious that Freud is merely analogizing from idea or wish to 'mental energy' and giving his account a 'sound' of the medical model while capturing a dialectical image of behaviour. Since such energy could be intentionally opposed to itself, the three parts of the psyche might wage an internal war—invariably over issues of value, morality or right *versus* wrong. The possible ways in which this energy can be transformed, altered or turned away from its natural object into diverse perversions and unrelated activities are limited only by Freud's genius in thinking up a new dialectical twist.

In 1914 Freud candidly observed that his libido theory stemmed not at all from his psychological studies, but drew rationale totally from a sort of analogy to biological principles (Freud, 1957a, p. 79). But Freud would have been aghast at our suggestion that he was a dialectician. He equated this style of thought with sophistry and senseless playing with words (see Rychlak, 1968, pp. 322–3). Freud most assuredly wanted his approach to be considered on a par with natural science. His effective combing of energic theory with his theory of wishes has to this day led many—probably most—of his interpreters to believe that Freud was a dedicated advocate of the medical model or, at least, a physicalistic theorist who wished to reduce behaviour to an instinctive (efficient cause) basis. But Freud's real model of illness gave birth to personality theory, for he saw in the delicate balance of 'mental adjustment' a dialectical ploy going on between internal factions. His psychology is a 'man-in-the-middle' view, with ego playing this role of arbiter and pacifier, striking the synthesis between the unacceptable intentions (wishes) of the id and the socially more appropriate but repressive and stultifying intentions (wishes) of the superego. This was to make mental illness an assessment of the adequacy of personality functioning—a breakthrough which was totally foreign to the mechanistic theories of those who preceded Freud in the medical profession.

The early Adlerian constructs of a neurotic's reversal tendencies (Adler, 1968, p. 143) or attraction to antithetic formulations (*Ibid.*, p. 34) are clearly dialectical in meaning. Indeed, Adler's major construct of compensation, as a reaction to inferiority, is dialectical in tone (Adler, 1930, p. 145). However, over the years Adler was to find that dialectical formulations were more helpful to a neurotic's defence (distance) than they were to his cure. Dialectical logic permitted the neurotic to twist any systematic presentation by the therapist into its illogical opposite (*Ibid.*, p. 63). This worked against the development of insight because the coherence of life style was easily masked by such sophistical manoeuvres. Adler also found the breaking up of human behaviour into opposites like those of Freud's life and death instincts to be unwarranted stretch of the theorist's dialectical imagination (Adler, 1968, p. 92).

Thus, in his mature thought Adler's image of humanity was *not* as an organism fraught with internal contradiction. This is not man's natural state. We only find contradiction when the individual is selfishly trying to maintain a life style in opposition to what he either now knows or *can* know is the proper (realistic) way in which to strive for perfection (that is, to cultivate social interest). The seeming contradictory nature of the neurotic is merely an artifact of growing social interest, which at one point makes the neurotic person seem doubt-laden. But to misconstrue this condition and somehow reify such inner turbulence as man's most basic nature is to confound the truth completely. This later rejection of dialectical formulations merges nicely with Adler's growing reliance on the force of organic evolution to explain how man 'ought' to behave. Adlerian psychology contains 'two teleologies'—one based on the life plan of the individual and the second based on the directional course of organic evolution (Rychlak, 1970b). And evolutionary theory is essentially demonstrative in meaning. Adler clearly saw the course of evolution as indicating the 'primary and true' direction which behaviour 'ought' to take (naturalistic ethic). Man advanced to the present by cultivating social interest, and only through this cultivation in the present will the neurotic find his way back to a sense of personal adjustment. Individual psychology is thus less 'dynamic' than Freudian psychology. Its solutions to problems in living are more direct and 'obvious', a fact which leads some of its critics to say it is superficial and simplistic.

This cannot be said of Jung, who was clearly the most outspoken dialectician of the analytical tradition. He once said, 'I see in all that happens the play of opposites . . .' (Jung, 1961, p. 337) and he specifically named the dialectical framework of therapy (Jung, 1953, p. 4). For Jung, the course of abnormality is via developing one-sidedly, affirming only one side to life and overlooking that other—equally valid!—shadow-side to our natures. As with Freud, Jung invoked a psychic energy conception, but he was careful to stress that his view of libido was teleological (Jung, 1961, p. 125). Libido is an *élan vital*, sensed phenomenologically as conation and desire. Jung was more critical of natural science conceptions than Freud and he made several attempts to discredit the more routinely accepted, demonstrative conceptions. His use of synchronicity, for example, was an effort to substitute a formal cause conception 'within time' for the customary conception of impetus changes taking place over time as antecedents-to-consequents.

According to Jung, each time the individual opts (final cause) to behave in one way, sending libido teleologically in one direction, an equal amount of libido is being sent in the opposite direction. Thus, for every behaviour affirmed in consciousness there is an equal degree of libido sent into the unconscious realm bearing the opposite behavioural intention. Such free libido collects around it a number of psychic contents into a 'complex', which acts as a smaller personality within the larger personality. This 'shadow-complex' has as its realm the unconscious portions of mind, putting it in touch with archetypal themes from out of the collective unconscious. If the conscious portions of mind fail to appreciate the existence of the 'other side' of its identity—if the masculine male fails to appreciate his feminine propensities or the gracious female neglects her meaner promptings—then in due time the darker personality might show itself in the psychological light of day.

Popping up as a cork from beneath the sea, a neurosis (complex formation) represents these unaffirmed, ignored or rejected sides to our personalities. The strong become weak, the graceful clumsy and the adequate inadequate. A kind of internal clash of thesis and antithesis is in progress, one which will eventuate in the total breakdown of the personality if a balance (synthesis) is not achieved. Jung's theory of cure is predicated on this balancing of opposites by way of an *individuation* process. It is possible to balance by way of a collective identity, as in the spiritual rituals of a religion or the political ideologies of a nation. But through individuation the 'self' emerges and, acting like a bridge across the levels of consciousness, it permits the individual to be 'all things' (the *many*) even as he retains his singular, total identity (the *one*). Jung's controversial conception of the collective unconscious is a variant form of the 'one and many' thesis, since it suggests that just as men have evolved organically to where they now have identical physical structures, so too have they evolved psychologically to have identical ways of knowing, experiencing and even suffering through a serious problem. A problem for a civilization is a problem for an individual. The schism in Christianity split the psyche of Western man, which means it touched all of us. Maladjustments issue from such a break in the collective psyche, and no borrowing from Eastern cults or religions (Buddhism, Yoga) is going to suffice as corrective factor in this schism (Jung, 1963, pp.537 and 549).

The final example of dialectic we might point in the psychoanalytical tradition is that of Rank—who provided a link to the phenomenological theory later formulated by C. R. Rogers (see below). We find Rank (1968) *externalizing* the dialectic, focusing on the *inter*personal in behaviour rather than on the dynamic intrapersonal forces which had so attracted Freud and Jung. Rank felt that Freud had become too enamoured with the scientific task of psychoanalysis, forgetting in the process that psychotherapy is for the client and never for the therapist. It does not make any difference to the client what sort of fanciful theory the therapist puts together to explain the neurosis. From the client's viewpoint, all such explanations are as good as one another, but they have no use for the neurotic if they fail to capture the central problem facing him. The client's problem stems from the fact that he is unable to exert a creative form of will (note the teleology here) in his interpersonal relations. He opts to give up (negative will) in the face of life's challenges and then suffers terribly both from the missed opportunities and the resultant self-hate this engenders. Regardless of the content of our theory, Rank argued, the essence of life is that it is a dynamic conflict in which will is either successful in creating the life wished for or it is not. The neurotic is a person who is steadily losing out in this con-test. He comes into therapy checkmated by life.

The Behaviouristic Tradition

John Watson (1924) early set the tone for behaviourism when he noted that this line of explanation was a 'natural science' (p. 11) and that its paradigm or 'measuring rod ... which the behaviorist puts in front of him always is: Can I describe this bit of behavior I see in terms of "stimulus and response"?' (p. 6). He might just as well have said 'efficient cause—effect', for this is the conceptual tie bind-ing all behaviouristic theorists and it is a clearly *demonstrative* one of uniform in-fluence pressing its way across time in the tradition of medical and other physicalistic models. The uniting of events across time is always fortuitous—due to contiguity, associative hook-up, reinforcements which happen by chance or through 'natural selection'—and *never* as directed meaningfully by some active agent (final cause ac-count). Meaning can be said to involve the influence of one event on another (possibly including mediation, see below), as in the case of event A taking on more reinforcing properties ('meaning') for event B. But meanings in an intentional (wishful, sym-bolical) sense are quite secondary, and at best helpful illusions which have spawned the erroneous teleological doctrines of antiquity (see Immergluck, 1964).

Insofar as bipolarity in meanings is concerned, as Dollard and Miller (1950, p. 184) have argued, the question is one of frequent contiguity in practice over time. When we are taught certain words such as 'boy', 'up', 'right' and 'good' as children we are virtually always being reinforced for 'girl', 'down', 'left' and 'bad' at the same time. It is this associative bond which accounts for the seeming bipolarity in language and not any implicit tie in the *meaning* (a word with the Anglo-Saxon roots of 'to wish' or 'to intend') of the word concepts being expressed. It is true to say that there is *no possibility of dialectic* in the behaviouristic view of mankind. Man is *not* a judging, evaluating animal as Freud would have it, using devious (dialectical) schemes to offset a wretching sense of guilt over some immoral prompt-ing. The grounds (moralistic teachings) for these conflicts are cultural, true enough, but the capacity to reason 'for the sake of' (final cause) such grounds—that is, judge and evaluate—is intrinsic to the Freudian account of behaviour. When Skinner (1971, p. 115) speaks of value judgements such as 'good' and 'bad' he conceives of these demonstratively, as separately determined behavioural events in the organism's response schedules. Whether there is wretching and guilt to be observed depends upon the schedules of behaviour being shaped rather than on any inner sense of turmoil over true judgemental deliberation.

The course of reinforcement theory is fascinating. Initially, the efficient- and material-cause restrictions of natural science were embodied in a 'reflex arc' psy-chology, wherein some literal stamping-in of a physical engram was presumed to take place in the central nervous system. This evolved rather quickly into a *drive* conception, so that it was held that only when a (primary or secondary) drive was being 'reduced' (i.e. rectifying a physical disbalance in body chemistry) did a bond-ing of response to stimulus come about. The drive-reduction model has continued to exert a major influence in behaviouristic theory, even though the highly simplistic reflex arc view of stimuli and responses has been changed dramatically by the introduction of 'mediation' theories (Rychlak, 1973a, pp. 286–7).

The idea here is that behaviour is never simply an input–output affair, but that it must ever rely upon a kind of 'middle term'—Tolman called it a signgestalt—which acted as an additional refinement in the now S–Mediation–R sequence. The mediator was itself 'brought into' the organism's functional capacities, of course, and at no time did the behaviourist contemplate the possibility that an organism could challenge this 'primary and true' item of experience. The organism can get 'new' or 'different' inputs in time, which might then contravene what earlier inputs had prompted in the way of behaviour. But each such input is a *unipolar* designation, combining to a final output performance in quasi-mathematical fashion with continuing mediational aides fixing a certain pattern to behaviour on the order of a regulating 'programme'.

Indeed, modern cybernetic conceptions are essentially identical to the efficient-cause constructs of behaviourism (Wiener, 1954). 'Thinking machines' think *only* demonstratively. They have 'primary and true' *bits* (Short for 'binary digits') of information stored away in their memories, and it is their inability to subdivide and rearrange these *uniform meanings* which gives their reasoning a wooden, uninspired, literally 'mechanical' quality. By processing vast amounts of data very quickly they can make proper comparisons and come to the 'correct' conclusions—as stipulated by their similarly unquestioned (primary and true) programmes which frame in their thinking operations. If the data on which they base their conclusions have been entered properly, a machine *cannot* make a mistake—itself a clearly human prerogative, the other side of making a creative contribution. This is the ultimate in Aristotelian toughmindedness—a process of demonstrative reasoning from fact to further facts without *ever* incurring error!

Note that the question of drive-reduction drops out of the account in cybernetic and other information-processing models of behaviour. Efficient causality reigns supreme, with material causality left unconsidered. It was B. F. Skinner (1957)—in another context—who was to lead the shift in modern times to what is now called an 'empirical law of effect', for he showed rather convincingly that it did not add a great deal to our predictions to focus on what was supposedly going on 'inside the organism' as drive-reductions or mediators of any sort. It was the S half of the S–R paradigm which Skinner was to focus his criticism on, even though he is most often known for his shift in the interpretation of the R (response) (Rychlak, 1973b). He thus spoke about responses *not* as elicited by antecedent stimuli (drives), but as acting independently as an *emitted* action. This is consistent with the demonstrative view of independent units associating, one with another (see above). But if this is true, what accounts for a reinforcement—a bonding of responses to certain stipulated situations in experience? Well, at this point Skinner fell back on his empirical thesis and said 'whatever' event which could be shown *empirically* to follow a response and by that fact lead to an increased likelihood of that response occurring on a subsequent occasion would be considered a (positive) reinforcement. The question is not what stimulates behaviour, but rather under what conditions is a certain level of behavioural emission made possible and sustained? Alter this empirical 'contingent reinforcement' and you can in turn alter the behavioural class being emitted in some preselected fashion (make it more or less frequent).

Theories of mental illness which issue from behaviouristic accounts follow their concepts of reinforcement. Drive-reduction models are probably still the most popular, and the favourite drive of these views is doubtless 'anxiety'. Both Dollard and Miller (1950) and Joseph Wolpe (1958) point to the fact that a reduction in anxiety is *ipso facto* positively reinforcing—resulting often in the ironic outcome of a maladaptive response being perpetuated. The woman who really does not wish to marry but has been rushed into saying 'yes' is fearful of the reaction of friends if she were now to negate the marriage. By 'stopping thought' about her possible humiliation ('repression') and simply going along with events, this woman senses a relief in the anxiety experienced and thus goes on her maladaptive way to the altar. Dollard and Miller (1950, p. 223) speak of this as a special form of 'stupidity' in which mediational aides of cue-producing responses (labels, words, signs) are never cultivated. They feel this is what Freudian repression and unconscious motivation really come down to. Wolpe (1958, p. 35) adds a contiguity thesis to this use of anxiety, which he views as an autonomic response which is easily attached to almost any coordinate association of events. For example, there was Wolpe's client who ate onions while in a state of (free-floating) anxiety. Following this, each time his intestines were distended due to gaseous condition this man also experienced anxiety.

For the Skinnerian, abnormal behaviour is strictly a matter of having been conditioned by circumstances to behave in a way not accepted in the culture within which one lives. The psychotic's 'emitted responses' or *operants* result in punishment, negative reinforcement or possibly no reinforcement at all. Tossed hither and yon by an erratic schedule of reinforcement, he may begin to appear quite odd in the extremes which his behaviour seems to be taking on. We rarely know the contingent reinforcements to which he is being shaped, but because he does appear 'crazy' we damn him all the more to a life of isolation and fantasy—in which the make-believe world is more contingently reinforcing than the real world. Once labelled 'sick', the abnormal individual also has a number of 'secondary gains' (reinforcements) to keep his level of emission in the abnormal realm at a significantly high rate per unit time observed.

The Phenomenological–Existentialistic Tradition

There has always been a decided affinity between those philosophies emphasizing the 'totality' (gestalt) aspects of things or events and dialectical formulations. Recall the 'many and one thesis' discussed above. Also, since dialecticians see an interconnectedness in all items of knowledge, the idea of 'error' is not viewed as a lack of something, but rather as an active principle of knowledge. Well, if error is related to truth, then what is 'the truth'? That *primary and true* given which demonstrative reasoning presumes is taken by dialectical theories as *not* so primary after all. It 'depends' on one's point of view and the phenomenological organization of events.

Facts are always personal and, indeed, subjective. This general strategy has been advanced in the dialectical line and Carl Rogers is a therapist in this tradition (the 'phenomenal field' defines reality subjectively, etc.). Actually, Rogers' 'self-consistency' (congruence) formulations are not friendly to dialectical (dynamic) constructions, but his early championing of non-directive two-person contacts is entirely in agreement with Socrates' view of dialectical as opposed to sophistical exchanges (see above) (Rogers, 1942, p. 176).

The point of Rogerian non-direction is to keep the conversation flowing between two individuals in as open and *non*-sophistical fashion as is possible. We cannot predetermine the direction which a therapeutic exchange will take and also come to know the emotive truth. This emphasis on the emotions is central to Rogerian thought and here we see most clearly the play of his dialectical leanings. One's emotions are rarely either/or; they do *not* follow the law of contradiction. One loves and also hates the same person. It is when the individual *denies* the emotive truth, when he accepts the standards of others in order to achieve interpersonal 'adjustment' (distorted symbolization) and forfeits thereby the opportunity to be his 'own person' that he sinks into maladjustment. Rogers does not dwell on accounts of abnormality, but he does make clear what it means to live 'the good life'. To do so, we must invest ourselves more fully in the oppositions of life—pain *and* pleasure, anger *and* love, fear *and* courage, and so on (Rogers, 1961, p. 195). The dialectic of the emotions cannot be distorted without harm, and the 'fully functioning person' trusts in his emotions for he realizes that they define what is truly unique (identity) about himself in the flow of events across time.

We see existentialistic psychologies developing the same line of thought, in that one's experience of life existence or *Dasein* is subjectively defined. Medard Boss is considerably less taken by dialectical formulations than Ludwig Binswanger, though neither thinker is anything like a demonstrative reasoner as regards the human image. Meanings are of utmost importance to existentialism. Boss feels that when a therapist takes the client's experience 'as unfolded' and contorts it into an opposite meaning-expression, he violates the basic tenet of extentialism (Boss, 1963, p. 235). If a client dreams of the death of a loved one with feelings of loss and great regret, the therapist has no right to turn this meaning into an opposite 'wish' that the loved one in question actually die (*Ibid.*, p. 264). Binswanger (1963, p. 254) has acknowledged the dialectical nature of dream life, as in the case of his client who dreamt he was floating 'above' the sky, which had a greenish hue far below him (*Ibid.*, p. 234). Binswanger also speaks of the dialectical movement obtaining between freedom and non-freedom (*Ibid.*, p. 313), and his concept of *shame* is also dialectical for he argues that this emotion reveals to others precisely what the individual wishes to hide (Binswanger, 1958, p. 338).

This view of emotion is reminiscent of Rogers, who in point of fact has begun citing existentialistic philosophers (Rogers, 1961, p. 110). The view of abnormality in inexistentialistic theories is also comparable to the Rogerian account. That is, an abnormal individual is seen as someone who has failed to affirm those possibilities open to him in life. Rather than take responsibility for his future, the abnormal dependently submits to being 'thrown' by the affirmations of others. He loses figural definition as a 'person' and slips into that ground of anonymity, or, his Dasein shrinks into a rigid oversimplification of right and wrong, good and evil, life or death, and so on (Binswanger, 1963, p. 254). With such rigid schisms a move in one direction or the other must ever be made, and we are back to that problem of identifying something as 'primary and true' (refer above). What *is* the right, good, life-giving thing to do? And, having done it, does that mean we are not *also* wrong, evil and death-promoting? Abnormals founder on such dialectical ruminations.

The image of humanity here as an active agent in life is underwritten by the concept of 'transcendence'. Immanuel Kant first used this term in conjunction with his distinction between the noumenal and phenomenal realms of experience. Kant held that thanks to man's capacity for reasoning by way of a 'transcendental dialectic', he could turn back on the more customary assumptions about what was plausible and self-evident in his thinking and, by way of this oppositional capacity, state alternatives which he had never before entertained. Using this ability man could therefore essentially study his thinking free of customary biases or biasing assumptions (see Rychlak, 1968, pp. 278–83). In similar fashion, claim the existentialists, an individual can always survey his life existence and via the fixed 'givens' transcend by way of the opposite meaning-implications to find new 'existential possibilities'. Teleologies are born in the simple recognition that a meaning-processing animal, standing now at the base of a mountain and knowing the meaning of 'I am down here', can by dialectical implication realize 'I could be up there, at the top'. Where one 'is' in relation to mountain sites or life situations is therefore always at least in part up to the person. We are all 'thrown' to some extent, but freedom is open to us within limits as well. Abnormals fail to transcend the circumstance, which they inappropriately define and then submit to without struggle. Normals transcend the 'given facts' and create their own 'new facts' (affirmed possibilities) more in line with what they want (that 'for the sake of which' they behave).

Some such transcendent capacity was also presumed by George Kelly in his philosophy of constructive alternativism. Kelly (1969, p. 11) properly appreciated that meanings are rarely unipolar and that man is generally incapable of saying merely 'one thing' about anything. To say that one event will take place is also to say that various other possible events will *not* take place (Kelly, 1955a, p. 124). As a meaning-processing animal, man's understanding is framed within bipolar formulations which Kelly termed 'personal constructs', recognizing thereby the same subjective factors which Rogers and the existentialists had pointed to. Kelly stated flatly that he was ascribing 'a dichotomous [in our terms, dialectical] quality to all human thinking' (*Ibid.*, p. 109). Moreover, the demonstrative canons of logic such as the law of contradiction just cannot be supported when we take a close psychological look at the human being (Kelly, 1970, p. 31). Kelly applied a dialectical conception to his view of clinical methods, the understanding of dreams, the resolution of moral dilemmas and even to Hamlet's soliloquy (Kelly, 1955b, p. 1062).

The abnormal individual in Kelly's scheme is someone who consistently presses a given set of constructs, even though the predictions about life that these dichotomous 'mental templets' afford continue to be invalidated (Kelly, 1955a, p. 158). The typical abnormal individual feels that his troubles result from the elements of his life rather than his construction of these events. He begins 'regressing' to the earlier, less mature dependency constructs he had [properly] employed as a child (Kelly, 1955b, p. 760). He turns to his parent, marital partner or physician for validation in all things, rather than relying on his abilities to reconstrue his circumstance. When the preverbal dependency constructs are in operation we often witness what the classical analysts have called 'acting-out' in his behaviour (*Ibid.*, p. 804).

Kelly like Freud was positively unfriendly to the dialectic as metaconstruct. Once, while speaking to Polish communists in Warsaw, Kelly was called upon to admit that his views basically supported dialectical materialism—the Marxian tenet on which communist economic and class-struggle theories rest (Kelly, 1969, p. 216). Kelly took such attempts to categorize his views in a mood of humorous disdain. He would have preferred to stay clear of the term 'dialectic' altogether, even though he seems to have been cognizant of the dialectical features of his approach (*Ibid.*, p. 169).

Practical Implications Which Flow From a Psychotherapist's Metatheory

It is hoped that at this point the reader will have sufficient 'feel' for our historical bifurcation and the 'causes' associated with it to begin seeing why certain trends and schools of thought in the practical treatment of the mentally abnormal person exist. We might now point to a few of the issues which often come up in discussions of 'what is?' or 'how to do?' psychotherapy. The other chapters of this volume will then provide further material for a testing of the metatheoretical scheme which has been advanced here.

A major practical issue is that of 'insight'. It is necessary in order for a cure to be provided the client? Clearly, since one has to deal in *meaning* for client insight to result, those assumptions about human nature which do not embrace meaning can hardly emphasize this aspect of cure. The classical medical model was of this type, and we are all familiar with the biologically oriented 'therapist' (it seems wrong to place the 'psycho-' prefix here) who searches for the chemical substrate to the behavioural problem which has been *diagnosed*. Factors having 'bedside manner' connotations are completely secondary to his therapeutic approach, for the patient is viewed in the same material–efficient-cause terms that one would view a salamander in the introductory laboratory courses which prepared this therapist for his professional calling.

Classical psychoanalysis was to change all this. Though Jung (1960, pp. 36–7) did speculate on the possibility of a toxic substance in the etiology of schizophrenia, his entire view on mental illness was opposed to such physical speculation—and in time he was to make it clear that 'psychological causes' were at the root of all mental illness. His therapy therefore amounted to a balancing of the psyche which had developed one-sidedly. Meaning-generation by way of *symbols of transformation* aided the patient to see that shadow-side of his nature which he had been letting pass unaffirmed to this point in life. Adler's therapy also emphasized the necessity of making the neurotic aware of the unproductive manoeuvres he was making in the game of life.

Adler and Jung were of course following in the tradition of Freud, whose approach to the client has rightly been likened to a psychic Sherlock Holmes (Hyman, 1962, p. 313). A clever opponent from within the client's psyche is [intentionally] at work and the psychic detective must get him to tip his hand. Freud has occasionally been ridiculed for having broken up the one person into three 'homunculi' (id, ego, superego) which now run the total machine by way of a Board of Directors or some such (note the 'one and many' thesis here). Well, if we now see how it is possible to view the same person dialectically formulating two (or more) intentions (wishes) directly in opposition with each other, then this no longer seems so excessive a theoretical suggestion. This does not necessarily violate scientific parsimony, so long as one's image of humanity is that of a dialectical being.

Drawing their tradition from natural science, the behaviourists consider all such talk of two or more intention-identities within the single person to be something like a medieval account of angels dancing on the heads of pins. Dollar and Miller (1950) tried valiantly to bring the two language systems together, subsuming in the process all of Freud's more teleological meanings under the material- and efficient-cause terminology of Hullian drive-reduction theory. But in translating 'repression' into what is *not* in mind and thereby making the neurotic 'stupid' (lacking in cue-producing, mediating responses) they show the impossibility of capturing a dialectical formulation in demonstrative terms. 'Insight' becomes 'putting more mediational cues into the mental hopper' rather than actually tipping the hand of an intentional opponent. Freud's neurotic is hardly stupid. He is cunningly wise. One side of his identity (unconscious) is literally using the other side (conscious) to further certain desired ends.

We see a similar divergence in the way Wolpe views anxiety and the role which Freud assigns to it. For Wolpe the symptom of anxiety *is* the illness. Though one might erroneously assign meaning to it, the manifestation of anxiety in a neurotic syndrome picture has no interpretable significance. Wolpe therefore teaches his client various methods of relaxation and then carries him up an (imagined) hierarchy of increasingly upsetting situations in the belief that a 'reciprocal inhibition' of anxiety by relaxation (responses) is taking place (Wolpe, 1958, p. 71). For Freud, anxiety is an instrumentality and *not* the illness. Anxiety is *not* a (bodily) drive in Freudian theory and it should never be confused with libido, which is the proper (mental) energizer of the personality system. Indeed, the id and superego do not even 'feel' anxiety. It is the unconscious portion of the ego which, after working out a compromise in the meaning-expressions to be made manifest in overt behaviour, literally *infects itself*—its conscious side—with the wretched physical emotion. In this way it prevents what is known (unconsciously) from being known (consciously). To have the meanings made manifest which were 'there' latently generated anxiety—but this anxiety was *intentionally* generated! It was the latent meaning of the symptom picture which Freud set his sights on, and *not* the anxiety.

It follows from the demonstrative assumptions of operant conditioning that symptom pictures such as anxiety are levels of response emission being sustained by certain contingent reinforcements. Therapy therefore becomes a question of finding what reinforcements influence the organism on an empirical basis and then altering the emission rates of normal and/or abnormal behaviours (as defined by cultural standards) accordingly. Hence we have the token economies and related efforts to 'shape behaviour' along its presumably efficiently caused direction.

Since Kelly's assumption is that abnormals are behaving according to a construct system which is continually invalidated, he has as his therapy a form of insight implied—really, a 'reconstruction' of life events. No doctrinaire theory of fixations and regressions is involved, of course, since Kelly affords each person the dignity of providing his own theory about life (the 'every man a scientist' theme of constructive alternativism). It is this reticence to press individuals into a prearranged scheme which typifies the phenomenological–existential school of thought. Rogers demands that the individual be allowed to rearrange his phenomenal field according to his own subjective perceptions. The existentialists accuse even Freud of 'reducing' Dasein to an underlying dynamic in the same way that the medical model reduces Dasein to a substrate of chemical and biological elements. To be frozen into another person's construct system, or 'thrown' by another person's possibilities, is often the *source* of mental abnormality, so how can a 'therapist' take this stance in relation to a client that he hopes to cure?

The historic debate between Rogers and Skinner (1956) was precisely on this point of 'who should be controlling the lives of whom?'. Since Skinner (1971, p. 114) finds the concept of 'autonomous man' to be an outmoded one, it is understandable that he should be nonplussed at all of the teleological talk he hears of supposed 'personal' growths, self-realization, the affirmation of possibilities and so forth. Based on his identification with natural science, such talk is held to be anti-scientific since it clearly denies the role of determinism in behaviour.

Actually, this is a hasty conclusion. If we take a dialectical view of things, it is possible to see how *both* determined and 'free' behaviour can be seen to function in the same individual. Many scholars have erroneously drawn direct parallels between the determinism of Freud and the determinism of, say, Skinner. Both men view behaviour as determined by 'antecendents' and therefore it is said that they share a common view. But do they really? Freud's determinism *follows* the taking of an intentional premise (compromise solution). As Jung, Binswanger and Kelly also make clear, the fact that a person knows or affirms one meaning implies by dialectical definition the opposite meaning. Knowing now two meanings, which course of action is to be carried out in the light of these bipolar opposites? Well, if it is possible to transcend the behaviouristic or cybernetic input in this fashion, making the demonstrative unipolar signal into a bipolar set of alternatives, then obviously what eventually takes place in behaviour depends upon the *precedent* premise which in turn will direct the *sequacious* behaviours to follow. Determinism *follows* the premise or construction (Kelly, 1955b, p. 926) taken (affirmed), just as we have noted in our opening comments that paradigms determine the kinds of scientific facts which are to be discovered (Kuhn, 1970).

The key issue here is whether or not human beings have some element of *arbitrariness* in their capacity to take 'this or that' premise, opposite ends of a construct dimension and so on. Basing his commentary on the demonstrative presumption, the behaviourist says 'no, there is no such thing as true arbitrariness in behavior'. Arbitrariness is simply ignorance of all the factors at play in the determination of a situation. If the dialectician feels he has some freedom in selecting alternative meanings to further (or not) in his behaviour he is deluding himself, because the (free will) decision he makes in order to arrive at his premise is *itself* determined by certain factual or other 'inputs'. And since these unipolar inputs are themselves fixed over time there *is no arbitrariness*. Skinner's determinism therefore *precedes* all else. If we insist upon speaking of mental freedom based on the illusion of contemplation in arriving at a course of action (premise, construction, compromise) that is something the behaviourist must live with (Immergluck, 1964). But in the demonstrative view of determinism there is no way of conceiving how a person could truly say to himself: 'I have a real choice here, in the situation facing me. Which alternative should I take?'

Another reflection of our historic bifurcation in discussions of psychotherapy has to do with the *relationship* between the client and therapist. We have already noted the detective-like approach of classical analysis. Though Adler did not accept the profound inner dynamics of psychoanalysis, he did proceed on the assumption that the neurotic was conforming to a life plan which he had quite intentionally laid down and was now furthering—albeit in an unconscious sense as time went by. Jung looked to the manifestation of shadow-side factors in the dreams and artistic productions of his clients, insisting that there was an intelligence speaking through such creative forms which had a meaning to express. Freud was of course locked in constant battle with his censoring opponent. All of this lends a certain 'authoritarian' air to the nature of the contact which was achieved between therapist and client. Once Freud had convinced himself by way of evidence from dreams, parapraxes, fantasies or the manner of a client in the consulting room, he took a more demonstrative tack. Resistance is another way of talking about what is 'primary and true' in the material unfolding before the analyst's interpretative gaze.

And insofar as there was anything germane in the actual therapist–client relationship, Freud made this play a secondary role to the 'underlying, internal dynamic'. Transference thus becomes extremely important to cure but this is *not* because of anything *real* in the two-person relationship. A 'transformed neurosis' has simply been generated within the four walls of the consulting room. It was Rank who was to change this view of the relationship. Rather than submerging the dialectic in the intrapersonal dynamics of the client calling for a 'fixed' insight, Rank moved the dialectic outward, into the dynamic and *real* relationship between the participants of therapy. He saw therapy as a 'battle' but one in which the client must emerge victorious. Without characterizing therapy in this aggressive sense, Rogers picked up on this interpersonal theme and—receiving an influence from Rank—came to the view of mental abnormality as something *begun* in how people treat one another. The existentialists follow pretty much in this vein.

Rogers employed the Socratic tactic of free and open discussion in his non-directive therapy to allow the individual and opportunity for self-growth and self-redefinition. Existentialists and phenomenologists are also more likely to have (interpersonal) ethical themes in their views of how therapy comes about—usually encompassing the values of individuality and 'freedom to choose' (taking us back to the question of whether or not this is possible in human behaviour).

The behaviourists, of course, are not so taken with relationship factors *per se*. They assign no responsibility to the client for his getting 'sick', as they assign no responsibility to *anyone* for his behaviour (non-teleological theory). Their view of the therapist is as someone who has sharpened his techniques in the laboratory and is now applying them much in the sense of a technician or a physician. What they are *primarily* interested in is demonstrating the great effectiveness which their approach has in comparison to other techniques of therapy. This takes us directly into the question of *outcome* or follow-up research, a favourite issue advanced by the behaviourist. It seems clear to him that therapists are in the business of therapizing and therefore presumably they should be only too ready to put their approaches to the test of outcome. Insight therapists are likely to resent this demonstrative assumption that it is always easy pointing to a 'good' outcome, even in the sense of removing certain clearly discernible symptoms. And sometimes even seemingly 'bad' terminations are not so clearly negative as they seem.

For example, Freud thought of his psychotherapeutic approach as a scientific tool, one which permitted certain truths about human nature to be brought to light. In 1910 he observed that occasionally his 'work of enlightenment' might actually lead to unhappiness for the individual who is brought to full awareness concerning his psychic constitution (Freud, 1957b, pp. 150–1). Even though this ironic outcome would occasionally arise—of someone being made 'worse' via therapy—it was Freud's view that the more realistic and honest attitude which would be the result (via the uncovering) could affect social changes in the outlook of an entire culture. It is not difficult to show that Freud actually thought of his *science* as promoting social revision *primarily* and individual cures only secondarily (Rychlak, 1968, p. 181). How then can outcome studies test with any hope of legitimacy the findings of psychoanalysis? How can one science decide for another what its fruits will amount to for mankind?

Though Rogers has been perfectly willing to put his views to an outcome test, he is not so taken with the race to prove therapeutic effectiveness as the behaviourists because of the manipulative technique orientation this engenders. And therapists in the existentialistic tradition are often open critics of the science mania which grips so many modern psychotherapists. In fact, existentialistic thinkers are likely to call for some alternative to modern scientific methods (see van Kaam, 1969). It is therefore not surprising to find them less than alarmed when the 'provable facts' on the removal of symptoms are not 100 per cent in support of any particular approach. Maybe anxiety is something which meaningfully unfolds in Dasein, calling for an affirmative action rather than a passive removal!

And so it goes. We cannot in good conscience hold out much hope that the differences to be seen across demonstrative and dialectical formulations will *ever* be resolved to the satisfaction of both sides. Hopefully, by using the terminology of this chapter the level of discussion among psychotherapists will benefit through greater clarity and a sense of the historical precedents which inevitably move us all.

References

Adler, A. (1930). *The Education of Children*, Allen & Unwin, London.
Adler, A. (1968). *The Practice and Theory of Individual Psychology*, Littlefield, Adams, Totowa, N.J.
Aristotle (1952). *Topics* and *Physics*, in R. M. Hutchins (Ed.), *Great Books of the Western World*, Vol. 8, Encyclopedia Britannica, Chicago, pp. 143–223 and pp. 257–355.
Bacon, F. (1952). *Advancement in Learning*, R. M. Hutchins (Ed.), *Great Books of the Western World*, Vol. 30, Encyclopedia Britannica, Chicago.
Binswanger, L. (1958). 'The case of Ellen West: An anthropological–clinical study', in R. May, E. Angel and H. F. Ellenberger (Eds.), *Existence: A New Dimension in Psychiatry and Psychology*, Basic Books, New York, pp. 237–364.
Binswanger, L. (1963). *Being-in-the-World* (translated and with a critical introduction by J. Needleman), Basic Books, New York.
Boss, M. (1963). *Psychoanalysis and Daseinsanalysis*, Basic Books, New York.
Breuer, J. (1955). 'On hypnoid states', J. Strachey (Ed.), *The Standard Edition of the Complete Psychological Works of Sigmund Freud*, Vol. II, Hogarth Press, London, pp. 215–22.
Breuer, J., and Freud, S. (1955). 'On the psychical mechanism of hysterical phenomena: Preliminary communication', in J. Strachey (Ed.), *The Standard Edition of the Complete Psychological Works of Sigmund Freud*, Vol. II, Hogarth Press, London, pp. 1–17.
Dollard, J., and Miller, N. E. (1950). *Personality and Psychotherapy: An Analysis in Terms of Learning, Thinking, and Culture*, McGraw-Hill, New York.
Freud, S. (1953). 'A case of hysteria, three essays on sexuality, and other works, J. Strachey. (Ed.), *The Standard Edition of the Complete Psychological Works of Sigmund Freud*, Vol. VII, Hogarth Press, London.
Freud, S. (1954). *The Origins of Psycho-analysis, Letters to Wilhelm Fliess, Drafts and Notes:* 1887–1902, Basic Books, New York.
Freud, S. (1957a). 'On narcissim: An introduction', J. Strachey (Ed.), *The Standard Edition of the Complete Psychological Works of Sigmund Freud*, Vol. XIV, Hogarth Press, London, pp. 67–102.
Freud, S. (1957b). 'The future prospects of psycho-analytic therapy (1910)', J. Strachey (Ed.), *The Standard Edition of the Complete Psychological Works of Sigmund Freud*, Vol. XI, Hogarth Press, London, pp. 141–51.
Freud, S. (1966a). 'A case of successful treatment by hypnotism', in J. Strachey (Ed.), *The Standard Edition of the Complete Psychological Works of Sigmund Freud*, Vol. I, Hogarth Press, London, pp. 115–28.
Freud, S. (1966b). 'Project for a scientific psychology', in J. Strachey (Ed.), *The Standard Edition of the Complete Psychological Works of Sigmund Freud*, Vol. I, Hogarth Press, London, pp. 283–397.
Hyman, S. E. (1962). *The Tangled Bank*, Atheneum, New York.
Immergluck, L. (1964). 'Determinism–freedom in contemporary psychology: An ancient problem revisited', *American Psychologist*, **19**, 270.
Jones, E. (1953). *The Life and Work of Sigmund Freud*, Vol. 1. *The Formative Years and the Great Discoveries*, Basic Books, New York.
Jung, C. G. (1953). *Psychology and Alchemy*, in H. Read, M. Fordham and G. Adler (Eds.), *The Collected Works of C. G. Jung*, Vol. 12, Bollingen Series XX. 12, Pantheon Books, New York.
Jung, C. G. (1960). *The Psychogenesis of Mental Disease*, in H. Read, M. Fordham and G. Adler (Eds.), *The Collected Works of C. G. Jung*, Vol. 3, Bollingen Series XX.3, Pantheon Books, New York, and Routledge and Kegan Paul, London.
Jung, C. G. (1961). *Freud and Psychoanalysis*, in H. Read, M. Fordham and G. Adler (Eds.), *The Collected Works of C. G. Jung*, Vol. 4, Bollingen Series XX.4, Pantheon

46

Books, New York.

Jung, C. G. (1963). *Psychology and Religion: West and East,* second edition, in H. Read, M. Fordham and G. Adler (Eds.), *The Collected Works of C. G. Jung,* Vol. II, Bollingen Series XX.11, Pantheon Books, New York.

Kelly, G. A. (1955a). *The Psychology of Personal Constructs. Volume One: A Theory of Personality,* Norton, New York.

Kelly, G. A. (1955b). *The Psychology of Personal Constructs. Volume Two: Clinical Diagnosis and Psychotherapy,* Norton, New York.

Kelly, G. A. (1969). *Clinical Psychology and Personality: The Seclected Papers of George Kelly* (edited by Brendan Maher), Wiley, New York.

Kelly, G. A. (1970). 'A summary statement of a cognitively-oriented comprehensive theory of behavior', in J. C. Mancuso (Ed.), *Readings for a Cognitive Theory of Personality,* Holt, Rinehart and Winston, New York, pp. 27–58.

Kuhn, T. S. (1970). *The Structure of Scientific Revolutions,* second edition, University of Chicago Press, Chicago.

Rank, O. (1968). *Will Therapy and Truth and Reality,* Knopf, New York.

Rogers, C. R. (1942). *Counseling and Psychotherapy,* Houghton Mifflin, Boston.

Rogers, C. R. (1961). *On Becoming a Person,* Houghton Mifflin, Boston.

Rogers, C. R., and Skinner, B. F. (1956). Some issues concerning the control of human behaviour: A symposium', *Science,* **124,** 1057.

Rychlak, J. F. (1968). *A Philosophy of Science for Personality Theory,* Houghton Mifflin, Boston.

Rychlak, J. F. (1970a). 'The human person in modern psychological science', *British Journal of Medical Psychology,* **43,** 233.

Rychlak, J. F. (1970b). 'The two teleologies of Adler's individual psychology, *Journal of Individual Psychology,* **26,** 144.

Rychlak, J. F. (1973a). *Introduction to Personality and Psychotherapy: A Theory-Construction Approach,* Houghton Mifflin, Boston.

Rychlak, J. F. (1973b). 'A question posed by Skinner concerning human freedom, and an answer', *Psychotherapy: Theory, Research and Practice,* **10,** 14.

Skinner, B. F. (1957). *Verbal Behavior,* Appleton-Century-Crofts, New York.

Skinner, B. F. (1971). *Beyond Freedom and Dignity,* Knopf, New York.

van Kaam, A. (1969). *Existential Foundations of Psychology,* Doubleday & Co. Image Book, Garden City, New York.

Watson, J. (1924). *Behaviorism,* Norton, New York.

Wiener, N. (1954). *The Human Use of Human Beings,* Houghton Mifflin, Boston.

Wolpe, J. (1958). *Psychotherapy by Reciprocal Inhibition.* Stanford University Press, Stanford, California.

3

PSYCHOTHERAPY, SOCIETY AND THE UNIVERSE

Grahame Leman

It is impossible to mediate on time and the creative passage of nature without an overwhelming emotion at the limitations of human intelligence—A. N. WHITEHEAD (1964, p. 73)

Apparently, whether we look at chromosomes, cathedrals, or even into the mirror, we always look at our own brain—ROLAND FISCHER (Fraser, 1968, p. 368)

Studying the literature, editing the articles, and writing my own sections, I could not suppress a sense of awe regarding the dimensions of man's existence, both in its horizons and in its limitations. This type of reaction is not currently widespread, for the success of the sciences tends to submerge the acknowledgement of these limitations. The forces of speculation and reverence which were so essential in creating the natural sciences and Western technology are not always attractive, because one must have courage to fear and wonder—J. T. FRASER (1968, p. xxiv)

The Function of Psychotherapies in Societies is to Deal with Outbreaks of Sanity

To write down an initial sentence like the one just above is to set up a kind of experiment. Not the kind of experiment you might do by running rats or student subjects in the immemorial way: rather the kind ordinarily done by philosophers, poets, cosmologists and mathematicians—who postulate some axioms with a promising smell and then go on to see what will happen when they grow a system from them. Which is what I propose to do here with my own initial sentence.

If, when I have done, you feel moved to venture empirical falsification of where I am by then *at,* you may like to adopt my own formal methodology: which is to read widely, keep my eyes, ears and other senses open as I go about the world, skim the newspapers and listen to the wireless . . . all in the spirit of a visiting anthropologist from somewhere on the far side of the Horse Head Nebula.

Psychotherapies, after all, are always and everwhere ordinarily concerned with correcting what were better called a *philosophical* than a 'psychological' difficulty of some sort. The padre, shaman, psychoanalyst, witch doctor, behavioural psychologist, confessor, sociotherapist, best friend, sensitivity trainer, interrogator, tutor, inquisitor, careers master, polcom or whoever finds himself confronted by some person whose perception of 'reality' differs from his own, or in any case from the official OK reality of the time and place; and he tries to goose this person, by talking to him and in other ways manipulating the shared symbolic environment, into perceiving (or at least pretending to perceive) a more acceptable sort of reality—what the pragmatical William James might have called a *workable reality*—in place of the reality which graunches, stalls and runs over others' feet when the owner tries to drive it through Socrates' Athens, Nero's Rome, nineteenth-century Vienna or Nixon's Washington, to say nothing of Skinner's Harvard.

Well, that which is a workable social reality inside some patch of planet Earth this year is not necessarily reality as it might be seen in the perspective of a cosmological time-scale by that three-eyed anthropologist from beyond the Horse Head Nebula; and I'm now going to move my argument along by nagging away at this key notion of *reality*.

What do you *see* when you look, well away from urban lights on a clear, moonless night, at the stars? A few hundred twinkling points of light, variously bright? A plough, a saucepan, a leading light to keep on your left hand if you want to march towards the sunrise? A goat or a scorpion determining your destiny? words like 'reality' and 'see' ought really to be subscripted like terms in a mathematical sentence; *reality* , *see* . What does the astronomer *see,* and what does he see it *through*? . . . eyes, telescope, brain, language, the accumulated astronomical and wider scientific knowledge of the world and the centuries? To the tourist on Palomar, awed by the bulk of the Hale telescope and the big Schmidt, it may seem obvious that the astronomer sees stars, and sees them through his telescopes. But an astronomer cannot *see* a star *as* he 'sees' it by looking through even the largest telescope: the stars are so far away that they still look like jiggling spots of light, and, even though the human eye is sensitive to a single quantum of light, it cannot *see* what can be recorded by a photographic plate exposed for several hours. About all an astronomer can *see* through his telescope, if he bothers to look, is whether or not the computer is pointing it at the part of the sky he wants to look through. The astronomer 'sees' the stars *as* he 'sees' them (huge, evolving globes of gas; receding galaxies; in curved space) not so much through a few bits of glass and metal as through a huge, living machine of language, in which these bits of glass and metal are located as minor components. The astronomer 'sees' his stars *through astronomy,* which is just such a living machine made of language, by the world and the centuries. Indeed, since he has to know a great deal of general science (such as physical optics and photographic chemistry) to be able to tell an observation from an artefact, the astronomer really 'sees' the stars *as* he 'sees' them *through the whole of science*. The unit of empirical significance, as Quine (following Duhem) has insisted, is not a point of light, or even Ayer's cigarette case on his desk in Christchurch, but the whole of science.

The whole of science is itself a living machine made of language; or, better, a living organism made of language and located in the entire human race through the whole of its existence in time. Robert Oppenheimer, trying to explain to a congressional committee what science was and what scientists are trying to do, once said that science is a language and scientists are trying to improve it. Sir Karl Popper has called this great, living telescope of language, through which inquiring man 'looks' at his universe and himself, 'the third world', the *inter*-subjective reality standing ontologically intermediate between the 'subjective' private dream and the 'objective' rifle butt smashing the teeth in, and compares it to the collaboratively built cathedrals of the middle ages: an inadequate figure, to my mind, since a cathedral suggests something finished and dead, where science is unfinished and (still, for how long?) alive.

All this is the more immediately obvious if we look away from the modern astronomer, up to his ears in hardware and decently clad in copper-riveted blue denim, at the old bare-assed astronomers, with their scanty instrumentation of a plumb well, a low, curved brick wall, a few notched sticks . . . and the continuingly unfolding mathematical model of the visible universe which made it possible for them to order their observations and discover that Phosphorus and Hesperus are one and the same wandering star, that the sun must be bigger than the whole of Greece.

It is perhaps less obvious today, given the greatly increased clutter of superficially impressive instrumental hardware, but remains no less undoubtedly true, that astronomers and other scientists 'see' the universe and man, not with their eyes through gadgets, but with their brains through language—through the whole of science, continuous with the rest of our whole linguistic inheritance as inhabitants of this planet in this corner of the universe.

The late George Alexander Kelly proposed that students of man (and especially those who proposed to try to do something about men in psychotherapeutic and other counselling enterprises) should take the scientist as their model man, at the core of their theory and practice. This is certainly a pleasingly elegant and parsimonius approach, avoiding as it does the bifurcation of the universe and ontological diseconomy entailed by assuming that there are two disparate kinds of people in the world—scientists and laymen.

Kelly's proposal falls nicely into line, too (like an iron filing in a magnetic field), with the ongoing tendency for science to turn epistemologically back on itself in the reflexive stance described by the pioneer cyberneticist Warren McCulloch (1965) as 'experimental epistemology', or by the Harvard philosopher Willard Quine (1969) as 'epistemology naturalised'. This revival of epistemology as a reflexive part of science itself, rather than as a propaedeutic to science handed down to the grubby technicians in the laboratory by philosophers enthroned in their armchairs, is everywhere apparent. Apart from McCulloch, trying to do experimental epistemology by making logico-mathematical models of the functioning of the individual brain and checking them out by neurological investigation, or Quine, trying to take the same fence by doing thought experiments in historical anthropology on the phylogenesis of language through the entire history of mankind, the thinkers who interest us most today seem to me to have been driven in along their various converging vectors (and no matter what they may have told their sources of funds they were doing) by this same, reflexive epistemological thrust.

In the autobiographical passages of his book *Tristes Tropiques,* the French anthropologist Claude Lévi-Strauss reveals a case history typical of the intellectual generation now in the chairs of power and being popularized in paperback trots to laymen, specialists in other specialties and a few students who still read books. As one of the French intellectual elite in training during the 1930s, years of triumph for Marxism and Freudianity, he experienced a kind of epistemological panic, felt driven to find some ground of knowledge to stand on that would be safe from the insurgent floods of the unconscious and the false consciousness; he thought he had found the model of method in geology, which is historical but also hard. Later, influenced by linguistics, he tried to find his epistemological rock in universals of language: what, he has been trying to discover, are the cross-cultural universals distilled from a wide range of cultures, languages, bodies of myth, musics, cuisines? These universals, he argues, must be the bases of all human knowledge; and he explicitly suggests (1968) that these epistemological universals in the symbol sphere of reality reflect structural universals in the somatic sphere of reality, in the physical structure and hard-wired functions of the animal human brain. Beauty and the beast are one.

Peter Berger (1969) claims epistemological status for religious thought, considered in his context (he is writing with his sociologist's hat on) as a kind of scientific method. He argues that mathematics, developed historically as a free invention of the human spirit at play, later turned out to have some structure in common with the universe at very large (deviant, counter-intuitive geometry finding a useful application as the model space of relativistic physics); and he asks us to wonder whether theology, considered in his context as also a free invention of the human spirit, could turn out to be useful in this sort of way.

You might say, this has already happened. When G. K. Chesterton was writing frequent Roman Catholic apologetics against Humean sceptics (and against his own melancholic temptations to nihilism), he would return again and again to the argument that God would not have given us deceiving senses and miscalculating brain. When Bertrand Russell, likewise confronted by the ubiquitous menace of Hume, could find nothing better to fall back on than his 'animal faith in induction', was he really saying anything different? And must not Charles Darwin have been led towards his theory of evolution by the religious notion of providence, the providential *fit* between organism and environment? The packages and the advertising campaigns may be very different, but the basic epistemological stuff inside the packages, the common active ingredient detected by the public analyst, is surely the same in all three cases.

The human eye is more sensitive to green light than to light of any other colour. This is what an evolutionist in epistemology would predict for an animal which evolved in an environment of terrestrial green vegetation. The shadows would be lighted largely by light filtered through, or reflected from, green leaves and grass; lurking prey and predator would be lit by green light. The human eye is sensitive to a single quantum of light; if it were any more sensitive, there would be nothing for it to be sensitive *to*; the retina has evolved in this direction as far as it is reasonable to go on this planet. There is evolution of the beast.

Beauty too evolves. Newton said of himself that he had stood on the shoulders of giants to get his view of the world. Newton and Leibniz developed the infinitesimal calculus independently at about the same time because there were in high European culture at that time both a set of problems about motion and a calculus-shaped hole in that set of problems. Newton and Leibniz were not so much Great Men who did things all by themselves as nodal points in a great net of human culture extended in time from the first beginnings of irritable ancestral life: without the unknown inventor of the cipher, no mathematics apt to Newton's purposes; without the unknown inventor of glass, no telescopes, no Pigeon League, no martyred Saint Galileo to justify the next foundation grant.

Now, where is the room (in this incarnation of beauty in the beast, in this historically specific twentieth-century society of animals looking at the stars and at everything else through its language) for the famed 'free inventions of the human spirit'? For *free* inventions? How far do the biological evolution of the brain of the beast and the historical evolution of the beast's cultured beauty limit our freedom to see, and, if we can't see everything, can we know what we can never see?

Consider first the beast itself. There is a growing mound of evidence that irremediable epistemological limitations have been built into the animal brain on this planet by its specific evolutionary history. To nail down this assertion, I offer some closely argued reinterpretation of the evidence presented in Lettvin's classic paper 'What the frog's eye tells the frog's brain', collected in McCulloch (1965), on the workings of the eye–brain complex of the frog *Rana Pipiens*. This work showed conclusively that the frog's eye and associated nervous tissue *code* raw information into a reduced and structured form, into something much more like sentences in a language than like bits of information.

We have to begin with some formal account of the information *available* at the outer surface of the frog's retina, and we can generalize the argument at the outset by disregarding our special knowledge of the structure of the frog's retina and associated nervous tissues. Any retina may be described as a discontinuous surface (mosaic) made up of individual photoreceptors. The *least* information available at this surface may therefore be represented symbolically as a sequence of sets of N ordered quadruples $(x, y; I; t)$, where N is the number of photoreceptors, the couple (x, y) identifies (like a map reference) the location in the surface of an individual photoreceptor, (I) gives the level of illumination at (x, y) and (t) gives the associated date. Although this representation is considerably oversimplified (for example, by neglecting the colour of the light), it is abundantly clear that a *minimal* symbolic representation of the *raw* information available at a retina is already much more complex and high structured than an atomic bit of information: even at this level, the frog is 'seeing', in a real sense, *through* his language.

Moreover, long before anything like a 'percept' or a 'sign' is available deeper in the brain for further processing, the frog's retina and associated nervous tissue *recode* this raw information into a reduced and more highly structured form.

According to Lettvin and his co-workers, the retina of the frog *Rana Pipiens* performs no less than *four* different peculiar operations on the raw information, each operation being associated with one of four sets of special-purpose nerve fibres, uniformly distributed and intermingled at their retinal ends; each of these four sets of special-purpose nerve fibres connects at its other end to a different one of four sheets of cells in the brain proper, which sheets are interconnected. The four peculiar operations associated with the four sets of special-purpose nerve fibres are:

52

(A)   sustained contrast detection;
(B)   net convexity detection;
(C)   moving-edge detection;
(D)   net dimming detection.

Each peculiar operation is practically independent of the *general* level of illumination, but each *is* functionally dependent on time in its own characteristic way. Thus, each of A, B, C and D represents an operation on a proper subset of quadruples of raw information (*x, y; I; t*), and each of these four operations has its own peculiar modality. If we now add to the quadruple (A, B, C, D) the usual date marker (*t*), it is clear that we need *at least* a sequence of quintuples (A, B, C, D; *t*)—where each of A, B, C and D represents an operation of peculiar modality or its result—to get a *minimal* symbolic representation of the coded information passing from the part of the frog that is more eye than brain to the part of the frog that is more brain than eye.

(Thus, A might represent in (say) a digital computer simulation a reduction routine r^A, reading data in the form (*I; t*) from a proper subset of retinal addresses $(x, y)^A$ and rewriting it by a reduction function σ^A to a smaller set of brain addresses $(m, n)^A$, and so on for B, C and D.)

To quote Lettvin, the frog's '... eye speaks to the brain in a language already highly organized and interpreted, instead of transmitting some more or less accurate copy of the distribution of the light on the receptors'. In other words, 'signs' and 'percepts' are, at least in the frog *Rana Pipiens,* not much like atomic bits of information or characters in an alphabet, but much more like words, sentences, even strings of sentences organized into paragraphs and narratives of history. The *ex*tensional reference of such a word or string (to an extralinguistic object or event outside the frog) together with the *in*tensional meaning of the same word or string (its relations to other words or strings inside the frog, such as motor instructions) have evidently been historically and socially determined by the evolution of frogkind in general and of *Rana Pipiens* in particular, in a peculiar ecology.

For *Rana Pipiens,* then, there can be no such thing as 'raw' information, as 'objective' data: his information is cooked, his data are capta, he has a theory built into his head as hard-wired lexicon and syntax, vocabulary and grammar incarnate, mathematics in the flesh; a language through which he must see this and may not see that; he is born in original epistemological sin.

In linguistics, logic and mathematics (which are really all one and the same subject and should be so taught in one course) there is another growing mound of evidence that we forked monsters are not much better off in this respect than little *Rana Pipiens*: that, epistemologically, we are by no means immaculately conceived.

It has lately become clear to linguists (Greenberg, 1966) that there are indeed *universals of languages,* structural properties of language found in all human languages known and studied: negation, alternation, lexical fields and so on.

Many of these universal structural properties of natural languages (conjunction, alternation, assertion, negation, existential quantifications, universal quantification, material implication and so on) turn up again, as we might expect, in formal logic, in artificial languages like *Principia Mathematica*; these, after all, are only attempts to give natural language a completely explicit and warranted consistent structure, so that any fool can tell by applying a mechanical test whether or not he is contradicting himself in the course of his argument.

Artificial languages like *Principia Mathematica* have been applied principally in the investigation of the foundations of mathematics. The main line here (Frege, Russell) has been an attempt to build up mathematics deductively from a very few, simple, evident axioms of logic. Logic was chosen simply because logic has traditionally been extracted as the structural essence, or essential structure, immanent in commonsense. Frege was a plain man, trying to use the essence of commonsense to clear up the frightful mess the mathematicians had made of their stuff. Unfortunately, commonsense failed: Frege used commonsense notions about sets in his account of number, and, as Russell discovered, commonsense breaks down when you push it that far—the paradoxes of set theory soon emerge and invalidate commonsense. Commonsense, as Quine says, is bankrupt.

This is alarming, because logic as the essential structure of commonsense is of course also the core structure of all discourse; and, though Frege pushed it a bit before it broke, he didn't push it very far. On the face of it, there is no vaulting *hubris* in supposing that commonsense will take you as far as you want to go in mathematics. But the core structure of *all* discourse, the most self-evident axioms of logic, are undoubtedly flawed.

Subsequent attempts to mend matters only made them worse and even more alarming. Goedel's investigations showed that this was not just a transient problem, soluble in principle by the invention of better logics, but an inherent limitation of all logics. Language is born in original sin, and there is no salvation.

Goedel's curious discovery—that we can know we can't know, can prove that proof is impossible—has been confirmed in subsequent work on the theory of computation and recursive functions by workers such as Turing, Post and Kleene (Minsky, 1967, with a good bibliography). The universal structural properties of language are fatally flawed.

Quine (1960; 1961; 1966; 1969; 1970) has argued the problem through in a series of books from the standpoint of one who has tried to pursue the original Frege–Russell line to a successful conclusion and has been obliged to admit failure. On the special question of the foundation of mathematics, he concludes that mathematics cannot be justified simply by logic; that mathematics can be justified, if at all, only insofar as she provides the core structure of a mode of behaviour, namely doing science. If science is all right, then mathematics is; and if not, not. Just as there can be no unit of empirical significance, in his view, smaller than the whole of science, so science cannot be justified by any structural property of her procedures, only by her procedures as a whole: there are no 'facts'; there is no such thing as a 'methodology'. There are fruits, or not: if the bang isn't big enough, the General is right not to stay to chat about the null hypothesis and the significance levels; if the bang is too big, there will be nobody around to attend symposia on the hypothetico-deductive method or ethnomethodology; put up or shut up. The argument generalizes beyond the status of mathematics in science to the status of all discourse in all human activity. I am inclined to extend Quine's dictum, arguing that *the unit of empirical significance* is *the whole terrestrial culture*, and the test survival.

We have seen that *Rana Pipiens* 'sees' his world through a language (lexicon, syntax) hard-wired into his tiny brain. We have seen that there are universal structural properties of all known natural languages, and that the essential core of these is also the essential core of logic and of mathematics and has been shown to be flawed. It seems probable to me that these core structural properties of language, because of their universality across cultures, emerge from hard-wired structural properties of our brains: the flaws in our logic (proved by Goedel and others to be beyond improvement) are as incarnate in us as our need of oxygen to support life or our vulnerability to plutonium poisoning. We may evolve out of our linguistic deficiencies (if we manage to survive long enough, in spite of them, to do so) but we can no more use a flawed language to make a better language than we can reach the moon by grasping out insteps and pulling hard.

However, I have precisely *not* been arguing that science or any other great human enterprise could be carried on by the individual brain, or turned over to some autonomous routine that could be drilled into the serfs or programmed into the machine by the master. I have been arguing, contrariwise, that human enterprises are carried on by *whole cultures*. We might look for epistemological salvation in this direction. Perhaps the whole is in some way bigger than the sum of its parts? Perhaps there is some emergent property of whole cultures which transcends the fundamental limitations of its individual biological carriers and of its shared language?

The properties and behaviour of whole cultures have also been thoroughly investigated. What Leslie A. White (1949) calls 'culturology' is a very old science, well begun in Lucretius. Sorokin (1963) has reviewed the major findings and speculations of recent workers in the field. Indeed, there is emerging in a disorganized way a massive body of work which might well be called 'a historical culturology of knowledge', which attacks epistemology by postulating that 'knowledge' is a whole culture's developing response to its whole developing environment and takes all history as its laboratory. One of the most interesting and lucidly accessible ways into this approach to the problem of knowledge is to be found in the work of the English philosopher R. G. Collingwood (1924; 1935; 1939; 1946). Collingwood was working in the tradition of idealist philosophy, and he therefore used a language unfamiliar to us and in some ways less useful than the language we would use to discuss the same problem; but, if you read Collingwood making sight transpositions from his language of 'mind' into our own language of 'culture', it is surprising how much of what sounds new today he was saying then, and how much better he said it. Collingwood liked to argue that history is the science of sciences, since you can't understand any special science properly (certainly not well enough to do creative work in it and change its direction) unless you know its history, unless you know how and why your contemporaries came to think as they do about the propagation of light, emission spectra or the causes of schizophrenia: the textbook and the handbook of constants and formulae won't get you any further than they go. Every science is a story, leading back through recorded history into the great darkness before the invention of writing. Collingwood also argued that, at a given instant in history, the thought of all men is constrained at the limits by the basic presuppositions of the culture of the day. This argument is not meant for a naive determinism: there is some freedom for all within the limits; there may be deviant sub-cultures within the larger culture, with variant presuppositions, including even sub-cultures of one individual. But thought is not truly thought unless it is widely communicable in the culture concerned and applicable in helping that culture to sove the problems it thinks it has: if it is neither of these things, we don't call it thought—we call if fantasy, dream, heresy, deviation, madness; we punish it, or license it as court jesting to ground the lightnings. Broadly speaking, the agenda, the questions on it, the rules of method, the allowable kinds of answer, constrain a generation as the rules of chess constrain a chess-player: if you can't or won't accept them, nobody will play with you. The rules shape rebellion too, in a mirror-handed way, since the rebel can fill out a deviant identity, a counter-self, only by breaking the rules there are: you can't be a *long*-haired rebel in a long-haired culture (Cromwell's saints were defiantly close-cropped, figure to ground of the hirsute cavaliers); you can't be an insurgent bourgeois without a bilking landed aristocracy to dispossess ('Get out of our way! You've had your day.'), a Bolshevik without Mensheviks or a romatic lover without arranged marriages and a censorious Society to challenge. But there will always be things that are strictly unthinkable, straight or mirror-handed, for thinkers of the day and culture: for instance, before the development of what the computer people call 'scientific notation' (representation of very large numbers as a multiple of a power of 2 or 10) it was strictly impossible to think or talk in any effective way about very large or very small quantities such as the diameter of the visible universe or the rest mass of the electron. Modern epistemological work in the science of science by people like Thomas Kuhn and Paul Feyerabend (Lakatos and Musgrave, 1970) or the reporter Dan Greenberg (1969) belatedly follows just this line of Collingwood's: that a science is a human story like any other, that the scientists are constrained in their conformings and in their deviations by the basic presuppositions of their culture and their day, and eschews the line that science is a discontinuous series of existential leaps by Great Men seized of notions from nowhere, or the line that science is a kind of free-floating computer programme, cooked up in Old Vienna and the diaspora from such magical ingredients as observation sentences and logical syntax, all untouched by the gnawed fingernails of anxious careerists.

Other examples of this historical culturology of knowledge may be found in (say) Farrington's (1961) story of the emergence of Greek science from Greek culture and decline in its decline; or in Gellner's (1964) historical account of the great modern epistemologists from Descartes onwards as men whose inherited epistemologies had been washed from under their feet by the surge of cultural change, who had been forced to try to find new epistemological ground to stand on. Gellner, incidentally, sees Marx as a merely life-sized figure in line in this perspective of historical culturology of knowledge, which may be an interesting way to take Marx for anybody who is still more interested in evolution than in revolution, or still more concerned with the search for elusive truth than with collapse into supine certainty. For my part, I would also include a lot of what is misleadingly called 'the sociology of knowledge', in what I have called here 'the historical *culturology* of knowledge': Mannheim (1936), for instance; or Peter L. Berger's and Thomas Luckmann's *The Social Construction of Reality* (1967), which reviews the history of the epistemological approach I have been sketching in the last few pages of this essay and then goes on (in a way which ought greatly to interest anyone responsible in any way for the pastoral care of souls) to apply the same approach in a new way, as a sort of culturological epistemology *of everyday life*, of the 'reality' in which you and I grow up, marry, work, raise kids, make money and war, run for office and end up on one end or the other of some therapeutic situation.

The upshot of all this is that there doesn't seem to be any prospect of epistemological salvation in the possibility that whole cultures might be able to transcend in some emergent way the *fundamental* limitations of the individual biological carriers of the culture and of their shared language. As Bertrand Russell (1962) deposed, in a phrase which has haunting reverberations for anyone concerned with the cure of souls, 'public knowledge is less than the sum of private knowledges'. While it is true that no human enterprise is carried on by individuals as such rather than by the culture as a whole, and that a culture can achieve through the centuries things (like the development of language) which could not be done by an isolated biological individual in his passing moment of life, a culture does what it does as an *inter*-action *of* individuals, there is a constant dialectical to-and-fro between the whole culture and each of the sub-cultures of one of which it ultimately consists. We may picture a whole culture as a sort of network of epistemological bottle-necks, each an individual brain with the kind of incarnate limitations we found exemplified in the tiny brain of the frog *Rana Pipiens* or in the vicissitudes of foundational studies in mathematics. If the visiting anthropologist from beyond the Horse Head Nebula were possessed, as well he might be, of a logic transcending our own, and if he were to try (as an *in vivo* experiment in interstellar epistemological engineering) to graft his logic into terrestrial culture, the graft would surely be rejected: our brains, evolved in different specific historical circumstances, would be incapable of working with it—rather as we are incapable of intuitively imaging a vector space of more than three orthogonal dimension. Fred Hoyle, in his interesting science fiction novel *The Black Cloud*, kills off his hero by having him volunteer for just such an experiment by an interstellar visitor. A planetary culture might, given aeons of time to do it in, *evolve* biologically and culturally out of the limitations of its brains and of its brain-constrained language, but I can't find any good reason to believe that *we* could bootstrap ourselves out of the ruck in a few decades as a result of some breakthrough in a Harvard seminar watered by a pious libation of dollars from the Ford Foundation or the USAF.

Wherever we look—at the brain, at language, at the whole terrestrial culture—we find nothing but original epistemological sin, no prospect anywhere of epistemological salvation; nothing for our comfort but 'animal faith in induction', justifiable to a very limited extent by the argument that, since we evolved in this universe, some sort of *fit* between structural properties of the universe and structural properties of our brain and nervous systems may reasonably be supposed to exist—a justification decidedly double-edged, since there is no warranty that evolution for survival in past conditions fits a creature for survival in new conditions (where are the dinosaurs now?).

Where are we at? Well, I have been trying in my own way to follow George Alexander Kelly's prescriptions for human scientists, that we should take the scientists as our model man and consider him in the perspective of the centuries rather than in the flicker of passing moments. Since the notion of 'reality' is a key notion in psychotherapy and its relation to society, I have been trying to work out what men know they can know of 'reality' by working through (so far as that is possible within the limits of a short essay on a large subject) a closely argued account of a naturalist epistemology, based on what scientific knowledge I have been able to glean over the years: not because I suppose science to be all that good (To deceive ourselves in that direction, I take it, would to be risk blowing up or poisoning the whole planet, let alone resting on what laurels we have), but because our poor science still seems to me that the best thing we own. The inescapable conclusion seems to be that, whatever 'reality' may be, we can't know much about it, save precisely that we can't know much about it.

If this is the upshot of thousands of years of intellectual endeavour by the whole of humanity, what can we say of the mayfly individual confronting his own 'reality' and trying to work it into some kind of humanly bearable or even rewarding shape?

On an earlier page, I planted a mention of Peter L. Berger's and Thomas Luckmann's book *The Social Construction of Reality* (probably one of the ten most useful books published since the turn of the century) against a return to it at this stage in the development of my argument. Berger and Luckmann argue most convincingly that our everday social reality—the reality in which you and I grow up, marry, work, raise kids, make money and war, run for office and end up on one end or the other of a therapeutic situation—is a gossamer artwork, insubstantial as a dream, constructed and constantly reconstructed as it blows away in our verbal conversations and other symbolic interchanges, face to face or through the media. It is a structure both precarious and indefeasible, not there and all there. It is precarious because, after all, it is woven only of words, images, clothes; because it can (as we may violently discover in the public upheavals of war, revolution, famine, economic collapse; or in the private upsets of divorce, desertion, bereavement, disability, bankruptcy or sudden unemployment) be destroyed or made altogether over in the space of an hour. It is indefeasible because, in the ordinary way, it seems to stand massively over against us as a concrete maze we must learn to run from whip to carrot, to squat solidly inside us as something we can't excrete or digest without losing our sense of self as something we know how to fly through the flak. Yet there remain those curious, ecstatic moments we all experience from time to time: when we wake in the small hours disorientated, or perhaps catch sight of a stranger's face (instead of the operative patch of bristled skin) in the shaving mirror, and find that we have forgotten who we are, or have some difficulty in convincing ourselves that we really are what we are used to thinking we are; or the recurrent feeling that we must be the only phoney in our racket, that the rest of them *are* what we are faking,

58

and that we are bound to be revealed by some accident or avenger as chinless under the beard, bald beneath the toupee and all round more codpiece than comforter. For what we are pleased to call 'practical' purposes, we ordinarily take these giddy passages of *ecstasis* for illusion, our accustomed social reality and social self as reality indeed. But, in the light of the sort of humble epistemological case I have been trying to make in earlier pages of this essay, I now want to argue that precisely in these *mad* moments are we at our most *sane*. Our model man the scientist (surely?) is at his most sane and useful not when he is stolidly beavering away at problem-solving in normal science, but rather when he is doubting everything he has been told and fooling around with alternative constructions of reality—the inquiring man who is playfully entertaining the strange and damnable notion that the earth may be a ball rather than a disc, or that it might usefully be considered (just as a mathematical trick, you understand, and no offence meant) to be going round the sun, is saner in his madness at that moment than the man who is robustly confident that the earth *is* a disc and that the sun *does* go over the top in the daytime and through underneath during the night, just as anybody will tell you. William James has written interestingly about the process of 'letting go' and the subsequent 'whirling' chaos from which he emerged with a new outlook and, so to say, *saved*; the notorious Guard Depot at Caterham, where raw blokes were turned into finished guardsmen for the British Army, used to reckon that they had first to smash a man to nothing before they could set to and make a guardsman of him; George Alexander Kelly, in the same vein, stressed the difficulty of working through to new constructs without transiently dissolving the old constructs into a broken system which doesn't predict outcomes and leaves you, so to say, without a self to fly through the flak. We do *not* know anything for certain, so we *must* be saner when in doubt than when in certainty. Even the dark night of the soul or existential despair (the religionists' and philosphers' equivalent of the salesman's 'dry spell') are arguably saner and healthier than a sunny, untroubled faith in resurrection of the revolution: they are at least a kind of openness to possibility, an invitation to change, invention or discovery, a questioning; the man who already knows all the answers he reckons he needs to know is *not* an inquiring man, and to that extent *not* fully human. Doubt is the greatest and most merciful of gods, and the only god fit for incarnation.

Societies, of course, have very little use for doubt or inquiry, openness or questioning: which is why all societies institute some kind of educational system designed to stop anybody learning anything. If we don't process our raw progeny into us, we vanish away: immanently, a society is a kind of machine or routine for processing raw babies into the kind of adults needed to keep that society in business. Jules Henry (1966) presents a delicately aware discussion of the problems of educa-tion, free of simple or comfortable answers, and he is especially interesting about the problem of educating people to be, as they say, 'creative'. The difficulty is that we don't really want people to be creative all through, we don't want them to be creative about *us* or about *our* way of life, we want them to be creative only here and there, to have bits of creativity inside them we can hire and harness to specific and narrowly limited tasks—we want *creative conformists*, like the 'creative' people in advertising agencies, who have beards and hair and strange clothes to show that they are not as other men and have special magics for hire, but whose beards, hair and strange clothes are very neatly trimmed, dressed and pressed to show that these magics are carefully insulated and earthed to protect the profane from shocks or injury; we want our coffee decaffeinated, to be sure it won't keep us awake, and are trying to find some way of getting the caffeine out without taking the lift out with it. Because people are unfortunately *not* loosely linked assemblies of autonomous gadgets—a ziptronic creativator here, a grade A intelligencer there—, not walking toolbags for the managers, but integrally whole persons, whose creativity or lack of creativity pervades them as part of their whole way of being a whole person in a whole world. What, for instance, is it to be a *writer*? It is surely not a matter of acquiring technical skills, such as knowing how to use the semicolon or clean out the bowl of the 'o' with the end of a wire paperclip, and then producing a steady 3,000 words or so of pay copy a day (come rose, come cabbage) for ever after? It is more a question of living the kind of life that will make you eventually the kind of person who has a few things worth saying when he does sit down at the typewriter. In fact, we can't have creativity if we don't let people be creative about everything all the time; and, if we did let people be creative about everything all the time, all unimaginable Hell would be let loose in every department of life, so in the end we settle for producing at vast expense an 'intellectual elite' of instant decaffeinated creators, consisting of a lot of anxious little careerists who copy from each other to make sure nobody could suspect them of being somehow unsound. I state the problem; I offer no programme for its solution.

To the extent that the problem does get solved, it solves itself as far as I can see. Nothing is perfect, and some people do survive their upbringing and their education in reasonably human shape. They do what little real work gets done.

Since indeed nothing is perfect (not even primary socialization, secondary socialization and induction into the sub-culture of the work group), even properly finished people tend constantly to waver out of the shape they are supposed to be holding: they freak out in a wild variety of ways, becoming alcoholics, addicts, sports car buffs, Casanovas, Jesus Freaks, revolutionists, Black Muslims, science fiction writers, phobics, anxiety states, schizophrenics, bums, melancholics, maniacs, followers of Tolkien. Technically speaking, they *alternate* into another reality, from a reality in which you aren't human without a swimming pool into a reality in which you aren't human in a decent pair of pants, from a script in which you are a ruggedly competitive heterosexual doing it his way to a script in which you are a gay homosexual getting by; and so on.

If these are 'disorders' at all, however untidy it may all look to the tidy mind, they seem to me (as I began by suggesting) to be *philosophical* rather than 'psychological' disorders. Given the kind of epistemological humility for which I have here made out a case, it seems inept to accuse these people, as we too often do, of being in a wrong relation to 'reality', needing loving or bashing back into the 'right' relation. But to *what* 'reality'?

I am haunted by a remark I saw somewhere in a newspaper at the time of the great row in the US about the *Pentagon Papers,* a massive study by the Pentagon

60

which concluded that the US ought never to have gotten so far into Vietnam in the first place and revealed the curious way in which she had been manipulated in by the people who wanted to go in. They were leaked by one Daniel Ellsberg, who had privileged access to them, to the press, because he thought the people ought to know a bit more about the way things get done in their name. Ellsberg was a Vietnam expert: knew the language, had studied the culture, had been studying the situation in the field for a year or so. When he got back to Washington, he found (and this is the remark that haunts me) that he could not make anybody there grasp that Vietnam was a real place with real people in it. To the people in Washington entitled to be concerned with the problem, of course, Vietnam and its people could not be as *real* as the bits of paper and the career prospects; Vietnam was not an inhabited place to them so much as an issue upon which they took one of a number of possible stances according to the interests of their own agency and the interests of their own career prospects. It is in this way, I suppose, that people who can't be too different from you or I, or any nastier, can encompass unimaginable indiscriminate destruction in a country as far away from the US as it is possible to go without starting to come back round the other side of the globe, all without noticing what they are doing. If madness is something to do with our relation to reality, this is madness indeed. After considering it, do we want to argue with the 'phobic' lady who doesn't like to go out of the house? After all, it *is* pretty dangerous out there; only, if everybody let themselves be frightened by the kind of world they are living in into staying indoors all the time, the whole house of cards would tumble down; so everybody doesn't. But it looks as if it is a philosophical dispute about danger and the right way to face it, rather than a difference between clear-cut illness and abundant health.

What I would like finally to suggest is just this: that, as members of a society which manifestly doesn't and can't understand the universe about it, or even itself, we shouldn't be too ready to try to change the strange (no matter how tenderly we do it) when they come to us in difficulties. I wouldn't want to go so far as Ronald Laing, who once suggested (if I remember correctly) that we should devote ourselves to a minute examination of the revelations accorded to the poet William Blake, but perhaps we should take the opportunity to help to join the strange in their epistemological adventures—to *know* that you are lost, it seems, is to be in the ideal epistemological stance; to *know* that it is hard to see through dark glasses on a moonless night is a pretty good way to start finding out how to see better. Meanwhile, we could always try to teach them our own trick of getting by in the social reality we have to deal with by pretending to be like enough to what all the others pretend to be.

Acknowledgements

Some of the material in this essay is based on consulting work done for the National Physical Laboratory, Teddington, England, on some aspects of artificial intelligence; other material relates to work in hand, on applied epistemology, for the management consultants Heirs Associates International SA, Geneva, of which the writer is an Associate.

Select Bibliography

Allport, G. W. (1949). *Personality: A Psychological Interpretation*, Constable, *London* (first published 1937).

Aristotle, *Nichomachean Ethics*, see Thomson, J. A. K. (1955).

Austin, J. L. (1964). *Sense and Sensibilia*, Oxford University Press, Galaxy paperback, New York.

Austin, J. L. (1965). *How to do Things with Words*, Oxford University Press, Galaxy paperback, New York.

Ayer, A. J. (1956). *The Problem of Knowledge*, Macmillan, London.

Bachelard, G. (1963). *Le Materialisme Rationnel*, Presses Universitaires de France, Paris.

Bachelard, G. (1966). *La Philosophie Du Non*, Presses Universitaires de France, Paris.

Bachelard, G. (1967). *La Formation de l'Esprit Scientifique*, Libraire Philosophique J. Vrin, Paris.

Bannister, D., and Fransella, Fay (1971). *Inquiring Man: The Theory of Personal Constructs*, Penguin Education, Harmondsworth.

Bannister, D., and Mair, J. M. M. (1968). *The Evaluation of Personal Constructs*, Academic Press, London, New York.

Barker, S. F. (1964). *Philosophy of Mathematics*, Prentice-Hall, Englewood Cliffs, New Jersey.

Barthes, R. (1953). *Le Degre Zero de l'Ecriture*, Editions du Seuil, Paris.

Barthes, R. (1964). *Essais Critiques*, Editions du Seuil, Paris.

Barthes, R. (1967). *Elements of Semiology*, Cape, London (translation).

Bartlett, F. C. (1932). *Remembering: A Study in Experimental and Social Psychology*, Cambridge University Press, Cambridge.

Benacerraf, P., and Putnam, H. (1964). *Philosophy of Mathematics: Selected Readings*, Prentice-Hall, Englewood Cliffs, New Jersey.

Berger, P. L. (1961). *The Precarious Vision*, Doubleday, Garden City, New York.

Berger, P. L. (1966). *Invitation to Sociology: A Humanistic Perspective*, Penguin, Harmondsworth.

Berger, P. L. (1969). *The Social Reality of Religion*, Faber & Faber, London.

Berger, P. L., and Luckmann, T. (1967). *The Social Construction of Reality*, Allen Lane, The Penguin Press, London.

Bloomfield, L. (1935). *Language*, Allen & Unwin, London.

Boulding, K. E. (1961). *The Image: Knowledge in Life and Society*, University of Michigan Press, Ann Arbor, Michigan.

Burke, K. (1962). *A Grammar of Motives* and *A Rhetoric of Motives*, World Publishing, Meridian Books, Cleveland and New York.

Burke, K. (1966). *Language as Symbolic Action: Essays on Life, Literature, and Method*, University of California Press, Berkeley and Los Angeles.

Burke, K. (1967). *The Philosophy of Literary Form*, second edition, Louisiana State University Press, Baton Rouge, Louisiana (first edition 1941).

Cantril, H. (1963). *The Psychology of Social Movements*, Wiley, New York.

Carpenter, E., and McLuhan, M. (Eds.) (1966). *Explorations in Communication*, Beacon Press, Boston.

Carroll, J. B. (Ed.) (1956). *Language, Thought, and Reality: Selected Writings of Benjamin Lee Whorf*, M.I.T. Press, Cambridge, Massachusetts.

Cherry, C. (1966). *On Human Communication: A Review, a Survey, and a Criticism*, second edition, M.I.T. Press, Cambridge, Massachusetts.

Chisholm, R. M. (1966). *Theory of Knowledge*, Prentice-Hall, Englewood Cliffs, New Jersey.

Chomsky, N. (1965). *Aspects of the Theory of Syntax*, M.I.T. Press, Cambridge, Massachusetts.

62

Chomsky, N. (1967). *Syntactic Structures*, Mouton, The Hague.
Cohen, S. (1971). *Images of Deviance*, Penguin, Harmondsworth.
Collingwood, R. G. (1924). *Speculum Mentis or the Map of Knowledge*, Clarendon, Oxford.
Collingwood, R. G. (1935). *The Idea of Nature*, Clarendon, Oxford.
Collingwood, R. G. (1939). *An Autobiography*, Clarendon, Oxford.
Collingwood, R. G. (1946). *The Idea of History*, Clarendon, Oxford.
Cooper, D. (Ed.) (1968). *The Dialectics of Liberation*, Penguin, Harmondsworth.
De Cecco, J. P. (Ed.) (1967). *The Psychology of Language, Thought, and Instruction: Readings*, Holt, Rhinehart and Winston, New York.
Dennis, N. (1960). *Cards of Identity*, Penguin, Harmondsworth.
Douglas, Mary (1966). *Purity and Danger*, Routledge and Kegan Paul, London.
Egner, R. E., and Denonn (1961). *The Basic Writings of Bertrand Russell 1903–1959*, Allen and Unwin, London.
Empson, W. (1961). *Seven Types of Ambiguity*, Penguin, Harmondsworth.
Empson, W. (1966). *Some Versions of Pastoral*, Penguin, Harmondsworth.
English, H. B., and English, Ava Champney (1958). *A Comprehensive Dictionary of Psychological and Psychoanalytical Terms*, Longmans, London.
Erikson, H. (1968). *Identity: Youth and Crisis*, Faber and Faber, London.
Farrington, B. (1961). *Greek Science: Its Meaning for Us*, Penguin, Harmondsworth.
Fenichel, O. (1946). *The Psychoanalytic Theory of Neurosis*, Routledge and Kegan Paul, London.
Fodor, J. A., and Katz, J. J. (Eds.) (1964). *The Structure of Language: Readings in the Philosophy of Language*, Prentice-Hall, Englewood Cliffs, New Jersey.
Fraster, J. T. (Ed.) (1968). *The Voices of Time: A Cooperative Survey of Man's Views of Time as Expressed by the Science and by the Humanities*, Allen Lane, The Penguin Press, London.
Frege, G., Writings, see Geach, P. and Black, M. (1960).
Freud, S. (1962). *Two Short Accounts of Psychoanalysis*, Penguin, Harmondsworth.
Freud, S. (1963). *Leonardo da Vinci: and a Memory of his Childhood*, Penguin, Harmondsworth.
Fromm, E. (1950). *Psychoanalysis and Religion*, Yale University Press, New Haven.
Fromm, E. (1960). *The Fear of Freedom*, Routeledge and Kegan Paul, London.
Fromm, E. (1963). *The Sane Society*, Routledge and Kegan Paul, London.
Geach, P., and Black, M. (1960). *Translations from the Philosophical Writings of Gottlob Frege*, Blackwell, Oxford.
Gellner, E. (1964). *Thought and Change*, Weidenfeld and Nicolson, London.
Gellner, E. (1968). *Words and Things*, Penguin, Harmondsworth.
Gerth, H., and Mills, C. W. (1954). *Character and Social Structure: the Psychology of Social Institutions*, Routledge and Kegan Paul, London.
Goffman, E. (1959). *The Presentation of Self in Everyday Life*, Doubleday, Garden City, New York.
Goffman, E. (1961a). *Asylums: Essays on the Social Situation of Mental Patients and Other Inmates*, Doubleday, Garden City, New York.
Goffman, E. (1963b). *Stigma: Notes on the Management of Spoiled Identity*, Prentice-Hall, Englewood Cliffs, New Jersey.
Gould, J. (Ed.) (1965). *Penguin Survey of the Social Sciences 1965*, Penguin, Harmondsworth.
Greenberg, D. S. (1969). *The Politics of American Science*, Penguin, Harmondsworth (first published in the US as *The Politics of Pure Science*).
Greenberg, J. H. (Ed.) (1966). *Universals of Language*, M.I.T. Press, Cambridge, Massachusetts (second edition with important revisions).
Guilford, J. P. (1965). *Fundamental Statistics in Psychology and Education*, fourth edition, McGraw-Hill, New York.

63

Hall, C. S., and Lindzey, G. (1957). *Theories of Personality*, Wiley, New York.
Hartmann, H. (1964). *Essays on Ego Psychology: Selected Problems in Psychoanalytic Theory*, Hogarth Press, London.
Hauser, R. (1965). *The Homosexual Society*, Mayflower Books, London.
Hebb, D. O. (1961). *The Organization of Behaviour: A Neuropsychological Theory*, Wiley, New York.
Heim, Alice (1970). *Intelligence and Personality: Their Assessment and Relationship*, Penguin, Harmondsworth.
Helmstadter, G. C. (1966). *Principles of Psychological Measurement*, Methuen, London.
Hempel, C. G. (1966). *Philosophy of Natural Science*, Prentice-Hall, Englewood Cliffs, New Jersey.
Henry, J. (1966). *Culture Against Man*, Associated Book Publishers, London.
Hoel, P. G. (1962). *Introduction to Mathematical Statistics*, Wiley, New York.
Horney, Karen (1937). *The Neurotic Personality of Our Time*, Routledge and Kegan Paul, London.
Humphrey, G. (1963). *Thinking*, Wiley, New York.
Hymes, D. (Ed.) (1964). *Language in Culture and Society: A Reader in Linguistics and Anthropology*, Harper and Row, New York.
James, W. (1950). *The Principles of Psychology*, Vols. 1 and 2, Dover Publications, New York (first published 1890).
Joachim, H. H. (1906). *The Nature of Truth*, Clarendon, Oxford.
Jones, E. (1964). *The Life and Work of Sigmund Freud*, Penguin, Harmondsworth (abridged).
Kaye, F. B. (Ed.) (1924). *The Fable of The Bees by Bernard Mandeville*, Vols. 1 and 2, Oxford University Press, London.
Kelly, G. A. (1955). *The Psychology of Personal Constructs*, Vols. 1 and 2, Norton, New York.
Kelly, G. A., Other writings, see Maher, B. (1969).
Kish, L. (1965). *Survey Sampling*, Wiley, New York.
Kleene, S. C. (1952). *Introduction to Metamathematics*, North Holland, Amsterdam and London.
Klein, Melanie (1948). *Contributions to Psychoanalysis 1921–1945*, Hogarth Press, London.
Klein, Melanie, and Rivière, Joan (1937). *Love, Hate, and Reparation*, Hogarth Press, London.
Koehler, W. (1957). *The Mentality of Apes*, Penguin, Harmondsworth (first published in German 1925).
Koerner, S. (1955). *Kant*, Penguin, Harmondsworth.
Koestler, A. (1964). *The Sleepwalkers: A History of Man's Changing Vision of the Universe*, Penguin, Harmondsworth.
Laing, R. D. (1960). *The Divided Self: A Study of Sanity and Madness*, Tavistock, London.
Laing, R. D. (1961). *The Self and Others: Further Studies in Sanity and Madness*, Tavistock, London.
Laing, R. D. (1969). *The Politics of the Family*, CBC Publications, Toronto.
Laing, R. D., and Esterson, A. (1964). *Sanity, Madness, and the Family*, Vol. I, Tavistock, London.
Lakatos, I., and Musgrave, A. (Eds.) (1970). *Criticism and the Growth of Knowledge*, Cambridge University Press, Cambridge.
Leach, E. R. (1966). *Rethinking Anthropology*, Athlone Press, London, revised paperback edition.
Leach, E. R. (Ed.) (1967). *The Structural Study of Myth and Totemism*, Tavistock, London,
Lévi-Strauss, C. (1955). *Tristes Tropiques*, Plon, Paris.
Lévi-Strauss, C. (1962). *La Pensée Sauvage*, Plon, Paris.

64

Lévi-Strauss, C. (1964). *Mythologiques: Le Cru et le Cuit,* Plon, Paris.
Lévi-Strauss, C. (1967). *The Scope of Anthropology,* Cape, London (translation).
Lévi-Strauss, C. (1968). *Structural Anthropology,* Allen Lane, The Penguin Press, London (translation).
Lewis, C. S. (1961). *An Experiment in Criticism,* Cambridge University Press, London, paperback.
Maher, B. (Ed.) (1969). *Clinical Psychology and Personality: The Selected Papers of George Kelly,* Wiley, New York.
Mandelbaum, D. G. (Ed.) (1949). *Selected Writings of Edward Sapir in Language, Culture, and Personality,* University of California Press, Berkeley and Los Angeles.
Mandeville, B., see Kaye, F. B. (1924).
Mannheim, K. (1936). *Ideology and Utopia: An Introduction to the Sociology of Knowledge,* Routledge and Kegen Paul, London (translation).
Marcuse, H. (1968). *One Dimensional Man,* Sphere Books, London, paperback.
McCulloch, W. S. (1965). *Embodiments of Mind,* M.I.T. Press, Cambridge, Massachusetts.
Mead, G. H. (1962). *Mind, Self, and Society: From the Standpoint of a Social Behaviorist,* University of Chicago Press, Chicago, Phoenix paperback.
Merleau-Ponty, M. (1945). *Phenomenologie de la Perception,* Gallimard, Paris.
Merleau-Ponty, M. (1960). *Signes,* Gallimard, Paris.
Merleau-Ponty, M. (1966). *Sens et Non-Sens,* Nagel, Paris.
Merleau-Ponty, M. (1969). *La Prose du Monde,* Gallimard, Paris.
Meyer, D. (1966). *The Positive Thinkers,* Doubleday Anchor, Garden City, New York.
Mills, C. W. (1959). *The Sociological Imagination,* Oxford University Press, New York.
Minsky, M. L. (1967). *Computation: Finite and Infinite Machines,* Prentice-Hall, Englewood Cliffs, New Jersey.
Mitchell, G. D. (1968a). *A Dictionary of Sociology,* Routledge and Kegan Paul, London.
Mitchell, G. D. (1968b). *A Hundred Years of Sociology,* Duckworth, London.
Morris, C. (1964). *Signification and Significance,* M.I.T. Press, Cambridge, Massachusetts.
Mumford, L. (1966). *The City in History,* Penguin, Harmondsworth.
Ogden, C. K., and Richards, I. A. (1949). *The Meaning of Meaning: A Study of the Influence of Language upon Thought and of the Science of Symbolism,* Routledge and Kegan Paul, London.
Parsons, T. (1951). *The Social System,* Routledge and Kegan Paul, London.
Parsons, T., Bales, R. F., and Shils, E. A. (1953). *Working Paper in the Theory of Action,* Free Press, New York.
Parsons, T., and Shils, E. A. (Eds.) (1962). *Toward General Theory of Action,* M.I.T. Press, Cambridge, Massachusetts.
Passmore, J. (1968). *A Hundred Years of Philosophy,* second edition, Penguin, Harmondsworth.
Peters, R. (1967). *Hobbes,* Penguin, Harmondsworth.
Pittman, D. J., and Snyder, C. R. (1962). *Society, Culture, and Drinking Patterns,* Wiley, New York.
Quine, W. Van O. (1960). *Word and Object,* M.I.T. Press, Cambridge, Massachusetts.
Quine, W. Van O. (1961). *From a Logical Point of View: 9 Logico-Philosophical Essays,* second edition (revised), Harvard University Press, Cambridge, Massachusetts.
Quine, W. Van O. (1962). *Methods of Logic,* second edition, Routledge and Kegan Paul, London.
Quine, W. Van O. (1966). *Selected Logic Papers,* Random House, New York.
Quine, W. Van O. (1969). *Ontological Relativity and Others Essays,* Columbia University Press, New York and London.
Quine, W. Van O. (1970). *Philosophy of Logic,* Prentice-Hall, Englewood Cliffs, New Jersey.
Reid, L. (1962). *The Sociology of Nature,* second edition (revised), Penguin, Harmondsworth.

65

Richards, I. A. (1926). *Principles of Literary Cricitism*, second edition, Routledge and Kegan Paul, London.
Riesman, D. (1961). *The Lonely Crowd*, Yale University Press, New Haven and London (abridged).
Robinson, Joan (1964). *Economic Philosophy*, Penguin, Harmondsworth.
Roszak, T. (Ed.) (1969). *The Dissenting Academy*, Penguin, Harmondsworth.
Rudner, R. S. (1966). *Philosophy of Social Science*, Prentice-Hall, Englewood Cliffs, New Jersey.
Ruesch, J. (1957). *Disturbed Communication: The Clinical Assessment of Normal and Pathological Communicative Behavior*, Norton, New York.
Ruesch, J. (1961). *Therapeutic Communication*, Norton, New York.
Ruesch, J., and Bateson, G. (1951). *Communication: The Social Matrix of Psychiatry*, Norton, New York.
Ruesch, J., and Kees, W. (1956). *Nonverbal Communication: Notes on the Visual Perception of Human Relations*, University of California Press, Berkeley and Los Angeles.
Russell, B., Writings, see Egner, R. E., and Dennon (1961).
Russell, B. (1962). *An Inquiry into Meaning and Truth*, Penguin, Harmondsworth (first published 1940).
Rycroft, C. (1968). *A Critical Dictionary of Psychoanalysis*, Nelson, London.
Ryle, G. (1963). *The Concept of Mind*, Penguin, Harmondsworth (first published 1949).
Sammett, Jean E. (1969). *Programming Languages: History and Fundamentals*, Prentice-Hall, Englewood Cliffs, New Jersey.
Sapir, E., Writings, see Mandelbaum, D. G. (1949).
Sapir, E. (1921). *Language: An Introduction to the Study of Speech*, Harcourt Brace, New York.
Sartre, J. P. (1938). *La Nausée*, Gallimard, Paris.
Sartre, J.-P. (1943). *L'Être et le Néant: Essai d'Ontologie Phenoménologique*.
Sartre, J.-P. (1965). *Esquisse d'une Théorie des Emotions*, Hermann, Paris (first published 1939).
Saussure, F. de (1966). *Cours de Linguistique Générale*, Payot, Paris.
Schlaifer, R. (1959). *Probability and Statistics for Business Decisions*, McGraw-Hill, New York.
Shaffer, J. A. (1968). *Philosophy of Mind*, Prentice-Hall, Englewood Cliffs, New Jersey.
Shepherd, M., et al. (1966). *Psychiatric Illness in General Practice*, Oxford University Press, London.
Siegel, S. (1956). *Non-parametric Statistics for the Behavioral Sciences*, McGraw-Hill, New York.
Sluckin, W. (1960). *Minds and Machines*, Penguin, Harmondsworth.
Snedecor, G. W. (1956). *Statistical Methods: Applied to Experiments in Agriculture and Biology*, fifth edition, Iowa State University Press, Ames, Iowa.
Sorokin, P. A. (1963). *Modern Historical and Social Philosophies*, Dover, New York.
Smith, F., and Miller, G. A. (Eds.) (1966). *The Genesis of Language: A Psycholinguistic Approach*, M.I.T. Press, Cambridge, Massachusetts.
Smith, J. M. (1966). *The Theory of Evolution*, Penguin, Harmondsworth.
Stebbing, L. Susan (1950). *A Modern Introduction to Logic*, seventh edition, Methuen, London.
Stouffer, S. A., et al. (1966). *Measurement and Prediction*, Wiley, New York.
Suttie, I. D. (1963). *The Origins of Love and Hate*, Penguin, Harmondsworth (first published 1935).
Talalay, P. (Ed.) (1964). *Drugs in our Society*, Johns Hopkins Press, Baltimore, Maryland.
Taylor, C. (1964). *The Explanation of Behaviour*, Routledge and Kegan Paul, London.
Thomson, J. A. K. (translator) (1955). *The Ethics of Aristotle: The Nichomachean Ethics Translated*, Penguin, Harmondsworth.
Thomson, R. (1968). *The Pelican History of Psychology*, Penguin, Harmondsworth.

Toulmin, S. (1967). *The Philosophy of Science: An Introduction,* Hutchinson, London.

Touraine, A. (1965). *Sociologie de l'Action,* Seuil, Paris.

Tylor, Sir E. B. (1958). *The Origins of Culture,* Harper and Row, Torchbooks, New York (first published 1871, as *Primitive Culture*).

Vaihinger, H. (1935). *The Philosophy of 'As If': A System of the Theoretical, Practical, and Religious Fictions of Mankind,* Routledge and Kegan Paul, London (translation).

Veblen, T. (1925). *The Theory of the Leisure Class,* Allen and Unwin, London.

Vygotsky, L. S. (1962). *Thought and Language,* M.I.T. Press, Cambridge, Massachusetts (first published in Russian, 1934).

Wann, T. W. (Ed.) (1965). *Behaviorism and Phenomenology: Contrasting Bases for Modern Psychology,* University of Chicago Press, Phoenix, Chicago and London.

Weber, M. (1962). *Basic Concepts in Sociology,* Owen, London (translation).

Wellek, R., and Warren, A. (1963). *Theory of Literature,* third edition, Penguin, Harmondsworth.

White, L. A. (1949). *The Science of Culture: A Study of Man and Civilization,* Grove Press, Evergreen, New York.

Whitehead, A. N. (1964). *The Concept of Nature,* Cambridge University Press, Cambridge, paperback.

Whorf, B. Lee, Writings, see Carroll, J. B. (1956).

Whyte, W. H. (1963). *The Organization Man,* Penguin, Harmondsworth.

Williams, R. (1963). *Culture and Society 1780–1950,* Penguin, Harmondsworth (reprinted with postcript).

Williams, R. (1965). *The Long Revolution,* Penguin, Harmondsworth.

Yates, F. (1960). *Sampling Methods for Censuses and Surveys,* third edition, Griffin, London.

Yule, G. U., and Kendall, M. G. (1950). *An Introduction to the Theory of Statistics,* fourteenth edition, Griffin, London.

Young, M. (1961). *The Rise of the Meritocracy 1870–2033,* Penguin, Harmondsworth.

APPROACHES

4

THE THERAPEUTIC COMMUNITY

D. J. Smail

As it is used in Britain, the term 'therapeutic community' may be employed on the one hand as a loose description of any institutional setting in which psychiatric patients are treated in a general, eclectic kind of way, or it may on the other hand be reserved as a name for a much more specific orientation to treatment, involving a comparatively clear-cut set of methods and beliefs. 'Therapeutic community' in its loose sense springs readily to the lips of administrative and medical staff of quite ordinary, traditional mental hospitals where treatment policies and staff attitudes may not have changed significantly over the past 15 years; in this case the usage seems to gain currency as a reassuring-sounding bromide for public consumption. It is the therapeutic community in its narrower sense—what Myers and Clark (1972) call 'the therapeutic community proper'—which will be considered here.

Therapeutic communities are primarily social organizations in a psychiatric setting, created to provide an alternative to the more prevalent kind of institutional organization to be found in this field, the baleful influences of which have been so well described by people like Goffman (1961) and Wing (1962). Probably most mental hospitals (and the writer can comment with confidence only on the British situation) have improved greatly in recent years in the degree to which the dehumanizing effects of institutionalization have been controlled and mitigated. Nevertheless, the social atmosphere differs widely—and, as we shall see, measurably—between hospitals, and true therapeutic communities are still very clearly distinguishable from the 'average', traditional mental hospital. One very central reason for this clear difference is that in the therapeutic community there is a definite, and often conscious, intention to break free of the medical model of mental illness.

Before we come to look in detail at therapeutic communities themselves, we should perhaps pause to consider how the medical model shapes the atmosphere and attitudes in the traditional hospital and why it is that the traditional approach is still so prevalent.

So far, the efforts of psychiatrists like Cooper (1967), Laing (1967) and Szasz (1962) and psychologists like Albee (1969), Bannister (1969) and Sarbin (1967) to put the view that the phenomena of mental disorder need not necessarily be construed in terms of symptoms of illness or disease (but rather as problems in living, results of interpersonal conflict, a natural—and even adaptive—reaction to social stress, etc.) have not met with much in the way of official or public approval. While there is some evidence that people are somewhat puzzled by the mental illness label when it is professionally applied to behaviour which they themselves see as signs of weakness or inadequacy (Reiff, 1966; Sarbin and Mancuso, 1970), it is still probably true that when faced with such 'weakness' or 'inadequacy' in themselves it is a lot more convenient to construe them as illness. It also seems humane, even reassuring, to proffer to the public an official view that behaviour they may fear as raving lunacy is simply symptomatic of 'an illness like any other'. Thus, the belief that mental disorder is mental disease, while it may sometimes strain credulity to a certain extent, is above all a *convenient* belief. Even if we have to resort to rather suspect logic on occasion, we can at worst treat patients *as if* they were ill. One should note in passing that one particular danger of this approach is that, as Szasz (1962) points out, we do not always *really* behave towards our patients (or our disturbed friends and relatives) as if they were ill, but are unable to work out a coherent view of *what* they are, because an illness model, as long as we stay within it, does not logically permit criticism of its own axioms. Thus we may say that X is ill, but treat him much more as mad, or stupid or dangerous.

A psychiatric patient in a mental hospital may frequently fall victim both to the expressed illness model and to the unexpressed negative valuation of madness or badness. The illness model determines that he shall be the passive host of a 'mental disease', and consequently shall submit to a ritual of diagnosis and treatment carried out upon him by experts who believe that his own conceptualization of his predicament can have little relevance. In the majority of cases this means in practice that after an initial diagnostic interview with a doctor his hospital life will consist largely of trying to busy himself (or 'being busied') in superficial social or occupational activities in between the times when he is given his tablets or capsules or administered electroplexy. The operation of the unexpressed valuation imposed upon him as mad, stupid or dangerous is likely to mean that he will be stripped of powers which enable him to make decisions about himself, significantly to influence what happens to him or to discuss his psychological reactions to his situation in anything but a cursory way. He will probably be gently and humanely treated, as a child by an uncle, but he will also have no more than the child's freedom of action.

In this (the physical treatment) application of the medical model are likely to be found a number of related attitudes among medical and nursing staff which find expression in varying proportions in different institutions. Discipline, in terms of strict ward routine and control of patient behaviour, is usually thought to be of central importance, as are cleanliness and tidiness. It is frequently thought unhealthy for patients to 'think about' their troubles, or to discuss their emotional difficulties with anyone but 'the doctor'. The doctor is seen as the central focus of authority, makes decisions which are not to be questioned by either staff or patients and is likely to be the only officially valid source of treatment policy. This will often be held to be true for the most inexperienced doctor even compared with much more experienced non-medical staff. Even in situations where physical treatments are accorded a secondary place—or possibly no place at all—by medical staff, the influence of the medical model is often still strongly to be felt: 'diagnosis' may appear under the guise of 'formulation' (in individual psychotherapeutic situations, for example); 'treatment', 'acute–chronic' distinctions, 'prognosis', will all find their place in the language of illness, and above all a similar set of doctor-centred, active therapist/passive patient concepts are likely to persist, where patients spend large parts of the day or week filling in time (often with the help of 'paramedical' staff such as occupational therapists) waiting for the next dose of 'treatment'. The therapeutic community has a different set of values.

The causal hypothesis underlying therapeutic community methods is likely to be that mental disorder or psychological disturbance arises from social, largely interpersonal pressures and conflicts, and that the social organization of the hospital or ward should mobilize all its resources to counteract the results of such experience. Different practitioners of the therapeutic community have emphasized somewhat different aspects of their work, but certain clearly discernible common trends are evident. Good accounts may be found in Jones (1968), Martin (1968) and Rapoport (1960), and much of this work is summarized in Caine and Smail (1969a).

Rather than being passive recipients of treatment, patients are encouraged to be active in helping themselves and others, and the emphasis is on communication, not only of information which will help the doctor to diagnose and treat, but much more of feelings and views which may be of therapeutic value to other members of the community. For this reason there is a heavy emphasis on group processes in therapeutic communities, as well as a marked 'blurring of role' between medical and nursing staff and patients—people accustomed to the traditional hospital commonly experience considerable unease when encountering a therapeutic community for the first time, since they are unable to distinguish staff from patients. The former will have given up not only their outward signs of office, such as uniform or white coat, but are also likely not to be immediately locatable in a geographically predictable place (e.g. nurses in the nurses' office) and to be generally referred to by their first names.

All time spent in the community is felt to be of potential therapeutic value, and so all activities are to be considered (usually in groups of one sort or another) from the point of view of the insights they provide into the behaviour, perceptions and assumptions on the individuals concerned.

As indicated, the vehicle of communication is the group, whether this is a meeting of the total community (the daily ward or community meeting which takes place in the morning in most therapeutic communities), a small group psychotherapy meeting of the conventional kind or a work group, which is formed usually only minimally for the carrying out of some kind of domestic, occupational or industrial work and which is aimed much more at providing experiences of the kind of interpersonal or intrapersonal difficulties individuals may have in the work situation. In the evening, social activities will also not be allowed to pass without some kind of therapeutic scrutiny in a group setting of the interpersonal relationships to which they give rise.

Staff members are not seen solely as purveyors of expert opinion or help, and hence are likely to be integrated into the community in a much more personal way than is the case in the traditional hospital. This, together with the fact that judgemental attitudes and conventional professional demeanour are likely to be felt unhelpful to the free expression of opinion, means that 'permissiveness' is a central feature of therapeutic communities, and behaviour which might be thought for one reason or another improper (for staff as well as patients) in a traditional hospital setting is much more likely to be tolerated in the therapeutic community. Further, staff will be exposed to, indeed will invite, the criticism of their colleagues and patients in an effort to gain as good an understanding as possible of their own contribution to social influences at work within the community and will keep patients fully informed of their own feelings and observations. Staff group meetings, in which staff at all levels can try to iron out their problems and difficulties in working together, are an important feature of most therapeutic communities, and here again decisions arrived at in them will be 'fed back' to the patients, or possibly patients will be invited to send their own representatives to staff groups. Emphasis on discipline, cleanliness, etc., is likely to be minimal (patients can scarcely learn to care for themselves if they are looked after, or regimented, like children), and the expression of painful, unconventional or negative feelings is unlikely to be officially inhibited. The emphasis on permissiveness should not be taken to suggest, as many of the opponents of the therapeutic community assume, that licence is given to sexual promiscuity or aggressive behaviour. It is a common observation of people who have worked in this kind of setting that sexual and aggressive 'acting out' are unusually infrequent, perhaps because of the searching social scrutiny which they would receive from the community if they did occur.

Perhaps most central of all to the therapeutic community philosophy is the concept of 'democratization'. Decisions concerning members of the community are not to be made autocratically or unilaterally, and even decisions traditionally seen as the sole province of the doctor, governed by his sacrosanct 'clinical responsibility', may be taken only after consultation with other community members or on the basis of a straight democratic vote: under this heading would be included decisions concerning the admission to or discharge from the community of individual patients. The attempt, of course, is to arrive at an informed democracy rather than a simple show of hands, and measures aimed at achieving this may involve the setting up of patient committees with their own elected officers or rules that decisions can only be taken on the basis of consensus. A consensus rule has the advantage that responsible medical staff in fact have the possibility of a veto, as well as turning the decision-making process into a potentially therapeutic situation in which a wide range of possible actions can be considered in all their implications. Because of the democratic structure of properly functioning therapeutic communities, patients are ultimately largely responsible for themselves and each other, and this is a very far cry from even the most benign of the paternalistic systems to be found in more traditional settings.

In practice, the functioning of most if not all therapeutic communities falls short of the ideals which may be set for them in terms of communications, permissiveness and democratization, and some of the practical difficulties will be discussed a little later. For the moment one should note that setting up and maintaining such a community is no easy matter, and this method of working imposes considerable strains on staff as well as patients: medical and nursing staff are for the most part used to working in a traditional, basically authoritarian and hierarchical system, and many find it impossible to adjust to the fundamentally different ways of the therapeutic community. The kind of problems involved in this area are discussed in detail by Jones (1968) and Martin (1968).

Having described in a somewhat concrete way some of the more salient features of the therapeutic community, it may be appropriate to look a little more closely at some of the theoretical reasons for their functioning which have been put forward.

The hypothesis that psychological disorder tends to be the result of interpersonal difficulties leads to the view that the nature of these difficulties will become evident as members of the community interact with each other and that the therapeutic resources of all members of the community can be brought to bear in an effort to correct faulty interpersonal perceptions, while the generally supportive and permissive atmosphere of the community will enable members of it to experiment with new ways of perceiving and relating to others. In most therapeutic communities, then, there is great emphasis on the 'here and now', and, in contrast with some of the more traditional form of psycho-analytically derived psychotherapy, not much attention is paid to raking over the past. While it is true that some therapeutic community medical staff in Britain may subscribe theoretically to some of the more mechanical views which are to be met with in the 'object relations' school, in practice their emphasis is likely to be on the adequacy or otherwise of the relationships formed by community members in the present.

The therapeutic community movements as a whole has yet to work out a reasonably viable theoretical background for the kinds of social techniques which are in fact used, and psychiatrists are probably hampered by the limitations of some of the more traditional approaches to group psychotherapy which have been prevalent. It is possible to find conceptualizations of group processes in the British literature which seem to offer a credible model for the therapeutic community approach (e.g. Walton, 1971, Chaps. 1 and 2, in which attention is paid to the kinds of learning experience which take place in groups). Yet, as Yalom notes in his excellent book on therapeutic groups (Yalom, 1970), British psychotherapists tend to come from the rather austere, fundamentally psychoanalytic schools which are likely to view present social interactions as the result of the intrapsychic hydraulics of past experience and disturbed parental relationships and are likely to approach the therapeutic group in a spirit of almost frightening professional 'neutrality', armed with extraordinary metaphysical concepts such as 'the group mind'. The kind of insights into psychotherapeutic processes which have emerged from the more pragmatic and liberated American schools, such as those of C. R. Rogers, G. A. Kelly and the Gestalt psychotherapists, have yet to make a significant impact on British psychiatry.

Having said this, however, one should point out that one of the more satisfactory conceptualizations of the therapeutic community approach is that of Maxwell Jones, himself one of the founders of this kind of treatment. A clear statement of these views may be found in his book *Beyond the Therapeutic Community* (Jones, 1968), in which he emphasizes that the social structure of the community should be set up to facilitate 'social learning' to the greatest possible extent. He argues that the hospital background of most therapeutic institutions and the nature of medical training are antithetical to the development of the atmosphere and relationships which foster social learning and suggests that the time is ripe for psychiatry to make a break with the traditional principles and practises of general medicine. Central to the concept of social learning is the idea of the 'corrective emotional experience', in which the therapeutic resources of community members will make positive use of instances of 'symptomatic' or disturbed behaviour to foster individual growth. It is also of interest that Jones views with disquiet the official policy of bringing treatment of mental illness into the orbit of the District General Hospital, since this serves to increase the influence of inappropriate medical methods of nursing and treatment.

One of the thorniest problems connected with the therapeutic community method is that of leadership. It is an ironic paradox that that method of treatment which seeks above all to break down the established administrative and medical hierarchy and to establish democratic processes a decision-making should in the end depend upon the presence of a strong leader. It seems to be a common experience that most therapeutic communities have been started, often in the face of considerable opposition, by one energetic and idealistic therapist (the names of D. Cooper, M. Jones and D. V. Martin once again spring to mind) and have been able to function in a largely antagonistic official setting mainly because of the skill such men have been able to muster in reconciling the liberal ideals of the community with the suspicions, fears and resentments met within the wider social context. Therapeutic communities very frequently attract intense hostility from the medical and administrative establishment, and whether he likes it or not the psychiatrist in charge of a community is answerable for what happens within it to these authorities, and hence he must, realistically, maintain ultimate control, even if this means on occasion temporarily abandoning democracy. In the National Health Service, certainly, therapeutic communities simple cannot exist independently of the bureaucratic and authoritarian structure surrounding them and sooner or later the values of the community are going to conflict with, and ultimately have to submit to, those of the larger environment. This of course generates very serious stresses and strains in the community, and even greater ones in the leader, who must appear democratic—indeed struggle to foster the democratic principles in which he believes—while at the same time preserving ultimate and absolute control in order to ensure that the community does not transgress the limits permitted by the statutory authorities. In an ideally functioning community, presumably, the leader would eventually be able to abdicate in favour of established democratic machinery—and some have managed to get close to this ideal—but more frequently the community must depend for its continued existence on the presence of one exceptionally able person. He, apart from resisting the pressures already mentioned, must also be able to tolerate and deal therapeutically with the difficulties and anxieties of staff and patients who may themselves find their values in conflict with those of the therapeutic community approach but who, either because of poor selection or the exigencies of training, must be contained within the system. It is perhaps not surprising then that, in the present writer's experience anyway, therapeutic communities tend to collapse when for one reason or another the leader departs. One hopes that this is not because of the fundamental unsoundness of the system, but rather because the system is too often in a situation where it has to be dependent on the good will of the surrounding administrative and medical structures.

Having considered some of the opinions and views on the nature of therapeutic communities commonly stated by those who have been responsible for setting them up, this would seem a reasonable juncture at which to turn to some of the 'tighter', more experimental literature. The kinds of questions which naturally arise concern the possibility of finding measurable differences between therapeutic communities and other types of institution in terms of staff and patient characteristics, treatment policies and effectiveness of treatment.

Several research workers have been interested in the variations in attitude to be found among mental health professionals. More obviously than seems to be the case in other branches of medicine, psychiatry cannot depend on a well-established body of scientific knowledge to justify its procedures, for, while the 'medical model' is widely subscribed to, there are not enough hard 'facts' to mould a uniform policy within that model, and this means that attitudes and value systems play a crucial role in the formation of a particular treatment orientation. Cohen and Struening (1963) were among the first to take a detailed look at this question and developed a questionnaire which identified five factors in the opinions of hospital workers about mental illness. These factors they labelled as authoritarianism, benevolence (kindly paternalism), mental hygiene ideology ('an illness like any other'), social restrictiveness and interpersonal ideology. They were also able to show that the attitudes revealed by the questionnaire responses were relevant to practical issues such as the discharge policy of some hospitals (Cohen and Struening, 1964). Similarly, Ellsworth (1965) was able to demonstrate significant relationships between expressed attitudes of ward staff, again measured by questionnaire, and the way in which the staff were actually perceived by patients—both authoritarian and benevolent–paternalistic staff tended to be perceived in negative terms by patients, while staff who repudiated 'traditional' attitudes of this kind were seen more positively. In later work, Ellsworth and Maroney (1972) have gone on to show that patients' 'perception of ward' may have a bearing on their adjustment to the outside community on leaving hospital; the important perceptions here concerned the degree to which staff were seen as accessible, receptive and involved. A slightly different note is struck in research carried out by Moos (1968), who suggests that there may be important variations in the way different patients see the same ward or in the way an individual patient may react to different activities in the ward. It would thus be wise not to generalize the kind of findings discussed above too hastily: while it seems on the face of it that 'liberal' staff attitudes are the ones which pay dividends, one may have to be fairly discriminating in selecting patients for a particular type of regime.

As part of a research programme aimed directly at clarification of attitudes of staff and patients in the therapeutic community setting, Caine and Smail (1969a) developed an 'Attitude to Treatment Questionnaire' which differentiated quite clearly between doctors subscribing to different psychiatric orientations, as well as between nurses and patients in traditional hospitals compared with those in therapeutic communities. The most powerful measure to emerge was a collection of items (forming a single factor from the questionnaire) which contrasts an emphasis on physical treatments, discipline, formal role relationships and authority with, on the other hand, a preference for interpersonal approaches, liberal ward organization, informal relationships and 'being oneself'. Using scores on these items, it was possible to distinguish a sample of physically orientated doctors from a sample of therapeutic community doctors, with almost no overlap between the two groups. Similarly, both nurses and patients in hospitals known for their traditional approach could be clearly distinguished on their scores on this instrument from those in therapeutic community settings. Thus, while many questions still remain unanswered, most of which would focus on the *reasons for* the differences between mental health professionals which have been observed, it seems clear that variations in attitudes to treatment among psychiatrists and others can be objectively demonstrated, and have in some cases been shown to be perceptible to others as well as having implications for what is actually done to patients.

Questions concerning how such attitudes are acquired have largely remained unanswered. Obviously enough, the part played by training needs close examination, but so far not much seems to have been done in the way of research into this problem. However, there is mounting evidence concerning the contribution of personality factors to the formation of treatment attitudes. Kreitman (1962) demonstrated differences between organically as opposed to psychodynamically orientated psychiatrists in that the latter were more introverted and emotionally sensitive (or possibly unstable than the former. Caine and Smail (1969a, b) arrived independently (if belatedly) at extremely similar findings, and developed a questionnaire measure of 'direction of interest' which seems to be consistently related to measure of treatment orientation of doctors and nurses as well as treatment (and symptom) preferences of patients (Caine and Leigh, 1972; Caine *et al.,* 1973; Smail, 1970). For example, there seem to be associations between a physical approach to treatment (or a somatic approach to symptoms), interests of an external (in the world 'out there') as opposed to internal ('all in the mind') nature and a tendency to view oneself and others in an objective, categorizing way rather than a more psychologically evaluative way—for example, as tall or shorter rather than as kind or unkind. A further point of interest is that Caine and his colleagues, in the studies just referred to, have found that conservatism may be a significant feature involved in treatment attitudes more typical of traditional as well as behaviour therapy approaches. Encouragingly, corroboration of some of the more significant of these findings has come from research recently carried out by Pallis and Stoffelmayr (1973), who, having studied a different sample of psychiatrists, again found attitudes to treatment on the Caine and Smail questionnaire to be related to social attitudes such as toughmindedness and conservatism. Thus the likely qualities of personality to be found in the (admittedly stereotyped) therapeutic community practitioner would be liberality, inwardly directed interests (possibly of a religious or philosophical kind) and emotional sensitivity, if not vulnerability. The opposite of this would be the organically orientated psychiatrist, tending to authoritarianism, with concrete, practical, down-to-earth interests, toughly resistant to emotional whims and fancies. It is of interest that the combination of authoritarianism and hard-headed pragmatism has also been demonstrated in a non-medical setting by Mirels and Garrett (1971), who investigated some of the psychological components of the 'protestant ethic' and found that people who had job preferences of a concrete, practical, as opposed to imaginative and theoretical kind tended to have higher scores on authoritarianism as well as believing that virtue lies in hard work and the just rewards thereof. One should perhaps insert at this point a reminder that the kind of 'personality differences' discussed above between groups of staff or patients are based on only moderate correlation coefficients or on tests of statistical significance which allow for great individual variation; it is still by no means impossible to find a liberal organicist or a bigoted and concretistic community therapist.

And now comes the question of the effectiveness of the therapeutic community method. In the writer's view the question 'How well does it work?' is a silly one, and to ask it is to fall straight into the trap dug by the medical model. Psychological therapies cannot be said to 'work' in the way that aspirins do, simply because nobody has yet been able to define a consistent or commonly accepted set of values by which to judge psychotherapeutic results. Indeed, much of the unresolvable controversy over what is or is not a 'good' method of psychological treatment probably stems from the fact that practitioners of different methods are unable to see that they are not verifying their usefulness against some 'real', external criterion, but are simply attempting to shove their own values down everybody else's throats. If one inclines to mechanistic manipulation, therapeutic paradise might consist of having everyone conditioned or 'shaped' to some ideal of socio-economic efficiency; or possibly we could be pressing buttons to stimulate our 'pleasure centres' all day, and all night, long. At the other end of the scale, a person could be judged a therapeutic success if he spent his entire life in an agony of self-actualization, laying bare his soul (and possibly his body) at every deep and meaningful encounter. Considerations such as these seems also to have played a part in the reasoning of Bergin and Strupp (1970), who conclude from their review of research in this area that questions of effectiveness in any global sense must be deferred until the phenomena involved in the process of psychotherapy have been examined somewhat more minutely.

A much more legitimate question, and one it should perhaps be incumbent on therapists at least to try to answer, is whether they have achieved what they set out to achieve, and if so whether they can demonstrate it to the satisfaction of others. Of course, not every treatment practitioner formulates his aims precisely enough for their success to be measured, or bothers to measure if he has. On the other hand, many have, and do. But again we come back to the problem of how acceptable the aims are in the first place to the rest of the psychotherapeutic or psychiatric community: it is not that it is impossible to submit treatment methods to a test, but that it is impossible to agree on what that test should be.

Having said this, it should be noted that studies using the conventional kinds of measure of improvement during and recovery after treatment suggests that results can be just as good, at least for some cases, in therapeutic community methods as in traditional ones, if not better. For example, Caine and Smail (1969a) demonstrated a greater degree of improvement, five years after treatment, in a group of neurotic patients treated in a therapeutic community compared with a group treated in a more conventional setting, in terms of both symptomatic relief and changes in more basic personality characteristics. Myers and Clark (1972) observed greater improvement in schizophrenic behaviour in patients on a therapeutic community ward when compared with patients on a traditional ward, and Whiteley (1970), surveying the results of treatment at the Henderson Hospital, one of Britain's foremost therapeutic communities, showed quite encouraging improvement rates for psychopathic patients.

Insistent advocacy of a particular brand of psychotherapy, or a particular view of psychological health, perhaps reflects the urge to generalize, to arrive at something akin to 'natural laws', met with so often in the wider sphere of psychology as a scientific discipline. To arrive at 'prediction and control' in any absolute sense, it is felt essential that psychological 'facts' should have equally absolute generality (and it seems still to be quite widely accepted that prediction and control are the proper aims of psychology). In psychotherapy, however, it would seem to be high time for us to recognize that what we are dealing with are systems of relative values, and we should abandon the search for some kind of externally specifiable, universally acceptable model of what man should be and how we can get him to be it. The apparent stability of natural scientific 'facts' resides in the widespread ability of natural scientists to agree about their observations and experience. They are perhaps fortunate in dealing with an area in which such agreement seems to be possible, that is where theories and hypotheses are usually capable of being checked by appeal in the last resort to sensory impressions which, for whatever reason, seem to be shared by all interested parties. In naive language, they can check their hunches against 'reality'. The social scientist, and perhaps most of all the psychotherapist, is not so lucky: wherever the criteria for the correctness of his hunches may be found, there seems to be no convincing indication that they reside in the same kind of commonly acceptable sphere of the immediately 'given'. It is not so much that we cannot easily check on our hypotheses in this way, but, even more difficult, we cannot agree on what kind of checking is relevant, nor on what kind of hypothesis is worth considering whether we can check on it or not. For example, I may be able to demonstrate to the satisfaction of all that a given kind of treatment leads to more patient days spent outside hospital. However, there is no guarantee that this particular criterion will be accepted by those who count as indicative of therapeutic success or, even if it is, that that is in itself any justification for the therapeutic method used. This kind of problem of values saturates psychology at every level. Psychological 'reality' is in an entirely relative domain, and there can be no appeal to an intersubjectively shared area of agreement concerning mental phenomena in the way that seems more possible with physical objects. Social scientists have a number of strategies for coping with this problem, and most of them boil down to a hostile (in Kelly's sense of the term) attempt to *constrain* people to a certain view—if we don't all agree naturally, we shall have to be in some way modified to make us agree by convention. This can be done at a theoretical level by turning people into machines—possibly S–R machines, or machines running on libido, etc.—by simple acts of denial of the more awkward facets of our subject matter ('there is no such thing as mind') or, more practically, by attempts to make everybody use the same concepts (e.g. by advocating a 'universal index' of personality factors or insisting that only *one* scheme of psychiatric diagnosis is permissible).

Behaviourism will only be 'true' when the whole population becomes behaviourist; if we all subscribed to the tenets of psychoanalysis, Freud would be infallible. But we shall not reach unanimity, simply because such theoretical positions as these ascribe values to different aspects of human behaviour and functioning and there is no scientific court in which the rightness of such values seems likely to be asserted.

It seems to be taking psychologists a terribly long time to recognize that there *are* no absolutes, and no objective criteria of psychological truth. Ironically, it is practitioners of sciences in which these problems are much less obviously apparent who are proffering us concepts which we can use to gain some control over our predicament; Bridgman (1959) and Oppenheimer (1956), both physicists, and the chemist and philosopher of science Polanyi (1958) all in their own way chide psychologists for their devotion to what amount to metaphysical ideals of objectivity, certainty and predictability, and point out that at the root of scientific enquiry man comes face to face with nothing other than himself and his own passion for understanding, channelled inescapably through his own perceptual and rational equipment.

What confounds the aims of prediction and control above all is our freedom. In those areas of behaviour popularly considered voluntary, we are free not to be predicted and controlled. There is no test which one could set up, even on logical grounds, let alone in practice, which could prove that men are mechanistically determined, and though we may have our *reasons*, we are, as de Charms (1968) points out, quite capable of inventing them ourselves; we have final causes as well as effective ones, an Aristotelian distinction which Rychlak (1970) suggests has been ignored by psychologists for too long. Instead, driven by what Bakan (1967) has called the 'mystery–mastery complex' (the urge to master others while keeping secret the means of mastery), they have twisted and turned to overcome this problem, again largely by attempting to replace freedom by mechanics. If people appear to have conscious motives, we say they are 'really' unconscious ones disguised. If people foil our attempts to experiment with them, we try to mislead them about our intentions or perhaps, if there is no other way, to hypnotize them—recommended as a possible solution by Brand (1971). In short, we seek in some way or other to deprive them of their ability to do to us what we supposed we were doing to them (Bannister (1966) gives a more detailed indication of the problems posed by reflexivity in psychology). Alternatively, it is quite possible to give up altogether and study animals instead.

When looked at from this standpoint, many if not most social institutions, whether familial, tribal, legal or political, are similarly aimed subtly or flagrantly at coercing human beings into some kind of predictability, at curtailing their freedom sufficiently to make them amenable to at least some kinds of laws and to make them measurable, even if by instruments no more sophisticated than social attitudes—and that attitudes are rudimentary measuring instruments, methods of ordering people, is a view interestingly developed by Kelvin (1970). In a covert kind of way, psychology has tended to line up alongside such forces of social control rather than limiting itself to studying them, and it is only recently, in the Anglo-Saxon world at least, that considerations of what to do about problems like freedom are beginning to creep into psychology from alien philosophies such as phenomenology and existentialism. It seems that if psychologists are to survive scientifically they must abandon the futile aims of prediction and control, the attempt to discover or impose on their subject matter one particular psychological system or language, and pursue instead the aims of clarification and understanding—a course suggested recently by both Bakan (1967) and Mair (1970) among others. In other words, it should be the psychologist's job to learn the rules of as many psychological 'languages' as possible and to develop skills in teaching people to learn each other's language. For example, it is quite possible that there is a language of physical symptoms and a language of psychological distress (Smail, 1970), that they are translatable in terms of each other but that speakers of one are likely best to understand and be understood by people who speak the same one. The first step for the psychologist is to suspend, for the present at least, any judgement he might wish to make that one is more correct than the other. People learn to speak that psychological language, operate with that system of values, which, for one reason or another, suits them best. Often labels are attached to such value systems, quite frequently by people who do not themselves operate within them; behaviourist, mystic, fascist, idealist, impressionist, schizophrenic, would be examples. The psychologist may attempt to clarify the operations of such different systems, but he has no hope of validating one rather than others, and every time he tries to do he will commit the naturalistic fallacy—whatever criterion of 'correctness' he chooses, he can always be asked whether or not it is *right*. As Smith (1961) has pointed out, disputation about values is possible, but can only be persuasive, not conclusive.

The dominant medical model of mental 'illness' offers little in the way of choice to those embraced by its methods, and the values which it involves are cloaked, at least in the public mind, by reverence for the march of medical science and the view that the expert knows best. Other treatment orientations, frequently seen as opposed to the organic, medical approach, in fact often display a similar blindness to the values which they espouse—one thinks of psychoanalysis or behaviour therapy—and so fall victim to what Polanyi (1958) has called 'moral inversion': the (sometimes fanatical) assertion of a value system precisely on the grounds of its 'objectivity' and freedom from values.

In its positive aspects, the therapeutic community comes some way towards meeting some of these difficulties. At the most obvious level, the emphasis on permissiveness dispenses with the (possibly covert) view that only certain kinds of behaviour are acceptable and allows people to try out ways of acting and reacting which even they themselves may have believed to be forbidden. To take an example already referred to, in the traditional mental hospital there is usually an unquestioning acceptance of the fact that cleanliness and tidiness are among the most essential characteristics of the hospital war, and patients are either regimented into complying with unusually fastidious rules or are cared for in these respects like babies by the nursing staff. In the therapeutic community patients may be allowed to discover for themselves how important such questions are to them and to act accordingly. The democratic organization of therapeutic communities likewise militates against the advocacy of any one particular view or the forcing of members of the community into a single generalized treatment mould. The recognition that every member of the community has a potential therapeutic contribution to make at different times to different people and, similarly, may find help from sources as diverse as a doctor, a fellow or a ward cleaner reflects a welcome emphasis on relativity and tolerance of uncertainty. The provision of opportunities for social learning in a permissive setting gives the individual freedom to behave as he chooses in the light of his experience: he need feel impelled neither by physiological nor psychical machinery, and through his freedom he may learn responsibility. It is of interest to note in passing that any psychotherapeutic system which places the onus for his behaviour on the patient himself at the same time as postulating mechanisms to account for it puts itself in a difficult theoretical position: presumably, where this difficulty arises it does so through a confusion between mechanisms and reasons. Social learning may provide people with reasons for changing their behaviour but will not, for example, condition changes in behaviour or 'shape' it in some mechanical way.

There are also, however, negative sides to therapeutic community life. The most obvious is the pressure to conformity, so that community values gather a force as ends rather than means. Such conformity may become embodied in a kind of community jargon—and this will be familiar to many people who have worked in or passed through therapeutic communities—and an intolerance of non-community views or preoccupations. It is a frequent fear of those who have observed therapeutic communities in operation that immersion for comparatively long periods of time (Probably between six and 18 months) in the somewhat artificial atmosphere of intense interpersonal scrutiny and mutual support may lead to difficulties in later adjustment to life in the wider social environment. Again, the emphasis on group sharing of experience may bring about an intolerance of individuality and 'differentness' and render unattainable the kind of 'community of freedoms' which Cooper (1970) advocates, resulting instead in what he calls a 'sterile "emptied-out" form of group existence'.

The therapeutic community method of coping with psychological disturbance is not, and need not be, suitable for everybody. Indeed, its relatively limited popularity would suggest that only a small minority of therapists and patients feel comfortable

82

in this kind of setting. From the purely practical point of view, it is likely that, as with other forms of psychotherapy, patients able to profit from a therapeutic community experience will be on the right side of average as far as intelligence and socio-economic level are concerned, though the fact that communities may set their own norms, rather than having the therapist's imposed upon them, may make these considerations less important than they might be in other areas. The evidence does suggest that psychological-mindedness and inwardly directed interests, together with social attitudes in the direction of tolerance and liberality, are fairly basic requirements for those likely to be able to make good use of the therapeutic community situation. More generally, however, as long as the social context in which they are set is structured hierarchically and oriented to absolute values, therapeutic communities may gain little ground, and some see hope for the future of these and related methods as lying much more in work outside institutions, in the population at large; Beier *et al.* (1971) describe an interesting experiment in which non-professionals helped members of their own local community to cope with problems which would more usually have been referred to psychiatric experts of some kind, and Maxwell Jones (1968) suggests that the techniques developed in hospitals can and should be extended beyond the institutional walls. As things are, it certainly seems unreasonable to except that a society which finds it difficult to afford freedom and democratic responsibility to its members when they are sane in any more likely to do so when they have gone mad, and for the moment one may expect the more frankly manipulative models of behaviour therapy, etc., to gain more ground.

It seems to the present writer that it remains to those psychologists who are still interested in a scientific (as opposed to scientistic or technological) approach to mental disorder to attempt to clarify the values that are involved in the therapeutic situation and thereby to make it more possible for people to make a rational choice between different psychotherapeutic languages, and perhaps to tolerate those they do not speak, even if not to learn them.

References

Albee, G. W. (1969). 'Emerging concepts of mental illness and models of treatment: the psychological point of view', *Amer. J. Psychiat.*, **125**, 870.
Bakan, D. (1967). *On Method*, Jossey-Bass, San Francisco.
Bannister, D. (1966). 'Psychology as an exercise in paradox', *Bull. Br. psychol. Soc.*, **19**, 21.
Bannister, D. (1969). 'Clinical psychology and psychotherapy', *Bull. Br. psychol. Soc.*, **22**, 299.
Beier, E. G., Robinson, P., and Michelletti, G. (1971). 'Susanville: a community helps itself in mobilization of community resources for self-help in mental health', *J. consult. clin. Psychol.*, **36**, 142.
Bergin, A. E., and Strupp, H. H. (1970). 'New directions in psychotherapy research', *J. abnorm. Psychol.*, **76**, 13.
Brand, C. (1971). 'Hercules' nervous breakdown? An appeal to psychology's pessimists', *Bull. Br. psychol. Soc.*, **24**, 307.
Bridgman, P. W. (1959). *The Way Things Are*, Harvard University Press, Cambridge, Mass.

Caine, T. M., and Leigh, R. (1972). 'Conservatism in relation to psychiatric treatment', *Br. J. soc. clin. Psychol.*, **11**, 52.

Caine, T. M., and Smail, D. J. (1969a). *The Treatment of Mental Illness: Science, Faith and the Therapeutic Personality*, University of London Press, London.

Caine, T. M., and Smail, D. J. (1969b). 'The effects of personality and training on attitudes to treatment: preliminary investigations', *Br. J. med. Psychol.*, **42**, 277.

Caine, T. M., Wijesinghe, B., and Wood, R. R. (1973). 'Personality and psychiatric treatment expectancies', *Br. J. Psychiat.*, **122**, 87.

Cohen, J., and Struening, E. L. (1963). 'Opinions about mental illness: mental hospital occupationl profiles and profile clusters, *Psychol. Rep.*, **12**, 111.

Cohen, J., and Struening, E. L. (1963). 'Opinions about mental illness: hospital social atmosphere and patient time in the hospital', *J. consult. Psychol.*, **28**, 291.

Cooper, D. (1967). *Psychiatry and Anti-Psychiatry*, Tavistock, London.

Cooper, D. (1970). *The Death of the Family*, Pantheon, New York.

de Charms, R. (1968). *Personal Causation*, Academic Press, New York and London.

Ellsworth, R. B. (1965). 'A behavioural study of staff attitudes towards mental illness', *J. abnorm. soc. Psychol.*, **70**, 194.

Ellsworth, R. B., and Maroney, R. (1972). 'Characteristics of psychiatric programs and their effects on patients' adjustment', *J. consult. clin. Psychol.*, **39**, 346.

Goffman, E. (1961). *Asylums*, Doubleday, New York.

Jones, M. (1968). *Beyond the Therapeutic Community*, Yale University Press, New York and London.

Kelvin, P. (1970). *The Bases of Social Behaviour*, Holt, Rhinehart & Winston, UK.

Kreitman, N. (1962). 'Psychiatric orientation: a study of attitudes among psychiatrists', *J. ment. Sci.*, **108**, 317.

Laing, R. D. (1967). *The Politics of Experience and the Bird of Paradise*, Penguin, Harmondsworth.

Mair, J. M. M. (1970). 'Experimenting with individuals', *Br. J. med. Psychol.*, **43**, 245.

Martin, D. V. (1968). *Adventure in Psychiatry*, Cassirer, Oxford.

Mirels, H. L., and Garrett, J. B. (1971). 'The protestant ethic as a personality variable', *J. consult. clin. Psychol.*, **36**, 40.

Moos, R. H. (1968). 'Differential effects of war settings on psychiatric patients', *J. nerv. ment. Dis.*, **147**, 386.

Myers, K., and Clark, D. H. (1972). 'Results in a therapeutic community', *Br. J. Psychiat.*, **120**, 51.

Oppenheimer, R. (1956). 'Analogy in science', *Amer. Psychol.*, **11**, 127.

Pallis, D. J., and Stoffelmayr, B. E. (1973). 'Social attitudes and treatment orientation among psychiatrists', *Br. J. med. Psychol.*, **46**, 75.

Polanyi, M. (1958). *Personal Knowledge*, Routledge & Kegan Paul, London.

Rapoport, R. N. (1960). *Community as Doctor*, Tavistock, London.

Reiff, R. (1966). 'Mental health manpower and institutional change', *Amer. Psychol.*, **21**, 540.

Rychlak, J. F. (1970). 'The human person in modern psychological science', *Br. J. med. Psychol.*, **43**, 233.

Sarbin, T. R. (1967). 'On the futility of the proposition that some people be labeled "mentally ill"', *J. consult. Psychol.*, **31**, 447.

Sarbin, T. R., and Mancuso, J. C. (1970). 'Failure of a moral enterprise: attitudes of the public toward mental illness', *J. consult. clin. Psychol.*, **35**, 159.

Smail, D. J. (1970). 'Neurotic symptoms, personality and personal constructs', *Brit. J. Psychiat.*, **117**, 645.

Smith, M. B. (1961). '"Mental health" reconsidered: a special case of the problem of values in psychology', *Amer. Psychol.*, **16**, 299.

Szasz, T. (1962). *The Myth of Mental Illness*, Secker & Warburg, London.

Walton, H. (Ed.) (1971). *Small Group Psychotherapy*, Penguin, Harmondsworth.

84

Whiteley, J. S. (1970). 'The response of psychopaths to a therapeutic community', *Br. J. Psychiat.*, **116,** 517.

Wing, J. K. (1962). 'Institutionalization in mental hospitals', *Br. J. soc. clin. Psychol.*, **1,** 38.

Yalom, I. D. (1970). *The Theory and Practice of Group Psychotherapy,* Basic Books, New York.

5

GROUP PSYCHOTHERAPY

Dorothy Stock Whitaker

A group is a versatile and flexible instrument. One of its potential uses is to form a setting in which individuals can change in directions which are personally advantageous to them. Thus, therapeutic communities, social clubs, activity groups and T-groups, as well as therapy groups as such, can all be utilized and exploited for the personal benefit of their members. Groups can also be organized for a variety of types of patient or client: seriously disturbed persons in mental hospitals; outpatients who manage to pursue their ordinary lives but are anxious, depressed or symptom-ridden; special problem groups such as alcoholics, drug addicts, the obese, etc.; and normal persons facing unusual stress, such as parents of subnormal or physically handicapped children, relatives of mental patients or persons facing bereavement, major surgery or other threats to life or identity.

It is probably true that all the groups just referred to have certain features in common, but they also differ in significant ways, depending particularly on the opportunities (or not) for face-to-face interaction amongst all the members and on the developmental maturity or seriousness of psychiatric condition of the persons involved. In this chapter I shall focus on small groups in which face-to-face interaction is possible amongst all the members, which are conducted by one or two therapists, which are understood by both therapists and patients to be organized for therapeutic purposes and which proceed through mutual sharing and discussion amongst the members. This specification excludes therapeutic communities (discussed elsewhere in this book), ward government groups, recreation groups, activity groups and other groups which are larger, do not always meet face-to-face and may be organized for other or additional purposes.

In the kind of group I shall be discussing, open discussion amongst members is the vehicle by which one hopes personal gain will be achieved, so this tends also to exclude younger children and very regressed or out-of-contact adults. In this chapter, then, the term 'psychotherapeutic group' refers to groups in which regular face-to-face interaction is specifically arranged for, with the explicit intent of providing a context for personal growth and change through mutual sharing and open discussion.

It will be useful to begin by point to the distinctive features of the therapeutic group. Many people who undertake to conduct therapy groups are more accustomed to offering help in a one-to-one context, and their theoretical orientation and previous training and experience naturally support this focus. It is therefore particularly important to point to those feature of a group which are different from the one-to-one relationship and which present the therapist with different problems and different opportunities (see Lieberman et al., 1968).

In individual psychotherapy one therapist and one patient confront one another and interact together. In group psychotherapy one or two therapists and five to eight (or more) patients confront one another and interact together. New phenomena inevitably come into play:

(1) The patients form relationships with one another as well as with the therapist. This means, first, that certain patternings of interaction can occur in groups which cannot appear in individual therapy. These include sub-grouping, cliques, scapegoating, etc. Second, it means that if one thinks in terms of transference it becomes possible for complex three (and more) persons' transference relationships to become established and played out in the group and for pairs and trios of patients to engage together in maintaining complementary transference patterns.

(2) The group includes persons (i.e. the other patients) who are not professionally trained therapists. Again, there are several implications. A patient may expect the therapist to display professional forbearance and acceptance; he does not expect this of his fellow patients and the group setting may be intrinsically more threatening on this account. A therapist, pursuing his professional role, may adopt a neutral stance and reveal relatively little of himself as a person. In consequence, the patient is free, as it were, to develop a fantasy relationship with the therapist determined largely by his own needs. The other patients, in contrast, are 'real' in the sense that they do not discipline themselves in terms of a professional role (or hide behind it). The relationship of patient-to-patient is in consequence a complicated and sometimes confusing mix of projection, accurate assessment of the other and appropriate or inappropriate response to the other as he presents himself. Times are changing, and many therapists are not so neutral as they once felt compelled to be. It is probably still true, however, that most therapists monitor their own behaviour in ways that patients do not.

(3) Each patient in a group necessarily exposes himself to the possibilities of reward or punishment, acceptance or rejection, by peers. This gives the patients power and influence over one another and is a further factor which makes the group an intrinsically more threatening place for many than one-to-one psychotherapy.

(4) The group establishes norms which attempt to regulate the behaviour of the patients and which define what is acceptable and what is not. Norms are an inevitable feature of all groups and contribute to the economy of the group's operation and the comfort of their members (or most of them). The way in which a therapy group establishes norms, the kinds of norms it establishes, its capacity to modify norms and the relationship of individual patients to the norms of the group are all important both for the effective functioning of the group and for the quality of the

experience of the individual:

(a) A group may establish norms which facilitate the therapeutic potential of the group. For example, a norm which states, in effect, 'We can all accept in one another feelings and behaviours which most people would criticize and condemn' is a liberating norm for a therapy group. So is a norm which conveys 'We are all alike in having problems which we wish to work on seriously'. So is a norm which states 'It is only human to have angry as well as loving feelings towards those to whom one is close'. Such norms support the therapeutic work of the group. Many more examples could be provided.

(b) A group may establish norms which work against or undermine the therapeutic potential of the group. Examples of antitherapeutic or destructive norms are: 'In this group it is only safe to talk about trivial issues', or 'It is valuable for us to talk about feelings of loneliness in intellectual and abstract terms', or 'Society is to blame for all our problems', or 'Peter is the only one here who has problems with hostility so let us help (e.g. attack) him'. Anti-therapeutic norms can also be thought of as collusive defences.

(c) Individual patients who support important group norms will be accepted in the group. Patients who deviate from or challenge group norms may be attacked, ostracized or encapsulated (and ignored) in the group.

(d) Individual patients who persistently challenge group norms may play an important role in forcing the group to make explicit, reconsider or modify its norms and thus may contribute significantly to the group's development.

(5) The group as a whole may develop shared views of reality which gain credence because they are held unanimously. These shared beliefs may be about some aspect of the outside world, or about the group, or about persons within the group, including, of course, the therapist. The unanimous opinion of a group can be markedly convincing to the individual who is the target of it. It is thus one of the factors which makes a group such a potent source of both support and threat.

(6) Under some circumstances, powerful emotional contagion can occur in therapy groups. The phenomenon of emotional contagion is easy to recognize. It involves the abrupt eruption of intense affect which seems to spread instantaneously through the group. The affect may involve anger, depression, elation, silliness, etc. An episode of contagion may be threatening to the therapist because he often feels powerless to control or influence it. An episode of contagion can have a powerful impact on the patient, with positive or negative potential, since a patient can be drawn into experiencing some affect against which he ordinarily defends himself.

(7) The group is an arena in which patients inevitably display characteristic interpersonal behaviour. They may present themselves in characteristic ways; they may (as it were) insist on being regarded as superior to others or helpless or no good or eternally understanding and warm, etc.; they may behave so as to 'pull' characteristic responses from others. This display of characteristic behaviour makes the group an ideal place, in fact an inevitable place, in which feedback can occur. The patient himself, the other patients and the therapist are all in a position to observe such behaviour and to comment on it. The situation thus can provide the individual with new and potentially useful information about his behaviour and its im-

pact on others. Feedback can be an entirely private process in which the individual simply *notices* how others respond to his behaviour or feedback can involve verbal exchange, in which one patient says to another 'When you do (say) that, I feel . . .'. Such a comment may be solicited or unsolicited. Of course, the feedback a patient receives from others may be so idiosyncratic that it reveals more about the person offering the feedback than about the recipient of it. However, the presence of a *number* of persons in the group makes it possible to check for idiosyncracy.

Feedback is a term which is often used rather loosely by group therapists and especially by T-group leaders. Sometimes it is used to cloak comments about the individual's motives or the sources of his problems ('I feel that you are depressed because your mother left you'). This, of course, is not a feeling at all, but an interpretation, speculation or projection. Sometimes the term 'feedback' is used to attach labels to people, and then is often simply a poor disguise for hostility (Let me give you some feedback about how childishly you are behaving'). Misuse of the idea of feedback can be useless at best and destructive at worst.

(8) Groups provide opportunities for social comparison among patients. In therapy groups patients inevitably compare themselves with one another. They see that they are anxious about the same (or different) things; that others have different (or the same) attitudes towards their own feelings of anger, tenderness, envy, etc.; that personal styles for expressing the various affects differ; and so forth. Sometimes social comparison can puncture cherished defensive fantasies, as when a patient who has believed that if only he were different in some way or had a different background all would be well sees that his magic formula did not work for someone else. In general, social comparison can contribute to reflections about one's self and identity; and to shifts in how one views oneself, the feelings one dares to acknowledge and the behaviours one dares to display.

(9) Groups offer opportunities for vicarious experiences. Patients spend a lot of time in groups observing others and observing the consequences of others' actions. Thus, a patient who is fearful of the consequences of expressing hostility may note that another patient who has expressed anger was not punished, etc. Sometimes vicarious experience seems to be a first step in the reduction of a patient's fears and can lead to the more direct and personal exploration of an issue. Most therapists doubt that vicarious experience alone can generate substantial therapeutic gain. Yet many group therapists have occasional patients who were virtually silent for months and then suddenly announced or displayed some striking therapeutic change. Internal experiences generated from observing others are hard to understand because they are so invisible, but they seem important for some patients. This phenomenon is also sometimes called 'spectator therapy'.

(10) Groups may be more or less cohesive. A highly cohesive group tends to have a clear sense of its own boundaries and of who is inside it and who is not. A member of such a group can often feel a comforting sense of belonging and reduced feelings of loneliness and isolation. In a group whose aim is personal therapeutic growth, very high cohesiveness may work against the therapeutic potential of the group if the members come to feel that the existence of the group is more important than anything else and stop daring to take risks.

(11) A group situation offers the opportunity for behavioural test-outs and for the practice of new behaviours. Most patients display a constricted range of interpersonal behaviours. They are frightened to display tenderness or anger or weakness or some other affect. Movement towards a greater range of expressiveness and more choice over whether or when one shall express one's feelings is often a mark of therapeutic progress. The real test of such therapeutic gain is the patient's ability to display a broadened repertory used more appropriately in his ordinary life outside the group. Often he moves towards this by testing out or practising new behaviours in the relatively protected context of the therapy group, thus gaining courage for further attempts outside.

Some of these special features of the group pertain to the group as a whole, some to interpersonal aspects of the situation and some to the behaviour and experience of the individual. They occur in varying combinations and continually change and shift. As a context for psychotherapy the small group is complex and distinctive. Two points follow from this. The first is that any therapist attempting to utilize a group for therapeutic purposes should pay attention to the distinctive features of his medium and try to take advantage of the special opportunities which they present. The second point is that the very complexity of the group situation leads most therapists to adopt some sort of conceptual framework which can help to introduce order into complexity and suggests ways of proceeding. The range of conceptual frameworks is considerable, and each tends to suggest procedures of its own. Some approaches overlap or are compatible; others are mutually incompatible. It is thus more appropriate to speak of 'group psychotherapies' rather than 'group psychotherapy', for there does not exist a unified theory or a single approach.

To illustrate the situation. A number of distinct and fairly well worked out conceptual frameworks have been presented in the group therapy literature. Foulkes (1948; 1957; 1964) has developed a group-analytic orientation which is based in psychoanalytic theory, regards the group as the matrix within which individual experience and growth occurs and focuses on all of the dynamic relationships within the group. Another approach, rooted in the Kleinian tradition, was put forward in the first instance by Bion (1961) and has since been developed and utilized by practitioners at the Tavistock Clinic in London. This approach conceptualizes the events of the group in terms of a series of basic-assumption cultures and the relationship of individuals to them. Whitaker and Lieberman (1964) describe a conceptual framework known as 'group focal conflict theory' which emphasizes shared conflicts and the solutions to them which emerge in groups. All of the approaches mentioned so far emphasize the importance of group-level features of the situation as the context in which individual change occurs. A further family of theoretical frameworks derives from the theory and practice of individual psychoanalysis. Sometimes called 'psychoanalysis in groups', this approach emphasizes the dynamics of individuals and is likely to employ as techniques dream interpretation, free association and the analysis of transference and counter-transference. In such an approach individuals may be focused upon in turn while the other patients function as auxiliary therapists. Group psychotherapists representing this orientation include Wolf and Schwartz (1962), Locke (1961) and others. Yet another orientation is presented by Yalom (1970), who has developed a point of view which, although eclectic, emphasizes the interpersonal features of the group. This list is by no means exhaustive. A fuller picture of the conceptual approaches available can be gained from consulting Rosenbaum and Berger (1963, currently being re-edited) and issues of the *International Journal of Group Psychotherapy*.

The conceptual framework which one adopts influences how one perceives the group and what one does as therapist. A 'psychoanalysis in groups' point of view leads one to focus on individual patients, perhaps in turn. A Bionic approach leads one to emphasize the transference relationship between the group as a whole and the therapist and to direct one's interpretations towards explicating this. A group focal conflict approach leads the therapist to be alert to shared concerns and solutions and to direct many interventions towards encouraging the recognition and reality-testing of shared fears. An interpersonal approach such as Yalom's leads the therapist to encourage feedback and social comparison.

All theoretical frameworks structure one's thinking; that is what they are for. All frameworks declare that something is figure and something is ground. Therefore all frameworks alert the therapist to some features of a group and incline him to disregard or de-emphasize others. This fact and the multiplicity of frameworks referred to above make the writing of a chapter like this one peculiarly difficult. The chapter is meant to be explicit and representative, and it cannot be both.

In an attempt to deal with this problem, I shall list and then discuss a series of core tasks which seem to me to confront any group therapist, regardless of his theoretical persuasion. These core tasks are as follows:

(1) to select patients and compose the group;

(2) to establish boundaries and ground rules;

(3) to monitor group-level processes and influence the group towards becoming (and maintaining itself as) a facilitating therapeutic environment; and

(4) simultaneously, to monitor individual and interpersonal aspects of the situation in order to exploit the total situation for the maximum benefit of each patient.

Selection and Composition

The first decisions which a therapist makes about a prospective group concern who is to be in it. Selection and composition are important because it is quite possible to compose a group that is virtually doomed to failure. It is not so easy to compose a group for which one can guarantee success, but at least certain gross errors of composition can be avoided.

Various answers have been given to the question 'Are there some patients who should not enter a group at all?'. In general, it seems best not to include patients who will be damaged by the group or who are likely to spoil the group as a therapeutic environment for others. With respect to the first point, one occasionally sees a patient who is so grossly frightened of the prospect of a therapy group that he seems likely, if pressed into one, to become immobilized or to decompensate. If one detects in a preliminary interview that such is the case some alternative form of treatment should be found. I do not refer here to the ordinary fears which many people display when the idea of a therapy group is first presented to them, but to a persistent and often inarticulate feeling of panic at the prospect of entering a group. Another kind of patient for whom a group is contraindicated is the person facing some acute crisis. Such a person cannot afford to wait until the potentially therapeutic qualities of the group environment have a chance to develop. He needs, at least initially, the kind of first aid which can be made available in a one-to-one situation. Some patients are not so much damaged by a group as not in a position to benefit from it. It is pointless to take into a group a psychotic patient who is in so florid a state that he literally cannot sit down or listen to anyone. The patients just described might also spoil an otherwise potentially useful group. The persistently threatened person will either frighten the others or (through the tyranny of the weak) force the group into a bland state which is overly restrictive for everyone else. The patient facing a crisis may, out of his own desperate need, turn the group into one-to-one therapy with an audience. The florid patient may threaten the others or his behaviour may make it virtually impossible for any interaction to occur which is not dominated by his behaviour. Some therapists would greatly extend this list of unsuitable patients. For a thorough discussion of this point and a report of relevant research see Yalom (1970).

Selection and composition are intertwined, because a patient who may fit well into one composition may be inappropriate for another. Often, the question is not 'Is this patient suitable for group therapy?', but 'Is this patient suitable for this group?'. Some compositions are intrinsically unworkable. The most common error is to compose a group which is so homogeneous with regard to preferred defence or preferred interactive style that the individual tendencies of the patients become translated immediately into group norms which are then very hard to displace. A group homogeneously composed of long-term paranoid patients will quickly generate an atmosphere of mutual mistrust likely to immobilize the group. A group homogenously composed of withdrawn patients will lapse into long periods of silence or force the therapist to adopt a questioning, probing style. A group composed of obsessive–compulsives will reinforce individual tendencies to intellectualize and transform intellectualization into a group norm. And so on. In general, a group which is too homogeneous with respect to preferred defences, preferred interactive style or preferred mode of affective expression is not likely to work well because the individual tendencies find mutual support and quickly become established as a persistent and intractable way of life. It is very difficult for a therapist to break into such a pattern.

If the first principle of group composition is heterogeneity with regard to preferred defence or preferred interactive style, a second principle is homogeneity with regard to level of vulnerability. This term does not refer precisely to severity of disturbance, but has to do with how vulnerable or readily threatened the individual is likely to be and how rapidly he is likely to be able to move. If a group is too mixed in this regard, the more vulnerable persons may be overly threatened and either squeezed out or damaged, or else the less vulnerable may be held back.

With many populations, this issue does not arise as a practical problem. It is most likely to arise in intensive treatment units in mental hospitals, where one often finds a very wide range of psychiatric conditions represented amongst the patients. One or more preliminary individual interviews may be very helpful to the therapist in forming the judgements about individuals which are necessary for composing a group. It is worth taking the time required to compose a potentially facilitating group. Frustration and failure for both therapist and patients can often be avoided.

Boundaries and Ground Rules

Like selection and composition, decisions about boundaries and ground rules are made before the group meets for the first time. The term 'boundaries' refers to such matters as the duration of the group, whether it is to be time-limited or open-ended, the frequency of sessions and the duration of each session. The term 'ground rules' refers to rules or agreements about confidentiality, individual outside contacts between therapist and patients, outside contacts among patients, and the like.

Decisions about boundaries depend a great deal on the kind of person with whom one is dealing in the group and on one's assessment of where they are, where they can be expected to move and how soon. For example, consider a group composed of mothers of subnormal children. These women are presumed to be 'normal' but faced with an unusually stressful and difficult reality situation. They may well profit from a time-limited series of group sessions—perhaps 10 to 12. Consider, further, a group of in-patients who have been psychotic but are considered sufficiently recovered to be discharged from a mental hospital. The intention of the group is to help them to cope with a potentially difficult transition period. Again, a limited number of sessions may be helpful. Different from either of these is an out-patient group composed of persons who are functioning in families and jobs but plagued by long-standing maladaptive patterns or unacceptable levels of anxiety or self-esteem. Such persons are likely to require a long-term, open-ended opportunity for extensive exploration. Decisions about boundaries are also influenced by the context in which the group is being conducted. Short-stay reception wards, for example, preclude long-term therapy, though it might be appropriate on other grounds. Conversely, some settings encourage interminable groups even though the group has become ritualistic and has lost its potential value.

Decisions about ground rules seem very much tied to the conceptual framework one adopts in trying to understand group events. Some therapists make explicit rules about confidentiality, outside contacts, etc., and others do not. Some therapists suggest that certain procedures be followed during the sessions and others do not.

The rationale for the therapist introducing explicit rules concerning confidentiality and the like lies in the undeniable fact that a group which observes such rules proceeds more effectively. Nevertheless, an argument can be made against the therapist introducing such rules. A rule about confidentiality or about avoiding outside contact amongst the patients can be stated by the therapist but cannot be enforced by the therapist. Patients will maintain confidentiality if they collectively see the point of it and if there is a group norm which supports this behaviour. Group norms in order to be effective and binding must evolve out of the interaction of the persons concerned. If no rule is made, a norm about confidentiality nevertheless is likely to become established simply because it operates to everyone's advantage. It may evolve as an unstated norm or it may become explicit, usually in consequence of an unstated norm being violated. If the issue of confidentiality is discussed explicitly in the group, the discussion constitutes an event which can be exploited for the therapeutic benefit of individuals (e.g. the patient's attention may be drawn to the position he takes, the role he assumes during the interaction, etc.). In general, making a rule about such issues as confidentiality, outside contacts and the like may be ineffective and may deprive the group of potentially valuable interactions.

Whether or not one suggests procedures to the patients seems to depend very much on one's theoretical orientation and what it suggests as a valuable way of proceeding. Some psychoanalytically-oriented group therapists, for example, encourage patients to associate to one another's dreams or specifically endorse periods of concentrating on particular patients. Therapists who emphasize working with and through group processes are less likely to structure sessions, on the grounds that the free-associational processes in the group will lead to the emergence of important shared concerns and will generate content and interaction which can be explored to the benefit of the patients. 'Accelerating devices' have recently been utilized by some therapists in an effort to move more quickly past initial defences and into more meaningful material. Whether or not it is advisable to utilize such techniques is a matter of controversy. My own view is that it is imprudent to attempt to attack or by-pass defences and preferable to work towards developing conditions of safety and mutual trust, so that patients in due course feel ready to give up their initial defences.

Monitoring and Intervening at the Group Level

It was pointed out earlier that all groups establish norms and that in a therapy group some norms support the therapeutic effort while others interfere with it. Antitherapeutic norms are those which constrict the area of free exploration within the group, in effect outlawing the examination of certain areas of human experience. For example, a group may use a rigid pattern of turn-taking to avoid confronting feelings of competitiveness for the therapist's attention; a group which projects all feelings of hostility on to one person is utilizing scapegoating as a device for avoiding owning up to such feelings; a group which persists in discussing trivial or remote or abstract topics is operating on a norm which may function to avoid a variety of issues. In group focal conflict theory such as anti-therapeutic norms are called 'restrictive solutions'. In more familiar language they may be called 'collusive defences'. Such anti-therapeutic patterns are not at all uncommon in therapy groups. In general, the therapist wants to avoid them or at least to prevent them from becoming chronic in the group. In order to do this he must first of all monitor the group situation so that he can be aware of them when they occur. Then, he must have some notion of when it is appropriate to intervene and when it it is not, and what sorts of interventions are likely to prove effective. Above all, it is useful for the therapist to be aware of any tendency in himself to collude in supporting anti-therapeutic norms, so that he can avoid doing so.

When a therapist becomes aware of the operation of some anti-therapeutic norm or collusive defence, his first impulse may be to interpret it—that is, to call the patients' attention to the anti-therapeutic pattern and either explicitly or implicitly call for its abandonment. This tactic can lead to undesirable consequences. One needs to keep in mind that the anti-therapeutic norm fulfils a defensive function for the patients. The patients are afraid to face some issues, and the norm or collusive defence helps them to avoid the issue and thus to contain their fears. A direct challenge to the defence either is disregarded or punctures the defence and exacerbates fears. Further, such an intervention is often experienced as punitive by the patients and may generate additional anxieties. A more useful approach is to work towards the alleviation or reduction of whatever fears may be present so that the anti-therapeutic norm or collusive defence becomes less essential for the group and can be given up. A therapist can contribute to the reduction of fears by encouraging the patients to make their fears explicit (a process which almost always leads to exploration, reality-testing and fear reduction) or by demonstrating through his own behaviour that the fears are exaggerated (e.g. by *not* being punitive when a patient dares to express something he fears will elicit punishment). The fears which are likely to arise in a group are many and varied. They often have an interpersonal character and may involve concerns about being ridiculed or criticized by other patients or the therapist, abandoned by the therapist, etc. Collusive defences, by definition, have an interpersonal character. They may involve role differentiation (e.g. encouraging one person to dominate the situation; scapegoating), but they may also involve the mutual support of individual defences (e.g. intellectualization; projection). The anti-therapeutic patterns which may emerge, and considerations about when and how to intervene and when it may be best not to intervene, are discussed in Whitaker (1974).

Occasionally a therapist may fall into supporting some anti-therapeutic group norm. This is particularly likely to happen when the norm in question is functioning not only to protect the patients but also to protect the therapist. Consider, for example, an in-patient group which is attacking the nurses on the ward for their uncaring attitude. Neither they nor the therapist may wish to see that they are displacing their angry feelings towards the therapist on to the nursing staff. Yet, unless they abandon this collusive defence, or are helped to do so, they will succeed in avoiding whatever benefits might accrue from the open exploration of hostile feelings towards an authority figure on whom they depend. It is not always easy for a therapist to avoid this kind of mistake. It is a mistake which is retrievable, providing he becomes aware of it. Repeatedly supporting shared defences may curtail the value of the group by preventing the patients from exploring and confronting core areas of experience.

Considerable attention has been paid to the issue of anti-therapeutic norms or collusive defences because their detection and management may be critical in generating a facilitating as opposed to an inhibiting therapeutic environment. Monitoring at the group level should also, however, include attention to other features of the situation. For example, a therapist may wish to notice and interfere with mood contagion before it becomes too pervasive and overwhelming. A therapist will wish to be aware of the building-up of shared beliefs and convictions. These vary as to character, target and import for the group. Some shared beliefs are an inextricable aspect of group norms or function as group norms. They may be facilitating or restrictive in their effects. Some shared beliefs are expressions of reality-based opinions. For example, a patient who believes himself to be unacceptable because of some physical defect may be confronted by a shared conviction on the part of the others that his defect is trivial. Shared beliefs are convincing to those who participate in them, but they may or may not accurately reflect reality. When they involve distortion or projection, the therapist will wish to encourage the patients to examine them; when they are accurate and supportive either of the group or if individuals within it, the therapist may wish to endorse and underline them.

A final point about group-level aspects of the situation deserves comment. Sometimes, during the emergence of some group norm or shared belief, one patient places himself in a deviant position and, despite all urging and threats of punishment, clings to it. Such a situation, though frustrating for everyone, usually offers useful opportunities for therapeutic movement. The individual can be urged to consider how it is that the group norm is so unacceptable to him; the other patients can be helped to be emphatic despite the threat the deviant is presenting to the group; the patients as a group may be forced to abandon or modify their norms and the deviant thus may influence the group's development.

Exploiting the Group Situation for the Benefit of the Individual Patient

Much of what has been said so far involves influencing the group towards being a constructive and facilitating therapeutic environment. In this section the focus turns to the individual and the ways in which the therapist can exploit the constantly shifting group environment for the specific benefit of the individual.

It is important to point out that, *given a facilitating environment,* much will happen in a group which is therapeutically useful for individuals without the specific attention of the therapist. For example, social comparison will certainly take place; feelings of isolation and loneliness may be alleviated; opportunities for vicarious learnings will emerge; patients will notice their impact on others and learn from this; feedback may be sympathetically offered; a patient's own motivations may lead him to try out new behaviours in the safe atmosphere of the group. Moreover, in a group, the therapist is not the only one present who can function in a therapeutically useful way. Often the patients display extraordinary understanding of one another. They empathically grasp what someone is experiencing and show sensitivity in understanding how far to go with him and what kind of support to offer.

While not wishing to deprecate the importance of any of the above, it is also true that the therapist will find many opportunities to intervene in ways likely to enhance the potential therapeutic value of a group for particular individuals.

Interventions introduced with the specific intention of benefiting some individual may or may not be directed explicitly to the individual. Comments directed particularly to an individual may involve a brief aside or an extended exchange. Other patients may or may not be drawn in. To explicate: a therapist may not refer to a particular patient directly but make a general comment to the group with the benefit of that patient in mind. For example, a therapist might be aware that a particular patient is ashamed of his envious feelings towards a sibling. With that patient in mind, he might remark to the group as a whole (given, of course, an appropriate opening): 'Most people here are beginning to recognize that envy is a very understandable human feeling'. His intention is that one patient in particular be helped to feel freer to explore his own feelings of envy. A therapist may point to some relationship between group events and the individual, for example, 'During the last twenty minutes or so when everyone was complaining about me, you were unusually quiet. What was going on for you?'. Or a therapist may point to some interpersonal event for the benefit of one of the individuals concerned, for example, 'Robert has been telling you that he finds you attractive, but it seems that even though you would like to believe him you are also afraid to'. A therapist might speak directly to a patient, much as he might do in individual therapy.

This point is being emphasized because inappropriate disctinctions are sometimes made between 'working at the group level', the 'interpersonal level', or the 'individual level', as if these had nothing to do with one another. In a group an intervention rarely, if ever, pertains to only one aspect of the situation. It is useful to be aware of the indirect, multiple or unintended effects of any given intervention, regardless of its primary target.

The general point being made here is that exploiting the group situation for the benefit of the individual does not always imply specific, exclusive or extended attention to that patient, though it may do so. Many useful types of intervention can be introduced. The therapist may question, interpret, share a feeling or reaction, summarize the events of a session and the like.

Certain additional interventions deserve special mention because they seem peculiarly appropriate to a group situation. These include underlining, modelling and a particular kind of teaching.

One of the more useful things a group therapist can do is to underline or call attention to some particular event likely to be important for an individual. The event has already occurred in the ongoing flow of the interaction and the therapist wants to make sure that the patients has noticed it and taken it in. For example, the therapist may underline what he believes to have been an important personal experience: 'Just now, you said you were as depressed as it's in you to be, and yet you didn't fall apart; you could stand it'. Or he may call a patient's attention to some group event in which the individual was not directly concerned, for example, 'Listening to others quarrel upsets you'. Or the therapist may comment more generally because he believes some event to have been important for a number of people, for example, 'It seems easier in this group to talk about angry feelings than to talk about tender and sympathetic feelings'.

The therapist can also function as a model in the group. By his behaviour he demonstrates to the patients how they can approach, confront, express understanding and acceptance, etc. Thus certain interpersonal behaviours first expressed by the therapist may be adopted by some of the patients. His therapeutic style may also be adopted by the patients to some extent. For example, while a therapist is monitoring group-level events and intervening to help maintain the group as a facilitating environment he is inevitably showing the patients how to do the same thing. He is alerting them (for example) to the fact that when they retreat to the trivial they are probably avoiding something; that when some outside event is being discussed it may be a symbolic way of referring to something in the group. In a group where the therapist frequently calls attention to interpersonal games, the patients are likely to become alert to this aspect of the situation. In general, patients may come to anticipate the therapist's behaviour. To a certain extent they internalize this role and learn to do his work for him.

To say that a therapist sometimes assumes a teaching role is to risk being misunderstood. The therapist ordinarily does not teach in the sense of lecturing the patients or telling them how to behave or how to see things. Yet modelling can be thought of as an indirect form of teaching and sometimes a therapist may teach more directly. He may tell a group what sorts of comments he considers useful and which he does not. For example, suppose a group is engaged in interpreting the behaviour of one of its members, and the patient in question consistently responds with a defensive 'Yes, but . . .'. The therapist may say directly, 'This way of going on doesn't seem useful. Every time someone comes up with a new idea about Peter, he shows us that it doesn't make sense to him and he can't use it'. Or, he may directly tell the group what sort of feedback is useful and what sort is not. He may, for example, suggest, 'When you come down to it, comments about *why* John behaves in a superior way are just guesses. There is only one thing you can speak about with authority, and that is how you feel when he behaves in this way'.

Some therapists who are accustomed to working with individuals find it hard to see how one can reach any given patient without focusing extensively on him and thus cheating all the others. I hope that the foregoing remarks have suggested some of the ways in which this can be done.

How active should a group therapist be? As with many important questions, the answer is 'It depends'. It depends partly on the kind of patient with whom one is dealing. Severely disturbed patients find it hard to tolerate longish periods of silence on the part of the therapist. They need more frequent reminders that he is there, listening and still sympathetic. In all groups there are periods when the therapist can afford to be less active simply because the group is going well without his direct intervention. At other times things are going well but he sees opportunities to intervene to someone's benefit. At still other times he may feel the group is in some sort of crisis and that he must intervene. He may feel this when some potentially overwhelming event has occurred (e.g. a suicide on the ward), when the group is being destructive towards one of its members or when the group persists for an overly long period in some collusive defence.

What are the goals of group psychotherapy? What is the nature of the complaint, and what constitutes cure? I do not believe that one can define any of these in terms which are so specific to group psychotherapy that they do not apply also to other forms of treatment. The way in which one conceptualizes goals, complaint and cure seems to have a great deal more to do with one's theoretical perspective than with the therapeutic medium being employed. Thus, with reference to goals, different therapists might speak in terms of the resolution of intrapsychic conflict, the easing of anxiety, the relief of symptoms, improving interpersonal skills and relationships, increasing the range of personal choice or moving towards self-actualization. 'Complaint' and 'cure' are likely to be formulated in ways consistent with one's thinking about therapeutic goals.

Most group therapists probably would not wish to define treatment goals too narrowly. If one appreciates the potential richness of the group as a medium for change, then one is likely to be reluctant to think only in specific terms such as reducing feelings of isolation or relieving symptoms. These and other specific gains may occur in the course of therapy, but if all goes well for the individual they are likely to be part of a wider and deeper reorganization of the self.

I personally have found it more useful to think in terms of expectations rather than goals. Goals are general, but expectations are specific to the person. One's expectations for a patient naturally will vary depending upon one's assessment of the potentialities of that person. For some persons, one hopes for significant personal change of the sort than can change the course of their life and set them on a path towards greater effectiveness and self-fulfilment. Some patients, one judges, have a more limited capacity, and here one might hope that a group might help them to establish greater contact with others or simply to lead a more rewarding life within a protected environment. One always hopes to work at what is the frontier for each person, facilitating what is for him the next possible step. If one looks at it this way, one's goals, or better, expectations, may continually change as the frontier changes or indeed as one's initial assessment is shown by events to require modification.

It is also possible to think of one's goal for the *group*. Is the point of the group to facilitate personal change or is it to do something quite different—to *supply* the patient with something which he needs and cannot otherwise get? Lieberman *et al.* (1973) suggest that many encounter groups may function as a source of supply rather than as an instrument for effecting change. Many individuals get rewards from an experience in an encounter group which they cannot get elsewhere: a sense of contact and closeness with others and the experience of meaningful interpersonal exchange. The same point can be made about some therapy groups. For example, one can set up a group on a regressed ward not with the expectation of decisive personal change, but with the expectation that a group may help the patients to lead a more satisfying life within their protected environment. Groups which go on over a period of years sometimes gradually shift their character from actively facilitating therapeutic change to providing support, maintenance and contact for the patients. Both supply and change are suitable goals for groups, depending on circumstances and clientele, but it is of course important not to mistake one for the other.

In addition to goal and expectation, one can also think in terms of benefit. Different forms of psychotherapy may work towards similar core goals but provide different side benefits. In a group, for example, an individual will have many opportunities to develop his capacity for empathy with others and to practise social skills. He will have relatively less opportunity to reflect without interruption on his past life and to construct a reinterpretation of his personal history. Individual psychoanalysis provides converse opportunities. In both settings, an individual may make significant personal progress towards (for example) freeing himself from a self-defeating life style. However, the ancillary benefits likely to accrue in the two forms of therapy may be different.

'Complaint' seems best defined from the perspective of the individual. A patient's complaint is whatever he says it is, or, since many patients cannot be articulate about such matters, it is the patient's experience of what is awry. If one adopts this view of the person's complaint then it follows that the complaint may change over time. A person who initially identifies his complaint as having persistent nightmares may later see it as a problem in experiencing and managing anger. An adolescent who first sees her complaint as not being able to lose weight may later see it as a problem concerning her attitude towards her own femininity.

'Cure' is a curious word. Of all the words borrowed from the medical model this seems to me to be most inappropriate and misleading. Psychotherapy can best be thought of as an episode in the unfolding, ongoing life of the individual. 'Cure' has a note of finality about it, as if now that one is cured of measles one is finished with it and can leave it permanently behind. This is not what happens in therapeutic work. Experience in a therapeutic group is an incident and hopefully a critical incident in an ongoing process. What one hopes for is not cure but a change of sufficient magnitude and importance such that the ensuing life experiences of the individual can maintain and continue the change process in a positive direction. One could, perhaps, use the term 'cure' if one thought of the goal of therapy as involving primarily the relief of symptoms. But in the kind of therapeutic activity I have been thinking of, symptom relief, though it may certainly occur, tends to be regarded as an incident in an ongoing process.

On the whole, the above discussion rejects the medical model. This implies that it does not seem appropriate to think of the relationships involved as those between doctor and patient. What, then, is appropriate? Teacher and pupil? Therapist and client? Conductor and group member? No set of labels seems exactly to describe the roles involved. In this article I have, for the most part, used terms traditional in the medical model: therapist and patient. Yet I believe that the relationship is more adequately described as a collaborative one in which different persons come together to serve a single goal—the personal benefit of the patients (=clients, =members)—through each assuming different roles and bringing different perspectives to the situation. The patients are the only ones who are in a position to know and reveal their present and past personal experiences, their inner feelings and their reactions and responses to one another. The therapist is in a better position than the patients to grasp group-level events, to detect shared covert fears and encourage the patients to explore them and test their reality and to call to the patients' attention potentially beneficial events and experiences which emerge during the group interaction. A group can proceed more effectively with a therapist than without one, providing, of course, that the therapist is reasonably sensitive and skilled and non-destructive. On the other hand, a therapist can do nothing useful without the ready and open participation of the patients and without the strengths they are able to bring to bear. The relationship, then, is a collaborative one in which the different participants being different and necessary information, perspectives and skills to the situation.

It is worth adding to the above that the medical model is so well entrenched that the idea of a collaborative relationship is foreign to most patients at first. Most patients are loyal to the medical model and once they have fulfilled their presumed obligation of providing information about themselves they are likely to expect the therapist to respond with advice and/or interpretations or at least to provide a procedural formula. Some of the material of early sessions can be understood in terms of the exposure of conflicts in role expectations and the renegotiation of the therapeutic contract.

The view presented throughout this chapter of the therapeutic processes and of therapeutic goals and expectations makes the evaluation of group therapy peculiarly difficult. It accepts that patients start from different places and that an end point which constitutes progress for one person might constitute no progress or even regression for another. It accepts that symptom relief might be a sign of therapeutic success for some but a sign of therapeutic failure for others (as when certain patients seem to utilize symptom relief as an excuse for fleeing from therapy). From time to time in either group or individual therapy one sees a patient for whom one is convinced that the therapeutic situation has averted some serious decompensation, but this is notoriously difficult to substantiate and may often be put down to the fantasies of the therapist. Sometimes, also, one feels that the change which occurs for a particular person may be tiny when measured by some objective criterion, yet crucial for that individual in setting him or her on a new life course which may in time accumulate to a significant gain. One is also sometimes aware that a gain which seems important may not be sustained because of circumstances in the person's home environment. All of these possibilities are part of the clinical experience of most therapists.

Many practising group therapists who are aware of these complexities place little confidence in formally constructed evaluation research, preferring to rely on their clinical judgement. At the same time, there is widespread recognition that clinical judgement is subject to bias and that systematic efforts to evaluate group psychotherapy and to understand its core processes are necessary. It is probably also fair to say that few group therapists are satisfied that adequate or definitive research has been done to date.

Two general types of evaluation research can be found in the literature. The first is usually referred to as 'outcome' research and the other as 'process-outcome' research. In outcome research the most typical design is one in which patients who have participated in a therapy group are compared with patients who have not and their progress is compared. Sometimes both pre- and post-measurements are employed; sometimes only outcome measures are used. The design may be simple (one experimental and one control group, one or only a few outcome variables, a single type of patient) or more elaborate, but the same basic paradigm tends to be employed. Two principal problems exist in this kind of research. One is the difficulty in identifying and isolating appropriate outcome variables; the other is difficulty in identifying appropriate control groups. With regard to outcome variables, it is natural enough to find that in research which purports to be objective and scientific an attempt is made to utilize readily identifiable, measurable (and countable) outsome variables. Thus one sees utilized discharge rates, readmission rates, symptom check-lists, anxiety scales, rating scales of social skills and the like. The problem is that it is very hard to find a measure which is on the one hand reliable and lends itself to summation and statistical tests and on the other hand pays appropriate attention to the subtlety and uniqueness of personal change.

If a study is to be accepted as convincing, it is necessary to show that changes have occurred because of the therapeutic experience and not because of some other factor. One ordinarily attempts to deal with this by introducing as a control group patients with similar problems who have not been exposed to the therapeutic situation. Several difficulties arise. One is that it is virtually impossible to match persons except with regard to relatively gross characteristics such as age, sex, diagnostic category, etc. Another is that one can never be sure that informal but nevertheless effective therapeutic experiences have not occurred for the control patients during the ordinary course of their lives. Nor can one guarantee that the therapeutic group is the only or most salient influence on the patients formally receiving treatment. These problems are well recognized, and researchers are inclined to assume that if sufficient numbers of patients are studied these individual differences will be cancelled out and confidence can be placed in overall findings. Opinions differ with regard to the extent to which this is true. In this form of research, the group is regarded as a 'black box'. That is, the internal characteristics or dynamics of the group are not examined. In consequence the assumption tends to be made that all therapy groups provide the same experience. Attempts may be made to ensure that groups are equivalent by including for study groups whose therapists are comparable in terms of experience or theoretical orientation. Whatever steps are taken, it is hard to defend the assumption of equivalency. It is for the reasons just outlined that outcome research of the traditional variety is open to criticism.

A second approach to evaluation could be called 'process-outcome' research. Here, the attempt is to relate what happens inside the group to specific outcomes. The special feature of this kind of research is that the group stops being the black box and the researcher tries to identify important features of the group situation which may be related to outcome. This approach promises richer results but also encounters methodological problems. All groups are unique and, if taken to its logical extreme, this approach could tell us a great deal about a single group and a small number of patients but very little about group therapy as such. If one attempts to design a piece of research which goes beyond describing a single example of the genre one encounters the problem of identifying just which features of the group situation are worth identifying as process variables. Should one, for example, examine the degree of cohesion of the group, the frequency and character of feedback, the therapist's style (and how does one assess that?), the types of norms established or some other variable? The situation is further complicated by the fact that a process variable which supports the therapeutic effort with one type of patient might well undermine the therapeutic effort with another type of patient. Relatively high cohesiveness, for example, might support the efforts of a group composed of neurotic patients but be excessively threatening to a group composed of schizophrenics. Thus, a useful process-outcome design would have to take into account type of patient. As in outcome research, it is difficult to identify meaningful outcome variables. If one allows that the outcome may be specific to individuals, subtle rather than obvious, or even that in some instances a positive outcome can consist of no change (i.e. a patient who otherwise would have gotten worse did not do so), then one obviously begins to rely on clinical judgements and becomes open to charges of subjectivity and bias.

Given these problems, it is no wonder that the research produced so far has been less than satisfactory. Much research has been undertaken, particularly of the 'outcome' variety, and some good summaries are available in the literature. A summary of outcome research has been presented by Gundlach (1967) and a review of process studies by Psathas (1967). For thoughtful commentary on problems intrinsic to research on group psychotherapy and possible remedies see Parloff (1967) and Lewis and McCants (1973).

As these articles suggest, some new and promising approaches to research appear to be emerging. Also potentially relevant is the comprehensive research on encounter groups and their effects recently presented by Lieberman et al. (1973). This book is of interest to group therapists for its substantive findings but perhaps even more so for its methodology, for it provides a possible model for integrating 'hard' and 'soft' data, using each to correct for, discipline and illuminate the other.

The training of group therapists has typically been accomplished through the traditional route of supervised practice, supported by reading and perhaps by the observation of groups. Such training methods seem effective, but there is no denying that they are expensive in terms of time. One therefore finds group therapists experimenting with other training techniques such as role-playing and other simulation procedures, tape-listening and participation in training groups or therapy groups. Morton A. Lieberman has suggested recently (in a personal communication) that one might be able to factor out the various sensitivities and skills required for conducting groups and design training methods specific to each. This seems a promising line of thinking, for it seems clear that some aspects of the therapist's task can be learned readily through reading (e.g. the kinds of structuring appropriate for different types of patient populations and settings) while others can only be learned through one or another kind of experience. An appreciation of certain group phenomena (such as the potency of shared beliefs, the power of sanctions applied against a deviant member and the threatening character of early sessions) can be learned best by participating as a member of a therapy group or training group. A great deal of practice in intervening and observing the consequences of one's interventions can be gained through simulation exercises. Testing one's capacity to confront and deal with crises arising in a group can perhaps only be done through supervised practice. With increasing demands for more training, it seems likely that a variety of innovative training programmes will emerge. The question of training is of central importance, for group psychotherapy can only make a positive contribution if it is used by persons who have an aptitude for the work and who have been trained appropriately. Groups have both a constructive and a destructive potential; they may provide a crucial experience for the persons concerned or they may be a waste of time. It is often not difficult to set up a group, but it is by no means automatic that the group will prove to be a beneficial experience. With care, with attention to selection and composition, with an aware and responsible attitude towards the interventions one makes and their consequences, a group can be a useful therapeutic device. Group psychotherapy can be used with a wide variety of populations and its applications are still expanding. It is already widely used to provide long-term uncovering therapy, short- or long-term supportive work, time-limited help in facing special stresses and preparation for important life transitions. As society invents new treatment settings, a role for group therapy may be found within them. For example, groups of several sorts could be utilized in conjunction with intermediate treatment for young offenders. Group methods are also particularly suited to preventive work. As the need for preventive work with normal populations becomes more fully appreciated, one may find groups used more extensively in such settings as medical wards, schools, parent associations and mother-and-baby clinics.

References

Bion, W. R. (1961). *Experiences in Groups,* Tavistock, London.
Foulkes, S. H. (1948). *Introduction to Group-Analytic Psychotherapy,* Heineman, London.
Foulkes, S. H. (1964). *Therapeutic Group Analysis,* Allen and Unwin, London.
Foulkes, S. H., and Anthony, E. J. (1957). *Group Psychotherapy: The Psychoanalytic Approach,* Penguin, Harmondsworth.
Gundlach, Ralph H. (1967). 'Overview of outcome studies in group psychotherapy', *International Journal of Group Psychotherapy,* **XVII,** 196.
Lewis, P., and McCants, Jane (1973). 'Some current issues in group psychotherapy research', *International Journal of Group Psychotherapy,* **XXIII,** 268.
Lieberman, M. A., Lakin, M., and Whitaker, D. S. (1968). 'The group as a unique context for therapy', *Psychotherapy: Theory, Research and Practice,* **V,** 29.
Lieberman, M. A., Yalom, I. D., and Miles, M. (1973). *Encounter Groups: First Facts,* Basic Books, New York.
Locke, N. (1961). *Group Psychoanalysis: Theory and Technique,* New York University Press, New York.
Parloff, M. B. (1967). 'A view from the incompleted bridge: group process and outcome', *International Journal of Group Psychotherapy,* **XVII,** 236.
Psathas, G. (1967). 'Overview of process studies in group psychotherapy', *International Journal of Group Psychotherapy,* **XVII,** 225.
Rosenbaum, M., and Berger, M. (Eds.) (1963). *Group Psychotherapy and Group Function,* Basic Books, New York.
Whitaker, D. S. (1974). 'Focal conflict theory and the formative phase of therapy groups', *Group Process,* In Press.
Whitaker, D. S., and Lieberman, M. A. (1964). *Psychotherapy Through the Group Process,* Tavistock, London.

104

Wolf, A., and Schwartz, E. K. (1962). *Psychoanalysis in Groups,* Grune and Stratton, New York.
Yalom, I. D. (1970). *The Theory and Practice of Group Psychotherapy,* Basic Books, New York.

6

FAMILY COUNSELLING

John R. Lickorish

Characteristics of Counselling

The word counselling has a comfortable and reassuring sound, as well as a long and honourable history in the English language. According to the *Shorter Oxford Dictionary* the word first appeared in the Middle English period (i.e. before 1450), when it had the meaning of 'deliberation' and the advice or direction which resulted from it. It was also associated with the notions of 'judgement' and 'sagacity'. In olden times, counsellors were wise men and women who were well known for their understanding of human affairs and for their ability to help people with their personal and social problems. Counselling therefore makes great demands upon the personal qualities of the counsellor, as well as requiring him to have a good grounding in the science of behaviour and a sympathetic understanding of human problems. Perhaps it is necessary to emphasize that counselling is *not* simply the giving of advice, nor is it a coldly legalistic procedure. It depends upon the establishment of a genuine personal relationship between the counsellor and his client and implies that each party trusts and cooperates with the other. If in some quarters counselling is currently regarded as a nondescript sort of activity, that is because the term is being used in a degenerate sense and not because of the nature of the counselling process.

The purpose of counselling is to enable the client to live a more creative and satisfying life. Sometimes this purpose is achieved by the removal of one particular difficulty that blocks the client's development. With other clients, it is necessary to alter the social and environmental pressures which are thwarting them. Nearly all clients need to restructure or 'reconstrue' (Kelly, 1955; Bannister and Mair, 1968) their world of personal relationships and so modify their attitudes towards both their environment and themselves. Most of them also need to learn to distinguish between those situations which can be changed and those which cannot. The latter require some degree of adaptation from the client, but that does not mean that he must necessarily conform to any particular social pattern. Some degree of conformity is essential to any kind of social life, but beyond that the client should be encouraged to 'be himself' (Trillich, 1962) and to 'become a person' (Rogers, 1967).

105

Personal development necessarily presupposes the existence of interpersonal relationships and they, in turn, inevitably raise moral and ethical questions. Whilst the counsellor is not expected to be an ethical philosopher, he must have a basic understanding of ethical principles. He must not suffer from the delusion that counselling is a 'value-free' activity, for the question of human values is implicit in nearly everthing he does (Bühler, 1962; Bugental, 1967; Reisman, 1971).

The client brings to the counsellor a problem which is stated, if only implicitly, in terms of a pattern, or patterns, of behaviour. Both counsellor and client have to examine this behaviour pattern and try to work out the system of psycho-social forces which maintains it. They must then attempt to devise a programme by which the client's behaviour may be modified and so made acceptable to himself, his family or to society. This approach in counselling is problem-centred and concentrates upon the total behaviour pattern of which the client forms a part. It does not simply regard the client as 'having a problem', and so possesses distinct advantages over the traditional type of individual psychotherapy. Firstly, the client's thoughts are directed away from himself towards a total situation, of which he is a part. In so doing an attempt is made to put the problem into a proper perspective. Secondly, not all the onus for improvements is laid upon the client himself, nor is he absolved from all responsibility. He is partly, but only partly, responsible for what has gone wrong. The concept of 'diminished responsibility' provides a realistic basis for the counselling process. Thirdly, since patterns of behaviour are learned, they can also be *unlearned* and therefore the client can himself do something to improve his condition. Fourthly, by starting with the behavioural complex, it is usually possible to show the family or the individual client how the undesirable behaviour is generated and maintained. As the situation is understood, so the client's part in it becomes apparent to him and he begins to realize the significance of 'action' and 'reaction' in human relationships. A fifth possible advantage is that the client may arrive quite quickly at the point where some small modification of his behaviour may be initiated. Thus he receives immediate encouragement to attend the counselling sessions, for he realizes that he can begin to 'improve' almost at once.

The Counsellor and his Resources

The counsellor must be able to use a wide variety of psychological techniques intelligently and creatively and therefore he must be thoroughly acquainted with the principles upon which they are based. Although many of the techniques have been devised by psychologists with widely differing or even antagonistic backgrounds, each technique is an application of one or more basic psychological principles. Thus Ellis's method relies largely on cognition and affect, Rogerians use empathy and semantics, Adler based his approach on social interest, Freudians rely on transference and free association, whilst behaviourists generally base their methods on the principles of learning and so on. If therefore the counsellor has a thorough grasp of general psychology, he will understand the principles upon which any specialized therapy or technique is based and so be able to apply it creatively to a problem that confronts him.

There are only a limited number of basic topics in general psychology around which the specialized techniques are built. Knowledge of these basic principles enables a counsellor to use any specialized technique and to weave it into his own counselling and therapeutic system. In this way he adopts a *synoptic* attitude towards the specialized therapies. He does not choose 'bits and pieces' from them in an eclectic fashion, but goes behind their surface structures to the fundamental principles on which they are built. Not all the specialized techniques are viable, and in order to discriminate between them the counsellor must have a good grounding in scientific method. It is equally important for him to acquire the habit of being critical of his own work and of attempting to evaluate the success of his counselling methods.

The behavioural problems with which the counsellor is concerned are commonly referred to as neuroses, emotional disorders, psychiatric disorders or mental ill-health. All these terms are based on a 'medical model' of disorder and imply that all deviant behaviour is some kind of 'illness' requiring psychiatric treatment. The absurdity of this quasi-medical description of behaviour is apparent when a child's refusal to attend school is designated a 'phobia' and regarded as an illness. The items included in these ill-defined psychiatric categories are for the most part psycho-social disorders and are in need of psychological rather than medical help.

The client who comes for counselling is not suffering because he 'has an illness' but because he *behaves* in an inappropriate manner. His behaviour, like all behaviour, consists of responses which have been developed in relation to the world as he perceives it. So often he has a distorted view of the world or the world treats him so badly that he gets into all sorts of difficulties and generally fails to develop adequate personal relationships. Often his inappropriate responses are integrated into complex patterns of behaviour and, inadequate as they are, they are the only means by which the client can react to his environment. His need, therefore, is not to be 'cured' of some 'illness', but to understand why he behaves as he does and then to learn how to respond more effectively to his environment. As Angyal (1965, p. 104) remarks, 'One of the frequent obstacles to therapy is that the patient conceives of the process of getting well as ridding himself of something within him'. Whereas, in fact, the client has to re-evaluate the data he has accumulated over the years, restructure his pattern of living and adopt a different attitude towards life. The counselling process is therefore concerned with 'helping' not 'healing'. It is based upon a psycho-social model of disordered relationships and rejects the 'medical model' of psychiatry. The counsellor tries to show his client how he can live a more satisfying and effective life. He does not try to restore him to some putative 'normal' condition of 'health'.

Family counselling employs basic psychological processes in a scientific manner. It repudiates any 'mystique' or esoteric knowledge and claims that the principles, processes and effects of counselling, as well as the attributes to the counsellor, are all open to rational, empirical enquiry. The words 'counsellor' and 'counselling' are used throughout this essay with meanings which are sometimes equivalent to the terms 'psychotherapist' and 'psychotherapy'. So although the counsellor covers a wider range of activities than the traditional psychotherapist, what he *actually does* is often (but by no means always) precisely similar to what the psychotherapist does. It follows that many of the experimental findings about the personality of the therapist apply equally well to the counsellor (Reisman, 1971, pp. 70–5).

The most important of these findings is that the counsellor must possess the qualities of 'warmth, empathy and genuineness'. These personal qualities have been extensively investigated by Truax and Carkhuff (1967) and scales have been developed for assessing them. It seems likely that these qualities cannot be deliberately acquired by the counsellor, but that they are part of his essential make-up. There is, however, some evidence to suggest that the counsellor may be able to cultivate these qualities, at least to a limited extent.

Another series of investigations shows that even successful therapists differ appreciably among themselves with respect to their personal qualities. They exert a differential effect upon their patients and tend to be classifiable into what are termed 'A' and 'B' type therapist groups. Whitehorn and Betz (1954) demonstrated that A-type therapists achieved better results with schizophrenic patients than did the others. Subsequent research has tended to confirm this classification. The main results of the studies are summarized by Betz (1962) and Stern and Bierman (1973). The A-type therapist, in contrast to the B-type, shows a more constructive attitude towards schizophrenic patients, understands them better and shows them more unconditional regard. He is 'field-dependent', makes better use of his intuitive and affective qualities and tends to be more interpretive and interactive.

The B-type therapist, on the other hand, is more factual, 'field-independent' and emphasizes cognitive clarity to a greater extent than the A-type. He encourages more self-exploration by his client and tends to work for symptom reduction rather than intuitive understanding. He is generally more successful with neurotic patients.

However, it may be that successful counselling is due just as much to the counsellor's interest in and commitment to his client as it is to his personality type (Swensen, 1971). No counsellor can hope to help anybody and everybody, since factors like his cultural background, social class, age or temperament may prove to be disadvantageous with some clients and helpful with others (Reisman, 1971, pp. 81 and 116). There is some evidence to show that the best results are obtained when counsellor and client are suitably 'paired' (Howard *et al.,* 1970). Whilst an ideal pairing may rarely be achieved, the limits within which an effective relationship can be established do seem to be fairly wide.

In addition to these basic personal qualities, the counsellor also needs a basic knowledge of psychology together with experience in the use of interview methods and the procedures for analysing and modifying behaviour. But it is equally important for the counsellor to have some experience of life as it is actually lived. This involves a first-hand knowledge of the workaday world outside the narrow confines of school, university, postgraduate training and professional practice. Indeed, the would-be counsellor might follow the advice given by Jung (1917) and 'wander through the world . . . experiencing in his own person love and hate and every kind of suffering'. Failing such a period of vagrancy, then some experience of teaching, community work, clubs or pastoral work would be a most valuable part of the counsellor's training.

There is, however, no doubt that the most important of the counsellor's personal resources is his ability to establish a good relationship with his client. Apart from the simple 'test-advisory' situation mentioned later, the counselling process is essentially a cooperative effort between two parties and therefore the relationship between them is of vital importance (Rogers, 1967; Steinzor, 1968; Wolstein, 1964). In family counselling the interaction between counsellor and client may be regarded as a recursive and branching form of dialogue. It is recursive because the counsellor often needs to 'refer back' to data already mentioned by the client; to explore it and weave it into the main behavioural analysis. The dialogue is 'branching' because discussion often goes off at a tangent. Such a branch sometimes leads to an impasse or it may reflect a defensive tactic on the part of the client. But frequently it produces useful information which must be 'looped back', or 'recursively' incorporated into the main discussion.

Although the counsellor must avoid adopting an authoritarian attitude towards his client, they do not meet as equals. The counsellor is in a somewhat superior position in relation to his client. His superiority is due to his knowledge and experience, his detachment from the problem and his ability to take the initiative in promoting a good relationship between himself and his client. During the counselling process it is to be expected that client and counsellor will move nearer to each other so far as the problem under discussion is concerned. This concept of the client–counsellor relationship may be compared to that between a brother and an elder brother. It is firm but kind, and seems a better model for the counselling process than that implied in the doctor–patient, priest–penitent or teacher–pupil type of relationship. Of course, the client may not at first accept this relationship. He may want to exalt the counsellor to an authoritative position and cast him in the role of Benign Provider, as father, mother, doctor or god. By doing this, the humble, dependent client hopes to receive, at little or no cost to himself, some quasi-magical 'cure' for his troubles. Alternatively, the client may cast *himself* in the dominant role and demand to know what the counsellor is going to do to help him. The counsellor must avoid accepting either of these positions vis-à-vis his client. He must persistently and patiently insist upon the brother: elder brother roles, even if he does not say so in as many words. Although the dominant–submissive relationships just mentioned are extreme positions of the client–counsellor axis, they may well form part of the client's preconceived notions about counselling. If they do, then the counsellor must take steps to correct these misconceptions and point out to the client that counselling can proceed only within a brotherly (or sisterly) type of relationship.

One important function of the client–counsellor relationship is to facilitate *self-disclosure* by the client. However much may be inferred about the client as a result of the counsellor's enquiries and observations, there is a body of personal data which the client will not deliberately disclose unless he wishes to do so. There is no reason to suppose that roundabout methods of obtaining information can succeed without the client's active cooperation. Even the subtleties of the Rorschach technique do not seem particularly successful in obtaining a valid account of the client's hidden life (Jensen, 1964). A patient enquiry, based on associative techniques, which enlists the willing and knowledgeable cooperation of the client may, however, disclose the hidden data. Such a cooperative effort is of the essence of the counselling process and one condition of its success. The client, however, can hardly be expected to undertake such exercises in self-exploration and self-disclosure unless a secure and trusting relationship has been established between himself and his counsellor. There is, however, a corollary to self-disclosure by the client and that is that the counsellor must be willing to be frank as well. Frankness does not involve the counsellor in telling *his* life story to the client, although there are occasions when experiences may be shared, but it does demand plain answers to plain questions. If the counsellor does not know he should say so, and if he wishes to delay an answer he should be equally frank about that and always he can confess his inability to give any guarantee of success. By thus disowning any pretensions to a god-like superiority the counsellor firmly seats himself alongside his client and emphasizes the fact that counselling is a cooperative effort in which the two of them must work together.

A further important function of the client–counsellor relationship is that it affords a base from which the client may launch his new *adventures in living*. Ultimately, the client himself holds the key to counselling success. In the last resort he has to set himself free, however much help he may receive in the process. For only he can actually put into practice the new patterns of behaviour which will enable him to live a more effective and satisfying life. In doing so, he must face the risk of failure and disappointment. Such risks can be faced if the client feels that he has his counsellor's wholehearted support.

An effective system of family counselling also depends upon the client being able to make contact with his counsellor without being subjected to a long and often inefficient referral procedure. This implies that the counsellor should work in a 'walk-in' type of consulting centre similar to the Free Clinic described by Freudenberger (1973) or to the Young People's Consultation Centre (1965) in Hampstead (Laufer, 1963) or perhaps like that of the Samaritan's Organisation. There are severe practical difficulties associated with this kind of immediate consultation service, as Freudenberger points out. But there are also distinct advantages. Clients would probably seek help from such a centre much more readily than they do from the existing services. So they would be more likely to ask for counselling at an early stage in their difficulties, rather than wait until their situation had become desperate before seeking help. Clients would also avoid the embarrassing experience of having to tell their problems first to a referring agency which is not actually going to help them and which sometimes adopts obstructive tacts. The direct approach of client to counsellor would also ensure a high degree of confidentiality between them, comparable to that between a solicitor and his client. Since there would be no referring agent, no reports would be furnished to any third party without the expressed consent of the client.

This kind of self-referral systems embodies the concept of 'sideways communication' which is often much more efficient than the vertical 'chain of command' and is rapidly replacing it in many organizations (Toffler, 1970, p. 123). Sideways communication has long been the accepted method of approach between priest and parishioner, client and lawyer and between doctor and patient. It is more efficient than the 'up-and-down' system of communication since it reduces the number of intermediaries and hence the opportunities for error. It cuts down on paper work, thus saving time and money, and enables more information to be transmitted more quickly than does the traditional hierarchical communication structure. Speed and accuracy are vital factors in a counselling system, but at present they are all too often inhibited by the administrative structure within which the counsellor works. It is sometimes argued that psycho-social disorders 'cure themselves' after a sufficiently long interval. That may be true, but many of them also get worse and the conditions which deteriorate are often the most dangerous. A 'self-referral' system might well reduce the incidence of the more serious disorders and on any showing the actual work of the counsellor must be based on a system of 'sideways communication', which is an excellent administrative means of encouraging responsible interpersonal relationships.

The number of counsellors required to operate an adequate service is extremely difficult to estimate. Lickorish and Sims (1971) suggest that one counsellor might provide approximately 1,600 interview-hours per year. If the average length of an interview is $1\frac{1}{2}$ hours and the average number per client is 10 (Reisman, 1971, p. 41), then one counsellor could help about 110 clients each year. The number of people needing help is variously estimated at from 10 to 30 per cent of the general population at any one time. Accepting the lower estimate and using some 'elastic arithmetic', it can be argued that there should be one counsellor for every 5,000 people in the general population.

The foregoing account of the counsellor and his work provides the outline for an *operational* definition of counselling. Such a definition is concerned with what a counsellor *does*, not with his authority or status. The definition leaves open the question of the counsellor's professional standing. So the concept of counselling may form a rallying point for all those trying to help people with their problems. On the other hand, an operational definition specifies very clearly the qualifications needed by the counsellor and the activities that he may be expected to undertake. Because counselling is intended to be 'open to all', it does *not* imply that the counsellor's level of competence is the lowest common denominator of all the helping professions. On the contrary, the standard of competence implied in this essay is at least as great as any demanded by the present social and psychiatric professions.

Since the counsellor operates within a wide theoretical and practical framework, he welcomes the assistance of 'helpers' or 'paraprofessionals' (Truax and Carkhuff, 1967). These could gain their experience by working under the guidance of a counsellor (Lickorish, 1972) and might eventually wish to qualify as counsellors themselves. The counsellor naturally wishes to work as closely as possible with members of the educational, health and social services, since many of the behavioural programmes he devises need the active cooperation of the workers in these fields if they are to produce the most beneficial results (Tharp and Wetzel, 1969).

The Family as an Interactional System

From a counselling point of view, it is much more important to understand the internal dynamics of a family than to be able to classify it according to a nosological system. Although families are frequently spoken of as nuclear, extended or foster, this method of classifying them provides no information about the *constitution* of the family, which often exercises a decisive influence upon the vital personal relationships within it. The constitutions of families vary so widely that they do not form a convenient basis for classification and for all practical purposes it is best to regard each family as a unique organization. Since it is now accepted usage to speak of 'single-parent families', it follows that the minimum size of a family group is two. The family necessarily implies a parent–child relationship which may be determined by biological, legal or social factors. The biological factor determines the relationship of the 'natural family', in which all the children are the physical offspring of the same parents. The legal factor regulates the adoption of children by one or both parents. Social factors determine the existence of a family of foster children and, of course, a family may include one or more step-children. So in one particular family there may be one or more of these four possible types of parent–child relationships. Since the parents themselves may be once married or divorcees, widows or widowers, there are literally hundreds of different possible combination of parent–child relationships for even a four-person family. With such a large variety of possible family constitutions it is usually pointless for the counsellor to attempt to classify his families. It is much more important to regard each one as a unique system of relationships and to refrain from trying to push it into some prefabricated pigeonhole.

It is, however, useful to have a conceptual *model* of the relationships within the family in order to facilitate behavioural analysis and the construction of a remedial programme. All models of interpersonal relationships are bound to be inadequate, but at the risk of oversimplification the system of forces operating within a family may be represented by a series of dyadic interactions. A dyadic interaction consists of what is taking place between any two individuals at a given time. The content of the interaction may be either verbal or non-verbal or both. The *inter*action may be analysed into two actions, what one person does to the other and what the other does in reply. These individual actions also include the more enduring attitudes and affections that each member of the dyad maintains towards the other. An analysis of the family situation must also include a record of the *personal* attributes of each individual member. Although it *is* possible to do more than one thing at a time, the number of simultaneous acts that one individual can perform is severely limited. Simultaneous actions can be recorded using the dyadic model, even if one action is directed towards several members of the family at one time. By combining a suitable coding system (Gutman *et al.*, 1972) with this interactional model of the family a very effective system of behavioural analysis may be built up.

The implications of this interactional model must not be pressed too far, but it is probably fair to regard the family at any one moment as analogous to a system of forces which is in temporary equilibrium, as indicated in Figure 1. The family's equilibrium changes from time to time and resolve itself into yet another set of more or less temporary forces. Since the family is a developing and not a homeostatic system, small changes are taking place within it nearly all the time. Sometimes a major change in the family's total system of forces may be effected by altering just one relationship within it. Thus if there is a change in father's attitude towards mother, it may well have repercussions throughout the family. The effects of it may theoretically in the example given take any path indicated by the arrows in Figure 1. This spreading of influence throughout the family is the theoretical basis for saying that *family* counselling may sometimes be effective when only one member is seen by the counsellor.

The interactional model of the family is illustrated by the diagram shown in Figure 1. This shows a hypothetical family with seven serious problems. The

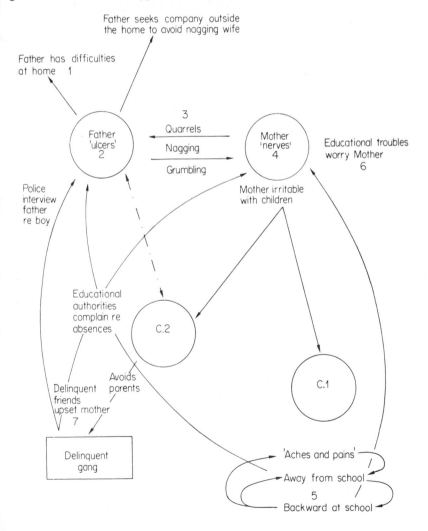

problem numbered 7 may reasonably be regarded as a result of the parents and the relationships at home. Any amelioration of problems 1 to 3 would almost certainly result in an all-round improvement in family relationships. Even if the family were suitable for group therapy this would not necessarily help father's work problem or his ulcers or the child's backwardness. The curved lines in this diagram indicate the reinforcing effects that the various activities have upon each other. The more stress father endures at work, the more he grumbles at his wife and the worse her nerves become, so she 'takes it out on' the children. Their backwardness and delinquency in turn cause anxiety and resentment in the parents, who not only become more punitive towards their children, but their physical symptoms may also be made worse. In this way a self-reinforcing *pattern* of family behaviour is maintained. Once such a pattern has become established, it is not easy to disrupt it. The counsellor's task is to break into this behavioural system at some point and endeavour to modify the harmful pattern or replace it with one that is more beneficial. Quite often the pattern may be broken into at several points more or less simultaneously. Thus medical help may be sought for father's ulcers and mother's 'nerves'. The child C.1 may receive some remedial education, whilst mother in particular may be instructed in the use of a Skinnerian programme to modify the behaviour of both children.

Assessing the Problem

Problems may be presented to the counsellor for a variety of reasons. Parents may come complaining about their children's behaviour. Husband or wife may ask for help in sorting out their marital relationships. An adolescent may need guidance regarding personal or sexual relationships or advice about a job or a career. Or someone may be just 'anxious' or 'worried'. Some clients come for counselling because they have been 'pressurized' into doing so. Others come because they themselves realize they are in need of help, whilst some are sent by a statutory body. Occasionally a whole family agrees to become a client *en bloc*, but usually one member or a married couple makes the initial approach. So the counsellor must be just as flexible in his acceptance of the problem as the client is variable in presenting it. Consequently it is sometimes necessary to work with only one member of the family, either because the others will not attend or the client is unwilling for them to know that he has seen a counsellor. Otherwise, unless the problem relates quite clearly to a single individual, the whole family should be interviewed severally and jointly as soon as possible after the initial interview. The family interview assists the counsellor in deciding whether there is a genuine *family* problem to be solved or whether it will be sufficient to arrange counselling for one or more of the family's members. During the first two or three interviews the counsellor tries to discover if the family has a 'core problem' or whether there are a number of problems and if they are specific or diffuse. It is not necessary to assume that just because one member of a family is in difficulties therefore the whole family is in need of counselling. On the contrary, if it is possible to identify a 'core problem' within the family it may be feasible to help the whole family by counselling only one of its members. The counsellor's 'client' may therefore be the whole family or one or more of its members. Such a 'variable-client' approach may be applied to the problems of the family shown diagrammatically in Figure 1.

In this family father would be the one member most likely to benefit all the others as a result of individual counselling. Any diminution of his antagonism towards mother would undoubtedly reduce family tension and lead to an improvement in the undesirable behaviour patterns indicated by the curved arrows. Obviously husband and wife should also attend as a 'dual client' and work out, with the counsellor, a behavioural modification programme for themselves and their children. After that has been accomplished, the whole family could meet as a 'multiple client' and attempt to consolidate and extend the behavioural programme. Such a procedure would be ideal when attempting to solve a complex family problem. In practice it is much more likely that one of the children would be initially 'referred' to the counsellor. Whether or not the rest of the family attended for counselling would depend partly upon the counsellor's skill in handling the initial interview. As a matter of experience, it seems that only about one whole family in five is able or willing to attend for more than two or three sessions.

The preliminary investigation will show whether a simple series of tests is all that is needed or whether a more extensive assessment must be carried out. It will also disclose whether or not the clients have recently consulted their own doctor or whether they must be requested to do so. If clients complain of symptoms which are likely to be organic in origin, then of course it is essential for them to consult a physician. It may not be possible for the counsellor to work conjointly with a physician, but there is no reason why medical and psychological treatment should not proceed side by side. Sometimes the counsellor must insist that his client consults a doctor before the counselling process begins. Thus both client and counsellor are safeguarded against the danger of mistaking an organic condition for a psychogenic disorder.

Whilst clients are always received with courtesy and kindliness, the degree of rapport which needs to be established between counsellor and client depends upon what is to be attempted. If it is necessary only to carry out a straightforward test of ability, then a polite, friendly relationship is all that is needed (Gathercole, 1968, p. 112). But if the counselling extends to a large number of sessions in which highly personal, intimate and embarrassing topics are being discussed, then a correspondingly deep relationship of mutual trust must be established. It may be true that 'the patient will show you all his problems in the first hour' (Fulweiler, 1967, p. 95) but some clients are much more diffident or defensive than others and they may attend for several sessions before they begin to discuss their 'core' problems. One must always remember, however, that the problem first mentioned by the client may not be the most important difficulty which confronts him or his family, real enough it may be. A minor problem is sometimes used as an excuse for gaining access to a counsellor so that the client may obtain help with more serious troubles. The initial problem, however trivial it may seem, must be assessed and discussed in its own right. By so doing the counsellor increases the client's confidence in him and encourages him to bring his other problems to light.

The best method of understanding the client's problem is to carry out a behavioural analysis of his situation. A detailed account of how to do so is provided by Kanfer and Saslow in their chapter entitled 'Behavioural Diagnosis' in the volume edited by Franks (1969). Essentially, behavioural analysis consists of cataloguing the client's actions within one or more specific areas of activity. These may include home, work, school or leisure. Of course not every action can be catalogued, and usually the client's unacceptable behaviour receives attention first. But as soon as possible the counsellor should enquire about the acceptable items in the client's behavioural repertoire as well as about his personal views and interests. All the items of behaviour are rated for frequency, intensity (or degree of seriousness) and duration. The acceptable and unacceptable items of behaviour are recorded separately, as well as the persons with whom the behavioural interactions take place and the factors which appear to facilitate the various behaviours. In addition it is important to discover any incipient or potentially good behaviour which the client might be encouraged to develop. The behavioural items are recorded on a chart or if they are not too numerous they might be located on a diagram like Figure 1. Either way, the analysis shows which behaviours are to be encouraged, which to be extinguished, what resources the client possesses and the means by which the counsellor proposes to modify each item of unacceptable behaviour. Such an analysis provides the base-line against which behavioural change can be assessed. It is rather tedious to carry out and it may require several sessions for its completion.

As the behavioural analysis for each client proceeds, there usually emerges a *pattern* of behaviour within the family. Thus behavioural analysis merges into pattern analysis since the two types of analyses simply emphasize different aspects of the total situation. Whilst behavioural analysis is primarily concerned with individual items in the client's behaviour, pattern analysis emphasizes the interconnections between the client and the significant figures within his 'life-space'. It may also be applied to the relation between the client's ideas and attitudes and his subsequent behaviour. The concept of pattern analysis is derived from Angyal (1965), who regarded 'neurosis' as an inappropriate pattern of behaviour which the client had made into a way of life.

Pattern analysis may reveal simple repetitive types of behaviour, like that of the executive who gave up his job each time he was expected to accept a post of greater responsibility. It may be applied to the problems of the family group shown in Figure 1. Here there are patterns within patterns. The curved arrows indicate how one kind of behaviour reinforces another and so maintains behavioural sub-systems within the family.

The following example shows how an initial, simple behavioural analysis must sometimes be replaced by a complex pattern analysis combining the client's ideational system with interpersonal relationships.

An attractive woman aged 50 complained that she dared not go out alone but could go anywhere with her husband. Taken at its face value it seemed to be a case of agoraphobia, and an orthodox desensitization programme was initiated but met with very little success. Further investigation showed that the client was specifically afraid of men younger than herself who, she said, made sexual overtures to her.

These 'advances' not only embarrassed but frightened her if she were alone. But in her husband's presence she felt quite excited if men 'made passes at her', because she knew that in his company she would not respond to them. She thus avoided the 'Suppose I did' thought which produced guilt and fear. Further analysis showed she was basically afraid of growing old. She exaggerated the attention that young men paid her in order to preserve her beautiful self-image. By insisting that her husband accompanied her everywhere, she not only controlled him but prevented her attractiveness from being put to the test! In addition, she could enjoy her fantasy life to the full with her imaginary paramours. This rather complex pattern of behaviour links together covert fantasies, thoughts and imaginations with overt behaviour and personal relationships. Together they form a locally consistent, self-reinforcing behavioural system which it would be very difficult to modify.

A further step in pattern analysis is the exploration of what Hadfield (1967, p. 237) calls *nuclear incidents*. These may give a clue to, or even explain, 'the whole problem' which is distressing the client. Although Hadfield restricts the use of this term to crucial phases in the child's development, there seems to be no reason why the term should not be applied to any event in the client's life if it has had a significant influence upon the development of his behaviour pattern. Thus in the case just quoted, the woman's fear of growing old (i.e. of losing her attractiveness) could be regarded as the 'nuclear incident' at the centre of her behaviour problem. By analysing what lay behind this fear and getting her to accept the reality of her life situation it would be possible to remove her fear of going out alone and enable her to live a reasonably normal life. Of course it does not necessarily follow that hers was a simple fear of ageing or even of death. Other fears may have clustered around this one fear, since some events do appear to form nuclei around which damaging and unpleasant memories cluster, along the lines suggested by Bartlett (1932) in his schemata theory of remembering. A special type of 'nuclear incident' which sometimes throws light upon the client's problem is the Early Recollection which Adler (1932) used regularly to request from his patients (Mosak, 1969).

The exploration of nuclear incidents and the elaboration of behaviour patterns may require the use of many techniques in addition to the interview. But the counsellor would do well to remember Kelly's First Principle, 'If you don't know what is wrong with the patient ask him, he *may* tell you' (quoted Bannister and Fransella, 1971, p. 78). Only when the client cannot elucidate his problem should the counsellor resort to indirect methods of investigation.

Among these indirect methods may be included the use of formal tests, which, generally speaking, are employed in one or more of the following situations. (1) When the required information cannot be obtained in any other way (e.g. an accurate estimate of intellectual ability). (2) When straightforward data can be collected by means of questionnaires. (3) When the investigation or the behavioural programme has reached an impasse and a projective or 'probing' technique seems to offer the best way forward. Tests suitable for these various purposes are described in the standard texts like those by Anastasi (1961), Mittler (1970) and Rabin and Haworth (1960).

It is, however, quite reasonable to regard even the most formal test as a highly structured interview, so that all types of counselling fall on the same continuum. At one pole are the highly structured tests of intelligence and educational attainments. At the other pole are the non-directive interviews. In between lie projective techniques, questionnaires, self-rating and grid methods and more or less structured conversations. It follows from this view of the counselling continuum that even the most formal test situation may have a therapeutic effect upon the client. It provides an opportunity for encouragement and shows him that someone can take an interest in him even when he is not very successful.

Counselling Methods and Techniques

The technique to be used in modifying a given behaviour pattern is determined by the nature of the problem and selected from the counsellor's repertoire. The counsellor does not simply apply his own favourite therapeutic method to all the problems presented to him but considers carefully what technique is best suited to a particular problem. This may seem rather too obvious to be stated but the point needs to be made in view of the fact that a wide range of behavioural disorders are still treated by whatever method the therapist happens to have learned. But effective counselling requires a knowledge of more than a dozen therapeutic systems and familiarity with literally scores of techniques which the counsellor may need to use at one time or another. Most of these methods and techniques are described by the following authors and the brief notes about each book mentioned give some idea of the topics it discusses.

An extensive survey of 15 different methodological approaches in counselling and psychotherapy is provided by Patterson (1966), whilst Harper (1959) gives much briefer surveys of 36 therapeutic systems. Yates (1970) describes the application of behavioural techniques to the main disorders of adults and children and gives a critical appraisal of behaviour therapy. He is a staunch advocate of the 'single-case' approach. Lazarus (1971; 1972) shows how behavioural methods may be integrated with other approaches and thus form a more comprehensive therapeutic system. Bandura (1969) is mainly concerned with conditioning and control techniques but he also discusses modelling and the function of 'awareness' and symbolic control in behavioural change. The text by Goldstein et al. (1966) discusses both individual and group therapies and is written from a research viewpoint. The discussions centre around a series of testable hypotheses and so firmly link therapeutic methods with general and experimental psychology. Franks (1969) is the editor of a symposium which critically surveys the field of behavioural therapy. Hadfield (1967) outlines his system of direct reductive analysis, which specifically avoids the traditional 'transference' situation and concentrates on the 'basic cause' of the problem. Rogers (1951) describes how the counsellor assists his client to clarify his thoughts and feelings and in a later work (1967) discusses the nature of personal relationships. The direct confrontational approach of Ellis (1962) emphasizes the cognitive factor in therapy. A somewhat oversimplified scheme of parent–adult–child relationships is outlined by Harris (1970) which may be used by the client himself in trying to sort out his own problems. Family counselling techniques are described almost in note form by Satir (1964), whilst Haley and Hoffman (1967) have provided an extensive and carefully annotated account of five different approaches to family therapy.

From such a wealth of material the counsellor must select the procedures most suited to particular clients and their problems. He must also learn to adapt and modify existing techniques when necessary and be able to devise new procedures to meet unusual situations.

It is not necessary always to carry out an exhaustive investigation before initiating a behavioural programme, for the sooner the client attempts to modify his behaviour the better. If at all possible, the remedial programme should begin at the end of the first interview. Further investigation may go hand in hand with behavioural modification. Sometimes it is necessary to teach the client to relax and this in itself is an excellent introduction to a behaviour modification programme. Instruction in relaxation is greatly facilitated by the use of the manual that Jacobson (1964) has specially prepared for the client. Whether or not relaxation is being taught, it is usually advisable for the client to carry out simple therapeutic actions in the intervals between the counselling sessions. These actions must be carefully chosen and discussed with the client. They must be very specific and likely to evoke a therapeutic response after a few repetitions. The client must, however, be warned against expecting instant success and be encouraged to give them a fair trial. Thus a husband who was highly critical of most of his wife's dresses was instructed to reduce marital friction by enquiring about the few dresses that he *did* like. Parents whose teenage daughter was verbally very aggressive were asked to ignore as far as possible her provocative remarks and to concentrate on praising her for items of acceptable behaviour. The very shy client may keep a log of the number of incidental greetings he gives during the day or the number of times he looks someone full in the face. Such activities as these, initiated after the first or second interview, encourage the client by making him feel that something is quickly done to help him and that counselling is not 'just talk', important as that may be.

Because of his flexible approach to family problems the counsellor may undertake group work with either the whole family or as many of its members as are willing to attend the counselling sessions. Or following Fulweiler (1967), he may deliberately try to divide the family into dyads or triads and interview each in turn. But however the group is formed, one of the objects of family group counselling is to improve the family's general system of interpersonal relationships and so produce a better 'atmosphere' in which to live. This beneficial effect may be brought about in a number of ways, even if only dyadic or triadic groups are formed. Thus marital counselling may reduce the tension and feeling of insecurity in the home, with consequent beneficial effects on the children. Specifically, parental counselling may show father and mother how to cooperate in handling their children better. Within a cooperative home atmosphere, a Skinnerian system of rewards may be easily devised to enable the children to gain enjoyment from creative and acceptable behaviour. If there are adolescents in the family, then a family group discussion may be able to modify the interpersonal demands and expectancies of the family members. As a result, tensions decrease, the youngsters get a fair deal and the parents learn that their children are growing up.

When only dyads or triads attend for counselling they may be regarded as an illuminated area of the family surrounded by a shadow formed by the rest of the family's internal relationships. Relationships within the shadow are more difficult to assess and modify, since they are accessible only through the members who are being counselled. But if the interactional view of the family is correct, then it is still reasonable to regard the *family* as the client even when only one or two of its members attend the counselling sessions.

If however the children in a family are too young to take part in discussion, it is hardly possible to undertake family counselling as such. Under these conditions observational techniques may be indicated or demonstrations of suitable parent–child behaviour may be arranged. If possible the demonstration should be 'live' and recorded on videotape, while the parents watch it on a suitable monitoring screen. The clients' own children should take part and the demonstration can be discussed with the parents when playing back the recording. In this way the parents are provided with a 'model' of desirable personal interaction which they can try to integrate into their own behaviour pattern. According to Bandura (1969), modelling is one of the most effective means of establishing new response patterns.

A second-best alternative is the use of instructional films. But these are obviously much less suitable, since they cannot be tailored to suit the needs of particular families.

Even when all the children are old enough to take an active part in a family discussion, the process still bristles with difficulties of which the following are perhaps the most important. (1) Lack of verbal ability on the part of one or more members. (2) A dominant or sulky member. (3) Too wide an age range amongst the children. (4) The presence of a handicapped member, unable to express himself adequately. (5) Fear, anxiety or diffidence which prevents one or more members from making an adequate contribution to the discussion. (6) The problem itself may be too embarrassing for members to discuss it freely. (7) The formation of an antagonistic or recalcitrant sub-group within the family. (8) The size of the family may make it extremely difficult, if not impossible, to evaluate the enormous number of interpersonal relationships and reactions which may occur even within a 50-minute hour. (9) Significant remarks by diffident members may go unnoticed or even be suppressed by the more voluble members. Certainly some of these unfavourable factors could be overcome, given enough time and perseverance. But it is often more advantageous to conduct dyadic or triadic interviews than to attempt to interview the family as a whole. Perhaps the best type of family for group counselling consists of three or four members, with teenage children, all of whom have a reasonable degree of verbal fluency.

Although the counsellor spends much of his time trying to modify the interpersonal relationships within the family, it is important to remember that it may be just as beneficial to attempt to modify the relationship between the family and its environment. As a psychological term, the 'environment' consists of both people and things. Personal environmental factors include the relationships at work and school, the contacts with in-laws, friends, clubs and societies. The non-personal or physical environment consists of the material conditions under which the family lives. These conditions include size and type of house, family finances, conditions at work and prospects of employment, the type of area in which the family resides and the local opportunities for recreational activities. Some or all of these personal and physical environmental factors may have therapeutic or psychonoxious effects upon the family. When carrying out a behavioural analysis, it is obviously important to examine the *extra*-familial relationships as carefully as one examines the internal relationships of the family.

The extent to which the environmental forces can be altered often depends upon factors quite beyond the counsellor's or the family's control. Where changes of physical environment can be made they may utilize the longing that people often have 'to get away from it all' and make a fresh start. Provided the client realizes that such a move by itself will not necessarily solve his problem, then a 'change of scenery' may help the client to establish new patterns of living. Thus the whole family may benefit from moving to a new house or a more congenial district or from taking a holiday. Other environmental changes are likely to be connected with father's move to a new job, the need to move near a school or mother's need to find employment outside the home. The lonely housewife may be able to join a club or cultural organization. The retiring, anxious child may be introduced via small group activities to a suitable club, team or other social activity. It must be emphasized, however, that in addition to a change of environment counselling is always necessary, if only to try to prevent the client from repeating his former mistakes in the new situation. Occasionally, some benefit may accrue to the whole family by systematically separating one or more of its members from the rest for a longer or shorter period. But the use of this separation technique frequently makes counselling doubly necessary. For, apart from the small child, the separated member usually needs help with his personal difficulties, whilst the rest of the family certainly needs to be shown how to establish better relationships with the 'difficult' member. The following examples indicate the kind of separation manoeuvres that may be carried out. A small child may attend a play group or nursery school in order to lessen the strain on a harassed mother. A babysitter may give young parents an opportunity for an evening out together. Husband and wife with deteriorating marital relationships may voluntarily agree to separate for a time. One or more children may go to boarding school or be taken 'into care' temporarily. Although much has been written about separation techniques, there is very little hard data to demonstrate their efficacy. Most of the research seems to have been based on the unsatisfactory psychiatric type of assessment (Wolkind and Rutter, 1973) and not upon behavioural analysis. Usually separation techniques must be regarded as a second-best procedure, and sometimes they are just desperate 'last resorts'.

Evaluating Family Counselling

The family counsellor employs many techniques which have been devised by members of a variety of schools of therapy. The effects of most of these methods have been extensively investigated and a critical review of 42 studies is provided by Truax and Carkhuff (1967, pp. 6–18). Most of the studies failed to show that psychotherapy was an effective agent of behavioural change. Some studies, however, definitely indicated 'that at least some kinds of psychotherapy under some circumstances are indeed effective' (ibid., p. 18). Bearing these findings in mind, it is reasonable to argue that family counselling may eventually prove more effective than the specialized therapies. First, owing to its object-centred approach, family counselling employs the type of behavioural modification best suited to the given situation. In so doing it capitalizes on the fact that different therapeutic methods produce differential effects (Di Loreto, 1971; Paul, 1966). Second, the client is regarded as operating within a field of psycho-social forces and so the counsellor attempts to modify the forces impinging upon the client from without, as well as trying to modify his intra-psychic activity. This dual approach should produce some gain over methods that concentrate upon either external or internal factors.

Third, the counselling process may be extended to the client's family or peer group, so that they also may become therapeutic agents. This is perhaps a subtle but useful method of increasing the beneficial effect of the external forces which influence the client. Yet, so far, the effects of these counselling methods are unproven and it is still open to the hardline critic to say that family counselling is just as ineffective as any othe type of therapy.

But acceptance of the hardliner's criticism does not remove the need for explaining why people are still willing to attend counselling sessions. One possible reason is that people 'get better' more quickly with a little help than they do without it. The 'spontaneous recovery' period may last as long as two years. If the client can 'get better' in, say, four to six months, then the time spent in counselling may well have been worthwhile. Another reason may lie in what Spearman is said to have called 'the changeling fallacy'. This may take one of two forms in the present context. It may be that the period of 'spontaneous recovery' coincides with the period of counselling and so counselling receives the credit for the improvement in the client's condition. Or, it may be that during the counselling process events occur which have an unrecognized, but decisive, therapeutic effect upon the client. Again counselling takes the credit for the improvement. At the very least, counselling provides 'a shoulder to cry on' or 'someone to talk to'—both comforting experiences which are not to be despised—or a temporary retreat from the storms of life or even 'the purchase of friendship' (Schofield, 1964). These last four items can be placed on the credit side in evaluating counselling, however difficult it may be to incorporate them into an acceptable statistic.

In order to demonstrate the probable effectiveness of counselling it would be necessary to carry out the following procedures. (i) Make a behavioural analysis at the beginning of counselling in order to form a base-line against which change can be assessed. (ii) Specify the items of behaviour which are to be modified. (iii) Specify the technique(s) to be used to modify the behaviour. (iv) Catalogue the forces which the counsellor cannot control but which influence the client. (v) Monitor these forces throughout the counselling process in order to detect any *change* in them which might significantly influence the client's behaviour. (As an alternative, control the client's 'life-space' (Lewin, 1936) so that extraneous factors are excluded.) (vi) After a given interval, make a second behavioural analysis and compare it with the first. If no relevant factors have been detected under (v) or if it has been possible to exclude all extraneous factors from the client's life-space, then any change in behaviour may be due to one or more of the following factors: (a) the counselling process; (b) a maturational and/or developmental process which was already at work when counselling started; (c) a process which was *initiated* by counselling, but which subsequently became autonomous; (d) a combination of (a) and (b).

If the change in behaviour could properly be ascribed to (a) or (c), it still would not follow that counselling was a *necessary* cause of behavioural change. Other procedures might be able to produce the same result if they were *substituted* for the counselling process. If they did so, then counselling would be an *efficient* cause of change, able to produce a result which could be equally well produced by other methods. However, it would be extremely valuable to demonstrate that counselling was even an *efficient* cause of behavioural change, for that would enable it to be subjected to a cost-benefit analysis and compared with other therapeutic methods. Thus it would be possible to decide whether to invest time and energy in counselling or in some other kind of therapeutic activity.

Although most of the investigations into the effectiveness of counselling and psychotherapy have been carried out by the method of group comparisons, there is much to be said for attempting to evaluate the the results of family counselling by using the 'single-case' method. Shapiro (1961) was a pioneer of this method, which is strongly advocated by Yates (1970, p. 380) and is especially suitable for the individual counsellor who is unable to collect large experimental and control groups. By regarding each case as an experimental investigation in its own right (which, in fact, it is) the counsellor turns his day-to-day work into a series of researches of which some may be selected for very detailed evaluation. The face validity of such research is as good as that of specially organized investigations. If it lacks some technical refinements, it is at least being conducted in a real-life situation and is not subject to the artificial conditions of the laboratory. Even if the individual results obtained by it are relatively weak, their cumulative effect may be quite impressive. As Goldstein *et al.* (1966, p. 18) point out—'A series of individually faulty researches with no consistent methodological weakness may add up to a fairly convincing conclusion'.

The results of investigations into counselling are all the more valuable if they are carried out in the conditions of everyday life. The results can also be more confidently generalized than those obtained under artificial or laboratory conditions. Moreover, any viable method of counselling must be applicable to the client's behaviour within his ordinary environment (Tharp and Wetzel, 1969, p. 200). If methods can be devised and tested within that environment, then research and counselling may be fused together into one on-going, self-correcting process.

As long as people feel they gain some benefit from counselling, so long will they continue to ask for it. They will not be impressed by the lack of scientific evidence for its effectiveness. Even if it proves impossible to demonstrate that counselling is effec-

124

tive, people will still seek help for their personal and family problems. When, time and again, one sees an obvious change in a client's behaviour even during just one interview, it is difficult to believe that counselling is entirely ineffective. Of course, no one ever said it was. But can the results of counselling be produced more efficiently by other means? The client, apparently, does not think so—and he has the last word.

References

Adler, A. (1932). *What Life Should Mean to You*, Allen & Unwin, London.
Anastasi, A. (1961). *Psychological Testing*, second edition, Macmillan, New York.
Angyal, A. (1965). *Neurosis and Treatment: A Holistic Theory* (Ed. E. Hannman and R. M. Jones), Wiley, New York.
Bandura, A. (1969). *Principles of Behaviour Modification*, Holt, Rinehart & Winston, London.
Bannister, D., and Fransella, F. (1971). *Inquiring Man. The Theory of Personal Constructs*, Penguin, Harmondsworth.
Bannister, D., and Mair, J. M. M. (1968). *The Evluation of Personal Constructs*, Academic Press, London.
Bartlett, Sir Frederic (1932). *Remembering: A Study in Experimental and Social Psychology*, Cambridge University Press, London.
Betz, B. J. (1962). 'Experiences in research in psychotherapy with schizophrenic patients', in H. H. Strupp and L. Luborsky (Eds.), *Research in Psychotherapy*, American Phsychological Association, Washington D.C., pp. 41–60.
Bugental, J. F. T. (1967). *The Challenges of Humanistic Psychology*, McGraw-Hill, New York.
Bühler, C. (1962). *Values in Psychotherapy*, Free Press, New York.
Di Loreto, A. O. (1971). *Comparative Psychotherapy: An Experimental Analysis*, Aldine-Atherton, New York.
Ellis, A. (1962). *Reason and Emotion in Psychotherapy*, Lyle Stuart, New York.
Franks, C. M. (Ed.) (1969). *Behaviour Therapy: Appraisal and Status*, McGaw-Hill, New York.
Freudenberger, H. J. (1973). 'The psychologist in a free clinic setting. An alternative model in health care', *Psychotherapy: Theory Research and Practice*, **10**, No. 1, 52.
Fulweiler, C. R. (1967). 'No man's land', in Jay Haley and Lynn Hoffman, *Techniques of Family Therapy*, Basic Books, New York, pp. 3–96.
Gathercole, C. E. (1968). *Assessment in Clinical Psychology*, Penguin, Harmondsworth.
Goldstein, A. P., Heller, K., and Sechrest, L. B. (1966). *Psychotherapy and the Psychology of Behaviour Change*, Wiley, New York.
Guttman, K. A., Spector, R. M., Sigal, J. J., Epstein, N. B., and Rakoff, V. (1972). 'Coding of affective expression in conjoint family therapy', *Amer. J. Psychotherapy*, **26**, 185.
Hadfield, J. A. (1967). *Introduction to Psychotherapy*, Allen & Unwin, London.
Haley, J., and Hoffman, L. (1967). *Techniques of Family Therapy*, Basic Books, New York.
Harper, R. A. (1959). *Psychoanalysis and Psychotherapy: 36 Systems*, Prentice-Hall, Englewood Cliffs, N.J.
Harris, J. A. (1970). *The Book of Choice*, Cape, London.
Howard, K. I., Orlinsky, D. E., and Hill, J. A. (1970). 'Patients' satisfactions in psychotherapy as a function of patient–therapist pairing', *Psychotherapy: Theory Research and Practice*, **7**, No. 3, 130.
Jacobson, E. (1964). *Self-operations Control*, Lippincott, Philadelphia.
Jensen, A. R. (1964). 'The Rorschach technique: A re-evaluation', *Acta Psychologica*, **22**, 60.

Jung, C. G. (1917). 'The psychology of the unconscious processes, in *Collected Papers on Analytical Psychology*, second edition, trans. C. E. Long, Balliere, Tindall and Cox, London, p. 356.

Kelly, G. A. (1955). *The Psychology of Personal Constructs*, Vols. I and II, Norton, New York.

Laufer, M. (1963). 'The help of an adult', in *New Society*, 19.12.63, 17.

Lazarus, A. A. (1971). *Behaviour Therapy and Beyond*, McGraw-Hill, New York.

Lazarus, A. A. (Ed.) (1972). *Clinical Behaviour Therapy*, Brunner/Mazel, New York.

Lewin, K. (1936). *Topological Psychology*, McGraw-Hill, New York.

Lickorish, J. R. (1972). 'Helping the helpers', *J. Association Educ. Psychologists*, 3, No. 2, 27.

Lickorish, J. R., and Sims, C. A. (1971). 'How much can a clinical psychologist do?', *Bull. Br. Psychol. Soc.*, 24, 27.

Mittler, P. (Ed.) (1970). *The Psychological Assessment of Mental and Physical Handicaps*, Methuen, London.

Mosak, H. H. (1969). 'Early recollections: Evaluation of some recent research', *J. Individual Psychology*, 35, 56.

Patterson, C. H. (1966). *Theories of Counselling and Psychotherapy*, Harper & Row, New York.

Paul, G. L. (1966). *Insight vs. Desensitisation in Psychotherapy*, Stanford University Press, California.

Rabin, A. I., and Haworth, M. R. (Eds.) (1960). *Projective Techniques with Children*, Grune & Stratton, New York.

Reisman, J. m. (1971). *Towards the Integration of Psychotherapy*, Wiley-Interscience, New York.

Rogers, C. R. (1951). *Client-Centred Therapy*, Houghton Mifflin, Boston.

Rogers, C. R. (1967). *On Becoming a Person: A Therapist's View of Psychotherapy*, Constable, London.

Satir, V. (1964). *Conjoint Family Therapy: A Guide to Theory and Technique*, Science and Behaviour Books, Palo Alto.

Schofield, W. (1964). *Psychotherapy: The Purchase of Friendship*, Prentice-Hall, Englewood Cliffs.

Shapiro, M. B. (1961). 'The single case in fundamental clinical psychological research, *Brit. J. Med. Psychol.*, 34, 255.

Steinzor, B. (1968). *The Healing Partnership: The Patient as Colleague in Psychotherapy*, Secker & Warburg, London.

Stern, M. I., and Bierman, R. (1973). 'Facilitative functioning of A–B therapist types, *Psychotherapy: Theory, Research and Practice*, 10, No. 1, 44.

Swensen, C. H. (1971). 'Commitment and the personality of the successful therapist', *Psychotherapy: Theory, Research and Practice*, 8, No. 1, 31.

Tharp, R. G., and Wetzel, R. J. (1969). *Behaviour Modification in the Natural Environment*, Academic Press, London.

Tillich, P. (1962). *The Courage to Be*, Collins Fontana, London.

Toffler, A. (1970). *Future Shock*, Bodley Head, London.

Truax, C. B., and Carkhuff, R. R. (1967). *Toward Effective Counselling and Psychotherapy: Training and Practice*, Aldine, Chicago.

Whitehorn, J. C., and Betz, B. J. (1954). 'A study of psychotherapeutic relationships between physicians and schizophrenic patients', *American J. of Psychiatry*, 111, 321.

Wolkind, S., and Rutter, M. (1973). 'Children who have been "in care"—an epidemological study', *J. of Child Psychology and Psychiatry*, 14, 97.

Wolstein, B. (1964). *Transference, Its Structure and Function in Psychoanalytic Therapy*, second edition, Grune & Stratton, New York.

Yates, A. J. (1970). *Behaviour Therapy*, Wiley, New York.

Young People's Consultation Centre, Second Report (1965), 11 King's College Road, London, N.W.3.

7

PERSONAL CONSTRUCT THEORY PSYCHOTHERAPY

D. Bannister

Personal construct theory is not a theory of psychotherapy. It is a theory of man which can be applied to the psychotherapeutic venture.

Since its original presentation (Kelly, 1955) there have been a number of summary accounts of personal construct theory (Sechrest, 1963; Bannister and Mair, 1968; Pervin, 1970; Bannister and Fransella, 1971) and more specific considerations of its implications for psychotherapy (Patterson, 1966; Kelly, 1969; Landfield, 1971; Fransella, 1972).

The theory offers as its model of man 'man the scientist'. Obviously, in suggesting that all men may be viewed as scientists Kelly is not arguing that all men wear white coats, have PhDs or are interminably dull in their discourse. He is suggesting that each man has a series of related notions (however incompletely articulated) about his own nature and about the nature of the universe he inhabits. These notions if he were a member of the Science Club would be called his 'theory', but since he is merely an ordinary person they are referred to as his 'personality' or his 'habits' or his 'central nervous system' or his 'attitudes' or his 'unconscious motivation' and so forth.

In the light of his general view of the world, a person attaches specific meaning to any particular situation with which he is confronted and thereby he has certain expectations about the events which will unfold from that situation. Were he an accredited member of the Science Club these expectations would be called hypotheses; in view of his humble status they are referred to as his 'set' or his 'anticipatory goal responses' or they may even be externalized right out of the man altogether and thought of as 'stimulus characteristics'.

In the light of his expectations (which reframed are his inquiries) a person moves into a situation, thereby hoping to affirm its nature and his own nature in relation to it. In formal science he would be said to be 'experimenting', but viewed by psychologists in their Science Club mood he is merely said to be 'behaving'.

As events unfold, a person reviews them in relation to his interpretations, his expectations and undertakings and thereby changes, to a greater or lesser degree, the philosophy in terms of which he framed his responses. He changes himself. In science, this is called revising a theory in the light of experimental outcome. The psychologist/scientist viewing the organism/man refers to such revision as 'learning' or 'acquiring a skill' or 'resolving intra-psychic conflict' and so forth if he approves of it, and 'acquiring a maladaptive learned habit' or 'fixating' or 'forgetting' and so forth if he disapproves of it.

Personal construct theory is an elaborate philosophy/psychology comprising a fundamental postulate and 11 elaborative corollaries, these in turn being amplied by a language for dealing with structure and change in construct systems and forms of operational definition such as grid method. Its central tenets can be sketched by considering closely the components of the term *a personal construct system*.

The term 'personal' denotes that the person is the irreducible unit of psychology as it is seen in terms of construct theory. It argues that each of us inhabits a unique and distinctive world, so that while we may communicate in terms of envisaged similarities and differences between our own world and that of others, we must at no point deny the uniqueness of an individual's experience. Psychological 'similarity' is seen in terms of similarity in the *ways* in which people interpret their world, not similarity in the worlds themselves. A bank clerk may communicate far more meaningfully with his friend the retired missionary priest than the bank clerk next to him at the counter, because bank clerk and missionary have come to make sense of their apparently disparate worlds in terms of the same issues and concerns while the bank clerk and bank clerk only occupy 'similar' worlds in the terms of the construing of a third person. They have not gauged their worlds in the same way.

A construct, defined at the most simple level, is a way in which two or more things are seen as alike and thereby different from one or more other things. It is bipolar in that we can never affirm anything without contrasting it implicitly with something else, which is thereby negated. If we say that someone is an *honest man* we are contrasting him with *dishonest men*, we are not saying that he is *honest* instead of being a *battleship*, a *greengrocer* or *the square root of −1*. A construct may have a verbal label but the verbal label is not the construct. The construct is the actual discrimination that the individual makes amongst the elements with which he is surrounded. Thus a baby may well construe *sweet* from *bitter* without possessing the verbal label *sweet–bitter*. Nor are the poles of a construct merely collections of elements, for a construct is an axis of reference. *North–south* is not a collection of 'north' things versus 'south' things, for we can readily transfer it around so that in a new juxtaposition previously 'south' things are seen as 'north'.

Thirdly, though we have verbal labels for some constructs, while others are not so articulated, all are essentially parts of a construct *system*. The system is such because constructs are related one to another, they imply and are implied by each other and thereby allow us to make predictions from one to the other. For one man, to be *traditional* rather than *modern* may be inevitably to be *moral* rather than *promiscuous* and thereby *serious* rather than *whimsical*. The system is hierarchical, with some constructs for an individual subsuming others as elements within their range of convenience. Thus for one behaviourist man *reward–punishment* may be an overarching and superordinate construct which articulates a series of subordinate constructions down to the level of *cigarette–electric shock*. Perhaps for all of us *within me–outside of me* definies countless other interpretable aspects of experience. The system is such that it exists over time as changeable yet continuous. A man may change his subordinate and immediately operational constructs with relative ease while modifying his superordinate principles relatively slowly.

Psychotherapy is not a bundle of set procedures. However formalized it may be, it is essentially a fast-flowing, interactive engagement between two or more human beings. The effect of using an elaborate theoretical framework such as personal construct theory to guide such an engagement cannot be defined, it can only be described. The following description focuses initially on what a personal construct theory therapist sees as the nature of the client–therapist relationship and the nature of complaint and 'cure'.

The Client–Therapist Relationship

The limitations of the 'doctor–patient' concept of the relationship in psychotherapy are now widely acknowledged. It is doubtful that anyone possesses the curative expertise in psychological matters implied by the term 'doctor', and certainly little good comes of the kind of passivity induced by undertaking the role of 'patient'. Equally, categorizing a person's problems in understanding himself and his relationships with other people (however severe and disabling these difficulties may be) as an 'illness' adds little to our understanding of them. The word client, rather than patient, is much used, these days, not in any fee-paying sense, but to avoid the implication of 'illness'.

Kelly suggested that following his model of 'man the scientist' the therapist–client relationship might be looked on as broadly equivalent to the relationship between a research supervisor and a research student. Such a metaphor suggests not an expert dealing with an ignorant unfortunate but a differential balance of expertise as between the two. The research student, in any scientific endeavour, is clearly the expert in the immediate field. He is the one up to date with the literature, the one fully involved in the research project. Equally, in Kelly's terms the client in psychotherapy is the only really informed expert on himself. On the other hand, the research supervisor's expertise has to do with familiarity with ways of testing theories, with ways of evaluating evidence, with exploratory strategies. It is in this kind, then, that the therapist may contribute to the endeavours of the client.

This approach stresses that the content of the whole undertaking will be provided by the client. He is not to be given particular 'insights', he is to be encouraged to be insightful. A particular content of his 'unconscious' cannot be specifically revealed to him by an outsider, but he can be helped to explore those constructions for which he has no verbal label. He may be unaware of discriminations he operates because they were discriminations elaborated in preverbal infancy; or because some of the contrast poles of his constructs have become submerged; or because a superordinate construct is too far-reaching in its implications to be readily categorized; or because his construing system is changing too rapidly for aspects to be pinpointed and labelled.

The notion of therapist and client as co-experimenters puts certain demands on both. It demands that the therapist be, above all, *useable*. He must be personally available as validating and invalidating evidence in the experiments conducted by his client during the therapy sessions. He must be ambiguous enough to be variously construable by his client but not so ambiguous that he cannot be construed at all. Thus his manner must not be remote, distant and 'abstract'. Nor must it be a vivid personal style which overwhelms the client and pre-empts his interpretation and response.

He must be willing to take part in an experiment that must necessarily be conducted largely in the client's language. The tendency to trivialize psychotherapy by prescribing it as treatment only for the young, articulate, intelligent, middle-class and 'not too disturbed' must not only be avoided but it must be replaced by a willingness to try to work in terms of construction which may initially be very alien to the therapist's personal experience—say the constructions of the so-called psychotic. He must strive for something of the talents of the novelist in entering into other people's worlds. He must broaden his own native tongue till it be not too particular and jarring upon the ears of his clients. His constructions must have a wide range of convenience so that they can readily communicate across boundaries of class, culture and age.

Above all, he must construe himself in the same terms as he construes his client. He too will be validated and invalidated, as will his client. He is likely to manifest hostility and bully the evidence to suit his own preconceptions, as may his client. He will have to tighten and loosen his constructions in order to achieve change, as must his client. He must not use a form of construction which distances him from his client or treats his client as a non-person. He must use constructions which acknolwedge that the client's talk and behaviour have the same degree of *meaning* as the talk and behaviour of the therapist. Thus the client's talk and behaviour must not be viewed in terms of pre-emptive 'nothing but' constructions. It must not be viewed as merely 'symptoms' or 'phobic' or 'paranoid' or as being nothing but 'sublimation' or 'inhibition' or 'not authentic'. What any person says or does represents some kind of bid for meaning and has the authority of the person behind it.

The client must reciprocate and be prepared to put his convictions at risk. He must undertake to experiment with his life, however, cautiously—or the therapy will be reduced to the level of hand-holding and misery-reciting.

These joint experimenters are each other's subjects. The present author was once driven by the repeated demands of a client to say what therapy was and why it could possibly do her any good to propose the following formula. 'The idea is that I should try and understand you because being understood has not been a common part of your experience. You should try and understand me because understanding someone else has also not been a common part of your experience. If we succeed it may do us both some good.'

The Complaint

The dangers of the overspecified, too readily agreed and too firmly adhered to 'complaint' are obvious. Inevitably a client enters therapy with a history—often a long history—of trying to explain his problem and of having his problem reframed for him by a variety of doctors and his Uncle Fred.

But this well-rehearsed form in which the problem is presented is likely not to be a good formulation. If it had been a well-formulated problem then most likely it would have been solved long before. It is the badly framed questions to which we can find no answers. It is essential therefore that the nature of 'the problem', 'the complaint', must itself be at issue in therapy, and both therapist and client must have the freedom to reconstrue and reformulate the problem, not once but perhaps many times. This means that the characteristic opening style of therapy in personal construct theory is one of circumspection and discussion of a wide range of ways in which 'the problem' can be viewed. In no sense is the patient's initial statement of the problem rejected but it is elaborated, extended, explored, looked at historically, rephrased in many ways and both its subordinate and superordinate implications considered.

This notion of superordinate and subordinate implications is derived from Kelly's argument that construct systems are hierarchical, with some constructions being governed by others. This idea can be readily illustrated by considering Hinkle's (1965) laddering procedure, which itself can sometimes be used as part of therapeutic exploration. A person has what might be a relatively subordinate construction, say *'reads novels—doesn't read novels',* and might answer the question 'Would you prefer to see yourself as a person who reads novels rather than one who does not?' by opting for *reads novels.* He can be further asked why he would prefer to see himself in such a way. He may reply that a person who *reads novels* is thereby showing an interest in *other people's lives* (rather than say being *only interested in his own life*). This gives us a more superordinate construction. This in turn can be questioned: why would he wish to show an interest in *other people's lives* to which he might reply that this would help him *to relate to people* (as contrasted with being *unable to relate to other people*). Querying this yet more superordinate construction might elicit some such reply as that this is desirable because it will help him to *develop his personality* (as contrasted with having his own *personality undeveloped*) and so on and so forth. Finally, some construction is reached which is, for the time being, the articulate ceiling of that particular pyramid of constructs. This whole issue can be rephrased by asking the question 'At what level of abstraction is the problem to be stated?'. Any problem can be stated in very immediate and concrete (subordinate) terms. 'My difficulty is that I quarrel so much with my wife.' This very same problem could be restated in even more concrete terms. 'My wife and I are always quarrelling about the way to bring up our children.' It could be restated at a much more superordinate level. 'My problem is a difficulty in understanding and relating to people which, for example, shows itself in my relationship with my wife.' It could be restated in yet more superordinate terms. 'My problem is that I am not worth much as a person and this shows itself in the poor quality of my relationships with people.' One of the startling things about much of the literature on psychotherapy and the issue of whether it 'cures' anyone is the arbitrariness with which problems are stated at one level of abstraction or another, as if it made no difference to the evaluation of the ultimate outcome how widely or how narrowly problems are framed.

Therapists of all persuasions, when they talk in terms of their most superordinate constructs, tend to state that *all* problems are of certain essential modal kinds. From the point of view of a behaviour therapist all problems are ultimately *maladaptive learned habits*. From the point of view of a psychoanalyst all problems are ultimately *unresolved psychodynamic conflicts*. From the point of view of a Rogerian all problems are ultimately *failures to actualize self*. Equally, in terms of personal construct theory all problems are ultimately *failures to elaborate one's personal construct system*.

Failure to elaborate personal construing can take any one of a number of forms.

It may be that the person's construing system has become too tight, too specific, too anchored into particular elements in his life, too restricted to particular strategies for handling experiment and evidence. Hence the obsessional, whose life has become circular, repetitive, trapped. He is endlessly successful in repeating his non-elaborating cycle but is in danger of death by boredom because it represents no kind of journey. This is the situation of the man who has proved beyond all doubt that by carefully avoiding any close contact with other people you can always avoid personal disaster only to find that this is itself a form of personal disaster.

It may be that the personal construct system has become too loose, too chaotic. The constructs are so vague and inconsistent that they generate no testable expectation, they cannot act as a guide to any formulated venture which would have a meaningful and evaluatable outcome. They may be so loose that people are tempted to refer to them and the person as 'psychotic'.

Again, the problem may have more specific and identifiable form in the shape of particular contradictory implications in a person's construct system which prevent elaboration. An example of such a contradiction is well analysed by Wright (1970).

In the initial circumspection of the patient's 'complaint' much may be made of the case history. But the case history must not be a recital of apparent facts and events from the point of view of an outside observer but the patient's case history as seen by him in his own terms. As Kelly repeatedly stressed, the person is not the victim of his autobiography but he may be the victim of the way he interprets his autobiography. His past does not decide his present except and insofar as he sees his past as generating certain inescapable and unescaped conclusions.

Therapeutic Method

Different therapeutic theories and approaches inevitably generate broad differences in method, so that the popular image of different kinds of therapists reasonably represents them as 'doing' different things. At a simple and summary level it would not be unfair to characterize say analytic, behaviour therapy and client-centred methods in something like the following terms.

The essence of psychoanalytic method is to bring to the surface repressed psychodynamic conflicts and to resolve these using the transference situation, i.e. using the therapist both as representing the other people who are significantly involved in these conflicts and ultimately as representative of reality. Change in the client is seen as resulting from the resolution of conflict and the gaining of insight.

The behaviour therapist sees his methods as focusing on the relearning of responses to groups of situations. The client is to be helped to re-enter say feared situations (either ideationally or *in vivo*) and to learn to handle them without either the anxieties or the inappropriate responses which have become characteristic of his reaction to such situations.

The Rogerian therapist seeks to use a context of warmth and understanding between therapist and client as a means of enabling the client to begin to express and realize himself in an undistorted way.

In construct theory psychotherapy, in line with the vision of 'man the scientist', change is seen as coming about because the person has construed, experimented in terms of his construction and thereby reconstructed himself and his life situation. The client must be encouraged to articulate his interpretation of himself and others and to specify his expectations in terms of his articulation; to subject these expectations to experimental test in his mundane life and within the therapy session; to elaborate his construing in terms of the outcome, as he has experienced it, of his experiment. This broad approach has particular implications for the relationship between 'talk' and 'behaviour' and the equivalent relationship between events *within* the therapy session and within the life of the client *between* therapy sessions. 'Talk' is essential because thus is reviewed the outcome of experiments. 'Behaviour' *is* the experiment.

There is no virtue in behaviour as such unless it becomes an experience, that is to say, it is interpreted, given meaning, significance is seen. Kelly used often to refer to the story of the Inspector of Schools who claimed to have had thirteen years' experience, whereas it was clear that he had had one year's experience repeated thirteen times. Never, after the first year, had he made any sense out of the events of which he was a part. This is an implicit comment on behaviour therapy in that it argues that simply to enable a person to go through a series of events, which he has previously avoided, is only of value insofar as he sees a new meaning in the events.

Equally, talk as such is of limited value. There is no good reason why a client should take up a new point of view and new stances towards life simply because the therapist has produced good arguments for them. The only ultimately convincing argument, for each of us, is our own experience. We are only really convinced of something *when we have found it to be so*. Thus the conversation must assist the client to venture a dream behaviourally, so that there is the possibility that he *might find it so to be*.

Within this argument, it must be noted that the therapy session is itself an event—it is part of the life of the client.

Thus one client of the author was a young man who appeared rarely to have been able to express anger or to act openly on the grounds of his anger. The following is a transcript of a part of one session.

Therapist: Try hard to think of one occasion when you were angry and expressed your anger.
Client: (after a long pause) I don't think I can.

Therapist: There probably was a time. Think of being angry and let your mind track back and forth to see if any event comes into your thoughts.
Client: Yes, once.
Therapist: Tell me about it.
Client: I had this appointment with a friend, we agreed to meet at three o'clock. I waited till after four o'clock. It was very cold. Then I rang him up to see what had happened. (long pause) He didn't sound bothered at all. He said 'I just forgot'.
Therapist: Were you angry?
Client: Yes, very angry. Very angry.
Therapist: What did you say?
Client: I said that I thought it was not very fair of him to just forget like that. (long pause)
Therapist: What else did you say?
Client: Nothing, I just said it was not very fair of him.
Therapist: (after a long pause) Listening to that I don't know whether to laugh or to cry. You produce that as an example of your anger and it is so comical and so pathetic I don't know what to say about it. It's just such a miserable example of anger.
Client: (voice rising sharply) I don't need you to tell me that it's miserable. I don't need you to just sit there and tell me I'm pathetic. I know it was pathetic, I know all about that. You're not helping me just sitting there all smug saying that sort of thing.
Therapist: (after a long pause) All right. I agree it was arrogant of me to say that and I apologize. It's just that I was disappointed that you hadn't been able to express your anger more strongly to the man who kept you waiting.

The relationship between client and therapist is the pivot on which therapy turns, and interestingly this is acknowledged in most therapies in one form or another, whether it be the psychoanalyst talking of the importance of transference, the behaviour therapist acknowledging the need for cooperation and support or the Rogerian specifying the importance of warmth, genuineness and accurate empathy. Thus the therapy session can be used as a kind of laboratory for experiments where the penalties for failure are not too severe, the boundaries of ventures can be thoughtfully defined and outcomes be clarified.

In personal construct theory psychotherapy a great many techniques may be used and new modes of interaction invented but the broad frame of the method always comprises an attempt to enable the person to reflect, to reconstrue and, by articulating his past and present experience, read it into his future.

The Mode of Change

While asserting that, in general, construct systems change in relation to varying validational fortunes, personal construct theory has a particular argument as to the mode of change itself. This argument is that we change by cycling from tight to loose construing on a continuous basis. The construct *tight–loose* is a construct about constructs. A tight construct is defined as one which leads to unvarying and unidirectional predictions. Thereby it is a construct which is part of a highly defined network, with articulated implications of which the person is well aware. It is a form of construing which readily generates operational definition and specific commitment in the life of the person.

For some people, for example, *criminal* (as contrasted with *honest citizen*) is a tight construct, part of a tight interpretive network. They see *criminal* as being exactly implied by law and as implying, in its turn, set liabilities to punishment and undeniable loss of respect, with this in turn entailing a whole series of unacceptable personal characteristics. On the other hand, it would be possible to use the construct *criminal* in a loose mode, so that an impoverished pickpocket, though convicted, was seen as no *criminal* while a wealthy and publicly praised businessman was seen as *criminal,* while speculatively the notion of *criminal* might be linked to a whole series of notions to do with the criminal as not so much characterized in himself as characterizing the society from which he has been alienated, and simultaneously criminality might be seen as a sickness, a form of protest or even as part of an alternative culture. Thus to construe tightly is strictly to define the focus of convenience of a particular construct as being a specific set of elements, to be almost obsessionally concretistic, to be precise and particular, to attempt a technology, to strive for quantification or its equivalent. To construe loosely is to traffic in undertones and overtones, to be open-ended, to use the dream, the poem and the speculation as strategies of argument, to range freely across experience quoting echoes and themes, reframing questions and answers at will. Kelly argued that to change effectively is essentially to range *between* loose and tight construing in a continuous cycling movement—loosening, tightening, loosening. To attempt to change from one tight construction to another tight construction is to be frustrated by the prescriptive nature of the starting point, which is so defined that we cannot meaningfully allow that it be an equally defined something else. Equally, to traffic only in terms of loose construing is to live always with the overture and never with the opera. It is to see all kinds of possibilities and realize none. To change forthwith from being *pub pianist* to *social worker* or *vice versa* is difficult because it is arbitrary. To brood on the desirability of serving mankind means little in terms of personal change until it is operationally defined and tightened into a particular service for particular men. To loosen (and thereby superordinate) the construction of *pub pianist* until it is seen as sociable and serving might be to echo personal themes which eventually recombine into the undertaking *social worker.*

It is unfortunate that a person's chances of readily moving between definition and extension are gravely diminished in a society which tends to glorify both tight and loose as ways of life, as complete in themselves rather than as turning points in a continuous movement. The classic divisions between science and art, practical man and theoretician, dreamer and man of action, tough and tender minded and so forth form part of our culture and some of the barriers which we have erected across our lives.

If we attempt now to tighten the construct *tight–loose* into terms of practices within psychotherapy, we can see that a wide range of techniques are permissible and necessary within the bounds of construct theory psychotherapy. Thus if a client needs to loosen his constructions in order to draw off from his particular involvements in a situation so that he can see it in terms of alternative perspectives, then we may well use loosening techniques. Many of these are traditional in other psychotherapeutic approaches. Free association and dream interpretation in psychoanalysis, fantasy in Gestalt therapy, the non-directive style of Rogerian therapy, are all ways in which clients may be encouraged to loosen their construing. The con-

136

struct theory psychotherapist is entitled, within his own framework, to use all these and to add to them any other strategies for loosening he may care to invent, such as forms of role-playing, self-characterization, laddering and so forth. Equally, classic forms of tightening from other forms of psychological therapy are entirely admissible. The procedures of behaviour therapy are often excellent strategies for tightening, in that they encourage the client to define vast fears into specific situations and undertakings and to quantify pervasive anxieties into hierarchies. To these the construct theory psychotherapist may add other forms of tightening, such as the use of grid method as a way in which the client can define his constructions and examine in quantified form their implications; attempting fixed-role therapy which requires the client to embody broad descriptions of persons into particular actions in life situations; and so forth.

Taking the client through tight–loose cycles can be on varying time-scales. Within a single therapy session it is advisable to loosen the client's constructions and then help him to retighten them towards the end of the session. On a longer time-line, over many sessions, the overall aim may be to move in some fairly major fashion from a tight formulation of situation, goals and problem through a long, loose, speculative period in which, at all levels from fantasy to speculative argument, the client may explore possibilities, ultimately to tighten again into plans of action and a defined stance. This broad conception of a mode of change has the effect of making the work of a personal construct theory therapist with one client or with a group very variable in style. He cannot be said to be generally 'directive' or 'non-directive' but may flow between the two possibilities as he detects the client is becoming either overbound to tight constructions or fearful and lost in loosening. The notion of tight or loose as a central mode of change liberates the therapist to use many techniques and styles of relationship with his client, while at the same time imposing on him the need to consider at any particular point whether tightening or loosening is most needed by his client if personal movement is to be achieved.

Limitations on Change

The central experience in psychotherapy, both for therapist and client, is the experience of stasis—the problem remains, the therapy is experienced as a repetitive and circular exchange. Any theory of psychotherapy must offer some kind of explanation of change–no change strategies for both client and therapist. Construct theory offers a series of constructions to do with the issue of change, and the ones which are briefly discussed here are hostility, guilt, anxiety and aggression.

Hostility, in construct theory terms, does not mean simply that someone is being antagonistic, stubborn or viciously resentful. It is interesting that 'nastiness' definitions of hostility are 'from the outside' definitions. That is to say, they define hostility as it is experienced by the person *towards* whom the hostility is directed. Kelly defines hostility 'from within' as a continued effort to extort validational evidence in favour of a type of social prediction which has already been recognized as a failure. This definition attempts to explain hostility in terms of what is going on *within* the hostile person. Kelly is saying that we become hostile when we simply cannot afford to be wrong. One way to see the point of the definition is to try to imagine it in personal terms. Imagine that you have a central belief about your own and other people's nature, a belief in terms of which you have explained much that has happened in your life, a belief on which you base much of your action. Suppose that you have no readily available alternatives to this belief. Suppose then that evidence comes to light that this belief of yours is flatly wrong, that things are not as you have imagined they were. What do you do? If you abandon your beliefs about this major part of your life then that part of your life becomes meaningless, it becomes chaotic. It becomes an area in which you cannot meaningfully respond because you cannot make sense of what is happening. The alternative is to become hostile, in Kelly's sense of the term. You try to force the facts to fit the theory, you cook the books, you bully people into providing the kind of evidence which you need to maintain your belief. You force people to behave in the manner appropriate to your belief, so that they still 'make sense'. The alternative is chaos, and chaos is not something you or I will readily contemplate.

As a passing example, this author once had in therapy a young man whose basic theory about himself seemed to be that he was loathed and persecuted by all men. Certainly he was able to explain a great deal of what had happened to him and what would happen to him and how he ought to react in these terms. The author was, at that time, unquestioningly using an amiable, approving style in therapy, rather of a Rogerian kind. It became obvious as the weeks of therapy sessions passed by that the young man was becoming more profoundly unhappy and disturbed. In the wisdom of hindsight, it now seems that he was faced by a lump of smiling evidence contradicting his basic theory about how people regarded him—and if he should cease to make sense of people as *enemies* he could make little of them as *friends* or *brothers* or *fellow citizens*. So he began to extort validational evidence for his theory. He ·sneered at all therapeutic efforts to help him—he blocked, fenced, argued, jabbed, sniped and gouged in all interchanges. Eventually he was successful, in that the therapist burst out angrily with a denunciation of his conduct and a revelation of how deeply he had come to dislike this particular client. A smile of surpassing beauty spread across the client's face. At last he was back again in business, his theory was safely re-ensconced—he had always known that the therapist (like all men) secretly hated him, it was only a matter of bringing this hatred to the surface.

Clearly the whole therapeutic strategy was in error in that it was abruptly challenging the validity of a basic assumption of the client. If you wish to help anyone to change, you do them no service by attacking in strength some central belief. In most cases the person simply cannot afford to abandon a central belief with no alternatives available *to them*. It is more appropriate to begin at the outer edges of a person's construct system, to begin with peripheral implications of his central beliefs. These he can explore and perhaps see as containing contradictions in terms of experiences which the therapist is helping him gain. Then, as each part of his network of arguments is abandoned, an alternative viewpoint covering that area is developed. As the examination proceeds inwards, towards more central beliefs, a complete alternative system is being elaborated. This view of therapy echoes the old philosophic metaphor which argues that life is akin to rebuilding a ship while at sea. It makes no sense to begin by stripping out the keel at one go. By removing a plank and *replacing* a plank, the ship is rebuilt while still sailing.

This is an inescapable problem of therapy: the client is sailing all the time that the therapy is going on. He has to continue to live during any change process. Hostility is of times a necessary counter, although in its most extreme form, as a paranoid reaction, it is a savage obstacle to change. Kelly (1969) offers a graceful and sympathetic view of hostility using the Procrustes legend.

It must be remembered that construct theory is reflexive, and thereby the notion of hostility is often equally applicable to the therapist. Many a client has been bullied into behaviours which validate the therapist's theories as to what man is like, what change is about and what behaviour ought to be. Clients are eminently capable of attacking the central beliefs of therapists, and if the therapist is inflexible and incapable of alternative construction then he is foredoomed to chaos or hostility.

Guilt, as a concept, occupies varying positions in different therapeutic approaches. It is central to psychoanalytic theory, has virtually no place in learning theory and behaviour modification approaches and is certainly part of the vocabularly of almost all clients. Kelly had a strange (yet, one surmises, deliberate) tendency to use terms which are in common use but redefined so that they are oblique to their common usage. Thus guilt, for Kelly, is defined as an awareness of dislodgement of the self from core role structure. He is here stressing that, just as we place constructions on other people in order to be able to understand and predict their behaviour, so we place constructions upon ourselves in order to be able to understand and anticipate our own behaviour. Sometimes our construing of ourselves proves faulty. We find ourselves doing things which we would not have expected to do if we were the sort of persons that we though we were. This is perhaps the most disturbing and disorganizing experience that any man can undergo. To live in an inexplicable world is frightening enough—to be to oneself an inexplicable person is even more frightening.

People who seek psychotherapeutic help are, by that token, likely to be in doubt as to who and what they are. The obsessional patient who says 'I know it's irrational but I can't help . . .' is saying that he is 'not himself'. The so-called psychotic who fluctuates wildly in his view of the nature of God or the nature of the universe is presenting explosively different theories as to what he is.

The practice of psychotherapy here walks a tightrope, for it is essentially dedicated to change and therefore likely to founder upon exacerbate problems of identity. For this reason many of the techniques in construct theory psychotherapy (fixed-role therapy and role-playing generally, the development of propositional construing) are designed to permit *exploration* of change without irrevocably dislodging the client from core role structure. The very notions of 'hypothesis' and 'experiment' are supremely useful in that they enable us to explore change without committing ourselves to an inevitable departure from our present standpoint. A hypothesis is a statement which can be explored without having to believe that is true. Thus, in therapy, there must be no intransigent demand for change. There must be an acceptance of the client's need sometimes to reassert his identity as he sees it, even though this reassertion may, for the time being, bring experimenting to an end and reinstate earlier behaviours and beliefs.

As in other therapies, anxiety is recognized as a significant monitor of change. Kelly specifically defines anxiety as an awareness that the events with which a person is confronted lie mostly outside the range of convenience of his construct system. This formulation does not define anxiety as a sort of generalized pressure within a hydraulic system. It stresses that we are anxious when we are unable to see the further implications of the situation in which we are placed. We may be familiar with the immediate subordinate implications of the situation but uncertain of its more far-reaching significance. A commonplace anxiety experience is 'exam nerves'. Here the student is thoroughly familiar with the immediate nature of the situation—the form of exam questions, time allotment, study methods and so forth. Yet his constructs may not extend to cover questions such as 'What will it signify about my capacities if I fail?', 'How will other people regard me if I fail?', 'What would be the long-term implications for my future if I cannot succeed academically?' and so forth. Perhaps death is a prime progenitor of anxiety because, lacking firm constructions about an afterlife, it must be the boundary of the range of convenience of our construing.

The progress of therapy should be marked by a supportable level of anxiety. If the client is bland then he is working well within the range of convenience of his construing and is not being challenged to elaborate. Equally, if he is forced too rapidly and too extensively to contemplate a variety of unknowns then he may become so anxious that he has to deal with them by strategies which may more seriously curtail change. He may constrict his perceptual field so that he is not even aware of challenging elements in his situation and so forth. Again, as so often in therapy or in any psychological undertaking, a balance between risk and certainty, between validation and invalidation is needed.

The aim of therapy, in a construct theory sense, is to facilitate change, to produce *aggression* in Kelly's meaning of the term. He defined aggression as the active elaboration of one's perceptual field, stressing thereby the exploratory and experimental aspects of personal behaviour and the need continuously to reconstrue. The inescapable limitation on change is the rate at which a person can develop permeable constructions which admit and make sense of new elements—constructions which affirm the familiar while accepting the novel.

Fixed-Role Therapy

Clearly, a prime value of personal construct theory in therapy is that it provides the terms in which the broad strategies of work with a single client or a group can be understood and allows for a wide variety of techniques to be intelligently used. However, there are particular techniques which have been directly derived from construct theory or are particularly consonant with it. A major venture of this sort is fixed-role therapy (Kelly, 1955; Bonarius, 1970; Skene, 1973; Karst and Trexler, 1970).

Fixed-role therapy is by no means an invariable part of construct theory psychotherapy. It is an occasional device for opening up a therapeutic dialogue that seems to have become blocked and circular. However, it is worth discussing in some detail because it exemplifies the total approach of construct theory psychotherapy.

The client is asked to write a self-characterization. He is asked to write a description of himself, a pen portrait, rather as if he were a character in a play. He is asked to write it in the third person so that it opens with the words 'Bill Bloggs is . . .'. It is to be written as if by a sympathetic friend who knows the person very well, perhaps better than anyone could really know him. The third-person form is used since the element of role-playing ('as if' by a friend) often enables the person to reveal himself more readily than the 'I' form.

The therapist uses this self-characterization as the basis for writing a second description of the person called the fixed-role sketch. Ultimately, the client is going to be asked to enact the role of the person described in the fixed-role sketch and this suggests some of the limitations to be borne in mind when it is being written. There would be little point in writing it as more or less an exact duplicate of the self-characterization, since there would then be no demand for change. On the other hand, to write it as the exact opposite of the self-characterization would be somewhat threatening, since it would demand that the person reverse all his current behaviours. More importantly, it would merely be asking the person to explore the contrast poles of dimensions he is already too well embedded in—it would not ask him to try to explore new and alternative constructions. The fixed-role sketch is written obliquely to the self-characterization. Thus, if the self-characterization described a person who is either very *dependent* on or fiercely *dominating* of other people, then the fixed-role sketch might describe a person who is *interested* in other people. The construct *interested* is, in a sense, at 90° to the *dependent–dominating* construction and thereby demands that the client really undertake a new role.

When the fixed-role sketch of the new personality (call him, say, Harry Hawkes) is ready, we first have him vetted by the client Bill Bloggs. Bill is asked whether he can believe in the existence of such a person as Harry Hawkes—does Harry seem credible? If Bill does not find the fixed-role sketch a believable one then it has to be altered until he can believe that such a person might exist. Secondly, Bill is asked whether he finds the fixed-role sketch to be that of an acceptable person—not necessarily a person Bill would love and admire but a person he could put up with, a person whom he would find more or less reasonable. If the fixed-role sketch is not acceptable in this sense, then it must be altered until it is.

Now that we have a credible and acceptable person portrayed in the fixed-role sketch, Bill Bloggs is invited to take up (for a fixed period, usually of the order of three weeks) this character and enact him. Enactment is to be complete so that, at all times during the three weeks, he will try to think the thoughts of Harry Hawkes, dream his dreams, eat his food, read his books, answer questions as Harry would answer them, react to the behaviour of others as Harry would react and so on and so forth. It is made clear to Bill Bloggs that he is *not* being offered this fixed-role sketch as some sort of 'ideal person' which he is aiming to become—indeed he will give up the enactment after three weeks and revert to his 'usual' self. It is offered to him as an experiment to be carried out in the role of a hypothetical character.

If the client agrees to this venture, then it is customary to arrange that he be seen fairly frequently—at least twice a week—during the few weeks of the fixed-role undertaking, so that he can be closely guided in and supported through his enactment. He has to read the fixed-role sketch over many times until he is completely familiar with it, so that he can readily interpret it into behaviour. During the therapy sessions the client stays in role and occasionally the therapist may himself offer an enactment of the fixed role if he feels that he can thereby reveal something additional about its nature to the client. Only the therapist and the client will know that this enactment is taking place.

What can be achieved by this sort of venture?

Firstly, it is an arduous and interesting psychological exercise to try to interpret a broad psychological portrait into the acts and talk of daily life. A great part of any therapy is concerned with arguing about the meaning, in terms of daily life, of psychological generalizations, both those offered by the therapist and those offered by the client. This kind of enactment is one way of testing out the possible meanings of such generalizations and exploring their operational detail.

Secondly, the enactment may make available to the client new responses from *other* people. It may be that in small but significant ways people will speak and react differently to this 'new' person. The client, like all of us, may have partly framed other people's responses towards him by his own behaviour and stance. The new behaviours which he manifests as a result of following the fixed-role sketch may elicit from other people kinds of reactions which are in some small degree novel for the client. Such reactions may provide him with new evidence, new material on which to base his ideas about the nature of his relationships with other people.

Thirdly, the client is inveigled, by his own behaviour, into exploring the idea that his personality is an *invention* and not an unalterable and unrefusable burden placed on him by his genetics. In the course of enacting a 'new personality' he may begin to suspect the extent to which he has, in the past, framed and ordered the person he has presented to others and to himself. He may become more aware of the possibilities of change. At the end of the fixed-role period, therapist and client will review the experience to see what has been learned from it before it is put on one side and other ventures undertaken. It is interesting to note that the ingenuity of clients often far outruns the ingenuity of therapists, in that they find lessons which are not apparent in terms of the way in which the venture was envisaged. Thus one client reported to the author that people had reacted to him in exactly the same way in his fixed role as they had always reacted to him previously—there had been no difference in their behaviours. The author's reaction was one of disappointment and a feeling that, thereby, the venture had been a waste of time. The client thoughtfully corrected this conclusion, pointing out that it was a very significant thing to discover that he could vary his behaviour quite substantially without causing vast disturbances in other people's responses. He had for long been convinced that any variation in his own behaviour from a rigid and set norm would cause catastrophic reactions in those around him—he saw them as demanding that his conduct remain absolutely regimented and fixed from day to day. Now he knew that he could experiment more freely with his deportment without initiating immediate confusion or disaster.

Fixed-role therapy then can be viewed as a model of the total approach which underlies personal construct theory psychotherapy. The theory sees man as self-invented. It sees behaviour as man's continuing experimentation, it sees exploration and change as the living aspects of life. From this point of view, fixed-role therapy is, in minature, a model of the total theory and the total view of what therapy is about.

Role-playing

Role-playing, in less formalized and elaborate ways than fixed-role enactment, is a technique native to construct theory psychotherapy. Within the therapy session the client is often asked to role-play his parent, enemy or lover in some significant situation and perhaps his own responses thereto. Once the client has understood that role-playing is not play-acting but a way of exploring and elaborating aspects of self in relation to other people and situations, it can become additionally a major mode of communication between client and therapist. The sociality corollary of personal construct theory reads to the extent that a person construes the construction processes of another person he may play a role in a social process involving the other person. Role-playing, in these terms, is a primary technique for unfolding the way in which one person construes the construction processes of another. It is essentially a method of discovery and not simply a rehearsal of the known.

Additionally, each act of role-playing reintroduces the client to the use of propositional constructs, to thinking in 'as if' terms rather than pre-emptive and 'nothing but' terms. Of itself, this is a prime agent of change. Radley (1973) elaborates this notion of change, emphasizing the movement from envisaging what it is to become X, to behaving 'as if' one were X, to becoming X.

Modes of Self-exploration

A basic theme in many forms of psychological misery is the experience of being alienated from oneself, being not in control of oneself, being unable to understand oneself. As a result a great deal of work in therapy is concerned with self-exploration, with revealing to the person his basic assumptions.

Construct theory has generated some formal methods for facilitating such exploration and these include grid method, self-characterization and self-other monitoring techniques.

Grid method (Bannister and Mair, 1968; Bannister and Bott, 1974), following the reflexive argument of personal construct theory, is perhaps best used not as a 'test' of a subject by a psychologist but as a format within which a client may examine his own construing. The therapist supplies a necessary expertise by way of designing a grid with appropriate elements, eliciting and supplying construct labels, analysing out the pattern of interrelationships between constructs and highlighting some of the structural and content features of the grid. But the crucial contribution of the grid will come when the client examines the results along with the therapist and tries to gain some insight into his ways of viewing other people and himself. Perhaps the best starting point for grid evaluation is for the therapist to consider how much of the pattern of construct relationships he would readily have predicted, how much he thereby seems to understand and to ask the client to clarify those clusters of constructs which seem surprising or inexplicable.

It is assumed that the therapist will use methods of self-exploration, such as the grid, on himself, both in relation to particular clients where he is not clear as to his own construction of the situation and in relation to the therapeutic venture as a whole.

Self-characterization procedure has been briefly described in relation to fixed-role therapy. It has a more general use as a way of articulating some of the superior ordinate constructs which the client uses to understand himself.

There is no standard scoring system for self-characterization but it can be analysed as a meaningful and intentional statement by the client. For example, the therapist can ask, of himself and then of the client, a series of questions in relation to self-characterization. What kind of overall theme is proposed in the opening sentence? What apparent contradictions exist within the description? What sets of cause—effect relationships are implied? How sympathetic is the 'sympathetic friend' who wrote the passage? Is change a theme of the portrait or is the person described as fixed? How does the biography relate to the client's statement of complaint? How are other people envisaged within the self-characterization?

Self-characterization is best used recurrently during therapy as a way of monitoring changes in the way in which the client sees himself, and in this way it serves purposes akin to those of diaries and other modes of continuing self-assessment.

Another self-monitoring technique—McFall's Mystical Monitor (Bannister and Fransella, 1971)—involves free talk into a tape-recorder in isolation, with a clear understanding that the client will erase the tape immediately he has finished his own consideration of the monologue. (The relationship between this and say free association methods in psychoanalysis is apparent.) Although the tape is erased (so that the monologue is audience-free) uncommunicative clients seem often to find it easier in therapy sessions following the tape experience to talk more freely of their major concerns.

Methods for exploring self—other viewpoints and relationships can be derived from the 'conversational model' argument (Mair, 1970a, b). Client and therapist or dyads in group therapy can write out a description of self, descriptions of the partner (both 'secret' and 'open') and predictions of how the partner will describe them and then jointly examine these descriptions in terms of the evidence on which they are based, the kind of relationship they imply, their degree of reciprocity and so forth. This kind of exercise has interesting implications, in construct theory terms, for identity problems. Kelly argued that we gain a picture of ourselves (core role structure) by construing the way others construe us. Clearly a man does not simply accept other people's view of him—their views will be varied and contradictory in any case. He filters their view of him through his view of them and sees this as evidence. ('View' here includes the implications of their behaviour towards him.) If a man you see as conformist thinks you are conventional this means something different from being thought inhibited by someone you regard as idiosyncratic to the point of madness. Yet clients—particularly adolescents—who are certain of their nature often seek it by withdrawing from people, by withdrawing, in effect, from the source of evidence and thereby deepening the crisis of identity. Personal experiments such as conversational model ventures are useful sources of self (through 'other') knowledge.

Group Therapy

Kelly (1955, p. 1160) suggests a particular strategy for group psychotherapy, and it is worth noting that it illustrates his general view of therapy as having an *evolutionary* quality so that concerns and methods change as the stages of therapy unfold.

Kelly proposes six main stages in the evolution of a therapy group. Clearly these phases will overlap but they are designed to help to give a kind of developing form to the life of a therapy group.

The first of the six phases is the initiation of *mutual support*. This is the very tentative opening phase in which no member of the group should be encouraged to put himself in a vulnerable position until he begins to feel that he is accepted by at least some members of the group—they show a readiness to see the world through his eyes. Discussion is kept away from deeply disturbing material until the therapist is satisfied that mutual supports are established. The second stage involves the initiation of *primary role relationships*. In this phase members of the group are encouraged to begin exploring their direct relationships with other members of the group in the face-to-face situation. Here the advantage of having several people as a kind of mutual experimental laboratory becomes apparent. The third phase involves the initiation of *mutual primary enterprises*. In Kelly's words: 'This is the phase in which the members of the group use their understanding of each other to propose and execute experiments. It starts when members of the group begin to suggest that the group ought to explore a certain kind of situation or attempt to discover the answer to a certain kind of problem'. The emphasis is now shifted from particular cross-relationships to group experiments as a whole. The term primary has been used to indicate that the group has essentially been dealing with events and interactions *within* the group. In the fourth phase, which is termed the *exploration of personal problems,* the group turns its attention to those personal problems of group members which have a *locus* outside the group. Be it noted that this is relatively late in the day when problems with an outside context are directly brought in for group examination. The previous three stages have all been concerned with building up relationships and experiments essentially within the group. During this fourth phase various members can enact (in role-playing form) their version of a particular client's predicament and indicate at a concrete level just how they would deal with his problems. The fifth phase, the *exploration of secondary roles,* involves what, in learning theory terms, would be called 'generalization' in the form of the generalization of role relationships from the group to persons outside the group. There can now be free discussion for the respects in which outside figures are like or unlike individual members of the group in the hope that, in this way, individuals can make their role constructs more permeable. The sixth and final phase is the *exploration of secondary enterprises*. As a member of the group enters this phase he will be turning his attention more to ventures which he has undertaken outside the group, with the group acting as a source of support, an insurance policy against outside failure. As the focus of individual members moves more and more to enterprises outside, so the group as such is moving to its end.

The Purpose of Construct Theory Psychotherapy

Although many techniques are admissible within construct theory psychotherapy, the approach is *not* eclectic. While it does not specify set techniques, it does provide principles in terms of which any given technique will be considered appropriate or inappropriate. While not particularizing a content for man's psyche, it does provide a framework within which any psychological content can be considered.

Like any approach, construct theory involves assumptions and it strives to make these assumptions clear. Perhaps its primary assumption, in relation to therapy, is that the client is in some essential sense 'trapped'. He is unable to elaborate his construct system, so that he cycles repeatedly through the same experience—whether this experience takes the form of the cloudy circlings of the so-called mad or the rituals of the neurotic. It follows that the therapist is dedicated to trying to help the patient to achieve movement again and to reach a position from which he can begin to explore and elaborate his life. The therapist assumes that, whether his client's system is blocked by hostility or by excessive tightness or loosening or by internally conflicting argument, the only ultimate way to elaborate a system is by experimenting with it. His purpose therefore is to encourage the client to explore his system. and to experience varying validational fortunes in relation to it.

The pivot of construct theory psychotherapy tends to subsist in queries of the kind, 'If you are right about X then what do you think would happen if you . . .?'. The client's answer is a testable hypothesis, and if tested the outcome may provide the point of change.

The fundamental postulate of personal construct theory is that 'a person's processes are psychologically channellized by the ways in which he anticipates events'. We can add to this that the ways in which a person anticipates events will change in terms of new interpretations of—and thereby new responses to—the unfolding of events.

Thus the therapist is continually striving to understand how the person he confronts sees the world by this very striving he is offering the person a model of human relationship.

146

References

Bannister, D., and Mair, J. M. M. (1968). *The Evaluation of Personal Constructs*, Academic Press, London.

Bannister, D., and Fransella, Fay (1971). *Inquiring Man—The Theory of Personal Constructs*, Penguin, Harmondsworth.

Bannister, D., and Bott, M. (1973). 'Evaluating the person', in P. Kline (Ed.), *New Approaches in Psychological Measurement*, Wiley, London.

Bonarius, J. C. J. (1970). 'Fixed-role therapy: a double paradox', *British J. of Medical Psychology*, **43**, 213.

Fransella, Fay (1972). *Personal Change and Reconstruction*, Academic Press, London.

Hinkle, D. N. (1965). 'The change of personal constructs from the viewpoint of a theory of implications', Unpublished PhD thesis, Ohio State University.

Karst, T. O., and Trexler, L. D. (1970). 'Initial study using fixed role and rationale-emotive therapy in treating public speaking anxiety', *Journal of Consulting and Clinical Psychology*, **34**, 360.

Kelly, G. A. (1955). *The Psychology of Personal Constructs*, Vols. I and II, Norton, New York.

Kelly, G. A. (1969). *Clinical Psychology and Personality: The selected papers of George Kelly*, Ed. B. A. Maher, Wiley, New York.

Landfield, A. W. (1971). *Personal Construct Systems in Psychotherapy*, Rand McNally, New York.

Mair, J. M. (1970a). 'Experimenting with individuals', *British J. of Medical Psychology*, **43**, 245.

Mair, J. M. M. (1970b). 'Psychologists are human too', in D. Bannister (Ed.), *Perspectives in Personal Construct Theory*, Academic Press, London.

Patterson, C. H. (1966). *Theories of Counselling and Psychotherapy*, Harper & Row, New York.

Pervin, L. A. (1970). *Personality: Theory Assessment and Research*, Wiley, New York.

Radley, A. R. (1973). 'A study of self elaboration through role change', Unpublished PhD thesis, London University.

Sechrest, L. B. (1963). 'The psychology of personal constructs: George Kelly', in J. M. Wepman and R. W. Heine (Eds.), *Concepts of Personality*, Aldine, Chicago.

Skene, R. A. (1973). 'Construct shift in the treatment of a case of homosexuality', *British J. of Medical Psychology*, **46**, 287.

Wright, K. J. T. (1970). 'Exploring the uniqueness of common complaints', *British J. of Medical Psychology*, **43**, 221.

8

GESTALT PSYCHOTHERAPY*

James S. Simkin

Gestalt is a German word meaning whole or configuration. As one psychological dictionary puts it, '. . . an *integration* of members as contrasted with a summation of parts' (Warren, 1934, p. 115). The term also implies a unique kind of psychotherapy as formulated by the late Frederick S. Perls, his co-workers and his followers.

Dr Perls began, as did many of his colleagues in those days, as a psychoanalyst, after having been trained as a physician in post-World War 1 Germany. In 1926 he worked under Professor Kurt Goldstein at the Frankfurt Neurological Institute, where he was first exposed to the tenets of Gestalt psychology but '. . . was still too preoccupied with the orthodox approach to assimilate more than a fraction of what was offered' (Perls, 1947, p. 5). Later, Dr Perls was exposed to the theories and practice of Wilhelm Reich and incorporated some of the concepts and techniques of character analysis into his work.

While serving as a Captain in the South African Medical Corps, Perls wrote his first manuscript in 1941–1942 outlining his emerging theory and application of personality integration which later appeared as a book, *Ego, Hunger and Aggression*. The term 'Gestalt therapy' was first used in 1949 as the title of a book on Perls' methods written by him and two co-outhors, Ralph Hefferline of Columbia University and the late Paul Goodman of New York City.

Group Psychotherapy and Workshops

In Gestalt therapy the emphasis is on the present, ongoing situation, which, of course, involves the interaction of at least two people—in individual therapy the patient and the therapist. This interaction becomes expanded to more than two people in the group situation and may involve an interactive process among several people or may involve the interactive process at any given moment between two

---

* This chapter is based primarily on a previous manuscript, 'Gestalt therapy in groups', written by this author for *Basic Approach to Group Psychotherapy and Group Counseling*, edited by G. M. Gazada. Copyright 1968 by Charles C. Thomas, Publisher.

people with each of the other participants involving themselves as they are ready. In Gestalt therapy it is not necessary to emphasize the group dynamics, although some Gestalt therapists do so. All Gestalt therapists focus at one time or another on the interactive process between the therapist and the group member in the here-and-now and/or the interactive process between group members as it is ongoing.

Perls preferred the term workshop to group psychotherapy and in a paper written in 1967 indicated the values of workshop *versus* individual therapy as follows:

> To the whole group it is obvious that the person in distress does not see the obvious, does not see the way out of the impasse, does not see (for instance) that his whole misery is a purely imagined one. In the face of this collective conviction he cannot use his usual phobic way of disowning the therapist when he cannot manipulate him . . . . Behind the impasse . . . is the catastrophic expectation. . . . In the safe emergency of the therapeutic situation, he (the patient) discovers that the world does not fall to pieces if he gets angry, sexy, joyous, or mournful. The group supports his self-esteem. The appreciation of his achievements toward authenticity and greater liveliness also is not to be underestimated. Gestalt therapists also use the group for doing collective experiments in learning to understand the importance of the atmosphere. . . . The observation by the group members of the manipulative games of playing helpless, stupid, wailing, seductive or other roles by which the neurotic helps himself in the infantile state of controlling, facilitates their own recognition (1967, p. 17).

Theoretical Foundations

Man is considered a total organism functioning as a whole, rather than an entity split into dichotomies such as mind and body. With the philosophical background of humanism, *à la* Otto Rank, the organism is seen as born with the capacity to cope with life. This is opposed to what I call the original sin theory of human development—that the organism must learn to repress or suppress its instinctual strivings in order to become 'civilized'. The emergence of existential philosophy coincides historically with the development of Gestalt therapy. Wilson Van Dusen (1960), in an article on existential analytic psychotherapy, believes that there is only one psychotherapeutic approach which unites the phenomenological approach with existential theory and that is Gestalt therapy.

The theoretical model of the psychodynamic schools of personality—chiefly the Freudian school—envisions the personality like an onion consisting of layers. Each time a layer is peeled away, there is still another layer until you finally come to the core. (Incidentally, in the process of 'analysis' of the onion, you may have very little or nothing left by the time you come to the core!) I envision the personality more like a rubber ball which has only a thick outer layer and is empty inside. The ball floats or swims in an environment so that at any given moment only a portion is exposed while the rest is submerged in the water. Thus, rather than inventing an unconscious or pre-conscious to account for behaviour that we are unaware of, I suggest that unaware behaviour is the result of the organism not being in touch with its external environment, being mostly submerged in its own background (internal environment) or in contact with (usually preoccupied with) fantasies.

In *A Review of the Practice of Gestalt Therapy,* Yontef (1971) summarized the theory of Gestalt therapy. He reasoned that organismic needs lead to sensory motor behaviour. Once a configuration is formed which has the qualities of a good Gestalt, the organismic need which has been foreground is met and a balance or state of satiation or no-need is achieved.

> When a need is met, the Gestalt it organized becomes complete and it no longer exerts an influence—the organism is free to form new gestalten. When this Gestalt formation and destruction are blocked or rigidified at any stage, when needs are not recognized and expressed, the flexible harmony and flow of the organism/environment field is disturbed. Unmet needs form incomplete gestalten that clamor for attention and, therefore, interfere with the formation of new gestalten (Yontef, p. 3).

As Perls (1948) puts it, 'The most important fact about the figure–background formation is that if a need is genuinely satisfied, the situation changes' (p. 571).

Example of a First Session in a Gestalt Workshop

The following excerpt is an example of how one workshop started. Following a short introduction, a suggested exercise involved each of the participants and very quickly one of the participants asked to work.

> *Jim:* Good evening. I'd like to start with a few sentences about contract and then suggest an exercise. I believe that there are no 'shoulds' in Gestalt therapy. What you do is what you do. What I do is what I do. I do have a preference. I prefer that you be straight with me. *Please* remember, this is a preference, not a should. If you feel that you *should* honour my preference, then that's *your* should! When I ask you, 'Where are you?' and the like, my preference is that you tell me—or tell me that you're not willing to tell me. Then our transaction is straight. Any time that you want to know where I am, please ask me. I will either tell you, or tell you I am unwilling to tell you—so that our transaction will be straight.
>
> Now for the exercise. Please look around the room and select someone you don't know or don't know well—whom you would like to know or know better . . . OK? Now here are the rules. You may do anything you like to 'know' the other person better, except talk! John?
> *John:* The lady with the brown sweater.
> *Jim:* Marilyn, are you willing to be 'known' by John?
> *Marilyn:* Yes.
> *Jim:* Elaine, please select a partner.
> *Elaine:* That man—I believe he said his name was Bert.
> *Jim:* Are you willing, Bert?
> *Bert:* My pleasure!
> *Jim:* Nancy?
> *Nancy:* I would like to know Agnes better.
> *Agnes:* That's fine with me.
> *Jonathan:* Well, that leaves me to Phil.
> *Jim:* Yes, unless you're willing to include me.
> *Jonathan:* No thanks. I'd rather get to know Phil! (group laughter)

The group breaks into dyads and for several minutes the person who has asked to know the other is the aggressor, 'exploring' the other with his sensory modalities (touch, taste, smell, etc.), lifting, pulling, dancing with, etc. Then the partners in the dyad are asked to switch and the 'aggressor' becomes the 'aggressee' as the exercise is repeated.

Jim: OK, I am interested in knowing more about your experience. If you have made any discovery about *yourself* and are willing to share, please tell the rest of us what you found out.

Bert: I discovered that I felt very awkward and uncomfortable when Elaine was the aggressor!

Elaine: I sensed your discomfort and found myself concerned with what you thought of me.

Bert: I would like to work on my always having to be 'masculine'—my avoidance of my passivity.

Jim: When?

Bert: Now!

(At this point Bert leaves his chair in the circle and sits in the empty chair across from the therapist.)

I feel anxious. My heart is pounding and my hands feel sweaty, and I'm aware of all of the others in the room.

Jim: Is there anything you would like to say to the others?

For the next 15–20 minutes Bert worked in the 'hot seat'. When he finished, the therapist turned his focus (awareness) back to the group.

'In The Now'

The following examples are taken from my training film *In The Now*. After my introductory comments, Al moved from the group circle to the 'hot seat'. He was very eager to start. His work with me is presented verbatim from the film. It concludes with the last several minutes of the film which involved, primarily, an exchange between Al and Colman, another participant.

Jim: Okay, now I would suggest we start with getting in touch with what we're doing in this situation now. Most people are interested, or at least they say they are interested, in changing their behaviour. This is what therapy is all about. In order to change behaviour; you have to know what you're doing and how you do what you do. So, let's start with your examining, focusing your awareness and saying what you're in touch with at this moment. Say where you are, what you're experiencing.

Al: I feel as though I got the catastrophe by sitting over there suffering, and I still feel it at intervals. But I really haven't felt so much like a patient in all the time I've been a psychologist. I think it's for this special occasion. Last night at four o'clock in the morning I awoke . . . well, it started at nine . . . I started blushing in the groin, you known. I thought it was a flea bite 'cause we got five new dogs . . . pups. I couldn't find the flea. By four o'clock in the morning, I was blushing here and here, in my head, and I couldn't sleep, I was itching so. And I got an antihistamine. By nine or ten in the morning the itching went away and then coming here I get this chest . . . my chest hurts.

Jim: How about right now?

Al: I'm sweating. I sweat and I'm warm.

Jim: What happened to your voice?

Al: It got low and warm and I wiggle a little.

Jim: And now?

Al: I feel a tension I carry around a good deal up here—a band that grabs my head like that and pulls me together like I'm puzzled.

Jim: Play the band that's pulling on Al. 'I am Al's band and I . . .'

Al: I am Al's band containing him. I'm his crazy megalomina—want to run the world his way.

Jim: Tell Al what your objections are to his running the world his way.

Al: He's a nut . . . to think he can run the world his way. Or a child.

Jim: Now give Al a voice and let Al talk to the band.

Al: I know how to run it as well as anybody else. Why shouldn't I?

Jim: You sounded like a fairly reasonable nut or child at that moment . . .. And now?

Al: Back to my gut. I make myself suffer to recognize I can't take what I want.

Jim: Okay, what is it that you want that you're not taking at this moment?

Al: Well, I very reluctantly thought of the milk and the world as one.

Jim: You're reluctantly not taking the milk and the world at this moment.

Al: I'm sure that's not what I said. I reluctantly *thought* of the milk. I didn't want to talk about that. I'd rather be a megalomaniac than an infant asking for warmth (mother's milk).

Jim: Can you imagine anything in between those two . . . the infant and the megalomaniac?

Al: It's a long way, yeah. You know I'm an extemist. Let's see a bite size. Yeah, how about just writing an article on art therapy, which I've scheduled for the last three years? I haven't done that. I would like it just to flow and to come out without any pain, without giving up anything else.

Jim: So you want to be the breast.

Al: I want to be the breast? To be a giver, to flow. Oh well, I hadn't thought of it that way.

Jim: Well, think of it that way. Take a couple of hours. Imagine yourself a big tit.

Al: It's a very feminine thing to be, a breast.

Jim: Yeah.

Al: Give a little. . . . Give a lot.

Jim: Yeah.

Al: You get . . . you capture your son with that milk. You hold onto him.

Jim: Al?

Al: Yeah?

Jim: Would you be willing to be as tender, soft, feminine as you know how?

Al: It's a threat.

Jim: What's a threat?

Al: To follow your suggestion would be a threat . . . of what? Makes no sense.

Jim: Okay. Do the opposite. Whatever the reverse of being soft, tender, loving, feminine is for you.

Al: Be masculine.

Jim: Show me.

Al: It's something like '*practice*' . . . you know fatherly, uh, '*shut-up!*'.

Jim: Yeah, do a little scowling with it. That's it.

Al: '*Shut-up!*' So it's not puzzling, it's uh, it's father. '*You burnt the soup!*', '*Leave the table*', and then a kind of fantasy of mother crying. I sort of regret that my father died before I became friendly with him again.

Jim: Say this to him.

Al: I'm sorry. (Sigh) Well, inside I said I'm sorry you died.

Jim: Outside.

Al: I'm sorry.

Jim: Say this to him outside.

Al: I'm sorry you died too soon (for me).

Jim: Give him a voice.

Al: I haven't the slightest idea what he would say. I thought of his excusing me. He says, 'You, you didn't know any better. You were young and angry'.

Jim: Your father sounds tender.

Al: He may be the father I wanted. I never, I don't think of him as a tender man but . . ..

Jim: It's the voice you gave him.

Al: Yeah. I may have underestimated him.

Jim: Say this to him.

Al: Dad, I guess I did, I underestimated you.

Jim: Say this to Al.

Al: Al, you underestimated me. You could have been closer . . ..

Jim: (Interrupts) No, no. Say this sentence to Al. 'Al, I underestimate you.'

Al: Al, I underestimate you. You can do a good deal more than you're doing. Then I put myself down and say, 'You're crazy to expect so much from yourself', and don't do anything . . . like going from do everything to do nothing. Just sit and don't create it. I feel a little phoney to accept your interpretation so easily.

Jim: You see what you just did?

Al: I puzzled myself?

Jim: You said, 'I feel a little phoney . . .'. There came your band.

Al: And it hurts here. It didn't hurt there for a long time. What happened? I'm supposed to know? So I've got a blind spot. I'm entitled.

Jim: Your blind spot happens to be Al Freeman.

Al: A total blind spot?

Jim: You're not entitled to that blind spot. What are you doing?

Al: Puzzling. You're playing God and telling me I'm not. I'm not God? That was a . . . I didn't expect to say that at all, really.

Jim: What just happened?

Al: I exposed something, I guess. It was quite unintended.

Jim: Yeah.

Al: I was just going to argue with you, and I came out with my manic side. I don't often do that.

Jim: You just did.

Al: It slipped. I'm sorry . . . I'm not sorry, I'm glad, I'm glad. Whew.

Jim: What do you experience right now?

Al: Warmth. I love having people laugh, especially with me. So I guess everybody wants it. Wants warmth and love.

Jim: God never makes excuses or gives reasons.

Al: No?

Jim: I know.

Al: I give you permission to be God. I understand. Yeah, you have warmth. I give you . . . I give you warmth. What else do you want? The world? You can have the world. Just be sure to give it back . . . in ten minutes. God is an imposter, because I'm God. And that other one is a fake. I really could do the whole thing myself.

Jim: Yeah. Now you're catching on.

Saying Good-bye

Jim: There's quite a bit of . . . unfinished business that sometimes accumulates during a workshop . . . especially in the area of resentments and appreciations. Now you don't have to have any appreciations or resentments, you may have some other unfinished business. If you have any unfinished business, now is the time to bring this out.

Colman: I want to talk to Al.

Al: Go ahead.

Colman: I left last night and you bothered me. And I feel that you're haunted, you're a mezepah (warlock) and you came here looking and you saw what happened to me. And you asked me a question which really was a statement. You've done that animal trainer bit before, is what your question stated. This guy showed you, and you wouldn't believe. And last night when I came to you . . . to relate to you, you almost took it.

Al: I pulled away because you damn near broke my glasses.

Colman: Yeah.
Al: That's why.
Colman: OK. Go ahead. Still with the mezepah.
Al: With your hug. No, you're perceiving it badly. I bought it; I did not have any notion whatsoever as to whether you had created that idea, the trainer, on the spot.
Colman: I don't want . . . don't give me that. When I came to you last night . . . and I tried to convey to you my feeling, it wasn't your glasses. OK. Your glasses were incidental, but you turned to me and you said: 'Oh, yeah, now I see why you do that'.
Al: I said I had no idea. . . .
Colman: Better late than never. You couldn't take it that I felt for you . . . you had to put it off on me that I had to do it . . . you can't eat it, you can't taste it.
Al: OK. I feel it's unfinished business. . . .
Colman: And I still like you.
Al: Let's, let's hear what's behind it then.
Jim: Oh, shut up!
Colman: And Jim . . . I don't mind crying: it makes it hard to talk. I . . . I did come . . . entirely as . . . I say, I think. Go ahead, do me. But I think it's beautiful, and I do appreciate it. Thank you, and all you beautiful people.
Jim: Could you add one more sentence, Colman? Remember that the 'it' in Gestalt therapy is 'I'. Your sentence was 'it's beautiful'.
Colman: I think I'm beautiful
Jim: I do too.

Therapist–Patient Relationship

Although some people claim they want to change their behaviour, I believe that most people seeking psychotherapy want relief from discomforts. These may be generalized malaise–anxiety, depression and the like or very specific discomforts like headaches, stiff necks, knotted stomachs, etc. Furthermore, their usual expectation is that this relief will be the result of the therapist doing the work, rather than through their own efforts.

Ideally, I see myself as a midwife in relationship to my patient. Having been present at many 'births' of new attitudes, feelings, conceptualizations, behaviour and the like (including my own), I can facilitate acceptance (reowning) of these attitudes, feelings, etc., on the part of the patient through my acceptance of where the patient and I are at the moment. My 'of course' attitude can be reassuring to the person I'm relating to as well as facilitate change through non-pushing.

At times, my relationship to my patient is that of a senior experimenter or scientist to the junior or novice experimenter. At other times, we are both risking (experimenting)—taking steps into the unknown and momentarily relinquishing centredness in the quest for growth and the excitement of growth.

I see each therapeutic encounter with my patient as a separate Gestalt. An event which can be complete unto itself and has the potential of a structure with a beginning, a middle and an end. Whatever is foreground at the beginning of the session is what is focused on and worked with—be it a rehearsed programme, an immediate awareness of some sensory or motor experience, a feeling of confusion, recall of unfinished business, etc.

Research in the Area of Gestalt Therapy

The final chapter in Fagan and Shepherd's *Gestalt Therapy Now* is the only research article in the book. It is concerned with the problems of the reluctant witness. Commenting on the difficulties in doing research in the area, Fagan and Shepherd said:

> Most often, hard data are difficult to obtain: the important variables resist quantification; the complexity and multiplicity of variables in therapist, patient, and the interactional processes are almost impossible to unravel; and the crudeness and restrictiveness of the measuring devices available cannot adequately reflect the subtlety of the process. However, the fact that the task is difficult does not reduce its importance, and the need for many questions to be asked and answered by the more formal procedures available to researchers (Fagan and Shepherd, 1970).

I have been interested in assessing the effectiveness of Gastalt therapy in workshops as contrasted with weekly therapy. During the years 1970 and 1971, I gathered systematic feedback from people coming to residential workshops, and I compared the feedback of these patients with feedback that I obtained from patients whom I had been seeing in a more traditional manner the previous two years. Seventy-five per cent of the patients who attended the residential workshop reported that they received what they came for or more. This claim was made by 66 per cent of those who were in weekly therapy with me. The percentage of patients who claimed that they received no help, or got worse, was approximately equal for those coming to residential workshops and those coming for weekly therapy (14 per cent). The remainder in both the traditional and the workshop style were people who claimed they 'got something' from the experience. (It is interesting to note that patients who had either the individual or group work on a 'spaced' basis and the workshop on a 'massed' basis favour the massed basis by a ratio of about 9 to 1.) Systematic feedback data have been obtained from over 200 people who have attended both workshops and traditional therapy.

I have also experimented with training in Gestalt therapy and have data on the results of an experiment massing close to 300 hours of training into a three-month period. What I attempted was to provide an intensive training experience for five therapists in a residential setting. The number of hours available was comparable to (or more than) the number of hours of training in the more formal institute training styles. Using personality inventories, peer group ratings, the A.B. Therapists Scale, my clinical impressions of the trainees and other systematic measurements, I have some preliminary evidence which supports the possibility of successfully massing training in a three-month period. A follow-up study, in which the five therapists returned for a week seven months after their training, indicated that the *direction* of change (shown during the three-month period) continued. In addition, the quality of their work in dealing with patients showed a consistent positive increase as reflected by both patients' and supervisors' rating of their work.

Yontef (1971) discusses some of the possible research areas in Gestalt therapy. He also discusses the attitudes of Perls and his co-workers concerning research (pp. 39–40).

Goals

In Gestalt therapy the patient is taught how to use awareness in the service of himself as a total functioning organism. By learning to focus awareness and thus discovering what *is*, rather than what *should be*, or what *could have been*, or the ideal of what *may be*, the patient learns to trust himself. This is called in Gestalt therapy the optimum development of self-support. Through awareness, the splits which have been developed can be reintegrated. The patient can become more whole as he begins to deal with his avoidances, which have created holes in his personality.

I sometimes use the simile of a cake in encouraging patients to reown the parts of themselves which they have considered noxious or otherwise unacceptable. Just as the oil, or flour or baking powder, etc., by themselves can be distasteful, as part of the whole cake they are indispensable to assure its success.

Selection, Composition, Frequency

Patients selected for inclusion in Gestalt therapy groups need to be screened to determine their willingness and ability to work within the Gestalt therapy framework. Ordinarily this screening is done through individual interviews in which the Gestalt therapist assesses through the therapeutic encounter rather than through psychodiagnostic evaluations the patient's willingness to work.

Most Gestalt therapists experience maximal involvement in heterogeneous groups—thus groups will be composed of males and females, young and old, range of occupations presenting problems, etc.

One such typical group had an actor, a student, two housewives, a physicist, an X-ray technician, an attorney, a nurse, a drama coach, a psychologist and a painter. The age range for this group was from the early twenties to the late fifties. There were equal numbers of men and women.

Usually therapists reserve the right to bring new people into groups, with group participants allowed to veto additional members during the initial session of that new member.

Gestalt therapy training groups consist of licensed or license-eligible psychotherapists. Emphasis in these training groups is on theory and techniques as well as experiential learning regarding overcoming personality problems, working through impasse situations, resolving interpersonal and intrapsychic conflicts, etc. There are also training groups for educators, physicians, attorneys, probation officers, school counsellors, etc. These training groups are labelled Gestalt awareness training, and the emphasis is on the use of awareness to facilitate growth.

Uniqueness of Gestalt Therapy

Inasmuch as in Gestalt therapy theory growth occurs as a result of allowing oneself to become who one is, emphasis on acknowledging one's behaviour at any given moment. Paradoxically, behavioural changes result from the acknowledgement and acceptance of how one is at any given moment rather than through declaration of intention, promising oneself or another to do better, etc.

The self-regulatory organismic barriers include disgust and/or shame. Both have strong impactful ways of reminding the organism what does or does not suit him. Suitability or appropriateness, thus, is not defined in terms of guilt (societal strictures) but rather in terms of individual morality or ethics.

This position argues that man recognizes one's own and others' needs and wishes without having to develop an external police force or internal introjected police force.

Respect for one's self and for others, if reinforced, would eliminate many of the problems now labelled neurotic or sociopathic.

Relationship to Academic Psychology

Gestalt therapy has used in both a practical and theoretical sense some of the research emanating from the Academy. Of special relevance is the work in perception and especially field theory and figure–ground formations as postulated by Gestalt psychologists.

Fritz Perls in attempting to define Gestalt therapy over a decade ago wrote that 'Gestalt Therapy (puts) the theory of Gestalt Psychology to practical use by exploring the emerging gestalten of the therapeutic situation as unresolved events' (unpublished personal communication). In addition, there is a good deal of emphasis on emerging figures as demanding attention and that most resolutions of phobic behaviour are dealt with by emphasizing attention to demand quality and persistence of emerging figures.

In this writer's opinion, Gestalt therapy more than any other psychotherapeutic system uses both experimental and theoretical academic psychology as support for its constructs and application.

Gestalt Therapist Qualifications

The typical Gestalt therapist who is currently being trained at one of the existing Gestalt therapy institutes is a licensed or license-eligible psychotherapist usually from one of the three major disciplines which are licensed to practise psychotherapy in the United States. In most states these are psychiatrists, clinical psychologists and clinical social workers. Typically, the Gestalt therapist is trained in an institute or in a closely supervised apprenticeship with a senior Gestalt therapist over a period of several months to two or three years.

I have experimented with intensive training and offered a condensed three-month training programme consisting of over 120 group hours and over 60 individual hours plus about 100 or more hours collateral training (reviewing tapes, peer group supervision, didactic session, etc.) (see research section).

In addition, I am currently experimenting with several one-month intensive training programmes to see whether it is possible to train Gestalt therapists via this modality as opposed to the more traditional spaced learning situations offered at the Gestalt therapy institutes throughout the country. In the spaced learning model, the Gestalt therapist trainee typically works two to four hours a week in both group and individual settings. In addition to a didactic or theoretical seminar once a month, he is required to attend a minimum of a weekend or a longer workshop every two to three months. At some of the Gestalt therapy institutes the advanced trainees co-lead introductory seminars with institute members as part of their experiential training.

Workshop Style—Training/Treatment

A good deal of the work done in Gestalt therapy is conducted in the workshops. Workshops are scheduled for a finite period of time, some for as little as one day. Some are weekend workshops ranging from 10–20 or more hours and others are more extended, ranging from a week through several months in duration. A typical workshop consists of one Gestalt therapist and 12 to 16 people treated over a weekend period. Given longer periods (ranging from a week on up to a month or longer) as many as 20 people can be seen by one therapist. Usually, however, if the group is larger than 16 there are co-therapists.

Since workshops have a finite life, there are just so many hours available to the participants. Usually, there is high motivation on the part of most participants to get into the 'hot seat', that is to be the focus of attention and to 'work'. Sometimes, rules are established so that no one can work a second time till each participant has had an opportunity to work once. At other times, no such rules are set. Thus, depending on a person's willingness, audacity and drive, some people may get to work several times during a workshop.

Use of the 'Hot Seat' and Other Techniques

In a recent article, Levitsky and this author have described is some detail the use of the 'hot seat' and other techniques used in Gestalt therapy. Many therapists follow Perls' lead in the use of the 'hot seat' technique and will explain this to the group at the outset. According to this method, an individual expresses to the therapist his interest in dealing with a particular problem. The focus is then on the extended interaction between patient and group leader ('I and thou') . . .

As therapist and patient work together, occasions arise in which the patient is asked to carry out some particular exercise, for example, 'Could you repeat what you just said, but this time with your legs uncrossed?' or 'Could you look directly at me as you say this?'. The attitude with which these exercises are carried out is an important element. The patient is gradually educated and encouraged to undertake these exercises in the spirit of experiment. One cannot really know the outcome beforehand even though a specific hunch is being tested. The spirit of experiment is taken seriously and the question raised 'What did you discover?'. The discovery is the most potent form of learning (Levitsky and Simkin, 1972, p. 140).

Ethical Considerations

Gestalt therapists view people as having the capacity to cope with life. Rather than impose on their patients their own values or structures on how to live, the Gestalt therapists are interested in having their patients/trainees discover for themselves what values fit their own way of looking at life. Thus, patients are asked to experiment, to examine, to pick and choose and to taste before swallowing.

An underlying corollary to the above is my conviction that there is enough room in this world for everyone. I do not need to force my views on others or 'justify my existence'. I can usually find a sub-culture which shares my values if I do not accept or agree with the majority of values of the larger culture. In the extreme, I can create my *own* sub-culture if need be.

The basic drive or energy in Gestalt therapy is oral aggression. Perls contended that this was necessary in order to be able to taste and to discover what is nourishing and what is toxic. Then one can destructure the ideas, or food or whatever and assimilate, following tasting.

On the basic assumption then that the person can be self-regulatory, the Gestalt therapist encourages experimentation to discover what 'fits'. Naranjo (1971), in his article titled 'Present centreredness, technique, prescription and ideal', says 'There are a number of implicit moral injunctions in Gestalt therapy', and he lists nine of these. He believes that these nine include living now, living here, stopping imagining, stopping unnecessary thinking, expressing, giving in to unpleasantness and pain, accepting no shoulds or oughts other than your own, taking full responsibility for one's own actions, feelings and thoughts, and surrendering to being who you are. He further indicates that although such injunctions as part of a moral philosophy are paradoxical to the point of view of Gestalt therapy, which is anti-injunctions, the paradox is resolved when these points of view or injunctions are looked at as statements of 'truth rather than duty' (p. 50).

I believe the basic ethical attitude of the Gestalt therapist is that if you experiment you have the possibility of discovering what is suitable for you. If you swallow whole, there is no possibility of growth, no matter now potentially nourishing the food, idea, etc., may be. A number of Gestalt therapists believe that the goal in Gestalt therapy *is* maturation and growth and that maturity, which Perls defines as 'the transition from environmental support to self-support', can only be accomplished through the focusing of awareness and discriminating what is useful for oneself.

Of great immediate concern in terms of ethics is the aptness of the Gestalt therapist. Shepherd points out that:

> Since Gestalt techniques facilitate access to and release of intense affect, a therapist using this approach must neither be afraid nor inept in allowing the patient to follow through and finish the experience of grief, rage, fear, or joy. The capacity to live in the present and to offer solid presence standing by are essential. Without such presence and skill the therapist may leave the patient aborted, unfinished, opened, and vulnerable—out of touch with any base of support, either in himself or available from the therapist. The therapist's capacity for I–thou, here-and-now relationships is a basic requirement and is developed through extensive integration of learning and experience. Probbly the most effective

application of Gestalt techniques (or any other therapeutic techniques) comes with personal therapeutic experiences gained in professional training workshops and work with competent therapists and supervisors (Fagan and Shepherd, 1970).

In addition, Shepherd points out the following as one of the possible consequences of Gestalt therapy:

> The consequences of successful Gestalt therapy may be that by teaching the patient to be more genuinely in touch with himself, he will experience more dissatisfaction with conventional goals and relationships, with the hypocrisy and pretense of much social interaction, and may experience the pain of seeing the deficiencies and destructiveness of many social and cultural forces and institutions. Simply stated, extensive experience with Gestalt therapy will likely make patients more unfit for or unadjusted to contemporary society (Fagan and Shepherd, 1970).

Limitations of Gestalt Therapy

I consider Gestalt therapy as the treatment of choice for people who are 'up in their head' most of the time. On the other hand, with people who are given to acting out, that is who do not think through or do not fully experience their behaviour, I would hesitate to use Gastalt therapy as a treatment of choice. A good rule of thumb is that for *experienced* therapists Gestalt therapy is usually an effective tool if used with populations they feel comfortable with. Gestalt therapy has been used successfully with a wide range of populations including children, adolescents and adults.

For some Gestalt therapists the use of Gestalt therapy in group is limiting. Shepherd maintains that the therapist may, by becoming too active, foster passivity of others in groups while working with someone in the 'hot seat'. Thus, facilitating the growth of one person may at the same time be:

> ... defeating his own goal of patient self-support. In this case, the group too responds passively, regarding the therapist as an expert or magician, and themselves as having little to contribute without his special techniques and skill (Fagan and Shepherd, 1970, p. 233).

John Barnwell's work with ghetto adults in a poverty programme (Simkin, 1968) and Janet Lederman's (1969) work with six-to-ten-year-old behavioural problem children in the heart of an urban poverty area underline the point of view that the therapist or educator's competence with certain populations is much more important than the technique as such.

Suggested Readings

There has been a sharp increase in interest in and the practice of Gestalt therapy during the past decade (1963–1973). At the time this chapter is being written (mid-1973) there are several Gestalt therapy institutes throughout the United States, with at least three offering systematic training (Cleveland, San Francisco and Los Angeles).

Several books have appeared in the last three years, ranging from a collection of

160

10 older articles in *Festschrift for Fritz Perls* (Simkin, 1968) to the excellent collection of 25 articles in the book *Gestalt Therapy Now* focusing on theory, technique and application of Gestalt therapy by Fagan and Shepherd (1970).

Kogan (1970), unhappy with the (then) absence of a systematic bibliography of source material in Gestalt therapy, collected and published a pamphlet which lists books, articles, papers, films, tapes, institutes and the *Gestalt Therapist Directory*. He includes approximately 90 references. Fagan and Shepherd list over 60 references. Yontef (1971) cites 45 references.

During 1972, two chapters dealing with Gestalt therapy appeared in two different books. In the Sager and Kaplan (1972) collection, Simkin's 'The use of dreams in Gestalt therapy' appeared under the 'New Approaches' section, and in Solomon and Berzon's (1972) collection Levitsky and Simkin have a chapter dealing with the use of Gestalt therapy in small groups.

Perls' autobiographical book *In and Out of the Garbage Pail* (1969b) and Simkin's interview of him in 1966 give much of the historical background to the development of Gestalt therapy. Also of historical interest are the two excellent papers written by F. Perls' widow, Laura Perls (1953; 1956).

Practically none of the Gestalt therapy literature has been channelled through conventional sources during the three decades of its existence. Major exceptions are Fritz Perls' (1948) article in the *American Journal of Psychotherapy* and Polster's (1966) more recent article in *Psychotherapy*.

Until 1969, the only films depicting Gestalt therapy were all made by F. Perls.* His are still the primary sources (over 30 varied films) with one exception: Simkin's (1969) training film. Simkin now has his training film (1969) available on $\frac{1}{2}$-inch video-tape as well as two later training videotapes made in 1971 and 1973.

No Gestalt therapy library is considered complete without the two basic books *Gestalt Therapy* by Perls *et al.* (1951; 1965) and *Gestalt Therapy Verbatim* by F. Perls (1969a).

References

Barnwell, J. E. (1968). 'Gestalt methods and techniques in a poverty program', in J. S. Simkin (Ed.) *Festschrift for Fritz Perls*, Los Angeles.
Fagan, J., and Shepherd, I. L. (1970). *Gestalt Therapy Now*, Science and Behavior Books, Palo Alto, California.
Kogan, J. (1970). *Gestalt Therapy Resources*, Lodestar Press, San Francisco.
Lederman, J. (1969). *Anger and the Rocking Chair: Gestalt Awareness with Children*, McGraw-Hill, New York.
Levitsky, A., and Perls, F. S. (1970). In J. Fagan and I. L. Shepherd (Eds.), *Gestalt Therapy Now*, Science and Behavior Books, Palo Alto, California.
Levitsky, A., and Simkin, J. S. (1972). In L. N. Solomon and B. Berzon (Eds.), *New Perspectives on Encounter Groups*, Jossey-Bass, San Francisco, pp. 245–54.

* A complete list of F. Perls' films may be obtained from Psychological Films, 205 West 20 St., Santa Ana, Ca. 92706; Films, Inc., 1144 Wilmette Avenue, Wilmette, Illinois 60091; and Gestalt Therapy Films, Science and Behavior Books, Inc., 577 College Avenue, Palo Alto, Ca. 94306. Each of these sources distributes some of Perls' films.

Naranjo, C. (1971). 'Present centeredness: technique, prescription and ideal', in J. Fagan and I. L. Shepherd (Eds.), *Gestalt Therapy Now.* Harper Colphon Books, New York.

Perls, F. S. *Ego, Hunger and Aggression,* Allen and Unwin, London, 1947: Random House, New York, 1969.

Perls, F. S. (1948). 'Theory and technique of personality integration', *American Journal of Psychotherapy,* **2,** 565.

Perls, F. S. (1967). 'Workshop vs. individual therapy', *Journal of the Long Island Consultation Center,* **5,** No. 2, Fall, 13.

Perls, F. S. (1969a). *Gestalt Therapy Verbatim,* Real People Press, Lafayette, California.

Perls, F. S. (1969b). *In and Out of the Garbage Pail,* Real People Press, Lafayette, California.

Perls, F. S., Hefferline, R. F., and Goodman, P. (1951). *Gestalt Therapy,* Julian Press, New York. (Republished: Dell, New York, 1965.)

Perls, Laura (1953). 'Notes on the psychology of give and take', *Complex,* **9,** 24.

Perls, Laura (1956). 'Two instances of Gestalt therapy', *Case Reports in Clinical Psychology,* Kings County Hospital, Brooklyn, New York.

Polster, E. (1966). 'A contemporary psychotherapy', *Psychotherapy: Theory, Research and Practice,* **3,** 1.

Pursglove, P. D. (1968). *Recognitions in Gestalt Therapy,* Funk and Wagnalls, New York.

Sager, C. J., and Kaplan, H. S. (Eds.) (1972). *Progress in Group and Family Therapy,* Brunner/Mazel, New York.

Simkin, J. S. (1966). Individual Gestalt Therapy: *Interview with Dr. Frederick Perls,* Audiotape recording, A.A.P. Tape Library, No. 31, Philadelphia, Pa.

Simkin, J. S. (Ed.) (1968). *Festschrift for Fritz Perls,* Author, Los Angeles.

Simkin, J. S. (1969). *In The Now,* A Training Film, Beverley Hills, California.

Simkin, J. S. (1972). In C. J. Sager and H. S. Kaplan (Eds.), *Progress in Group and Family Therapy,* Brunner/Mazel, New York, pp. 95–104.

Solomon, L. N., and Berzon, B. (Eds.) (1972). *New Perspectives on Encounter Groups,* Jossey-Bass, San Francisco.

Van Dusen, W. (1960). 'Existential analytic psychotherapy', *American Journal of Psychoanalysis,* 310.

Warren, H. D. (1934). *Dictionary of Psychology,* Houghton Mifflin, New York.

Yontef, G. M. (1971). *A Review of the Practice of Gestalt Therapy,* Trident Shop, California State College, Los Angeles.

9

RATIONAL-EMOTIVE PSYCHOTHERAPY

Albert Ellis

Rational–emotive therapy (RET) is a theory of personality, a system of philosophy and a technique of psychological treatment. It has many facets and complications, but I shall do my best to present some of its main aspects in this relatively brief chapter; and, if I do fail to do a perfect job, well, I (according to my own theories) am only a fallible human being. Anyway, let me present the main tenets of RET; also mention some of the main experimental and clinical evidence in their support; show how they are related to the major issues in psychotherapy; and conclude with a case presentation.

Well, what *are* some of the basic hypotheses of the rational–emotive approach? These:

The Importance of Values

RET emphasizes the importance of values in human affairs. It assumes that beliefs, constructs, attitudes or values are central to what we call 'personality'; that rational or empirically based values lead to healthy, and irrational or magical values to unhealthy emotional functioning; and that when people's basic value systems are changed concomitant change is also effected in their 'self' or 'being'. Considerable evidence has accumulated in recent years that values exist and importantly influence humans, including studies by Kelly (1955), Murray (1951), Hartman (1967) and Rokeach (1968).

Rational and Irrational Behaviours

RET holds that rational goals or behaviours can be fairly clearly defined (Ellis, 1968; 1971; 1973c) in that practically all humans want to survive, to be relatively happy, to live amicably in a social group and to relate intimately to a few members of this group. If it is assumed that these basic values are good, then behaviours that abet them are rational and those that sabotage their attainment are irrational.

163

Rationality, then, is a method or technique of effectively gaining certain values. It does not exist in any intrinsic or absolutistic sense.

The A–B–C Theory of Disturbance

Like George Kelly's theory of personal constructs (1955), RET states that when you have an emotional reaction at point C (the emotional Consequence), after some Activating event or experience has occurred at point A, it is *not* A that causes C; rather, it is your Belief system, B, that you hold *about* A (Ellis, 1962; 1971; 1972d; 1972e; 1973a; Ellis and Harper, 1961a). If you feel depressed at point A after you have been rejected for a job at point C, the rejection does *not* cause your depression. Rather, it is your *beliefs* about this rejection at point B.

RET precisely distinguishes your rational Beliefs (rB's) and their appropriate emotional Consequences from your irrational Beliefs (iB's) and their inappropriate or disturbed Consequences. Thus, when you are rejected, you first may hold a rational Belief—'I don't like being rejected; what a drag!'—that results in your appropriate feelings of sorrow, irritation and annoyance. But you also may hold a highly irrational Belief—'It's *awful* to be rejected; I *shouldn't* have got myself refused; I am a worthless slob because of this rejection!'

Your first set of Beliefs is rational because, in accordance with your basic value system of *wanting* to stay alive, be happy, live well in your social group and relate intimately to a few others, it *is* unfortunate for you to be rejected and you'd *better* feel appropriately saddened about this. Your second set of Beliefs is irrational because it isn't *awful* (that is, *more than* unfortunate) for you to be rejected; there's no reason why you absolutely *shouldn't* or *mustn't* be rejected (though *it would be better* if you weren't); and you are not a worthless slob, but at worst a person with some slobbish *traits,* when you are rejected.

Your rational Beliefs and appropriate Consequences of feeling sorry and annoyed about your rejection, moreoever, will help you work harder to get accepted in the future. But your irrational Beliefs and inappropriate Consequences of feeling depressed will encourage you to mope, to feel future acceptance is hopeless and discourage others from accepting you.

When I first clearly propounded the A–B–C theory of emotional reaction almost 20 years ago, there was little experimental evidence to support it. Since that time, cognitive psychology has come into its own and literally hundreds of experiments have shown that emotion and behaviour are highly dependent on cognitive mediating processes. Excellent studies in this area have been published, for example, by Bannister (1971), Bannister and Mair (1968), Blum and Wohl (1971), Carlson *et al.* (1969), Cook and Harris (1973), Davies (1970), Davison and Valins (1969), Marica *et al.* (1969), Miller (1969), Nisbett and Schacter (1966), Schacter and Singer (1962), Valins and Ray (1967), Velten (1968) and Wine (1971). More specific clinical experiments backing the A–B–C hypotheses of RET have also been done by numerous investigators, including Cautela (1970), Lazarus (1971), Maes and Heimann (1970), Maultsby (1971a), Meichenbaum (1971), Rotter *et al.* (1972), Sharma (1970) and Trexler and Karst (1972).

Confronting and Attacking Irrational Beliefs

Although many systems of psychotherapy, from that of Alfred Adler (1929) to that of William Glasser (1964), recognize that dysfunctional beliefs or attitudes lie behind so-called emotional upsets, RET is perhaps the one that most vigorously helps disturbed individuals to confront, attack and change these beliefs. It holds that the most efficient and elegant road to personality change is to confront these individuals with their magical philosophies, to explain how these cause disturbance, to attack them vigorously on logico-empirical grounds and to teach people how to change and eliminate disordered thinking. RET extends this view to work with 'normal' children as well as 'disturbed' adults. The Institute for Advanced Study in Rational Psychotherapy in New York City runs The Living School, a private elementary school, where rational–emotive psychology is regularly taught to the pupils in the course of regular classroom presentations. Empirical studies demonstrating the active–directive teaching methods used in RET-oriented emotional education have been published by several investigators, including Bersoff and Grieger (1972), Breen (1970), Daly (1971), Ellis (1973d), Gustav (1968), Hartman (1968), and Sydel (1972).

Homework Assignments

From the beginning, RET has said that there is no better way for people to surrender their emotional disturbances than by working and practice, or vigorously acting, against them; and it has advocated activity homework assignments or *in vivo* desensitization to minimize or eliminate disordered behaviour (Ellis, 1962; 1971). RET studies as well as work in the general field of cognitive-behaviour therapy have recently provided a number of controlled studies that have not only shown the validity of using homework assignments but have also indicated that this kind of method is usually more effective than imaging or other forms of desensitization. Relevant publications in this field include those by Cooke (1966), Davison (1965), Dua (1970; 1972), Hodgson *et al.* (1972), Hoehn-Saric *et al.* (1968), Leitenberg *et al.* (1971), Litvak (1969a; 1969b), Marks (1971), Maultsby (1971a), Mitchell and Mitchell (1971), Perlman (1972), Rimm and Madeiros (1970), Ritter (1968), Rutner and Bugle (1969) and Zajonc (1968). RET has also taught self-management methods to clients for the past several years (Ellis, 1971; 1972d) and considerable evidence supporting the effectiveness of this kind of homework methodology has been published by Goldfried and Merbaum (1973), Flexibrod and O'Leary (1973), Homme (1965), Stuart (1969) and others.

Operant Control of Thinking and Emoting

RET theorizes that humans tend to be reinforceable or hedonistically motivated. Consequently, if they are to learn to engage in difficult and disciplined pursuits, they often do better if they reinforce themselves after they have done these things and sometimes also penalize themselves when they fail to do them (Ellis, 1972d; 1973b;

166

Ellis and Harper, 1961a; Homme, 1965; Skinner, 1972). Specifically, I have helped my clients for the last decade to give up their irrational Beliefs by reinforcing themselves with something they truly enjoy doing (such as eating, smoking or having sex) after they work 10 or more minutes a day at disputing one of their main self-defeating notions, and by penalizing themselves (by doing house-cleaning, engaging in exercise, contributing to a political party they abhor or doing something else they consider obnoxious) if they do not work at this kind of disputing. Applying operant conditioning to changing crooked thinking and inappropriate emoting often works beautifully in clinical practice (Ellis, 1969b; 1973b). The validity of this kind of procedure has been experimentally determined by several researchers, especially Donald Meichenbaum and his associates (1971).

Group Therapy and Marathon Encounters

Because of its educational emphasis, RET has always emphasized its own special brand of group therapy (Ellis, 1962; 1973e; Ellis and Harper, 1961b). It has also developed a unique cognitive–emotive approach to marathon encounters, which stresses the encounter groups may do more harm than good when they are almost entirely experiential and abreactive and when they do not include a considerable amount of cognitive teaching and restructuring (Ellis, 1969b; 1972b; 1973e).

Group therapy is usually an integral part of RET because it provides an educational-type setting where several individuals can be seen at once, where they learn how to talk other group members out of their irrationalities and thereby get practice in dealing with their own, and where they get active–directive participation in modelling, role-playing, assertive training and behavioural rehearsal. Risk-taking and shame-attacking exercises are frequently employed in RET group work. Members are asked to do something risky or foolish in the group itself and are shown how their irrational Beliefs *make* most of these acts 'risky' or 'foolish'. They are given shame-attacking homework assignments—such as wearing conspicuous buttons or going around all week with a headband and a large feather—to show them that they can publicly perform 'shameful' acts, suffer few or no consequences and learn to change their thinking and feelings about such acts.

Logico-empiricism and Anti-magic

RET theorizes that emotional disturbance is little more than another name for devout religiosity, intolerance, whining, dogmatism, magical thinking and anti-scientism; and if people rigorously follow the logical-empirical approach and forego all forms of magic and absolutism it is virtually impossible for them to be seriously disturbed. More specifically, it traces deep-seated feelings of anxiety, depression, guilt and hostility to the human tendency to 'awfulize', terribilize', 'horibilize', and 'catastrophize'—that is, to go beyond empirical data and to assume that unpleasant and disadvantageous experiences absolutely *should, ought* and *must* not exist (Ellis, 1957a; 1958a; 1962; 1968; 1970; 1971; 1973a; 1973f).

Rational–emotive therapists show their clients that their emotional upsets stem from their fascisistic insistences on deifying and glorifying or on devilifying and damning themselves and others. They explain and reveal how the clients demand, command and dictate that (1) they do outstandingly well and be incredibly popular and loved; that (2) others treat them kindly, considerately and justly at all times; and that (3) the world perpetually provide them with easy rewarding fulfilments. RET teaches clients how to dispute and attack these unrealistic expectations and demands, how to accept themselves and others unconditionally and undamningly and how to put up with inevitable annoyances and frustrations.

I first hypothesized that there are only a limited number of major irrational ideas that people devoutly believe and by which they disturb themselves in talks given in 1955 and 1956 (Ellis, 1957a; 1957b; 1958b). Since that time, a large number of experimental studies have confirmed the thesis that disturbed individuals hold irrational, illogical and unrealistic ideas significantly more often than do less disturbed people. These include studies by Argabrite and Nidorf (1968), Beck (1967), De Wolfe (1971), Hoxter (1967), Jones (1968), Lidz et al. (1958), MacDonald and Games (1972), Platt and Spivak (1972) and Trexler and Karst (1973).

The Semantics of Emotional Disturance

Following some of the principles laid down by Alfred Korzybski (1933), RET theorizes that if people consistently defined their terms, shied away from overgeneralizations and were more objective in their language and thinking they would find it difficult to be severely disturbed. During RET sessions, clients are often stopped and forced to change their irrational for more rational statements. For example, 'I *should* succeed' becomes 'I'd better succeed'; 'You are no good' becomes 'You have some poor traits'; 'I can't do this' becomes 'I won't do this'; 'I like myself' becomes 'I like many of the things I do'; 'I need your love' becomes 'I strongly wish you would act favourably towards me'; 'You made me angry' becomes 'I made myself angry at your performances and wrongly concluded that you were a louse for doing them'; 'It is awful that his happened' becomes 'It is highly inconvenient that this happened'; 'I can't stand injustice' becomes 'I don't like injustice and intend to work to prevent it'; 'I deserve to get good marks' becomes 'If I study diligently, I shall probably increase my chances of getting good marks'.

The Theory of Human Worth

RET has a somewhat unique theory of human worth, which has been changed since my original formulations. In *A Guide to Rational Living* (Ellis and Harper, 1961a), I concluded that an individual's worth or value would be better measured not by his traits, deeds or performances—since these may easily change—but would more safely and wisely be based on his or her aliveness. I became increasingly sceptical of this practical but philosophically inelegant solution to the problem of human worth and now believe that a human really has no 'intrinsic value', as Robert Hartman (1967) claims that he does, and that it is better if we do not rate or measure ourselves *at all,* but merely rate our traits and performances, for the purpose of increasing our enjoyment. I discuss this view in detail in my paper 'Psychotherapy and the value of a human being' (Ellis, 1972c) and in my book *Humanistic Psychotherapy* (Ellis, 1973a). Some of the main reasons for believing that people do better to rate their traits and acts and *not* their totality or their 'selves' are these:

(1) Intrinsic worth or value is a Kantian thing-in-itself that is not observable or verifiable. (2) The 'self' that you value when you say 'I like myself' is a higher-order abstraction or overgeneralization (Korzybski, 1933) that is not very definable and that is in the same category as 'soul' or 'spirit'. (3) When you rate your 'self' or 'ego', you invent a kind of heaven or hell, for your 'good self' is really heavenliness, holiness or holier-than-thouness and your 'bad self' is hell, damnation or shithood. The main purpose of ego-rating is to prove that you are better than other humans and that, in a sense, you are superhuman. But since you are inevitably fallible and inferior to others in many respects, you will tend to feel inferior and devilifiable. (4) If you believe in intrinsic worth and self-rating, you will tend to bring on other important evils: such as your becoming self-centred rather than problem-centred and joy-seeking; your becoming self-conscious and narrow in your range of interests and involvements with others; your tending to hate yourself and other people; and your giving up desires and preferences in favour of assumed absolutes, needs, demands and compulsions.

Humanism

RET is doublejointedly humanistic in that it first takes the view that people are to be studied and helped so that they can live a happier, more self-actualizing and more creative existence; and also takes the view that people are better off when they emphasize human interests rather than those of inanimate objects, of lower animals or of some assumed 'natural order' or of gods. RET is also one of the few modern therapies that rigously parses feelings of anger and aggression into their healthy or assertive aspects and their unhealthy or grandiose aspects and that teaches people how to eliminate rather than merely suppress, repress or ventilate disturbed aspects of anger (Ellis, 1973c).

The rational–emotive hypothesis is that what we call anger and hostility usually consist of (1) healthy displeasure and determination to rid yourself of this displeasure (that is, 'I definitely do not like your unjust behaviour and am determined to try to get you to modify it!') and (2) unhealthy whiningness and commandingness (that is, 'I loathe *you* for committing this behaviour and I must vindictively punish and damn you for exhibiting it! You absolutely *must* not do what displeases me!'). RET teaches you how to become more *assertive* and less *hostile* by showing you exactly what your magical anger-creating cognitions are and how you can minimize them. It hypothesizes that if its methods are consistently employed, particularly in the education of children, the humanistic values of tolerance, love and peace will tend to prevail.

The specific RET thesis that anger and hostility result from the individual's Belief system rather than from the Activating experiences that occur to him or her, and that therefore cognitive restructuring instead of abreaction or cathartic release of feelings is desirable has been substantiated by a large number of experiments clinicians and social psychologists—including those reviewed by Berkowtiz (1970), Bandura and Walters (1963), Schacter and Singer (1962) and Singer (1968).

Hereditary and Environmental Influences

RET, unlike many modern psychotherapies, stresses the influence of *both* heredity and environment and often teaches people that they may have great trouble in changing their disturbed behaviour patterns because they have strong biological as well as sociological tendencies to perpetuate them (Ellis, 1962; 1971; 1973a). An enormous amount of evidence exists today to back this RET claim, and has been summarized by such investigators as Bender (1963), Chess *et al.* (1965), Kallmann (1960), Meehl (1962), Rosenthal (1970), Rosenthal and Kety (1968) and Slater and Cowie (1971). Another group of historical, anthropological, religious and psychological studies indicate—as predicted by RET theory—that virtually all humans, at all times and places, have been exceptionally irrational and that, in all probability, they have inborn as well as environmentally acquired tendencies to behave this way (Ellis, 1942; Frazer, 1959; Hoffer, 1951; Jahoda, 1969; Lévi-Strauss, 1962; Pitkin, 1932; Tabori, 1959; 1961).

Comprehensive Approach to Personality Change

From its inception, RET has hypothesized that human cognition, emotion and behaviour are transactionally related and that for effective personality change a comprehensive, multi-faceted attack on the disturbed individual's presenting symptoms and basic philosophies is desirable (Ellis, 1962; 1968; 1969a; 1971; 1973a). It also assumes, however, that since humans are uniquely cognizing creatures, they can practically all use liberal amounts of rational–persuasive therapy or emotional education and that, more often than not, this type of treatment would be better employed as the core method.

Considerable evidence for the importance of rational–persuasive methodology has been reported and summarized by a number of investigators, including Bednar (1970), Dolliver (1971), Frank (1973), Hovland and Janis (1959) and Rosnow and Robinson (1967). Evidence for the thesis that a comprehensive attack on disturbed symptomatology is likely to be effective, especially when it includes cognitive therapy, has also been presented by many specialists, including Cautela (1965), Davison (1968), Harper (1959), Hobbs (1962), Lazarus (1971), Lovaas (1971), Sloane (1969) and Thorne (1973).

Issues in Psychological Therapies

What position is taken, in the rational–emotive approach, concerning some of the major issues in psychological therapies that are discussed in the present book? Let me give my own views in this regard.

The Nature of the Complaint

The rational–emotive therapist normally begins with C, the emotional Consequence, or complaint, presented by the clients. It is assumed that if clients say they are coming for treatment because they are, say anxious, depressed or underproductive they have genuine complaints in this respect and one of the first jobs of the therapist is to explore these complaints, to find their basic philosophic source and to help the clients change this source and thereby rid themselves of the complaints. Usually, the therapist starts where the clients are—or think they are. If they present a symptom (e.g. overeating) that 'really' masks another symptom (e.g. self-castigation), they may be shown that they have 'deeper' problems than they know about. But these 'deeper' symptoms or causes will usually be discovered while client and therapist are working on the presenting issue and dealing with that.

The reason why I, personally, usually start where clients are at, and work with them on whatever bothers them most, is because even if this complaint turns out to be relatively trivial, it can immediately be used as a starting point by which I teach the individual the A–B–C's of virtually *any* disturbance, including the presenting one. Thus, if a client overeats because, she cliams, she is angry at her husband for degrading her for being fat, I quickly show her that A, her husband's defamation could not possibly cause C, her anger, her feeling of being degraded, and her overeating. Rather, I prove to her, it is her Belief system, at B, *about* her husband's 'unfair' and 'horrible' defamation that is upsetting her. If I can get her to see *this,* then it doesn't really matter if overeating is one of her minor problems and something else (e.g. fear of failure) is her 'real' problem. Once she learns the A–B–C's of emotional disturbance, we can fairly easily go on to these 'deeper' issues and show her how to apply her new knowledge of herself to them.

When I employ RET, my relationship to a client may be close or involved (if I happen to like him or her); or it may be minimal, as it frequently is, since RET is largely an active–directive *problem-solving* approach and does not require close relating between therapist and client. Even though severely disturbed, the client is *not* viewed as being 'ill' or 'sick' but as being an individual with *crooked thinking* and *inappropriate emoting.* Consequently, an educative, often highly didactic and informative, approach is taken: much more along the lines of teacher–pupil than doctor–patient relationship. The therapist, however, is authoritative rather than authoritarian; can largely be himself or herself; can directly answer personal or impersonal questions; and can actively engage, in rational encounter groups, as an individual in his or her own right. It is not assumed, however, that the therapist is as disturbed as the client; is primarily interested in personal friendship or gratification during therapy sessions; and has just as much to gain, in terms of personal help, as the client.

The Nature of Cure

It is largely assumed, in RET, that the client sees himself or herself as having serious problems and as not achieving one or more of the main human goals of surviving, being happy, living amicably in a social group and relating intimately to a few selected members of this group. 'Cure' is rarely attempted, since it seems utopian to assume that anyone will ever *completely* achieve these basic goals or eradicate present and future symptoms; but significant improvement is sought. This is defined as the individual's becoming minimally anxious, depressed, self-hating and hostile to others and maximally capable of achieving his or her own basic goals and values. Since the individual normally chooses to live in a social group (rather than to be a hermit), some degree of social acceptability and adherence to the morals of his or her group is usually discussed and sought in RET. But a thoroughly social or conventional concept of 'mental health' is hardly prompted; and clients are often helped to adjust happily, unguiltily and effectively to goals (such as homosexual relationships or living in a commune) that are disapproved of in their general society.

Although, as noted above, particular complaints or symptoms are specified and attacked in the course of RET, this form of therapy does not usually stop there and does tend to have an ideal goal, which may never be achieved (and, according to RET theory itself, of course, doesn't *have to* be) but which the therapist nonetheless keeps in mind. That goal is not only to help the client surrender or be 'cured' of the symptom, but to significantly minimize his or her *disturbability* and the consequent chances of the return of this or any other symptom. Thus, a client who is depressed because, he reports, he has just been rejected by a woman he deeply loves is shown, first, how not to awfulize and horribilize about *this* rejection, and how therefore to rid himself of his depression. But he is also normally shown how to acquire a general philosophy of self-acceptance and anti-demonizing that will help him, for the rest of his day, to refuse to awfulize about *any* kind of rejection—including sex, love, social or business rejection. In this sense, RET is far from being a symptom-removing or a palliative kind of therapy (though temporarily or at times it will strive for these kinds of results). It is a form of psychological treatment that usually aims for basic philosophic restructuring, hence for far-reaching personality change.

The Evaluation of Therapy

RET holds that although the state of research in psychotherapy is still such that clear-cut measurement of therapeutic change is exceptionally difficult, there is no intrinsic reason why this cannot ultimately be achieved. Just as it sees human disturbance as consisting of disordered thinking, emoting and behaving, it would like to see evidence for psychotherapeutic effectiveness in all three of these realms. Thus, if a person has a snake phobia, it would tend to put him in the 'cured' or 'non-phobic' category when (1) he fully believes that snakes (and similar animals) may well be ugly and undesirable but hardly awful or horrible; when (2) he can think about or contact snakes without feeling anxious and without having physiological correlates of anxiety, such as a fast pulse, profuse sweating and a pain in his gut; and when (3) he can easily approach rather than avoid snakes.

Social Implications of Psychotherapy

RET believes that ethics and values are an important part of therapy, in that

172

almost all men and women want to live in social groups and relate intimately to some members of these groups. Their enlightened self-interest therefore involves their first striving for their individual pleasure and relative freedom from pain; but at the same time refraining from interfering needlessly with the satisfactions of other members of their group (largely because these others would then tend to interfere with their own, the individuals', satisfactions). RET therefore importantly considers both individual *and* social interest. It does not, however, advocate that therapy be mainly or only designed to try to establish 'socially acceptable' behaviour or even that all clients be ultra-interested in establishing loving interpersonal relations. Although a rational–emotive therapist would probably not be interested in helping a client be a successful thief or murderer, he might well agree to help one be an unabashed political maverick, a devoted scientist or artist who hardly cares for intimacy with others or even a happy hermit.

Training of Psychotherapists

In the training of rational–emotive therapists it is considered to be desirable, though not absolutely necessary, for the trainee to experience some amount of RET himself or herself. In our most intensive training programme at the Institute for Advanced Study in Rational Psychotherapy in New York City, we have a special therapy group for all the fellows in training at the Institute; and if in the course of their participation in this group or their other work as fellows it is discovered that they have fairly serious problems, they are asked to get individual RET as well. But we do not believe that all therapists absolutely must have a considerable amount of therapy themselves—as most psychoanalytic schools tend to believe. Nor do we even believe that therapists must have scores of hours of personal supervision. Practically all our supervision is group supervision: where several therapists have their cases simultaneously supervised by a highly experienced rational–emotive therapist and where they all help supervise each other. We find this a better and more active kind of supervision than the usual type of supervision that most schools insist upon.

We also make sure that our trainees, in addition to being trained in individual RET procedures, are trained in (1) regular group therapy; (2) marathon groups; (3) public workshops; and (4) other kinds of applied uses of rational–emotive psychology. As noted previously in this paper, RET uses an educational model rather than a medical or a psychodynamic model. RET therapists, therefore, are trained in various kinds of ways to do different kinds of emotional education and to do it with children, with adults, with married couples and in small and large group settings.

Case Presentation

To get a real feeling for how RET works, it is usually desirable to see how it is applied with an individual who has severe emotional problems. To this end, let me present the case of Walter R, a 27-year-old who came to see me because of several symptoms: he was shy and inhibited when trying to relate to members of the other ex; he had some degree of sexual impotence, particularly in regard to very rapid jaculation; and he was exceptionally hostile to authority figures, including his arents and his immediate supervisor at the firm where he was employed as a junior ccountant. Since it became fairly obvious, in the course of his first few therapy essions, that Walter's main problems were largely connected with his enormous ears of failure and his long-standing and deep-seated feelings of worthlessness, I rst worked with him on these problems. During our second session together, part of ur dialogue went as follows:

Therapist: You seem to be terribly afraid that you will fail at making good initial contacts with a woman and also at succeeding sexually.
Client: Hell, yes! To say the least, I'm scared shitless in both these areas.
Therapist: Because if you fail in either area, what—?
Client: If I fail, I'll be an utter slob!
Therapist: Prove it!
Client: Isn't it obvious?
Therapist: Not to me! It's fairly obvious that if a woman rejects you, socially or sexually, it'll hardly be a great thing. But how will that prove that *you*, a total person, will be no good?
Client: I still think it's obvious. Would this same woman reject *anyone*?
Therapist: No, probably not. Let's suppose that she accepts many men, but not you. Let's also suppose that she rejects you because she finds that, first, you're not terribly good at conversation and, second, you come quickly in intercourse. So she finds you doubly deficient. Now, how does that still prove that you're no good?
Client: It certainly proves that I'm no good for *her*.
Therapist: Yes, in a way. You're no good for her conversationally and sexually. You have two rotten *traits*.
Client: And she doesn't want *me*, for having those traits.
Therapist: Right. In the case we're assuming, she rejects *you* for having those two traits. But all we've proved is that one woman despises two of your characteristics; and that this woman therefore rejects you as a lover or a husband. Even she, mind you, might well accept you as a nonsexual friend. For you have, don't forget, many other traits—such as intelligence, artistic talent, reliability, etc.
Client: But not the traits she *most* wants!
Therapist: Maybe. But how does this prove that *all* women, like her, would find you equally wanting? Some, actually, might like you *because* you are shy and *because* you come quickly sexually—when they don't happen to like intercourse, and therefore want to get it over rapidly!
Client: Fat chance!
Therapist: Yes, statistically. For *most* women, presumably will tend to reject you if you're shy or sexually inadequate, in their eyes. But a few, at least, will accept you for the very reasons that most refuse you; and many more, normally, will accept you in spite of your deficiencies, because they nonetheless become attached to you.
Client: Who the devil wants *that*!
Therapist: Most of us do, actually, if we're sane. For, since we're all highly imperfect, we're happy that some people accept us *with* these imperfections. But let's even suppose the worst—just to show how crooked your thinking is. Let's suppose that, because of your shyness and fast ejaculation, *all* women rejected you for *all* time. Would you still be a worthless slob?
Client: I wouldn't exactly be a great guy!
Therapist: No, you wouldn't be Jesus Christ or Napoleon; or, certainly, Casanova! But many women, remember, wouldn't want you if you were one of them. Jesus, if he ever

really existed, seems to have been pretty shy with women; and Napoleon may well have come quickly. As for Casanova, most women, at least today, wouldn't want him just *because* he was so sexy. Anyway, we're evading the question: *would* you be a total slob?

Client: Well, uh, I, no, I guess not.

Therapist: Because?

Client: Well, because I'd still have other, uh, good traits. Is that what you're getting at?

Therapist: Yes, partly. You'd still have other good traits. And *you,* if you were rateable at all, would equal *all* your traits, and not merely two of them, such as shyness and sexual prematurity. Moreover, even—and let's deliberately suppose the worst now—*All* your characteristics were bad or inferior and, again, *every* attractive woman you ever met rejected you. Would you *then* be worthless?

Client: Damn right I'd be!

Therapist: Wrong again! I don't think you're stopping to define what you really mean by the term *worthless.* When you consider yourself, rotten, no good, a turd, what do you really mean by that?

Client: That I'm incompetent and can't get what I want.

Therapist: No, you—and practically everyone else—really mean *more* than that. You *first* mean that you're totally incompetent— which is invariably false, but we're assuming it in this special case we're making up. But you also mean—don't you?—that you will *always* be totally incompetent and *never,* therefore, get anything you want. Isn't that what the term *worthless* or a *rotten person* means?

Client: Yes, I guess that's what I mean.

Therapist: But is that really provable, that hypothesis? That you'll *always* be utterly inept and *never* get what you want?

Client: (pause) Uh, no. I guess it isn't.

Therapist: Say that with more conviction! 'No, it *isn't* provable—that I'll never do anything well and never possibly be accepted by *any* woman I want.' For is *that* ascertainable?

Client: (pause) Uh. No. No, it really isn't.

Therapist: But let's even suppose more. Suppose, by some miracle of prediction, we could even legitimately say that you *never* will do anything well and win the favor of *any* woman? You're just, we're imagining, a *completely* inadequate person—though we never, actually, could prove that. Even so, imagining that, doesn't your term *worthless* mean something more?

Client: You mean it means that I don't *deserve* to get what I want?

Therapist: Yes. Exactly! *Worthless* doesn't merely mean that 'because I'm so incompetent, I *can't* ever get what I desire'—which, again, is pretty unprovable. It *also* means, 'I only *deserve* to get good things in life *when* I fulfil certain requirements, such as being socially bold and very sexy. The powers that run the universe *know* I am lacking in these respects and they therefore won't *allow* me to get what I want. They *damn me,* and plunge me into some kind of eternal hell, for lacking these essential requirements and therefore being worthless'. Isn't *that* what the term means?

Client: I never thought about it that way.

Therapist: Well, stop for a moment and think about it.

Client: (long pause) Uh, I think you're, uh, probably right. I *do* think I don't *deserve* to succeed at anything if I am seriously lacking in some important trait. And, although I though I had given up all formal religion, I, I guess I *do* still believe in some kind of damnation. At least, for *schnooks* like me!

Therapist: Ah, see! There you go again! '*Schnooks* like me!' See the overgeneralization. What you really mean is, 'I believe that people like me, who *act schnookily* on many occasions, don't deserve to succeed at anything important'. Your acts, deeds, performances, traits, characteristics, may indeed be schnooky or shitty—but *you* are not *a* schnook. You are *you*: a human individual, with all kinds of schnooky and nonschnooky behaviors.

Client: Am I never, then, a 'good person', either?

Therapist: Right! You're never *a* good person, *a* great guy, *a* genius, or *a* god. You're only, at most, a person *with* various good, great, or genius-like traits. And crummy ones and mediocre ones, as well!

Client: Hmm. You have quite a different way of looking at things, there.

Therapist: Yes—a different and a more scientific way. And if I can get you to see that you *aren't* anything, but that you *have* various traits and *do* various deeds, you'll almost automatically begin to see what you can do when you foul up on those traits and deeds.

Client: You mean, try to change my foul-ups the next time?

Therapist: Right. And, in the case we're discussing, try to become *less* shy and *more* sexually adept. But you won't, probably, won't either try or succeed at trying, if you keep rating *yourself,* putting *yourself* down when you presently fail. Why is that?

Client: Oh, I guess for the same reason I tell some of the bookkeepers I work with, and one in particular who blames herself mightily for even minor errors that she makes. 'If you spend time and energy blaming yourself'. I often say to her, 'you won't have that same time and energy available to correct your errors.'

Therapist: Precisely. Also, you might tell her: 'If you put *yourself* down for your bookkeeping mistakes, you are really saying, "Because *I* am a lousy bookkeeper and a rotten person, I *have* to keep making errors and behaving rottenly all the time. For what can *a* rotter do but invariably act rottenly?"'.

Client: I see. In fact, uh, isn't it interesting that I see it so clearly for her, but, uh—

Therapist: 'But not for *me!*'

Client: Right. Not for *me.*

Therapist: Because? What, uh, do you think is the reason for that? Why not for *you?*

Client: I, I—I guess I see myself as different.

Therapist: Just *different?*

Client: Uh, no. I—. Oh, yes, I see now: *special!* I've got to be special!

Therapist: Yes, isn't *that* really the issue? 'I, special creature that I am, *should* be great, glorious, noble, and perfect. And if I'm anything *less* than that—even above average, but not truly *special*—I'm—what?'

Client: Right. I'm a nothing!

Therapist: You see, the *should* then, or the *must?* Do you see that, just about invariably, when you put *yourself* down, damn *you,* there's some idealistic and unrealistic *should?*

Client: Yes, I remember your famous phrase, now, which I've heard on a tape recording of one of your lectures: *'Shouldhood* equals *shithood!*'.

Therapist: And do you see what it means?

Client: I think I really do, now. I saw it vaguely, when I first heard you say it on the tape. But now I see how it specifically applies to *me.*

Therapist: How?

Client: Well, uh, I—yes, that's it!—I should, I absolutely *must* do well, uh, practically all the time; and whenever I don't do what I *must* in this respect. I'm totally lacking, a worthless slob. Even if I do well but not well *enough.* It's an all or nothing thing. Perfection—or slobbishness! Nothing in between.

Therapist: Yes. And perfection not merely about your *traits,* but about *you,* about your *youness.* If you're lacking in some important traits or areas; your whole *being* is slobby. Well, how do you expect to win, in this game of life, with *that* basic philosophy?

Client: I guess I can't.

Therapist: Theoretically, you *can*—for pratically nothing is utterly impossible. But the chances are astonomically high that you *won't.*

I kept working, along these cognitive lines, revealing to Walter R what his underlying philosophic assumptions were, how they led to his 'emotional' problems, such as his extreme anxiety, fear of failure and semi-impotence, and how he could clearly understand them and change them. I especially used the A–B–C's of RET in getting him to attack his disturbance-creating Belief system. We started with his emotional Consequence (C), his shyness and inhibition when approaching attractive woman. Then we went to his Activating experiences or Activating events (A), that occurred just before he felt shy and inhibited at A. A usually consisted of the times when he went to a social affair, saw a woman he considered attractive and decided that he would like to approach her. Immediately therafter, at C, he felt self-conscious and normally made no move whatever to meet her. Even if, by some accident, she started talking to him, he still felt very inhibited and normally spoke to her hesitatingly and badly; and, finally, he practically never tried to make a subsequent date with her.

I showed Walter that A (the Activating experience) never, as he first thought it did, caused C (the emotional Consequence). Instead, B (his Belief system) directly caused C. First, he had a rational Belief (rB): 'I'd like to become friendly with this woman, but I may fail and get rejected by her, and wouldn't that be unfortunate. How annoying that would be!' If he had stayed rigorously with this kind of rational Belief, he would feel, at C, *appropriately* concerned and somewhat cautious; and would also feel sorry, regretful and frustrated, in case he did try to make contact with this woman and did get rejected by her. His rational Belief (rB) would be sensible and realistic because it generally *would be* unfortunate, disadvantageous and annoying if he were refused; and his emotional Consequence would be appropriate, since why should he be totally *un*concerned about approaching this attractive woman and happy about being rebuffed by her?

But the real issue, I showed Walter, was his irrational Belief (iB): 'Wouldn't it be *awful* if this woman rejected me. I couldn't *bear* it! What a worm I'd then be!'. This set of Beliefs led to his *in*appropriate responses of overconcern, anxiety and almost complete inhibition in approaching the woman; and to his feelings of horror, depression and panic if he did make contact with her and was refused. His irrational Beliefs (iB's) were senseless and unrealistic for several reasons.

(1) It clearly wasn't *awful* if a woman rejected him because *awful* really means (when it is operationally defined): (a) extremely disadvantageous or noxious (in terms of the individual's basic goals of surviving and getting what he wants out of life); (b) *more* than one hundred per cent obnoxious; and (c) not legitimately allowed to exist, *because* it is so undesirable. Although the first of these hypotheses is empirically provable, the last two are magical and are unverifiable. Nothing, clearly, can be *more* than obnoxious or unfortunate; and there is nothing that *should* or *must* not exist simply because it is highly undesirable to the individual to whom it occurs.

(2) Although he might never *like* being rejected by an attractive woman, he clearly could *bear* such a rejection. It wouldn't kill him; he could go on to other rejections—and acceptances; and the pain (the sorrow, regret and frustration) would be *tolerable*. Only his foolish *belief* that he couldn't bear it would make it 'unbearable'.

(3) How could his being rejected make him a *worm*? It might prove that his *behaviour* was wormy—or it might not prove that at all, since he could get rejected if a woman liked a man with blue eyes and his were brown. But even if his behaviour was poor, inept or inadequate that would only be a *part*, and never the *whole*, of his

existence and his being. He, as a total *human,* could never be *a* worm. Technically, he as a whole would always be too complex to be rated at all—to be given a single report card or evaluation. Moreover, he would always be a *process,* an ongoingness—and how can this kind of ever-changing process be rated?

As I showed Walter how he was illegitimately rating himself, rather than merely evaluating his traits and performances, and how this kind of self-rating would lead him to feelings of worthlessness, depression, the conviction that he could *never* be accepted by a woman he found attractive and to consequent shy, withdrawn and inept behaviour with females, he tended to see clearly what we were discussing and to accept most of the points I was making about him and his self-defeating philosophies. 'But how', he asked, 'can I get rid of my irrational beliefs myself? What can I do to change them?'. I replied as follows:

Therapist: Let me show you three major, though overlapping, techniques of changing your irrational Beliefs about yourself and the world. First, use our regular Homework Report to zero in on what your main irrational Belief or nutty idea is when you feel hurt from a rejection or withdraw from trying to be accepted. Look at one of these Reports.
Client: (Taking Report and looking at it) It says 'ANSWER QUESTION C FIRST; THEN ANSWER THE OTHER QUESTIONS'.
Therapist: Right. And what is Question C?
Client:'CONSEQUENCE of your Irrational BELIEF (iB) about the Activating Event listed in Question A. State here the one most disturbing emotion, behaviour, or CONSEQUENCE you experienced recently.'
Therapist: All right; and what emotion or CONSEQUENCE are we dealing with in your case?
Client: Rejection.
Therapist: Right. So write, in the blank space after Question C. 'Feelings of rejection.' Or 'hurt'. Or 'withdrawal'. Or 'anxiety'.
Client: I'll write 'anxiety and withdrawal'.
Therapist: Fine. Now fill in A, the Activating Event or Activating Experience. What happens before you feel anxious and withdraw?
Client: I meet a woman I find attractive and whom I'd like to get to know better.
Therapist: O.K.: fill in—'Meeting with an attractive woman'. Now how about rB, your rational Belief about seeing this woman and, perhaps, talking to her.
Client: I guess it's, 'I would like her to like me'.
Therapist: Right. But we're more interested in your negative rational idea. 'And if she doesn't like me—?'
Client: That would be terrible!
Therapist: No, that's your irrational Belief. We'll get back to that in a minute. But before you tell yourself that, you first tell yourself something quite sane and rational. What do you think *that* is?
Client: Uh. 'It would be pretty bad, uh, uncomfortable, if she doesn't like me'.
Therapist: Yes, something like that. 'It would be bad, uncomfortable, unfortunate, frustrating, if she didn't like me.' O.K. And suppose you stayed *only* with that. You *merely* told yourself that. How would you then feel, at C, instead of anxious and withdrawn?
Client: Uh, I guess I'd feel cautious.
Therapist: Yes: cautious or concerned or thoughtfully planning. But not really anxious—which means *over*concerned and self-downing. Now, let's go on to your irrational Belief. You've already stated that.
Client: 'It would be terrible if she didn't like me!'
Therapist: Yes, that seems to be it. That's what's making you overconcerned, anxious,

withdrawn. Now: how would you Dispute, at point D on the Homework Report, that irrational Belief?

Client: It wouldn't be terrible, because——.

Therapist: No, you're trying to give E, the Effect, or answer to the Disputing. But how about Disputing itself? In what manner do we Dispute, or challenge, virtually *any* hypothesis, once we set it up?

Client: By asking why or how it is true?

Therapist: Right. And in the case of your specific hypothesis of irrational Belief?

Client: '*Why* would it be terrible if I approached a woman I found attractive and she didn't like me?'

Therapist: Exactly. And what's the *answer* to that Dispute?

Client. Uh. Because I would feel destroyed if she refused me.

Therapist: No, that's only an answer that holds true *if* you maintain, rigidly and foolishly, your hypothesis. If you insist on *thinking* it's terrible if you get rejected by a woman, then, because of that insistence, you feel destroyed if you do get rejected. But that is no evidence, your feeling of destruction, for the validity of the original hypothesis.

Client: It isn't?

Therapist: No, of course it isn't. If you have the hypothesis, 'I am a turd unless I have a million dollars', and you ask me, 'Why are you a turd when you don't have a million dollars?' and I answer, 'Because I then feel destroyed and feel like a turd', is my answer *proof* of my original hypothesis?

Client: Uh, no. It is only proof that you feel worthless because you insist that you must have a million dollars to feel worthwhile.

Therapist: Right. So your conclusion that you feel destroyed if you got rejected by a woman and *therefore* it is awful to be rejected is no evidence for your original proposition, 'It would be terrible if I approached a woman I found attractive and she didn't like me!'. It's only evidence that you most probably would foolishly *make yourself* feel awful—and not that it *would* be.

Client: Oh. I see. Only my *belief* in the hypothesis makes me feel the crummy way I feel. There, uh, *is* no evidence that being rejected *is* truly awful or terrible.

Therapist: No, there isn't any such evidence; nor, probably, can there ever be any. 'It's *awful* for me to be rejected' is a magical, unvalidatable hypothesis. Why is that so?

Client: Because, uh, of what we discussed before. *Awful* means *more than* disadvantageous. And that is unprovable.

Therapist: Right, And *awful* means 'I *shouldn't* be rejected, because I find it so unpleasant to be!'. Well, *shouldn't* I be, no matter how unpleasant I may find rejection?

Client: Of course you—or I—*should* be rejected. I simply *am*—or *will be,* many times.

Therapist: Right. So if you keep Disputing, at D, your irrational Belief, at iB, you'll keep coming to the conclusion that it *is* irrational and unverifiable, and you finally won't believe it any longer.

Client: Is that the main way for me to Dispute it, then, as we've just done?

Therapist: Yes, but there are other variations on this way. For example, for ten minutes every day, you can take *any* irrational or nutty Belief that you have—such as the one that it's terrible for you to be rejected by a woman you find attractive—and prophylactically practise it, even when you are not being rejected.

Client: How?

Therapist: By using the logico-empirical method of seeing whether your hypothesis is consistent with your other goals and hypotheses, and by asking for factual evidence to sustain or invalidate it.

Client: Can you be more specific?

Therapist: Yes, in my group therapy sessions, recently, I have been giving most of the members of the group Disputing assignments and also using operant conditioning—a self-management technique adapted from B. F. Skinner's theories—to help them carry out these ten-minute-a-day disputations.

Client: What do you mean by operant conditioning?

Therapist: I'll explain in a minute. But first, the point is for you to decide exactly what hypothesis or nutty idea you want to work on for at least ten minutes a day. And, in your case, it would be the idea, again, that it's terrible for you to get rejected by a woman you find attractive. You would take this idea, and ask yourself several basic questions, in order to challenge and dispute it.

Client: What kind of questions?

Therapist: Usually, four basic questions—though they have all kinds of variations. The first one is, 'What am I telling myself?' or 'What silly idea do I want to challenge?'. And the answer, in your case, is: 'It's terrible if a woman whom I find attractive rejects me'. The second question is: 'Is this, my hypothesis, true?'. And the answer is—?

Client: Uh, well, uh. No, it isn't.

Therapist: Fine. If you had said it was true, the third question would have been: 'Where is the evidence for its being true?'. But since you said, it isn't true, the third question is: 'Where is the evidence that it's not true?'. Well—?

Client: Well, uh, it's not true because, as we said before, it may be very *inconvenient* if an attractive woman rejects me, but it's not *more,* uh, than that. It's *only* damned inconvenient!

Therapist: Right. And there's other logico-empirical evidence that it isn't terrible. For one thing, because *this* woman rejects you hardly means that *all* will. For another, you obviously have survived, so far, even though you have been rejected. For still another, lots of other people in the world have been rejected by the woman they most love, and it has hardly been terrible for all of them, has it?

Client: I see. There are several evidences that my being rejected isn't awful. And there is no reason, as we again noted before, why I *should* not get rejected. The world simply isn't a totally non-rejecting place!

Therapist: Yes. I think you're getting that well. Now, the fourth question is: 'What's the worst thing that could happen to me, if an attractive woman rejects me?'.

Client: Very little, I guess. I uh, was at first going to say that the worst thing that could happen to me was that I would be very depressed for a long time. But I now see that such a thing would not happen from any rejection but from my *view* of the horror, uh, of being rejected.

Therapist: Really, then, not so much could happen to you, if you got rejected. Is that right?

Client: Yes. As a matter of fact, I would learn something about approaching an attractive female. And I might learn something valuable about myself.

Therapist: Right. Now, this method of asking yourself these four questions, and persisting till you get sensible answers to them, is something you can do at least ten minutes every single day, even when there is not much going on in your life and you are in no danger of being rejected. And you can combine it with operant conditioning, to increase the probability of your actually spending the ten minutes a day working at doing it.

Client: Oh, I know now. That's Skinner's reinforcing technique.

Therapist: Yes, basically. You first discover what you really like to do and tend to enjoy—or would enjoy if you did it—every day. Like sex, eating, smoking, talking to your friends, etc. What would you say was the thing you like best, along these lines?

Client: How about eating ice-cream?

Therapist: You really eat some, or try to eat some, every day?

Client: Oh, yes. I rarely eat less than a pint a day. I love it!

Therapist: Fine. Now, what do you intensely dislike doing, that you intend to avoid doing?

Client: Uh. Cleaning my apartment. I keep putting it off. I rarely do it.

Therapist: O.K. Then, let's say, let's you agree with me—really, with *yourself*—that if you work at least ten minutes a day at contradicting and disputing your nutty idea, 'It's awful to be rejected by a woman I find attractive', you will then, and only then, allow yourself to have any ice-cream that day. And if you fail to work at it, this idea, you will not only not have the reinforcement, the ice-cream, but you will also take on the penalty of cleaning your apartment for at least an hour.

Client: But suppose the apartment gets too clean?

Therapist: Dirty it—and clean it over! Or ask your friends for their permission to clean their houses! O.K.?

Client: (laughing) O.K.

Therapist: But no nonsense! You only reinforce yourself when you do the ten minutes of questioning and challenging your nutty idea. And you specifically penalize yourself when you don't do it. Keep up this kind of reinforcement schedule, and the chances are that your will keep working against this irrational Belief—and that you will start to give it up.

The client agreed to this kind of anti-awfulizing, combined with operant self-management, and within the next three weeks he began to give up his idea that he *had* to be accepted by women he considered attractive. He did so well, in this respect, that he also began to attack his irrational belief that he had to last a long time in intercourse; and, as he began to surrender this notion, his fast ejaculation slowed down considerably.

At the same time as Walter was shown how to dispute and challenge his basic self-defeating philosphies, I also employed a number of other cognitive, emotive and behaviour therapy techniques with him, since RET is a comprehensive form of treatment that includes several important modalities and that, somewhat like Arnold Lazarus' (1971; 1973) multimodal or BASIC ID approach, stresses somewhat different methodologies with various clients. On the cognitive side, I used sensory imaging and rational—emotive imagery with Walter. In the course of sensory imaging, I got him to practise seeing himself in bed with a woman, able to get a perfectly fine erection and able to use it in many ways, including penile—vaginal copulation, to last for five minutes or more of active sex play. Using rational—emotive imagery (REI), as outlined by Maultsby (1971b) and Ellis (1973b), I showed him how to vividly picture himself failing to date a new woman and failing, at times, to last very long in intercourse; and, while imagining failure, to change his 'normal' feelings of depression and panic to those of sorrow and disappointment, and concomitantly change his awfulizing about failing.

Cognitively, I also explained some common myths and facts about human sexuality to Walter. I showed him how he could easily satisfy a female non-coitally, in case he did not get an erection or last long in intercourse; how he could employ the sensate focus that has been made famous by Masters and Johnson (1970)—and that was also used in RET during the 1950s (Ellis, 1958a; 1960; 1961); and how he could use a number of other methods, both palliative and curative, to divert himself from sexual awfulizing to more enjoyable forms of sex.

Emotively, I and other members of Walter's therapy group used direct confrontational methods to help him face some of his basic problems and to discuss them openly in group. We showed him, via feeling feedback from group members, that he was more attractive to females than he dreamed that he was. We provided him, at times, with direct support from a few people in the group, who volunteered to go with him on some of his dating homework assignments and make sure that he actually approached some attractive women. We gave him several kinds of risk-taking and shame-attacking exercises in the group itself, to show him that expressing his positive or negative feelings to others usually brought about immediate good results rather than the bad consequences he kept predicting. We continually gave him unconditional acceptance as a person, along with non-condemnatory feedback about some of his ineffectual interpersonal behaviours.

Behaviourally, I employed several active–directive homework or *in vivo* desensitizing assignments with Walter. I (and his group members) gave him graduated assignments in regard to meeting, talking with, trying to date and make sex–love overtures to attractive and non-attractive women. I also, while working on his hostility to authority figures, gave him the activity assignments of deliberately having more contacts with his parents, whom he normally avoided like the plague, in order to experience his intense feelings of hatred towards them, to observe exactly what he was irrationally telling himself to create these feelings and to work at changing his hostility-creating beliefs. I used assertion-training methods with Walter and role-played with him, in individual and group sessions, how he could speak up to his parents and his supervisors and determinedly tell them what he disliked about their behaviour instead of holding his displeasure in for a long time and finally expelling it as violent anger. I also did some amount of modelling and behaviour rehearsal with him, to help him to see how he could forthrightly confront me and others and become habituated to 'being himself' instead of 'proving himself', which he had inflicted upon himself for many years.

In the course of 14 sessions of individual and 37 sessions of group RET, Walter achieved significant improvement in all his presenting symptoms. He lost almost all his shyness about making contact with members of the other sex and he was able to encounter them, in new situations, and almost always make suitable overtures to those whom he found personable. He was able to last for five or more minutes of active sexual intercourse, particularly with a woman with whom he was having steady sex relations; and, for the first time in his life, he found that in some instances he even would have some difficulty in coming to orgasm, after 15 or 20 minutes of copulation, and would tend to resort to intense sensory imaging in order to do so. He was no longer hostile towards his parents, though he had no particular yen to be with them and only rarely was intimate with them. He lost his anxiety and his anger towards his immediate supervisor at work and, by using RET educational techniques with this person, became quite friendly with him, so that the supervisor became rather dependent on Walter.

In general, Walter felt at the close of therapy that the chances of his consistently denigrating himself again were virtually nil. As he reported, during one of his closing sessions, 'I know that I shall continue to screw up, in various ways, for the rest of my life. I've come a long way during the last several months; but I still haven't been able to maintain a steady love relationship with one woman, which I really want to do. But I'm sure—well, I'm *practically* sure!—that I'm just not going to put myself down any more, no matter how stupidly I behave. I am determined to accept *me*, in spite of my nutty, self-defeating behaviour. At least, I'm going to *try*!'. Two and a half years have now passed since Walter was in therapy, and I now see him once in a while as one of the active participants in my regular Friday night workshop in

182

problems of living at the Institute for Rational Living in New York City. He reports, when I speak to him after the workshop, that he has not only maintained but increased his gains and that he is still determinedly refusing to put himself down about anything.

Summary

Rational–emotive therapy is a comprehensive form of psychological treatment that heavily stresses the cognitive, philosophic, value-oriented and phenomenological aspects of human personality and of the creation and minimization of emotional disturbance. It holds that the individual largely manufactures his or her own psychological symptoms and has the ability, with consistent work and effort at changing basic attitudinal premises, to eliminate these symptoms and make himself or herself much less disturbable. It takes a transactional view of the relationships among cognitive, emotive and behavioural aspects of human living, and consequently heavily evocative–emotive and active–directive behaviouristic approaches to personality change, along with its persuasive–rational methodologies. It is not, however, interested in symptom removal so much as an elegant philosophic solution to the individual's fundamental 'emotional' problems. It is increasingly supported by a number of controlled clinical and experimental studies; and it has become an intrinsic and vital part of the newly developing field of cognitive-behaviour therapy. Although hardly a panacea for all ills, RET is an improtant aspect of today's armamentarium of psychotherapeutic methodologies.

References

Adler, A. (1929). *Understanding Human Nature,* Greenberg, New York.
Argabrite, A. H., and Nidorf, L. J. (1968). 'Fifteen questions for rating reason', *Rational Living,* 3(1), 9.
Bandura, A., and Walters, R. M. (1963). *Aggression,* National Society for Education, Chicago.
Bannister, D. (Ed.) (1971). *Perspectives in Personal Construct Theory,* Academic Press, New York.
Bannister, D., and Mair, J. M. (1968). *The Evaluation of Personal Constructs,* Academic Press, New York.
Beck, A. T. (1967). *Depression,* Harper-Hoeber, New York.
Bednar, R. L. (1970). 'Persuasibility and the power of belief', *Personnel and Guidance Journal,* 48, 647.
Bender, L. (1963). 'Mental illness in childhood and heredity', *Eugenics Quarterly,* 10, 1.
Berkowitz, L. (1970). 'Experimental investigations of hostility catharsis', *Journal of Consulting and Clinical Psychology,* 35, 1.
Bersoff, D. N., and Grieger, R. M. (1972). 'An interview model for the psychosituational assessment of children's behaviour', *Rational Living,* 7(1), 14.
Blum, G. S., and Wohl, B. M. (1971). 'An experimental analysis of the nature and operation of anxiety', *Journal of Abnormal Psychology,* 78, 1.
Breen, G. J. (1970). 'Active–directive counseling in an adult education setting', *Journal of College Student Personnel,* July, 279.

Carlson, W. A., Travers, R. M. W., and Schwab, Jr., E. A. (1969). 'A laboratory approach to the cognitive control of anxiety', Paper presented at American Personnel and Guidance Association Meetings, Las Vegas, March 31.

Cautela, J. R. (1965). 'Comprehensive desensitization and insight', *Behavior Research and Therapy*, **3**, 59.

Cautela, J. R. (1970). 'Covert reinforcement', *Behavior Therapy*, **1**, 33.

Chess, S., Alexander, T., and Birch, H. G. (1965). *Your Child is a Person*, Viking, New York.

Cook, S. W., and Harris, R. E. (1937). 'The verbal conditioning of the galvanic skin reflex', *Journal of Experimental Psychology*, **21**, 201.

Cooke, G. (1966). 'The efficacy of two desenitization procedures: an analogue study', *Behavior Research and Therapy*, **4**, 17.

Daly, S. (1971). 'Using reason with deprived pre-school children', *Rationa Living*, **5**(2), 12.

Davies, R. L. (1970). *Relationship of Irrational Ideas to Emotional Disturbance*, Masters Degree Thesis, University of Alberta.

Davison, G. C. (1965). 'Relative contributions of differential relaxation and graded exposure to *in vivo* desensitization of a neurotic fear', *Proceedings 72nd Annual Convention of the American Psychological Association*, 209.

Davison, G. C. (1968). 'Systematic desensitization as a counterconditioning process', *Journal of Abnormal Psychology*, **73**, 91.

Davison, G. C., and Valins, S. (1969). 'Maintenance of self-attributed and drug-attributed behavior change, *Journal of Personality and Social Psychology*, **11**, 25.

De Wolfe, A. S. (1971). 'Cognitive structure and pathology in associations of process and reactive schizophrenics', *Journal of Abnormal Psychology*, **78**, 148.

Dolliver, R. H. (1971). 'Concerning the potential parallels between psychotherapy and brainwashing', *Psychotherapy*, **2**, 170.

Dua, P. S. (1970). 'Comparison of the effects of behaviorally oriented action and psychotherapy reeducation on introversion–extraversion, emotionality, and internal–external control', *Journal of Counseling Psychology*, **17**, 567.

Dua, P. S. (1972). 'Group desensitization of a phobia with three massing procedures', *Journal of Counseling Psychology*, **19**, 125.

Ellis, A. (1942). *A History of the Dark Ages: the Twentieth Century*. In manuscript.

Ellis, A. (1957a). *How to Live with a Neurotic*, Crown Publishers, New York; Award Books, New York, 1969.

Ellis, A. (1957b). 'Outcome of employing three techniques of psychotherapy', *Journal of Clinical Psychology*, **13**, 334.

Ellis, A. (1958a). *Sex Without Guilt*, Lyle Stuart, New York; revised edition, Lancer Books, New York, 1969.

Ellis, A. (1958b). 'Rational psychotherapy', *Journal of General Psychology*, **59**, 35.

Ellis, A. (1960). *The Art and Science of Love*, Lyle Stuart, New York; revised edition, Bantam Books, New York, 1969.

Ellis, A. (1961). *The American Sexual Tragedy*, Lyle Stuart and Grove Press, New York.

Ellis, A. (1962). *Reason and Emotion in Psychotherapy*, Lyle Stuart, New York.

Ellis, A. (1968). *Is Objectivism a Religion?*, Lyle Stuart, New York.

Ellis, A. (1969a). 'A cognitive approach to behavior therapy', *International Journal of Psychiatry*, **8**, 696.

Ellis, A. (1969b). 'A weekend of rational encounter', in A. Burton (Ed.), *Encounter: The Theory and Practice of Encounter Groups*, Jossey-Bass, San Francisco, pp. 112–27.

Ellis, A. (1970). 'The case against religion', *Mensa Bulletin*, September, Issue No. 138, 5.

Ellis, A. (1971). *Growth Through Reason: Verbatim Cases in Rational–Emotive Therapy*, Science and Behavior Books, Palo Alto.

Ellis, A. (1972a). 'Psychotherapy without tears', in A. Burton (Ed.), *Twelve Therapists*, Jossey-Bass, San Francisco, pp. 103–26.

Ellis, A. (1972b). 'Helping people get better rather than merely feel better', *Rational Living*, 7(2), 2.

Ellis, A. (1972c). 'Psychotherapy and the value of a human being', in J. W. Davis (Ed.), *Values and Valuation: Essays in Honor of Robert Hartman*, University of Tennessee Press, Knoxville, pp. 117–39; reprinted: Institute for Rational Living, New York.

Ellis, A. (1972d). *Executive Leadership: A Rational Approach*, Citadel Press, New York.

Ellis, A. (1972e). *How to Master your Fear of Flying*, Curtis Books, New York.

Ellis, A. (1927f). *The Sensuous Person: Critique and Corrections*, Lyle Stuart, New York.

Ellis, A. (1973a). *Humanistic Psychotherapy: The Rational–Emotive Approach*, Julian Press, New York.

Ellis, A. (1973b). 'Are rational–emotive and cognitive–behavior therapy synonymous?', *Rational Living*, 8, 2.

Ellis, A. (1973c). 'Healthy and unhealthy aggression', Paper presented at The American Psychological Association Convention, Montreal.

Ellis, A. (1973d). 'Emotional education at The Living School', in M. M. Ohlsen (Ed.), *Counseling Children in Groups*, Holt, Rinehart and Winston, New York, pp. 79–93.

Ellis, A. (1973e). 'The group as a facilitator of personality change', in A. Jacobs (Ed.), *The Group as an Agent of Change*, Behavioral Publications, New York.

Ellis, A. (1973f). 'What does transpersonal psychology have to offer to the art and science of psychotherapy?', *Voices*, 1972, 8(3), 10. Revised version, *Rational Living*, 8(1), 20.

Ellis, A. (1973g). 'The no cop-out therapy', *Psychology Today*, 7(2), 56.

Ellis, A., and Harper, R. A. (1961a). *A Guide to Rational Living*, Prentice-Hall, Englewood Cliffs, N.J.

Ellis, A., and Harper, R. A. (1961b). *Creative Marriage*, Lyle Stuart, New York. Also published as *A Guide to Successful Marriage*, Wilshire Books, Hollywood, 1972.

Felixbord, J. J., and O'Leary, K. D. (1973). 'Effects of reinforcement on children's academic behavior as a function of self-determined and externally imposed contingencies', *Journal of Applied Behavior Analysis*, 6, 241.

Frank, J. D. (1973). *Persuasion and Healing*, Johns Hopkins University Press, Baltimore.

Frazer, J. G. (1959). *The New Golden Bough*, Criterion Books, New York.

Glasser, W. (1964). *Reality Therapy*, Harper and Row, New York.

Goldfried, M. R., and Merbaum, M. (Eds.) (1973). *Behavior Change Through Self-control*, Holt, Rinehart and Winston, New York.

Gustav, A. (1968). ' "Success is—" Locating composite sanity', *Rational Living*, 3(1), 1.

Harper, R. A. (1959). *Psychoanalysis and psychotherapy: 36 Systems*, Prentice-Hall, Englewood Cliffs, N.J.

Hartman, B. J. (1968). 'Sixty revealing questions for twenty minutes', *Rational Living*, 3(1), 7.

Hartman, R. S. (1967). *The Measurement of Value*, Southern Illinois University Press, Carbondale, 1967.

Hobbs, N. (1962). 'Sources of gain in psychotherapy', *American Psychologist*, 17, 741.

Hodgson, R., Rachman, S., and Marks, I. M. (1972). 'The treatment of chronic obsessive–compulsive neurosis: follow-up and further findings', *Behavior Research and Therapy*, 10, 181.

Hoehn-Saric, R., Frank, J. D., and Gurland, B. J. (1968). 'Focused attitude change in neurotic patients', *Journal of Nervous and Mental Disease*, 147, 124.

Hoffer, E. (1951). *The True Believer*, Harper, New York.

Homme, L. E. (1965). 'The control of coverants. The operants of the mind', *Psychological Record*, 15, 501.

Hovland, C. I., and Janis, I. L. (1959). *Personality and Persuasibility*, Yale University Press, New Haven.

Hoxter, A. L. (1967). *Irrational Beliefs and Self-concept in Two Kinds of Behaviour*, Doctoral dissertation, University of Alberta.

Jahoda, G. (1969). *The Psychology of Superstition*, Penguin, London.

ones, R. G. (1968). *A Factored Measure of Ellis' Irrational Belief System*, PhD Thesis, Texas Technological College.

Kallmann, F. J. (1960). 'Heredity and eugenics', *American Journal of Psychiatry*, **116**, 577.

Kelly, G. (1955). *The Psychology of Personal Constructs*, Norton, New York.

Korzybski, A. (1933). *Science and Sanity*, Lancaster Press, Lancaster, Pa.

Lazarus, A. A. (1971). *Behavior Therapy and Beyond*, McGraw-Hill, New York.

Lazarus, A. A. (1973). 'The BASIC ID' Paper presented at the Annual Meeting of the New York State Psychological Association, New York City, April 14.

Leitenberg, H., Agras, S., Butz, R., and Wincze, J. (1971). 'Relationship between heart rate and behavioral changes during the treatment of phobias', *Journal of Abnormal Psychology*, **78**, 59.

Lévi-Strauss, C. (1962). *La Pensée Sauvage*, Plon, Paris.

Lidz, T., Cornelison, M. S. S., Terry, C., and Pleca, S. (1958). 'Intrafamilial environment of the schizophrenic patient. II. The transmission of irrationality', *Archives of Neurology and Psychiatry*, **79**, 305.

Litvak, S. B. (1969a). 'A comparison of two brief group behavior therapy techniques on the reduction of avoidance behavior', *Psychological Record*, **19**, 329.

Litvak, S. B. (1969b). 'Attitude change by stimulus exposure', *Psychological Reports*, **25**, 391.

Lovaas, O. I. (1971). 'Certain comparisons between psychodynamic and behavioristic approaches to treatment', *Psychotherapy*, **8**, 175.

MacDonald, A. P., and Games, R. A. (1972). 'Ellis' irrational values', *Rational Living*, 7(2), 25.

Maes, W. R., and Heimann, R. A. (1970). *The Comparison of Three Approaches to the Reduction of Test Anxiety in High School Students*, U.S. Department of Health, Education and Welfare, Washington.

Marcia, J. E., Rubin, B. M., and Efran, J. S. (1969). 'Systematic desensitization: expectancy change or counterconditioning?', *Journal of Abnormal Psychology*, **74**, 382.

Marks, I. M. (1971). 'Recent advances in the treatment of phobic obsessive–compulsive and sexual disorders', Paper presented at the Second Annual Conference on Behavior Modification, Los Angeles, October 9.

Masters, W. H., and Johnson, V. E. (1970). *Human Sexual Inadequacy*, Little, Brown, Boston.

Maultsby, M. C., Jr. (1971a). 'Systematic written homework in psychotherapy', *Psychotherapy*, **8**, 195.

Maultsby, M. C., Jr. (1971b). 'Rational–emotive imagery', *Rational Living*, 6(1), 24.

Meehl, P. (1962). 'Schizotaxia, schizotype, and schizoprenia', *American Psychologist*, **17**, 827.

Meichenbaum, D. H. (1971). *Cognitive Factors in Behaviour Modification: Modifying what Clients say to Themselves*, University of Waterloo, Waterloo.

Miller, N. E. (1969). 'Learning of visceral and glandular responses', *Science*, **163**, 34.

Mitchell, K. R., and Mitchell, D. M. (1971). 'Behavior therapy in the treatment of migraine', *Journal of Psychosomatic Research*, **15**, 137.

Murray, H. A. (1951). 'Some basic psychological assumptions and conceptions', *Dialectica*, **5**, 266.

Nisbett, R. E., and Schacter, S. (1966). 'Cognitive manipulation of pain', *Journal of Experimental and Social Psychology*, **2**, 227.

Perlman, G. (1972). 'Change in self and ideal self-concept congruence of beginning psychotherapists', *Journal of Clinical Psychology*, **28**, 404.

Pitkin, W. B. (1932). *A Short Introduction to the History of Human Stupidity*, Simon and Schuster, New York.

Platt, J., and Spivak, G. (1972). 'Problem-solving thinking of psychiatric patients', *Journal of Consulting and Clinical Psychology*, **39**, 148.

Rimm, D. C., and Madeiros, D. C. (1970). 'The role of muscle relaxation in participant modeling', *Behavior Research and Therapy*, **8**, 127.

Ritter, B. (1968). 'The group desensitization of children's snake phobias using vicarious and contact desensitization procedures', *Behavior Research and Therapy*, **6**, 1.

Rokeach, M. (1968). *Beliefs, Attitudes and Values*, Jossey-Bass, San Francisco.

Rosenthal, D. (1970). *Genetic Theory and Abnormal Behavior*, McGraw-Hill, New York.

Rosenthal, D., and Kety, S. S. (Eds.) (1968). *The Transmission of Schizophrenia*, Pergamon, Elmsford, New York.

Rosnow, R. L., and Robinson, E. J. (Eds.) (1967). *Experiments in Persuasion*, Academic Press, New York.

Rotter, J. E., Chance, J., and Phares, E. J. (Eds.) (1972). *Application of Social Learning Theory of Personality*, Holt, Rinehart and Winston, New York.

Rutner, I., and Bugle, C. (1969). 'An experimental procedure for the modification of psychotic behavior', *Journal of Consulting and Clinical Psychology*, **33**, 651.

Schacter, S., and Singer, J. E. (1962). 'Cognitive, social and physiological determinants of emotional state', *Psychological Review*, **69**, 379.

Sharma, K. L. (1970). *A Rational Group Therapy Approach to Counselling Anxious Underachievers*, Thesis, University of Alberta.

Singer, J. L. (1968). 'Sex and violence on the screen: catharsis or stimulant', *New York State Psychologist*, **16**, 19.

Skinner, B. F. (1972). *Beyond Freedom and Dignity*, Knopf, New York.

Slater, E., and Cowie, V. (1971). *Psychiatry and Genetics*, Oxford University Press, London.

Sloane, R. B. (1969). 'The converging paths of behavior therapy and psychotherapy', *American Journal of Psychiatry*, **125**, 586.

Sydel, A. (1972). *A Study to Determine the Effects of Emotional Education on Fifth Grade Children*, M. A. Thesis, Queens College.

Tabori, P. (1959). *The Natural Science of Stupidity*, Chilton, Philadelphia.

Tabori, P. (1961). *The Art of Folly*, Chilton, Philadelphia.

Thorne, F. C. (1973). 'Eclectic psychotherapy', in R. J. Corstini (Ed.), *Current Psychotherapies*, Peacock, Itasca, Illinois, pp. 445–86.

Trexler, L. D., and Karst, T. O. (1972). 'Rational–emotive therapy, pacebo, and no-treatment effects on public speaking anxiety', *Journal of Abnormal Psychology*, **79**, 60.

Trexler, L. D., and Karst, T. O. (1973). 'Further validation for a new measure of irrational cognitions', *Journal of Personality Assessment*, **37**, 120.

Valins, S., and Ray, A. A. (1967). 'Effect of cognitive desensitization on avoidance behavior', *Journal of Personality and Social Psychology*, **7**, 345.

Velten, E. C. (1968). 'A laboratory task for induction of mood states', *Behavior Research and Therapy*, **6**, 473.

Wine, J. (1971). 'Test anxiety and direction of attention', *Psychological Bulletin*, **76**, 92.

Zajonc, R. B. (1968). 'Attitudinal effects of mere exposure', *Journal of Personality and Social Psychology*, **9**, Part 2, Monograph.

10

PSYCHOANALYTIC
PSYCHOTHERAPY

Sidney Crown

Everyone contributing to this book is, to some extent, exhibiting a false self. Cast as 'psychoanalytical' psychotherapist, 'behavioural' psychotherapist, 'rational–emotive' psychotherapist or what have you, we obey the Editor, our puppet master, and play our tune. This is justified because each author is playing a tune central to his psychotherapeutic value-system. But, first, I fear that if our actual performances were videotaped and rated by a number of outside judges (ignorant of what types of therapy we were 'doing') they might embarrass us by not assigning us 'correctly'. There is, I think, far greater overlap between different approaches than we admit. Secondly, in terms of the tumultuous social–cultural, political and economic changes taking place in Western industrial society, psychotherapistis of all approaches can only remain profoundly modest, perhaps saddened, at how little they are able to alleviate human misery. Further, it is more and more clear that any psychotherapy, while appropriate for one area of human psychological disturbance, is valueless or even harmful in others; conversely, there may be a form of psychotherapy more appropriate than one's own. I welcome the format of this book, therefore, because it forces us to outline our therapeutic philosophy and method as clearly as we are able around a number of basic issues and it encourages us to state our doubts.

Psychoanalytic Psychotherapy

Psychoanalytic psychotherapy takes its theoretical core and its practical techniques from psychoanalysis. The major changes are in the greater activity of the therapist, the frequency with which the patient is seen and the length of treatment. One to three sessions per week for between six months and two years, in the writer's opinion, is likely to be the time-span of the psychoanalytic psychotherapy of the future.

Theory

The theoretical principles of psychoanalytic psychotherapy are outlined succinctly by Rapaport and Gill (1959). There are five principles: dynamic, economic, structural, developmental and adaptive.

By dynamic is meant a theory which is drive-based. Most personality theories postulate a motivational component but psychoanalysis is unusual in the detail with which it describes drive development, in its emphasis on two major drives, sexuality and aggression, in the importance attached to early drive development (infantile sexuality) and in the suggestion that the drives are biologically based although their expression is environmentally determined.

The clearest and most clinically apposite account of psychoanalytic drive theory is that of Erikson (1965). He postulates that, during early development, sexuality and aggression involve successively and are expressed through the mouth (oral phase), the sphincters (anal phase) and the genitals (phallic phase). In each of these phases a characteristic psychological conflict takes place. The conflict of the oral phase is between the development of basic trust *versus* mistrust; of the anal phase between the achievement of autonomy (over bowel and bladder control) *versus* self-doubt; and in the phallic phase between initiative (in relation to the child's relationship with its parents) *versus* guilt. In each of these phases too there are characteristic relationships with important caretaking figures: the dependency of the oral phase is replaced by the conflict for autonomy in the anal phase and the attachment to the parent of the opposite sex and conflict with the parent of the same sex in the phallic–oedipal phase. The later vicissitudes of drive development (latency, adolescence, adulthood), important though these are, are accorded less weight in psychoanalytic drive theory because it is considered that the fundamentals of the personality are established in the early years.

From the clinical point of view, drive theory is relevant because a patient is assessed for strength of drive and for negotiation, successfully or less successfully, of the early stages of psychosexual development. Excessive attachment (fixation) to a particular phase may lead to a return to that phase when under stress (regression). Personality traits, symptoms and inhibitions are examined for clues as to the patient's psychosexual (drive) development.

The economic principle is a quantitative principle involving the concept of psychic energy, its expression, blocking, deflection, transmuting. An important subsidiary concept is that of 'cathexis': this involves the putative investment of energy in persons or things of psychological significance to the patient ('objects'). A related concept is 'narcissism'. This concerns the amount of energy with which the individual invests his own identity or self compared with that which he has available for objects outside himself. An appropriate balance is relevant to psychoanalytic psychotherapy because a patient must have the ability both to relate to the therapist and to persons and things outside himself (e.g. spouse, children, job).

The structural principle in psychoanalysis uses a tripartite model—of id (drive), ego and superego (conscience). Drive has been discussed. The ego is a structure closest in conceptualization to the non-psychoanalytic concepts of 'personality' or 'identity'. Its task is to help the organism's adaptation to the pressures of the drives, the real (outside) world and the conscience. It has at its command from earliest days the basic cognitive modalities—perception, learning, memory, motility, speech—and also certain measures to deal with anxiety. These are the defence mechanisms (see next section: Technique).

The superego or conscience develops as the ego's co-control component in the personality. It develops as a viable entity during the conflicts of the phallic–oedipal period and expresses itself both in normal guidelines to conduct acceptable to an individual and also, in normality and pathology, as feelings of guilt. A further concept based on the structural principle is that of mental conflict. Both intra-psychic conflict between component structures and extra-psychic conflict between the whole personality and the outside world constitute an important part of the human condition. The normal person possesses a frustration tolerance able to deal with the average stresses of life. Psychoneurosis represents an adaptation which is partially successful in that reality sense is preserved although the person suffers from a subjectively unpleasant symptom (anxiety, phobia, depression, hysterical conversion, obsession). If there is more or less permanent skew to the whole personality this represents a personality disorder (e.g. sociopathic personality).

The developmental principle states that the present can be understood in terms of the past. 'Psychic determinism' is important here; thus an 'unaccountable' choice of career or spouse or an impetuous decision can be seen as a comprehensible outcome given sufficient bio-psycho-social background knowledge of the person.

The principle of adaptation states that behaviour is in part related to adaptation to the world, both its physical and human aspects. For psychoanalytic psychotherapy, adaptation or maladaptation to human relationships, particularly to those with the opposite sex, are a frequent source of disturbance and suffering.

Psychoanalysis has been criticized both from outside (Hinde, 1960) and from within (Rosenblatt and Thickstun, 1970) for its theoretical reliance on the concept of psychic energy, useful though this is clinically in understanding the vicissitudes, of drive, the structure and function of 'defence', 'blocks' to personal fulfilment, etc. The developmental and adaptive principles are not energy-based concepts, but the dynamic, economic and structural principles rest heavily on the concept of psychic energy. Extensive revision is needed to bring this area of theory into line with advances in physiological and psychological knowledge. Rosenblatt and Thickstun (1970) in particular have made a systematic attempt to do this and to restate these metapsychological principles in terms of the concepts of information theory, learning and contemporary neurophysiology.

Technique

The clinical tools of psychoanalytic psychotherapy can best be discussed in the order of their appearance in a developing therapeutic interaction. These are: free association, transference, defence, interpretation and working through. The basic interaction between patient and psychoanalytic therapist is through the patient's free associations. He is asked to say what comes into his mind so far as possible without conscious selection of topics. It is, of course, impossible not to 'select' topics; the mind does not function as a computer programmed to draw at random from its memory and emotion's store. Following from the theoretical principles previously outlined and particularly from the idea of psychic determinism, the thoughts and feelings that occur to the patient as he free associates and the order in which these present are taken by the psychoanalytic psychotherapist to say something of significance about the patient and his problems. One of the possible effects of a patient's working with therapists of different age, sex, social background, etc., is not so much to effect the final result of therapy but to change the order in which events occur in a patient's associations. An example might be the early or later appearance of a homosexual conflict if the therapist is a man compared with if it is a woman. Another relevance of the free-association technique is that, compared with other psychotherapies, particularly the behavioural psychotherapies, the major responsibility for choosing topics for discussion or not topic (silence) rests with the patient. Psychoanalytic psychotherapy using free association is diametrically different from an individual psychotherapy such as Gestalt psychotherapy or group techniques such as psychodrama, where the emphasis is on the expression by doing (gesture, action, drama) rather than saying.

Transference means that from an early stage in psychoanalytic psychotherapy the patient will feel about and interact with the therapist in a way in which he or she has felt about significant figures in the past. The concept of transference is central to psychoanalytic psychotherapy and is the technical method most typical of it in contrast to the majority of other therapies. In clinical terms, the therapist attempts to show that a piece of behaviour such as an association, an emotion or an expressive gesture or other non-verbal communication simultaneously represents something of significance in the relationship with the therapist, of significance in the current (extra-therapeutic) life of the patient and of significance in the past. This tripartite understanding is felt to lead to increased insight and behavioural modification. Transference manifestations may make their appearance early in therapy or later. Classical psychoanalysis, by its emphasis on the passivity of therapist, encourages a deep transference (transference neurosis). Psychoanalytic psycotherapy, with less frequent sessions and greater activity of the therapist, while using the transference as a tool of central therapeutic importance does not encourage the development of a transference neurosis. The emphasis on transference in psychoanalytic psychotherapy has fairly been criticized because it directs excessive attention to the relationship between the patient and the therapist and minimizes the importance of significant other relationships in the patient's life, particularly family relationships.

The theoretical concept of the triadic personality structure (id, ego, superego) leads directly to the clinical concept of coping or defence mechanisms. These are mental mechanisms at the service of the ego whose function is to help the organism to adapt to stress, whether this stress arises internally (from the drives or from the superego) or externally (from the outside world). Defence mechanisms include repression, denial, projection, reaction formation, isolation of affect, intellectualization and others. The range of these defences together with their balance and effectiveness is taken to characterize the various personality styles (hysterical, obessional, paranoid, etc.) as well as broad clinical groupings, for example 'psychoneurotic', 'psychotic' or 'personality disorder'. In the course of the psychotherapeutic process it is postulated that the defences show themselves initially by the patient experiencing a block to his free associations. This is due to 'resistance'. Resistance may, firstly, be related to unacknowledged feelings for the therapist (transference resistance). Secondly, resistance may relate to arousal of the defences characteristic of the personality: thus the hysteric tends to repress or deny; the obsessional to intellectualize, isolate affect or use magical rituals to 'undo' an intrusive aggressive or sexual thought or feeling; the paranoid tends to project. Thirdly, resistance may relate to superego arousal (guilt). An important clinical phenomenon relating to superego arousal is the 'negative therapeutic reaction'. In this, as a patient appears to be improving clinically or when termination of therapy is discussed with him, he becomes ill again. This relates to a paradoxical fear of enjoying the gratification of personality fulfilment or freedom from symptoms because such pleasure arouses guilty feelings which need to be assuaged by clinical relapse and further punishment. The negative therapeutic reaction tends to occur in persons with a punitive conscience; the commonest clinical groupings are depression and obsessive–compulsive neurosis.

Interpretation means that at certain stages in the psychotherapeutic process the therapist aims to make the patient aware of facets of his mental functioning of which he was not aware prior to the interpretation. Thus he will, when he sees evidence from the patient's communications, interpret any of the phenomena described above: transference, defences or negative therapeutic reaction. The interpretation of dreams is, like transference, unique to psychoanalytic psychotherapy. The dream described by the patient ('manifest' dream) is interpreted (translated) in terms of how it relates to conflicts of the present to conflicts in infancy, for example to current interpersonal difficulties' to infantile problems in the same area (oedipal conflict).

It is not clear what factors are necessary to achieve personality change with the various psychotherapies. Increased insight or selfawareness seems an essential part of all of them including psychoanalytic psychotherapy. Some form of changed behaviour also seems to be necessary. On the whole it is not enough to achieve change only in thought or speech. The psychotherapies could, interestingly, be classified and rated according to the role they assign to altered behaviour both at the end of treatment and during treatment. Psychoanalytic psychotherapists tend to be suspicious of alteration in behaviour that occurs early in treatment. Terms such as 'acting out' or 'flight into health' are used. Acting out means carrying out an action as a defence instead of analysing the unconscious source of the action with the therapist. Thus acting out in the transference might apply to a patient who at some level of awareness senses unwanted negative feelings to the therapist but who, instead of allowing himself to grasp and verbalize the negative feelings, precipitates a quarrel with his boss at work or with his wife. 'Flight into health' is applied to a patient who notes minor alterations in mental conflict (e.g. lessened depression) and leaves treatment rather than pursues more basic personality change. Despite these *caveats* a change in behaviour is considered necessary in psychoanalytic psychotherapy. The technical term 'working through' applies to the patient who understands the infantile basis for a neurotic symptom or behavioural inhibition and then practises this altered behaviour in his life outside therapy.

This relative emphasis on work done within therapy before carrying the change into the outside world contrasts, for example, with certain of the behavioural psychotherapies, for example assertiveness training, in which the altered behaviour is the therapy; or with Gestalt therapy where the patient, talking, say, about a disliked ornament, is encouraged by the therapist to 'be' the ornament and to describe his (the ornament's) feelings. Similarly, encounter groups and psycho- and sociodramatic techniques encourage clients to do things as the essential part of the therapeutic process. 'Working through' or 'practise' is a therapeutic parameter that requires systematic research.

Therapist and Patient

In psychoanalytical psychotherapy the relationship between therapist and client is that of doctor and patient. Aspects of the classical psychoanalytical situation are preserved: there is a relative lack of intrusion of the analyst's personality and the therapy is disciplined in that the length and the time of sessions are fixed and changes in these, either by the therapist or the patient, are discouraged. The patient may lie supine on a couch with the therapist sitting behind him and out of his range of vision. This technique is unique to psychoanalytical psychotherapy and is an attempt to produce conditions of relative sensory deprivation for the patient so that he has to rely to a greater extent on his feelings, conflicts, emotions and difficulties and is absorbed relatively less with extrinsic aspects of the therapeutic situation such as the consulting room or the therapist's clothes, appearance, manner, etc.

The Complaint

The theoretical structure of psychoanalysis has a direct relationship to the way in which the patient's complaint is formulated. This in turn relates to assumptions about the patient's suitability for psychotherapy and the way treatment should be managed. It relates also to the 'ideal' conception of normality implied in the psychoanalytic concept of 'cure'. Psychoanalytic psychotherapy makes a tripartite formulation of the complaint: symptoms, personality structure and interpersonal relationships. Symptoms are described as in general psychiatry (anxiety, phobia, depression, hysterial conversion, obsessions) but, especially as compared with all forms of behavioural psychotherapy, their importance is relatively unaccentuated. Also, psychoanalytical psychotherapists regard the presence of certain symptoms as indicative of positive features of the personality. Great suspicion would, for example, be aroused by a patient who said that he had never experienced depression, as this would be taken to imply that the patient was out of touch with his inner feelings. Formulations about the personality in which symptoms are embedded follow from the considerations of the previous section: thus sexual development is expressed in terms of progress towards genital primacy; aggression is examined to see whether or not there is excessive evidence of early ('pre-genital') expression such as touring, manipulating passive–aggressive interpersonal relationships characteristic of the 'anal' phase. Drive development is also examined for evidence (from symptoms, personality traits, interpersonal relationships) of excessive fixation (hold-up) to early phases of development or of return, under stress, to an earlier phase (regression). Ego functioning is examined for the intactness of 'conflict-free' functions such as perception, learning, memory, etc., and more particularly in terms of the form, effectiveness and balance of the defence structure. Superego functioning is also looked at with a view to the balance between the guiding functions of the normal conscience as compared with the punitive, punishing, guilt-producing functions of the 'harsh' superego. Finally, the relationships between the patient and people around him are examined in relation to the patient's ability to sustain these, especially with the opposite sex.

This formulation leads to a number of assumptions about 'complaints'. The earlier the basis for the disturbance the greater its severity. Thus paranoid attitudes, feeding difficulties (anorexia nervosa, obesity), dependency problems, obessional difficulties, disorders of the patient's self-image ('narcissism'), clinging ('anaclitic'), depression, drug dependency, all these relate to problems laid down in the earliest years and are regarded as severe complaints. The converse follows: late disturbances are regarded as less severe. Thus disturbances in heterosexual relationships are considered to relate to the phallic–oedipal phase (3–6 years) of development with a relatively good prognosis, as with conditions whose basis is established later than infancy, for example, latency (5–12 years), adolescence or young adulthood. Other assumptions are also made about the relation of the complaint to the ego structure. Thus relatively crude defences such as projection or denial are assessed negatively, as are behaviour patterns such as impulsiveness because this suggests a defect in ego strength.

From these considerations about the formulation of the complaint assumptions follow about the appropriateness or otherwise of psychoanalytic psychotherapy. Thus late-onset problems involving interpersonal relationships and good ego strength will be felt to be suitable. Although many psychoanalysts feel that there is a linear relationship between severity of complaint and frequency of psychotherapeutic sessions there is a paradox because most psychoanalytic psychotherapists feel that if a complaint is too severe or too early or involves too inadequate an ego structure then such a patient is not suitable for 'deep' psychotherapy. A fundamental problem, underlined by Gelder (1972), is that therapeutic effectiveness has not been proved to relate to increased 'depth' or frequency of sessions. This is an area of psychoanalytic psychotherapy in urgent needs of systematic research.

Cure

Psychoanalytic psychotherapists frequently fail to specify their criteria of 'cure'. In this respect psychoanalytic psychotherapy compares unfavourably with behaviour therapy where the symptom is the illness, but also with brief psy-

194

chotherapy where a considerable effort is made to specify the complaint precisely, to hypothesize the underlying aetiology using as simple a psychodynamic formulation as possible and to explicate the criteria of cure. In any system of psychotherapy criteria of cure relate to the therapist's concept of normality. Of all the psychotherapies discussed in this book psychoanalytic psychotherapy is probably the one that most depends on an 'ideal' definition of normality. Thus Erikson (1965) suggests that 'genitality' should include mutuality of orgasm with a loved partner of the other sex with whom one is able and willing to share a mutual trust and with whom one is able and willing to regulate the cycles of work, procreation and recreation so as to secure satisfactory development for the offspring. I have previously reviewed various criteria of cure in psychotherapy (Crown, 1968). While all psychotherapies specify symptomatic criteria (relief of symptoms) and better adjustment in important life areas (work, social relationships and sexuality) the particular insistence of psychoanalytic psychotherapy is that there should be some evidence of psychodynamic change. This may include the resolution of conflicts between components of the tripartite structure of the personality; progress towards psychosexual maturity ('genitality'); evidence that ego strength has increased so that it is less vulnerable to, and more capable of controlling stresses from the drives, the external world and the conscience; evidence that the balance within the superego has been shifted towards the normal guiding functions of the conscience and away from the harsh, punishing functions leading to excessive guilt; and evidence that interpersonal relationships have improved, in particular with the opposite sex. Some psychoanalysts, as, for example, Freud et al. (1965) and Freeman (1972), have developed detailed psychodynamic 'profiles' suitable for rating patients of all ages and all degrees of severity of disturbance. The rating of complex changes via the intermediary of hypothetical constructs (defence, superego, etc.) is, however, difficult and the inter-rater reliability problem and the problem of inference are as yet unsolved (see Evaluation).

Whether 'cure' consists of social conformity or something more than this is a problem that has to be faced by all psychotherapies and all psychotherapists and is difficult to answer. Speaking personally, I would consider social conformity alone as equivalent to rehabilitation; cure would have to include some successful movement towards self-fulfilment which would not necessarily be equivalent to social conformity. Other writers such as Rapoport (1960) in relation to the therapeutic community approach have discussed the possibility that the goals of self-fulfilment and social adaptation may conflict. The anti-psychiatry movement is particularly challenging on this issue. This movement did not begin when it was 'labelled' by Cooper (1967). Some of the writers involved published their most influential work many years previously. Szasz (1962) in his Myth of Mental Illness can perhaps be regarded as the founder of the movement. Other influential writers include Frank (1961), Goffman (1968) and Laing (1967). Their work is important for psychotherapy: in particular their criticism of the behavioural engineering aspects of all psychotherapies; of the monumental detachment of many psychotherapists; of the pressure to conform, as with group therapy or the therapeutic community approach in their encouragement of 'togetherness' and discouragement of individual non-conformity. While, as with the lunatic fringe of any movement, an extreme position tends to absurdity, psychotherapists being presented as evil front men of the 'establishment', the warnings presented by this diverse movement, which has no homogeneity other than its memorable name, are salutary for orthodox psychotherapists of all approaches. Anti-psychiatrists sometimes forget, however, that anti-psychiatry of the existential do-your-own-thing variety can equally become a straitjacket, forcing a person into non-conformity where some may get most help from a structured therapy and conventional way of life.

Evaluation of Psychotherapy

Psychoanalytic psychotherapy has not been adequately evaluated; there has been less systematic attempt at evaluation than with many other forms of psychotherapy. The evaluation of psychotherapy is inextricably related to individual views on science and scientific method, on the nature of 'meaningful' questions and on how far the complex phenomena of psychotherapy can be scientifically investigated. If, as I feel, there are limits to the strictly scientific evaluation of psychotherapy, what methods can be used to establish what is 'true'? Where might it be profitable to investigate? Many contemporary psychiatrists, bored with discussions about the nature of science, have made Popper's criterion of disprovability their scientific touchstone. No theory or method which cannot lay down criteria by which it may be disproved can be regarded as scientific. This criterion is not easy to satisfy in the evaluation of psychoanalytic psychotherapy. Human behaviour and human decision-making assume the stochastic form: what comes after depends very largely on what has gone before. Any piece of behaviour has in its antecedents biological factors, psychological factors and social factors. In psychoanalytic terms, behaviour is 'overdetermined'. Human behaviour also depends on what is to come later; the paradox that the future is in the present complicates the problem of predicting behaviour, including psychotherapy behaviour. Because of this complexity the grand overall design, planned like an experiment with fertilizers and plots of land, seems most unlikely to yield dividends—even assuming that enough investigators with different approaches and varied personal philosophies could be persuaded to take part in the planning and stay the course necessary until completion.

Two recent, contrasting books, both excellent in their way, polarize present attitudes to psychotherapy research. Bergin and Strupp (1972) take a purist approach, talk with eminent researchers of diverse backgrounds and interests and, for me, succeed in making research and methodological standards impossibly high. Meltzoff and Kornreich (1970) try to salvage what is good about a piece of research even if aspects of it are open to criticism. I find their approach more productive. If this is taken to mean that psychoanalysts are slipshod in their thought, proof to the contrary may be found in a recent critical review by Wallerstein and Sampson (1971). These writers convey the awareness within psychoanalysis of the need to bring its research up to acceptable methodological standards. The problem is: what are acceptable methodological standards?

Part of the function of this book is to state problems authors believe to be unique to, or particularly relevant to, a given psychotherapy. The related problems of consensus and inference are fundamental to the evaluation of psychoanalytic psychotherapy. There can be no research progress unless there is agreement between observers on the phenomena under observation. In the particular context of consensus in psychoanalytical psychotherapy, Seitz (1966) describes a group of psychoanalysts whose basic plan of investigation was for members of the team to make independent interpretive formulations of the same psychological case material, for example, first dreams from different cases and ongoing material from a single continuous case. The group found itself unable to make adequate progress and disbanded after three years. Inference is a related problem. In addition to judging relatively simple aspects of behaviour directly (e.g. hostility), psychoanalytic psychotherapy emphasizes unconscious mental processes and is concerned with hypothetical constructs such as 'ego strength', 'punitive superego', 'defence', etc. The more inferential a concept the harder it is to rate and the lower the consensus. A number of empirical studies in this area are reported by Strupp et al. (1966), for example, judgement of the degree of inference entering into ratings of variables such as depression or anxiety (low inference) compared with working through or oral strivings (high inference). For research to be soundly grounded, precise definition of concepts is needed and evidence adduced that valid and reliable measurement or ratings can be made. Consensus and inference are two areas in which considerable future research is required.

Other suggestions emerge from a consideration of the psychotherapy research literature. Firstly, psychotherapy researchers are individualists and they should be encouraged to carry out intensive studies of careful design even if limited scope in areas of their special interest and competence. The choice is wide enough; there is as yet no proof of the relevance of even the most platitudinous of psychotherapy selection factors such as youth, intelligence and social class. This ignorance also applies to therapist variables and interactive variables. The 'new' operationism in the field of psychotherapy research must be taken seriously by psychoanalytic psychotherapy; concepts such as 'counter-transference', for example, must not be allowed to stand unchallenged and unmeasured—almost metaphysical in their complexity—but attempts must be made to develop appropriate methods for their definition and measurement. Another essential research area is the analysis of the psychotherapeutic process. One attempt at analysis of this (Crown, 1973) suggested that relationship factors, conditioning factors, insight factors and practise factors may be involved. Each of these needs minute definition, subdivision and investigation.

If it is accepted that the grand overall design is not practicable and if no individual or research team is likely to advance more than a small distance, other desiderata are needed. Two of these are replicability and cross-validation. Studies should be meticulously described so that they can be repeated. Further, a number of different methods may be used to approach a particular problem; in so complex a field consensual validation seems to me acceptable as a research method. A promising approach is the comparison of psychotherapeutic methods: psychotherapy with behaviour therapy; group psychotherapy with individual psychotherapy; marital psychotherapy with marital behaviour therapy; psychoanalytic group therapy with non-psychoanalytic group therapy. From educational research the work of Bernstein and Henderson (1969) is of relevance to psychotherapeutic practice and research. These authors have demonstrated how patterns of interaction relate to social aspects of speech which relate in turn to social class differences. It is often felt that psychoanalytical psychotherapy is unsuitable for non-middle-class patients. If this was so the mediator might well be speech habits. Psychotherapeutic research might well be advanced by a number of intensive studies of the speech habits of patients from different social classes, the speech habits of therapists, the interaction between these and the possible modifications needed in order for a middle-class therapist adequately to communicate with a working-class patient.

Psychotherapy and Society

Psychoanalytic psychotherapy and many other psychotherapies are socially 'unaware' in that they deal with the individual and 'his' problems in a consulting room. Only the therapeutic community, marital and family therapy and community-based ('peer group') therapies introduce a parameter from the outside world. This lack of a social dimension expresses itself in clinical practice and in the non-use of relevant sociological theory and concepts. Clinically, individual psychotherapists by a combination of academic instructions and supervised clinical relationships—with parents, spouse, lover, children. At the level of theory, sociological concepts are highly relevant to evaluation or treatment, for example, status, the sick role, illness behaviour, stigma, labelling, deviance (Mechanic, 1968). The individual psychotherapies also fail to pay attention to the interaction—goodness or badness of fit—between the patient–therapist dyad and the social–cultural milieu. Psychotherapy has failed to learn the lesson being learned in other fields: thus modern industrial management theory stresses interaction—the consumer is part of the organization—and, a second example, research on study difficulty in students emphasizes the transaction between the student, the institution and the social–cultural milieu (Crown et al., 1973). Psychoanalytic psychotherapy must progress towards greater social awareness; it should be concerned with, although not necessarily blindly adapted to, the socio-cultural scene.

Training and Status

As in the selection of patients for psychotherapy so in the selection of therapists it seems likely that the most important, but highly complex, variable is the psychotherapist's personality. Certain persons seem to be 'natural' psychotherapists, although it is extremely difficult to analyse what makes this so. Given a reasonably sound basic personality persons can become effective psychoanalytical psychotherapists by a combination of academic instructions and supervised clinical practice. The most controversial point concerns whether or not there should be a systematic attempt to produce psychological changes in the therapist. Formal psychoanalysis, of course, specifies personal psychoanalysis. My own feeling is that for all forms of effective psychotherapy, including the behavioural psychotherapies, some form of psychological change in the practitioner is necessary. This might be obtained through a spectrum of personal experiences of increasing complexity. For many some form of sensitivity training, such as the patient-orientated discussions called for in England–Balint type groups, may be sufficient. For other therapists brief individual psychotherapy might be helpful and for others formal psychoanalysis may be necessary; in certain individuals it is probably essential.

Professional status is a further controversial area, particularly in the relations between psychologists and psychiatrists. It seems to me that psychotherapists should work in a team where a medically qualified psychiatrist is available for the preliminary screening of patients. This is necessary because of the possibility of disguised presentation of conditions, such as 'masked' depression with suicidal impulses, unusual (e.g. pan-neurotic) presentations of early schizophrenia, and organic or metabolic conditions masquerading as anxiety or obsessionality. With these and other conditions there is a risk to the patient or client unless he is appropriately diagnosed and assigned to treatment. Psychotherapists in my opinion also need hospital back-up. Medical responsibility should not be a status quarrel but is related to training and division of labour in society at the present time.

Conclusion

Psychoanalytic psychotherapy is not, in my opinion, going to be seen off stage by newer techniques of psychotherapy despite the huffing and puffing particularly of therapies based on learning theories. For better or worse all the psychotherapies are severely limited in the degree to which they are capable of modifying man's aberrant behaviour or sweetening his experience. Every one of the psychotherapies needs, through research, to explore to the full its strengths and its weaknesses. What really is important: a particular therapeutic process? the therapist? the patient's personality? or the interaction between these? Clarifying the answers to these questions is the overall research task for the next decade. It will not be solved, I think, by attempting a grand overall design but by a number of researchers doing their research 'thing' and by others approaching the same problems from different angles (consensual validation).

Psychoanalytic theory chiefly needs to reformulate its economic principle so as to replace outmoded 'energy' concepts with concepts expressed in terms of learning, information theory and contemporary neurophysiology. Psychoanalytic clinical techniques must continue to attack basic problems of consensus and inference so that, for example, quantitative observational techniques such as videotaped interviews can be used to validate (or refute) theoretical constructs such as transference, resistance, defence, interpretation, guilt, etc. From this will come increased understanding of the psychoanalytic psychotherapeutic process and more precise demonstration of the criteria of cure, particularly evidence of psychodynamic personality change. Psychoanalytic psychotherapy must also include the social–cultural dimension wholeheartedly and admit the relevance of sociological concepts such as role, stigma, reference groups, illness behaviour, etc.

Psychoanalytic psychotherapy remains unrepentent in casting the patient in the role of patient and the therapist as therapist; mutual respect and discipline are expected in practical arrangements; and, so far as the training of the therapist is concerned, some opportunity for increased self-understanding is expected whether by individual psychotherapy, group therapy or sensitivity training.

References

Bergin, A. E., and Strupp, H. H. (1972). *Changing Frontiers in the Science of Psychotherapy*, Aldine, Chicago.

Bernstein, B., and Henderson, D. (1969). 'An approach to the study of language and socialization', in L. Hudson (Ed)., *The Ecology of Human Intelligence*, Penguin, Harmondsworth, pp. 159–76.

Cooper, D. (1967). *Psychiatry and Anti-psychiatry*, Tavistock, London.

Crown, S. (1968). 'Criteria for the measurement of outcome in psychotherapy', *Brit. J. Med. Psychol.*, **41**, 31.

Crown, S. (1973). 'Psychotherapy', *Brit. J. Hosp. Med.*, **9**, 355.

Crown, S., Lucas, C. J., and Supramaniam, S. (1973). 'The delineation and measurement of study difficulty in University students', *Brit. J. Psychiat.*, **122**, 381.

Erikson, E. H. (1965). *Childhood and Society*. Penguin, Harmondsworth.

Frank, J. D. (1961). *Persuasion and Healing*, Johns Hopkins Press, Baltimore.

Freeman, T. (1972). 'Anna Freud's metapsychological profile: its use in the management and treatment of schizophrenic and schizophreniform psychoses', in D. Rubinstein and Y. O. Alanen(Eds.), *Psychotherapy of Schizophrenia*, Excerpta Medica, Amsterdam, pp. 69–76.

Freud, A., Nagera, H., and Freud, W. E. (1965). 'A metapsychological assessment of the adult personality', *Psychoanal. Stud. Child.*, **20**, 9.

Gelder, M. G. (1972). 'Individual psychotherapy', in B. M. Mandelbrote and M. G. Gelder (Eds.), *Psychiatric Aspects of Medical Practice*, Staples Press, London pp. 54–69.

Goffman, E. (1968). *Asylums*, Penguin, Harmondsworth.

Hinde, R. A. (1960). 'Energy models of motivation', *Symp. Soc. Exper. Biol.*, **14**, 199.

Laing, R. D. (1967). *The Politics of Experience*, Penguin, Harmondsworth.

Mechanic, D. ('1968). *Medical Sociology*, Free Press, New York.

Meltzoff, J., and Kornreich, M. (1970). *Research in Psychotherapy*, Atherton Press, New York.

Rapaport, D., and Gill, M. M. (1959). 'The points of view and assumptions of matapsychology', *Internat. J. Psychoanal.*, **40**, 153.

Rapoport, R. (1960). *Community as Doctor*, Tavistock, London.

Rosenblatt, A. D., and Thickstun, J. T. (1970). 'A study of the concept of psychic energy', *Internat. J. Psychoanal.*, **51**, 265.

Seitz, P. F. D. (1966). 'The consensus problem in Psychoanalytic Research', in L. A. Gottschalk and A. H. Auerbach (Eds.), *Methods of Research in Psychotherapy*, Appleton-Century-Crofts, New York, pp. 209–25.

Strupp, H. H., Chassan, J. B., and Ewing, J. A. (1966). 'Toward the longitudinal study of the Psychotherapeutic Process', in L. A. Gottschalk and A. H. Auerbach (Eds.), *Methods of Research in Psychotherapy*, Appleton-Century-Crofts, New York, pp. 361–400.

Szasz, T. S. (1962). *The Myth of Mental Illness*, Secker and Warburg, London.

Wallerstein, R. S., and Sampson, H. (1971). 'Issues in research in the Psychoanalytic Process', *Internat. J. Psychoanal.*, **52**, 11.

11

PSYCHOANALYTIC BRIEF PSYCHOTHERAPY AND SCIENTIFIC METHOD

D. H. Malan

The Nature of Scientific Method and its Application to Psychotherapy

The field of psychotherapy abounds with scientific problems, philosophical, theoretical and practical, most of which appear to remain as unresolved now as they were 20 years ago. In descending order of generality we may list the following.

What is the scientific status of concepts used in human psychology, particularly those of the psychodynamic school?

Are the rules of evidence appropriate to this field in some way different from those in more exact fields such as the physical sciences?

How can scientific method be applied to the investigation of psychotherapy?

How is it possible to strike an appropriate balance between subjective and objective evidence?

Does psychotherapy help people to a greater degree than life experience in general?

If so, whom does it help, under what circumstances, by what methods?

What, if any, are the therapeutically effective factors?

Are such factors specific to any given technique, or general and non specific?

Can the great length of psychoanalytic psychotherapy be reduced?

If so, how do the patients, the techniques and the outcome differ from those of longer methods?

I shall start by stating my own position on the more general of these questions and go on to describe some work that has a bearing on all of them.

It seems to me that philosophers of science may become somewhat divorced from reality, first through taking physics as their main example, and then by exaggerating and idealizing the rigour and exactness even to be found in physics. Karl Popper himself, who takes most of his examples from physics, does not entirely avoid this pitfall. The statement that the essence of a scientific theory is not that it should be *provable* but *refutable* is a move towards the de-idealization of science and a brilliant piece of insight; but the de-idealization needs to be carried further. Most things in the world are blurred, and 'refutable' is a relative term. Certain theories about the past, for example evolution of continental drift, do not seem to me truly refutable short of the invention of a time machine—and if this were possible then they would be provable as well. Thus the statement, often heard, that the theories of dynamic psychology are in some way special because they are not refutable seems to me to be based on a misconceived view of other sciences.

One author who never fell into this kind of pitfall and saw into the heart of the matter was the late Helen Sargent of the Menninger Foundation. In one of her papers (Sargent, 1961, p. 100) she quotes a long passage, part of which is reproduced with slight modification below:

> It is an obvious fact that no one has ever seen a(n) . . . ., no one has ever weighed a(n) . . ., felt a(n) . . . ., or in fact made any observations whatsoever of a(n) . . . .. What we have seen are . . . ., ..., ..., ...

She says that it would be easy for a psychologist to fill in the first four blanks with such a word as 'ego' and the last four with such words as 'symptoms', 'attitudes', etc. She then springs her surprise—the passage was in fact written by Dancoff, a physicist, the word in the first four blanks was 'electron' and those in the last four start with 'scintillations on a screen'. She continues, 'The ego, then is in powerful company'.

This is a crucial point. The concepts of dynamic psychology are surely inferences from observations or ways of understanding observations, ready to be modified in the light of fresh evidence or to be abandoned when the lose their usefulness, in the same way as concepts in any other science.

Similarly, there are many elements often thought to be essential to scientific method which may of necessity be absent owing to the nature of the subject under study and sometimes simply because of chance. Whether or not *prediction* is possible may depend on whether most of the observations have been made before anyone thinks of an explanation for them. If all the relevant observations have been made already, there is nothing to predict and theory-building has to be retrospective. *Experiment* is not always possible—it is certainly much less possible in, say, evolution than in particle physics, simply because of the time-scale. *Crucial experiments* may be even less possible, and if they are not possible no one should be discouraged from making observations. One of the most frequent ways in which science advances is by the convergence of marginal evidence. Another may be called by a most unpretentious name such as the 'crossword puzzle principle'—which is based essentially on no more than *internal consistency*. The logic of internal consistency is essentially circular: in a crossword puzzle, the fact that a second word fits in with the first convinces the solver not only that the second word is likely to be correct but the first word also. Enough of such interlocking circular arguments result in an overall pattern that is highly convincing—until one remembers the type of prize crossword set in the newspapers, to which there may be several thousand convincing solutions only one of which is correct. Yet often the search for this kind of convincing pattern is the only logic that we can use.

I often wish that philosophers of science knew more about the history of chemistry than of physics and I hope I may be forgiven the following diversion, which illustrates some of these basic points in the clearest possible way. It concerns what is perhaps the most fundamental concept in all chemistry, the periodic table of the elements.

In the early part of the nineteenth century there was no crucial experiment possible by which the atomic weights of the chemical elements could be determined. The reason was simply that there were always more unknowns than equations. Nevertheless, with the help of various devices, which included the *assumption of simplicity*, *empirical laws* which seemed to hold in spite of the total absence of any theoretical explanations for them (and to which there were equally unexplained exceptions) and arguments of an *intuitive* kind based on *subjective* views about the resemblance between one element and another, a system of atomic weights was built up which had an internal consistency and received general acceptance. It is worth emphasizing the *logically indefensible* nature of the principles used to reach this end—yet these are principles that are used universally in science when more rigorous methods are not available. Put in another way, *in*ductive methods have to be used where *de*ductive methods fail. Then in 1869 a Russian chemist, Mendeleyev, discovered that if the elements were arranged in a table in ascending order of atomic weights a 'periodicity' emerged in which similar properties began to recur in the same order after a certain number of elements had been listed. Yet, in order to preserve this effect, he had to cheat in various ways—he had to change the periodic number to suit the data, he has to leave gaps, he sometimes had to put more than one element into a single place in the table and in two places he had to put a pair of elements in reverse order. This kind of retrospective juggling with data can hardly be described as the most convincing of scientific methods—more modern analogies could be found in the work of the Baconians or the prophecy of the Great Pyramid, where similarly the unit of measurement had to be changed halfway through—and it is hardly surprising that Mendeleyev's ideas did not find a ready acceptance. Yet the odds against his pattern being due to chance (though obviously even now no one could give a significance level) seem to me to be enormous. This was an example of the 'crossword puzzle principle' *par excellence*. And then Mendeleyev made a bold move: where there were gaps in his table he *predicted* that new elements would be discovered and by simple interpolation he predicted their properties. The final acceptance of his table came when these predictions were fufilled. Yet *such predictions would have been impossible if these new elements had already been discovered* and then the crossword puzzle principle would have been all that anyone had to rely on.

We now realize, of course, the meaning of every detail of Mendeleyev's complicated pattern, almost all of which can be *restrospectively predicted* by calculations in quantum physics.

To sum up, the essence of science is surely no more than the dispassionate examination of evidence, the seeking of patterns, the consideration of all possible explanations and the testing of these by seeking fresh evidence—where this is possible—by methods as rigorous as the situation will allow.

All these considerations have a particular relevance to research in psychotherapy, because they mean that no one should be ashamed of lack of 'refutability' in our theories, lack of exactness or objectivity in our observations, lack of properly controlled experiments where these are not possible or lack of conclusiveness in our evidence. The assumption that such qualities are indispensable is based on an idealized and mistaken view of the nature of science. Indeed, the search for these qualities *beyond what the nature of the phenomena will allow* has in my opinion been responsible for almost total despair and withdrawal on the part of the psychodynamic school and thousands of wasted scientific papers from other schools, leading ultimately to the state of general disillusion with research described so clearly by Bergin and Strupp (1972). Only a balanced amount of exactness and objectivity, based on a realistic and commonsense view of the nature of science, can lead to any substantial advances in our field.

The History of Psychoanalysis and the Problem of Brief Psychotherapy

Anyone who has kept a garden must have observed the need to be constantly tending it. If the flowers are simply left to themselves they will be overwhelmed by other plants—in many parts of the world first by tall grasses, then by shrubs and finally by trees, and the end result after many years will be forest. This is the phenomenon known in plant ecology as 'succession' and in it we can recognize a tendency towards *increasing height* in the dominant vegetation. This tendency is driven by powerful forces and requires constant effort if it is to be successfully opposed.

What has all this to do with the subject in hand? The answer is that it illustrates a similar phenomenon in the development of psychoanalysis, namely a constant tendency towards *increasing length*. This tendency also has been driven by powerful forces. The problem in brief psychotherapy is to identify the lengthening factors and to try specifically to oppose them.

Regarded in this light, the history of psychoanalysis may be summarized as in the following passage adapted from my book on brief psychotherapy (Malan, 1963). Each of the lengthening factors, of which there are surprisingly many, is shown in italics.

The original observation, made by Joseph Breuer (incidentally, the same as the joint discoverer of the Hering–Breuer reflex in the physiology of respiration), was that hysterical symptoms could be relieved by making the patient relive, under hypnosis, painful memories and feelings that had been forgotten ('repressed'). Freud, finding that not all patients could be hypnotized, replaced this method by suggesting forcefully to the patient in the waking state that there were things that she had forgotten and could remember (then, as now, hysterical patients were usually young women). He now found, however, that suggestion was often insufficient to overcome a marked *resistance* put up by the patient against recovering these memories. He was able to bypass this difficulty when he found that if he simply asked the patient to say what came into her mind in connection with her symptoms the memories returned in a disguised and symbolized form. When he learned how to translate the disguise the memories returned undisguised. With more experience he began to realize that whatever came into the patient's mind (not necessarily in connection with her symptoms) had a bearing on the memories or on the resistance against them; he concentrated on the latter, finding that when the resistances were pointed out the memories could be recovered without any forcing. In this sequence, from hypnosis through suggestion to 'free association', the tendency for the therapist to become *increasingly passive* is clearly to be observed.

During this time a quite unexpected complication had appeared, namely that patients inevitably began to have intense feelings about the therapist. This was already present in the first case treated by Breuer—the patient fell in love with him and had a phantom pregnancy, of which he was clearly the phantom father, and so shocked him that he gave up his work altogether. Freud later discovered that such feelings could also be of other kinds, including hate. He then recognized that these were really unresolved feelings directed towards an important person, usually a parent, in the patient's past and were thus simply 'transferred' on to the therapist. If he interpreted this to the patient, the feelings could be handled without jeopardizing the therapy and could finally be resolved. He therefore referred to such feelings as *transference,* 'positive' and 'negative' for love and hate respectively. Since the resolution was almost always time-consuming, the transference became one of the most important lengthening factors.

Yet there was always present the tendency for each new technique, initially successful, to become less and less reliable. Whereas early patients seemed to be cured through the recovery of comparatively recent memories and the interpretation of the related transference feelings, later patients tended to relapse and could be cured only by uncovering further memories and transference feelings belonging to increasingly *early childhood.* Analyses were prolonged by two further phenomena: the fact that a single symptom was usually found to have its roots in many quite separate memories and feelings, each of which had to be uncovered before the symptom could be relieved (*over-determination*); and the fact that each root often had to be uncovered many times in different contexts, and not once for all, before relief was permanent (necessity for *working through*).

It was eventually recognized that early relief of symptoms was often simply due to the satisfaction of the patient's need for love provided by the analytical situation ('transference cure'). The relapse that frequently occurred at threat of termination could be reversed only by interpreting the patient's grief and anger at being abandoned (*transference at termination*) and relating this to its true source in childhood. Meanwhile the importance of transference has steadily increased. The following is now a standard pattern for an analysis: there is an initial period in which both transference and non-transference interpretations seem to be effective and everything seems to be going well (the 'analytic honeymoon'); there is then a period of resistance in which insight is often lost and interpretations that were previously effective become useless; finally there develops a state known as the *transference neurosis* in which the patient's whole illness is expressed in his relation to the therapist, on whom he often becomes extremely *dependent.* Now, to a large extent, only transference interpretations are of any value; only after this transference has been interpreted again and again and related to its true source in childhood can the situation be resolved.

In the meantime the emphasis has gradually shifted. The transference has come

206

to be regarded not as a necessary evil but as the main therapeutic tool—thus transference is welcomed and especially negative transference, since the patient's unconscious hatred is felt to be a powerful source of neurosis. Memories, especially those concerned with traumatic events, are regarded as of less importance and emphasis is now laid on the repetition of neurotic childhood patterns in the relation with the therapist and the gradual acquisition of insight into these. Finally it is held that one of the most important factors is not so much the insight itself as the actual experience of a new kind of relationship with the therapist, through which the neurotic patterns can be corrected.

It has by now become clear that the steady increase in the length of analyses is due not only to these factors in the patient but also to factors in the therapist—one of which, passivity, has already been mentioned. The whole list of lengthening factors may then be presented as follows.

Factors in the patient

1. Resistance
2. Over-determination
3. Necessity for working through
4. Roots of neurosis in early childhood
5. Transference
6. Dependence
7. Transference at termination
8. The transference neurosis

Factors in the therapist

9. A tendency towards passivity and the willingness to follow where the patient leads
10. A 'sense of timelessness' conveyed to the patient
11. Therapeutic perfectionism
12. The increasing preoccupation with ever deeper and earlier experiences

The result of all these factors has been that, whereas early analyses tended to last a few months, nowadays an analysis that lasts twice as many years is nothing remarkable.

It is clear that a rationally based technique of brief psychotherapy must be based on a conscious opposition to these factors, and the problem of brief psychotherapy is how this can be done.

The Technique of Brief Psychotherapy Seen in the Light of the Lengthening Factors

Almost all techniques of brief psychotherapy involve primarily an opposition to the four factors in the therapist and are thus based on *abandoning therapeutic perfectionism,* conveying to the patient that therapy is *time-limited, planning* a *limited aim* from the beginning and guiding the patient towards this by an *active technique* of selective attention and selective neglect. These themes, for instance, are summed up in a passage written by French in Alexander and French's classical book *Psychoanalytic Therapy* (1946):

> ... the temptation is very great merely to treat the patient's problems as he brings them to us and thus, as it were, to let the patient drift into an analysis. ... It is highly important, therefore, to outline as soon as possible a comprehensive therapeutic plan, to attempt to visualize in advance (even if only tentatively) just what we shall attempt with our patient, what we hope to accomplish. ...
> In order to do this, it is necessary, first, of course, to make a dynamic formulation of the patient's problem .... After outlining all the possibilities and rejecting those that may be dangerous or impractical he [the therapist] will outline his plans for helping the patient to achieve those that seem realizable.

In our work, Balint summarized these principles most succinctly in the words: 'Go in, do something quickly, and get out.'

The factors in the patient have always been more problematical, and of all these the most problematical is the transference. It is clear, for instance, that the transference *neurosis* must at all costs be avoided; but how this is to be done is not so clear. Should—or can—all transference be avoided or discouraged, be ignored if it develops, be diverted on to someone in the patient's current life, be interpreted only when absolutely necessary, be interpreted without fear or even be welcomed (as in full-scale analysis) as the factor most likely to lead to permanent therapeutic results? It seemed that no one knew. As will be seen, much of our thinking was based on a fear that interpretation of the transference would lead to an intensification of transference; hence on the feeling that one had to be in a hurry and make the maximum use of a very brief honeymoon period before the transference neurosis would inevitably appear and therapy would develop into an analysis.

The Tavistock Work on Brief Psychotherapy: Pilot Study

Michael Balint had a sometimes healthy and sometimes not so healthy disrespect both for the application of scientific methods to psychotherapy and for much previous work on subjects that he was investigating. As a result, anyone undertaking the task of writing up his research on brief psychotherapy was left with a mass of highly subjective clinical data on a series of patients selected by rather undisciplined natural processes without regard for questions posed or answers given by previous workers. Now one could write up such material in a purely descriptive way, in the form of 'these are the patients we treated, these are the methods we used and this is what happened'. Yet it is practically impossible to write in this way without the implication of generalizations such as 'this is the appropriate method to use in patients of this kind'. The moment this element enters, one is forced into a systematic examination of evidence; one cannot stop until every aspect of the data has been scrutinized—from methods of selection, through the problem of controls and spontaneous remission, the direction of cause and effect, the measurement of factors in patient and therapy, to the most intractable of all, namely the measurement of therapeutic outcome.

Now the point at which I started examining the data coincided with the first publication from the Psychotherapy Research Project of the Menninger Foundation (Wallerstein *et al.,* 1956). I half-consciously recognized in this a fundamental principle, in the words of Helen Sargent, 'there is no substitute for a judgment made by a properly trained clinician' and consequently that psychotherapy research must consist of the *objective* handling of *subjective* judgements according to the rules of scientific evidence. With this, I could start in earnest.

The problems that this work had been concerned with, in the most general terms, had been: what kinds of result can be achieved in brief psychotherapy, by what methods, in what kinds of patient? These are respectively the problems of *outcome, technique* and *selection.* It is immediately obvious that nothing can be said about selection and technique without reference to outcome; therefore the first requirement must be a method of measuring outcome—which, as I said above, is one of the most intractable problems in all research in psychotherapy.

And yet, intractable as it is, a firm base on Helen Sargent's principle mentioned above guides one towards a solution. My thought on this subject has gone through a good deal of development (see Malan, 1959; 1963; Malan *et al.,* 1968), but the essentials are:

(1) to lay down criteria that need to be fulfilled if the patient is to be regarded as mentally healthy;

(2) to tailor the criteria for each individual patient, formulating them essentially as the undoing of the disturbances found in him;

(3) to keep as a basic principle that a disturbance in a patient must not merely disappear, but must be replaced by something positive;

(4) in addition, to define *specific stresses* that may be inferred from a patient's history, which should have been faced without relapse during the follow-up period and not merely have been avoided, whether voluntarily or involuntarily;

(5) to match the findings at follow-up to the criteria already laid down, considering the patient, his subsequent history and his environment *as a whole;* and

(6) to score the result on a simple scale, using certain anchor points as a guide.

I realized that ideally these criteria should be laid down in *in advance* of seeing the patient for follow-up, but since the above ideas developed retrospectively from these particular cases this was not possible. We later showed, however, that this could be done, and examples of the rigorous use of the whole method will be given below during the description of the replication.

Having scored outcome in the first 18 cases, I then regarded these scores as immutable and turned my attention to other variables.

Here, under Balint's leadership, we had started with three main hypotheses, the first two concerned with selection criteria and the third with technique.

(A) That most suitable patients for this form of therapy would be those of *good basic personality* with *'mild' illnesses* and complaints of *recent onset.*

(B) That the most suitable patients would show from the beginning an aptitude for working in interpretative therapy, manifested by *high motivation* and clear *response to interpretation.*

(C) That attempts to work with the transference would tend to result in an intensification of transference in the direction of increasing primitiveness, would hasten the development of the transference neurosis and would lead to difficulties over termination and ultimately to failure of therapy.

As far as Hypotheses A and B were concerned, I undertook an exhaustive study of the evidence and came unequivocally to the negative finding that neither *severity of pathology* nor *recent onset* bore any relation to outcome in these particular patients and to the positive finding that the only selection criterion that could be made to correlate with favourable outcome was *motivation.*

As for Hypothesis C, concerning the adverse effects of transference, this had been peremptorily swept aside by our early experiences. It had become quite clear, and it was easy to show on clinical grounds alone, that the most successful therapies tended to be those in which transference arose *early,* full attention was paid to the *negative* transference and feelings about *termination* became a major issue and were to some extent worked through. Not only this, but our fears of primitive transference were completely contradicted by the finding that those therapies were most successful in which the transference had been related to feelings about *parents*

When I came upon this latter finding, I had already reinforced the evidence on transference by means of a quantitative content analysis of the accounts of sessions dictated by the therapists from memory. For this purpose I had marked off each interpretation recorded and had made a judgement of whether or not it referred to the transference. As a measure of the 'transference orientation' of each therapy, I had taken the number of interpretations that referred to the transference divided by the total number of interpretations recorded for that particular therapy, thus eliminating as far as possible the effects both of fullness of recording and length of therapy. I had shown that this proportion, the 'transference ratio', correlated positively (though not significantly) with the scores for outcome.

I began to realize that, buried in these case notes, there might be a finding far more valuable than anything hitherto manifest, namely some relatively objective evidence about the therapeutic effectiveness of the transference–parent link, one of the fundamental concepts in theories about the therapeutic action of psychoanalysis. Yet I had made no quantiative judgements relevant to this and if I were to extract this evidence I would have to start all over again—and there were 1,300 interpretations to score. I wasted several months trying to evade this in various ways but eventually saw that it must be done. The result was that the 'transference–parent ratio', i.e. the proportion of interpretations that made the transference–parent link, was found to correlate positively and *significantly* with scores for outcome.

There was a final observation that needed to find its place. I had long been aware of a chance observation in our own work that had linked with remarks of Balint's and of Edward Glover's about the apparent successes of the early analysts, namely that there was a strong tendency for the therapists in this work to achieve striking successes with their first case—presumably when their enthusiasm was highest. Suddenly I realized that these favourable factors, motivation, transference, therapeutic enthusiasm, contained the common element of *involvement in the therapeutic process*. All the findings then made sense as a whole, each supporting the others, as in the crossword puzzle principle mentioned above.

And then—dare I say it—I started to read what other authors had written about brief psychotherapy. And yet this mattered not at all, because the questions that we had answered were in fact the questions posed by the confusion in the literature.

This confusion can be summarized by two opposite views of brief psychotherapy, together with a complete spectrum in between. According to the conservative view: only the mildest and most recent illnesses can be helped, the technique should be superficial and should avoid transference interpretations and the results are usually no more than palliative. According to the radical view: patients with severe and long-standing illnesses can sometimes be helped, in a permanent and far-reaching manner, by a technique containing all the essential elements of psychoanalysis. It will be quickly seen that our own views started near the conservative end of the spectrum and that the evidence eventually obtained was almost entirely in favour of the radical view of all three major aspects—selection criteria, technique, outcome.

It is worthwhile to pause at this point and to consider the scientific status of the findings. The following can be said to be major defects of the study:

(1) the sample was very small;

(2) there were considerable problems of interpretation caused by the way in which the patients had been selected;

(3) the absence of a control sample meant that one could never be absolutely sure that the improvements observed might not have occurred without treatment;

(4) the intercorrelation of retrospective, contaminated judgements made by a single observer—like Mendeleyev's work, but much more so—can hardly be called the most convincing of scientific methods.

Of these defects, the problem of a control sample has never been fully solved, though we did later undertake a systematic study of changes in a series of untreated patients (see Malan *et al.,* 1968). However, it was possible to provide quite strong evidence that therapy was responsible for changes in certain patients. This occurred when improvements began to appear during the course of *brief* therapy in *very chronic* conditions. The problem to do with selection could in fact be overcome by a careful consideration of the actual way in which these particular patients had been selected. The other two defects had for the time being to be accepted.

It then seemed to me that the following could be said:

(1) that the evidence that remarkable changes could be brought about by relatively brief therapy in certain patients was quite strong (over the whole series, the number of sessions in those cases successfully terminated by mutual agreement ranged from 5 to 40, with a median of 14);

(2) that the evidence against the conservative view that interpretation of the transference *did harm* was overwhelming; and

(3) that the way in which every finding fitted into a pattern suggesting that *involvement* was the important factor was at least very striking.

Nevertheless it had to be admitted that this retrospective reasoning, especially in so small a sample, was very dangerous and that, at best, it could lead to nothing more than the generation of hypotheses for further testing.

Tavistock Work on Brief Psychotherapy: Replication

It so happened that, since the writing of my book had taken several years, during which time Balint's team had continued to operate, there had accumulated a further 39 patients treated by the same methods. A combination of this, the refusal of a research grant dealing with the follow-up of untreated patients and my scientific conscience finally led me to seek support for a replication of this work, this time with as many safeguards built into the design as were possible with the resources available.

Anyone who plans a research project of this kind gives many hostages to fortune. Most of the patients might have disappeared or refused follow-up; ratings of outcome by more than one judge might have ended in total confusion and been unusable; and—a possibility that I only realized after the work had been under way for several years—later follow-up of the original patients might have destroyed the original correlations, so that there would be nothing to cross-validate. In the event, none of these disasters occurred. In particular, we succeeded in following up 30 out of the 39 patients, the length of follow-up since termination lying in almost all cases between four and nine years.

We had the help of a number of colleagues, all but one of whom had not been involved in the original work and could make entirely uncontaminated judgements.

The design was as follows.

(1) The basic material consisted of the clinical notes, all of which had been dictated by therapist or interviewer from memory soon after each interview.

(2) Outcome was scored by four judges independently, two contaminated by knowledge of therapy and two blind.

(3) Selection criteria were scored, on the initial assessment material only, by two independent judges uncontaminated by knowledge of any later events.

(4) Two variables (motivation and 'focality', see below) were scored, session by session, on the first eight contacts with the Clinic by two independent judges, one blind and one contaminated by knowledge both of therapy and outcome.

(5) The content analysis of the therapist's recorded interpretation was carried out by two independent judges, both contaminated by knowledge of outcome. These were the only two judges with the time and motivation to carry out this laborious operation on over 3,000 interpretation. The fact of contamination matters much less with these particular judgements, as they can be made according to relatively objective criteria. Quantitative measures were thus obtained of a number of different types of interpretation.

Finally, the variables judged as in (3) to (5) above were correlated with outcome.

Reliability of Judgements of Outcome

This was one of the crucial tests that the whole work had to undergo. I had

212

devoted years of thought to judging outcome and months of conflict-laden work to the actual scores in the original patients; but a judgement of outcome on psychodynamic criteria is immensely complex. No one would be surprised if disagreement between judges became great enough to jeopardize the whole project.

Events contradicted these fears to an unhoped-for degree. It soon became clear that the criteria and anchor points were defined in such a way that psychoanalysts could grasp them quickly and needed practice on no more than three or four cases before reasonable agreement could be reached. The final inter-rater reliability on the 30 patients was always in the region of $r = +0\cdot80$. Most important, the reliability between the mean of the two contaminated judges and that of the two uncontaminated judges was $+0\cdot83$. There was thus no difficulty in taking the mean of these four independently made scores as the final score for outcome in each patient. I should add that we have used this same method in a follow-up study of patients treated in groups and have obtained an equally high blind–contaminated reliability (mean of two judges each, as before) for a sample of 42 patients.

Examples of the Method of Measuring Outcome

The scale measures 'improvement' on dynamic criteria, and ranges from 0 ('essentially unchanged') to 4 ('apparently recovered') with half-points allowed. Negative scores, representing a judgement of 'worse', are also allowed, but in the present series these occurred in one patient only. Since the overall score is taken as the mean of four judgements, the final scale rises by intervals of one eighth of a point $(0\cdot125)$.

Here I should say that long experience has given me the greatest faith in this scale, differences even as small as the minimum being clinically meaningful. As an example, an overall score of $2\cdot625$ rather than $2\cdot5$ might reflect the fact that, whereas three judges scored $2\cdot5$, the fourth felt the improvements merited a score of $3\cdot0$. This is a clinically meaningful distinction which *ought* to be reflected in the final score.

Four clinical examples follow, all taken from the second series of brief psychotherapy patients. Because of the necessity for choosing examples that are simple and clear, the reliability of outcome scores is somewhat higher than in the series as a whole; but the first example will give an impression of the scope for genuine disagreement on a single case. For clarity of comparison all four examples are of the same sex, consisting of men in whom disturbances which psycho-analysts would term 'Oedipal' are prominent. Length of treatment tends to be less than the median, which for all cases successfully follow up was about 19 sessions—but this includes eight cases in whom there was failure to terminate within an arbitrary limit of 40 sessions. The smallest number of sessions that gave a really satisfactory result (mean score above $3\cdot0$) was 11.

The Military Policeman, 38, Married, Officer in the Military Police

Psychiatric diagnosis: acute on chronic anxiety state.

Disturbances: 14-year history of severe tremor in his right hand which interferes with his writing, together with anxiety in the presence of superiors. Recent severe anxiety attack when giving evidence at a court martial, in which he behaved as if he himself were guilty. Lack of tenderness with his wife. At interview, an air of rock-like strength, threatening to break down into tears.

Additional evidence: the tremor had first come on when he was an infantryman during the War and had been about to return to his unit in the Western Desert, after an attack of dysentery. His father, also in the Military Police, had never been promoted but had encouraged the patient in his highly successful career. The father had suffered a depressive breakdown, in which he had become difficult and can-tankerous, and had finally died nine years ago.

Hypothesis: we believed that (1) for reasons that were not clear, the patient had adopted a life pattern of denying strong feelings of all kinds, which he regarded as showing weakness, and (2) he suffered from guilt about successful competition with his father.

Criteria for successful outcome: these emphasized the ability to express all kinds of strong feeling without regarding this as a weakness and without the loss of his efficiency and strength.

Therapy (5 sessions): the patient became able to admit some of his softer feelings and was greatly reassured to discuss his breakdown with a colleague and to hear of others who had suffered something similar. The symptoms disappeared and the therapist felt there was little point in trying to go further.

Follow-up (7 years): he had been entirely symptom-free during the follow-up period. He had been able to attend courts martial without anxiety. He had then left the Forces, in which he had been unhappy, and taken a civilian job of comparable earning capacity. The follow-up interview was extremely uneasy; the patient seemed entirely out of touch with his feelings, the interviewer felt unable to ask searching questions and all questions about the patient's relation with his wife were met with the blanket statement 'I am sure we are very happily married'.

Scores: in spite of the complete symptomatic recovery, all four judges were uneasy about the extent of his true improvement, as reflected in their scores: $0 \cdot 5$, $2 \cdot 0$, $1 \cdot 5$, $1 \cdot 5$; mean $1 \cdot 375$. (It is interesting to note that the score of $0 \cdot 5$ was given by the therapist, who alone was able to judge that although the patient was symptomatically recovered, this was balanced by the fact that he was *less* in touch with his feelings than he had been during therapy.)

The Oil Director, 49, Married, Director of an Oil Company

Psychiatric diagnosis: acute anxiety state with depression.

Disturbances: breakdown into anxiety, depression and inability to work over the past year, starting four months after the death of his mother, whom he had been unable to mourn. Lifelong need to drive himself and others. Intolerance of all kinds of softer feelings in himself and others, which are felt as a weakness. Autocratic attitude in the home, with intolerance of rebellion in his children.

Additional evidence: his father was not very able; his mother was extremely ambitious for him and he enjoyed her admiration for his successes.

Hypothesis: an intense wish to prove his manliness and strength, as a defence against (1) a wish to be looked after, (2) rebellious feelings against his mother and (3) guilt about successful competition with his father.

Criteria: these emphasized the loss of compulsive self-driving; the ability to tolerate rebelliousness; the ability to tolerate weakness and dependence in himself and others without loss of effectiveness.

Therapy (46 sessions): this was largely concerned with getting him to admit and tolerate the passive, dependent part of himself, which he did with relief and satisfaction.

Follow-up (3 years 10 months): he had been symptom-free for much of the follow-up period, but six months ago had suffered a partial relapse, treated by tranquillizers. The major change had been that his self-driving had completely disappeared, without loss of effectiveness. He still accepted the softer part of himself and regarded it as valuable; but, as far as personal relations were concerned, after considerable initial improvement there seemed to have been a partial re-establishment of former patterns.

Scores: all judges were agreed that there had been moderate but not marked improvement: 2·0, 2·0, 2·0, 2·0; mean 2·0.

A comparison with the previous patient suggests that the latter had shown symptomatic recovery at the price of repression of most of his feelings, while the present patient, although showing incomplete symptomatic improvement, had made some real gains in terms of loss of compulsiveness and tolerance of softer feelings.

The Pesticide Chemist, 31, Married, Industrial Chemist Developing Pesticides

Psychiatric diagnosis: an acute outburst of uncontrollable feeling in an obsessional personality.

Disturbances and recent history: he has always been perfectionist and over-anxious at work, and he worries that the materials he develops may not have been tested properly. He takes criticism very hard, particularly from his boss. He has always suffered from premature ejaculation. He gives the impression that work is more important to him than his home life.

He came to consultation because of the following incident. He went to his doctor one morning complaining of loss of energy, and when he returned his wife suggested that he might stay at home for the day. He refused this suggestion and his wife then said that in that case she might get on with treating their house for woodworm. (He had been doing this gradually, room by room, but his wife had criticized the way he had done it.) He had a sudden uncontrollable outburst of rage, hit his wife, poured a gallon of anti-woodworm solution down to the sink and then cried for three hours.

Additional evidence: the chief factor in his childhood seemed to be that his father overworked and consequently the patient hardly knew him.

Hypothesis: he seems to be continually appeasing a sense of guilt. This makes him compulsive at work and this in turn makes him neglect his wife, which increases his guilt. When his wife complains, he breaks down because of his dilemma between these two areas of guilt.

Criteria: emphasized ability to relax and tolerate imperfections; an increase in warmth and companionship and improved potency between him and his wife.

Therapy (14 sessions): the main theme was repeated interpretation of his resentment at not getting what he wanted, which he defended himself against by redoubling his efforts to satisfy everyone else's demands—it was the last straw when this defence itself became the object of criticism. This was linked to the patient's childhood, in which everyone expected him to grow up and be responsible in spite of having no adequate relation with his father. During therapy the patient became able to be spontaneously angry at work; and he then had a showdown with his wife about her lack of enthusiasm for sex. The result was a great improvement in both situations.

Follow-up (4 years): he seemed to have completely recovered from his compulsiveness and in addition showed a marked improvement in his ability to be constructively aggressive both at work and at home. There as also an improvement in his potency; but there was not very much improvement in his ability to express love and both he and his wife felt the situation to be unsatisfactory.

Scores: 2·5, 2·5, 2·5, 2·5; mean 2·5.

The Indian Scientist, 29, Single, Scientist Working in Industry

Psychiatric diagnosis: anxiety state, premature ejaculation.

Disturbances: premature ejaculation and anxiety about it; intense dislike of male authority; difficulty over competition; inability to attain his potential academically and in work.

Additional evidence: his father was a very successful and pugnacious man, who used to thrash the patient when he was a boy. The patient's mother was warm and he felt very close to her.

Hypothesis: guilt and anxiety about hostile rivalry with his father.

Criteria: these emphasized that he should lose his anxiety and guilt about attaining any form of masculinity, to be shown in the ability to attain full potency and a satisfactory relation with a woman; ability to get on with male authority, yet to be constructively aggressive where appropriate; ability to attain his potential in a job that satisfies him.

Therapy (12 sessions): his guilt about hostility and rivalry towards his father was repeatedly interpreted. The male therapist somehow succeeded in avoiding becoming identified with this male authority. The patient worked very hard and responded very well, and in the fourth session experienced tremendous relief on confessing that he had once read his father's love letters to his mother. This enabled the therapist to go into the patient's rivalry with his father for his mother's love.

Follow-up (7 years 4 months): the patient now married and described most convincingly a passionate and mutually satisfying relation with his wife; his relation with male authority improved beyond recognition during therapy; he has now become a leader in his field; he was formerly much troubled by colour prejudice in England but has now emigrated to a country where this is no problem.

Our only reservations were that (1) follow-up was by letter only (since he was abroad), and (2) on two occasions he had had to have leadership thrust upon him. These were the reasons for the rather conservative scoring by some judges about a patient who, to all appearances, was recovered.

Scores: 3·5, 4·0, 3·5, 3·0; mean: 3·5.

Selection Criteria at Initial Assessment

During the course of our clinical work, Balint's team had formulated 20 selection criteria which needed testing. Two independent judges rated these on simple scales, using the initial assessment material only (psychiatric interview and projective test), in complete ignorance of either outcome or the events of therapy. At first glance the results were disappointing. Inter-judge *reliability* coefficients failed to reach the 2 per cent level of significance on 10 of the 20 criteria studied, so that there was no point in going on to correlate these criteria with outcome. When the remaining 10 criteria were compared with outcome, not one of the correlation coefficients reached the 5 per cent level of significance.

Nevertheless, this result was not quite so meagre as might be thought. In the first place, the failure of criteria concerned with hypothesis A—that results are best in mild illnesses of recent onset—is not a negative but a positive finding, since it both confirms the same observation on the original series of patients and indicates that help can be given in more severe and chronic illnesses than might be expected. As clinical confirmation of this, the most dramatic of all therapeutic results in the first series occurred in a lifelong character problem in a man of 54 who had been on the waiting list for psychoanalysis for 15 years—with a therapy of 14 sessions. The result that scored highest (3·75) in the second series was in a man of 45 suffering from crippling paranoid jealousy, the history of which went back 20 years (for a full acount of this 29-session therapy see Balint *et al.,* 1972). It also needs to be added that since, at the upper end, our scale measures 'degree of recovery' rather than 'extent of change', this result is not simply an artefact due to the fact that greater severity of initial pathology gives greater scope for change.

Moreover, of the 10 selection criteria, the one that gave the highest correlation with outcome ($p = 0·07$) was *motivation,* thus confirming the original finding that if any useful prognostic factor is to be discovered it is likely to lie here.

Prognostic Factors to do with Therapist–Patient Interaction in the First Eight Sessions

The original hypothesis about the importance of motivation had come out of a study of this factor not merely at initial assessment but during the initial stages of therapy. Therefore, together with an independent and uncontaminated judge, I scored motivation during the first eight contacts with the Clinic (this included the projective test). In addition, we scored a new variable called *focality,* which may be defined as the extent to which the therapist can stick to a therapeutic plan, or a single theme for his interpretations, in each session.

The results are too complex for presenting in any detail, but suffice it to say that both these two variables showed no significant relation to outcome in the first four contacts, but tended quite strongly to show a significant relation in contacts 5 to 8. Moreover, the two variables started by being unrelated, but in the second four contacts became strongly positively correlated with one another. The clinical significance of these observations will be discussed later.

Transference

When further follow-up on the *original* cases came to be examined, among the most striking findings were the following.

There were three patients who needed no further treatment and whose major improvements stood the test of time. (1) In all three of these transference arose early; (2) in two of them termination was a major issue; and (3) these three ranked first, second and third respectively in terms of the quantitative measure of the transference–parent link. When the overall correlations were considered, both early transference and termination gave significant results, but the factor that correlated most highly of all variables was the *sum of the two*.

The results of the second series were as follows.

(1) Of all the results, those on *early transference* and *termination* were the least satisfactory because they were equivocal. Neither variable correlated significantly with outcome by itself, but the sum of the two almost did so ($p = 0.056$). This is a rather artificial variable and therefore one could easily say that the results on the second series were essentially null. On the other hand, this variable does very strongly contain the element of *involvement* on the patient's part and the correlation suggests that those therapies tend to be the most successful in which the patient is involved both early and late; those of intermediate outcome are those in which he is involved *either* early *or* late; those of poorest outcome are those in which he is involved neither early nor late.

(2) As far as *negative* transference is concerned, the result can be dismissed quickly. There were a number of successful therapies in which interpretation of the negative transference played little part, and the overall importance of this factor was not confirmed.

(3) Of all the transference variables, I had laid greatest emphasis on the transference–parent link, and in the replication the whole of the content analysis was designed around this variable. The analysis was carried out by myself and another judge independently. It was so designed that not only was a measure of the transference–parent link obtained, but also of a number of other types of interpretation that could serve as controls. The result was most striking: the transference–parent link correlated significantly with outcome for both judges ($p < 0.02$) and none of the control interpretations did so.

The Therapist's Involvement

When the final results for each therapist's first case were considered, however, the original observation suggesting the importance of the therapist's involvement failed to be confirmed.

Discussion of the Results of the Replication

The positive results were as follows.

(1) Of all selection criteria at initial assessment *motivation* was the most important.

(2) During the fifth to eighth contacts with the Clinic, both *motivation* and *focality* tended to correlate significantly with outcome and also with each other.

(3) Of transference variables, *early transference + termination* gave a correlation with outcome 'significant' at the 0·06 level and the *transference–parent link* significant at the 0·02 level.

The clinical and theoretical significance of these findings now needs to be discussed.

Of all these factors, *motivation* and *transference* contain the element of *involvement on the part of the patient*, the importance of which is now confirmed—though somewhat less strongly—on the second sample. The importance of *involvement on the part of the therapist* suggested by the first sample is, however, not confirmed.

On the other hand, the significance of *motivation and focality* taken together has an important explanation to do with a particular kind of *interaction between patient and therapist*, which may be formulated as follows.

The dynamic therapist's main therapeutic tool is *interpretation*. The tool is double-edged and it needs both to be correct and to be carefully adjusted to what the patient can bear. In the initial stages of brief therapy, the therapist is all the time searching for the line of interpretation, the 'focus', on which he can base his work. He does this by offering partial interpretations to the patient and testing out the reactions to them. Incorrect interpretations produce no response; interpretations that are too disturbing arouse resistance, i.e. a decrease in motivation; correctly adjusted interpretations produce a clear response, a deepening of rapport and an increase in motivation. Thus, when therapy is going well, both motivation and focality will tend to increase—the patient will respond positively and the therapist will get the feeling that he knows where he is going. Correspondingly, when therapy is going badly, the patient may begin to withdraw and the therapist to lose his way. Each of these situations is likely to set up a self perpetuating cycle; thus there will tend to develop a divergence between those therapies that are 'going well', in which motivation and focality increase or remain high, and those that are 'going badly', in which these two variables remain low or decrease. It is easy to see that under these circumstances the two variables will tend to become positively correlated. In the present work, apparently all this has begun to develop clearly by the fifth to eighth contacts. But now comes the important point: 'going well', in these terms, has nothing intrinsically to do with therapeutic effects, yet therapies that are going well tend to lead to improvements at follow-up and those that are going badly do not.

This observation has two important consequences. First, we have now formulated an operational definition of 'going well' and 'going badly', which can be used in prognosis and therefore in selection. And second, we have obtained some evidence that a particular kind of therapist–patient interaction is *therapeutically effective*.

This latter inference is further strengthened by the observation on the therapist–parent link. The interpretation of the link between the transference and important people in the patient's past has long been regarded on clinical grounds as the psychoanalyst's major therapeutic tool. There is a considerable degree of unanimity on this. We have now obtained some *scientific* evidence tending to confirm the correctness of this long-held principle of psychoanalytic technique and thus partly substantiating the validity of psychoanalytic psychotherapy.

Lest I be felt to be claiming too much, this statement needs some discussion. What has been observed is a *correlation* between favourable outcome on the one hand and (1) a certain kind of therapist–patient interaction, and (2) a certain kind of interpretation on the other. For brevity we may call these two latter factors X and Y respectively. Now correlations are notoriously treacherous when one tries to interpret them in terms of cause and effect. This is particularly true when, as here, the variables studied are the result of natural processes rather than of deliberate experimental manipulation. The correlations mentioned above can be explained in a number of different ways. For instance, patients who interact in a particular way with their therapists (i.e. those high on variable X) might be those with the healthiest personalities and thus the most likely to show spontaneous remission quite independent of therapy. In this case it is not that variable X causes favourable outcome, but that both X and outcome are the consequence of a third variable, healthy personality. Similarly, it may be not that variable Y causes favourable outcome but that patients who are getting better cause the therapist to feel more confident and more able to give his favourite kinds of interpretation—i.e. that favourable outcome causes Y. In spite of these fallacies, however, the *simplest* explanation is that X and Y tend to cause favourable outcome, and since one of the themes of the present chapter is the advance of science by *converging* rather than *conclusive* evidence, these observations need to be given due weight.

Practical Considerations

All this work has led to very clearly understood principles of selection for this form of therapy, clear indications that the technique should involve the transference and strong evidence that radical and lasting improvements can be achieved. The evidence against the conservative view of brief psychotherapy in properly selected patients is by now conclusive, and this view—still widely expressed—should disappear from the literature.

The principles of selection need more detailed discussion.

First of all, where our series of patients was heavily weighted either *in favour of* or *against* a particular factor, then we can provide no scientific evidence about the effects of this factor but only clinical impression. This applies to certain contra-indications and one essential pre-condition.

The contra-indications, apart from such obvious factors as potential suicide, destructive acting out and psychotic breakdown, are factors that make successful brief work highly improbable. Those that recurred most often in our work were severe dependence, rigid defences and a feeling that therapy would inevitably become involved in complex and deep-seated issues. The fact that we largely succeeded in avoiding these dangers suggests that our criteria of exclusion were basically correct.

The essential pre-condition is *response to interpretation*. Extensive subsequent experience has convinced me that patients who show no response, especially after several sessions, should be automatically excluded.

The principles of selection are then based on the interaction between motivation and focality discussed above. Where both these variables start high, i.e. where a clear-cut therapeutic plan can be made and evidence can be provided that there is motivation to work with it, then the patient can be accepted immediately. Where there is any doubt, an extended diagnositic period will show whether the trend in these two variables is upward or downward. Only if it is upward should the patient be accepted.

Chronicity of complaints and, within limits, severity of pathology are not contra-indications in themselves.

With the help of these principles, I have been running a seminar for some years at the Tavistock Clinic in which patients are selected for brief therapy and treated by trainees under supervision. Though we have certainly had some disasters, we have also had some remarkable successes. Thus it has been demonstrated that whereas a high degree of *skill* is probably necessary, wide *experience* is not—though experienced supervision may possibly be—and the practical application of this form of therapy has been extended.

Conclusion

The collection and interpretation of all this data again took several years, and once more I found myself in the position of reading most of the literature after the main conclusions had been reached. It then became possible to put this work more clearly in the context of the whole history of research in psychotherapy as follows.

In the 1950s there was a great upsurge of optimisim, illustrated by the Psychotherapy Research Projects of the Menninger Foundation and the Phipps Clinic, the outpouring of research papers by the client-centred school and the three Conferences on Research in Psychotherapy. Yet the Menninger study clearly met enormous difficulties, with the result that no conclusions were published until nearly 20 years later; the Phipps Clinic studies gave ambiguous results; and only the client-centred studies gave rise to any definitive conclusions, and these—for the amount of work involved—were somewhat meagre. It is clear that there has crept into the field a progressive disillusion with research in general, which has finally been brought into the open by Bergin and Strupp (1972) in their interviews with psychotherapy researchers throughout the US. The main themes are as follows.

The flight from outcome into process.

Discouragement by the lack of impact on clinical practice.

Disillusion with psychoanalytic methods of therapy.

Disenchantment with statistical methods.

Emphasis on non-specific factors as the therapeutic agents.

Despair about ever being able to demonstrate the effectiveness of psychotherapy.

221

Yet in the work reported here we can observe the following.

Studies based on psychodynamic assessment of outcome.

Clear-cut results, based on statistical methods, the essence of which have been cross-validated.

Strong evidence about specific factors in technique that are therapeutically effective.

Some degree of validation of psychoanalytic principles.

Some evidence on the validity of psychotherapy.

A marked convergence between clinical and scientific evidence.

Immediate impact on clinical practice.

Why should this be so? I suggested that there are five main reasons.

First, accumulating clinical experience convinces me that patients who are suitable for interpretative or dynamic psychotherapy are a special category of person, who probably represent a small proportion of those routinely taken on in psychotherapeutic clinics or private practice. This is something that psychotherapists have never properly faced. Our own careful methods of selection, in which the obviously unsuitable patients were elminated, have probably concentrated the suitable patients to the point at which, instead of being swamped, they have exerted a major influence on the overall results.

Second, if patients who are suitable for dynamic psychotherapy are a small proportion, those suitable for *brief* psychotherapy must be even fewer. Most previous studies of psychotherapy have in fact used brief methods, which is essential if results are to be obtained during the life-span of most research projects. Yet, in spite of this, often neither the selection nor the technique used have been specifically tailored towards this special method of treatment. It may, therefore, not be surprising that the results have often been indeterminate. Our own method of working is likely to have reduced this problem to manageable proportions.

Third, the use of brief methods of therapy has made it much easier to handle the material and to isolate factors in technique that correlate with outcome.

Fourth, the use of well-trained and experienced therapists has probably given the therapy the best chance of being effective—although with experienced supervision it seems that similar work can also be carried out by trainees.

And finally, with the aid of Helen Sargent's principle that there is no substitute for experienced clinical judgement, I believe that the development of a valid measure of outcome has been of overriding importance. Armed with this, perhaps we may learn the truth about psychotherapy during the next few decades.

Acknowledgements

My grateful thanks are due to the David Matthew Fund of the London Institute of Psycho-analysis and the Mental Health Research Fund for generous financial support; and to E. H. Rayner, P. Dreyfus, H. A. Bacal, E. S. Heath, F. H. G. Balfour and R. Shepherd for making independent judgements in the work reported here.

222

References

Alexander, F., and French, T. M. (1946). *Psychoanalytic Therapy,* Ronald, New York.

Balint, M., Ornstein, P. H., and Balint, E. (1972). *Focal Psychotherapy,* Tavistock, London; Lippincott, Philadelphia.

Bergin, A. E., and Strupp, H. H. (1972). *Changing Frontiers in the Science of Psychotherapy,* Aldine, Chicago; Atherton, New York.

Malan, D. H. (1959). 'On assessing the results of psychotherapy', *Brit. J. med. Psychol.,* **32,** 86.

Malan, D. H. (1963). *A Study of Brief Psychotherapy,* Tavistock, London; Lippincott, Philadelphia.

Malan, D. H., Bacal, H. A., Heath, E. S., and Balfour, F. H. G. (1968). 'A study of psychodynamic changes in untreated neurotic patients. I. Improvements that are questionable on dynamic criteria', *Brit. J. Psychiat.,* **114,** 525.

Sargent, H. D. (1961). 'Intrapsychic change: Methodological problems in psychotherapy research', *Psychiat.,* **24,** 93.

Wallerstein, R. S., Robbins, L. L., Sargent, H. D., and Luborsky, L. (1956). 'The Psychotherapy Research Project of the Menninger Foundation: Rationale, method, and sample use', *Bull. Menninger Clin.,* **20,** 221.

12

BEHAVIOUR THERAPY

Victor Meyer and Andrée Liddell

In recent years we have witnessed an enormous and unparallelled increase in the research and application of behaviour modification principles in clinical and non-clinical settings, such as hospital wards, schools, prisons and business concerns (Ernst, 1971; Krasner, 1971). In clinical settings this approach is gradually being adopted by many members of the usual team of professionals who are involved in the care of psychiatric patients, for example, social workers (Jehu, 1972) and counsellors and nurses (Ayllon and Azrin, 1968). In certain cases even parents are utilized to ensure that generalization outside the clinical setting occurs and can be maintained (Berkowitz and Graziano, 1972). Here we shall be concerned only with behaviour therapy as applied to a psychiatric population. This enforced narrowing of the field nevertheless leaves an uncomfortably large, varied and continually changing area to summarize and evaluate.

Definition

There have been several definitions of behaviour therapy offered by various 'experts' in the field. Some of them have emphasized the development of techniques directly derived from learning principles (Bandura, 1969), while others have conceptualized behaviour therapy as an approach utilizing available knowledge from the whole of experimental psychology and its allied or complementary disciplines (Yates, 1970).

The way in which one conceptualizes behaviour therapy greatly depends on one's past training in psychology, for example, whether Skinner or Pavlov was emphasized; whether one works basically in research or as a clinician; and on the type of population treated. On the last point, for instance, if one is working with institutionalized mental defectives or autistic children, one is more likely to conceptualize behaviour therapy as the application of Skinnerian principles for the development and maintenance of new behaviour. On the other hand, if one is working in a health service with university students or other intelligent adult patients with existential problems, the relevance of simple conditioning begins to be

223

watered down and cognitive factors often appear more important than reflexes and other autonomic responses.

We see behaviour therapy as an approach to changing behaviour by means of procedures derived from learning principles. These principles serve to guide the current and aetiological analysis of the patient's complaints, to select goals for treatment and to design the actual treatment so that gains will be extended to the natural environment. The emphasis is on the modification of behaviour in its widest sense: autonomic, motor and cognitive aspects of behaviour are considered equally amenable to treatment. Since we are dealing with people, the whole of psychology and its related disciplines cannot be ignored and the understanding of their various models is often necessary for the realistic application of learning principles. We are not arguing that learning principles are the only processes to affect behaviour. We recognize the part played by various neurological and metabolic processes—but even if behaviour develops as the result of primarily organic determinants, treatment based on learning principles can alter their effects. Therefore behaviour therapists should not be put off, for example, by the diagnosis of 'brain damage'.

Behaviour therapists are experimentalists in the widest sense of the word: they adhere to operational knowledge and concepts only if they can be anchored to antecedents and consequences. They choose learning principles in preference to any other model of normal and abnormal behaviour because learning principles are derived from experiments carried out in the laboratory using the methodology of experimental psychology. The onus is on the behaviour therapist to extrapolate this knowledge to the clinic.

In summary, a behaviour therapist is constantly guided by learning principles, whether he is structuring his behaviour to his patient, whether he is trying to understand him and his complaints or whether he is designed and implementing treatment. It follows that behaviour therapy is not viewed as a selection of techniques into which patients can be rigidly fitted nor is it an approach derived from any one abstract learning theory. It is a flexible approach which uses relatively well-established principles founded on experimental studies.

In getting down to details we shall discuss under the loose divisions of diagnosis, 'techniques', treatment and research.

Diagnostic Interview

Behavioural Analysis

The diagnostic interview is the most important aspect of the work of the behaviour therapist as well as the most difficult one to carry out. In spite of this it is also totally ignored in the literature except for Kanfer and Saslow (1969). Interviewing is not designed to classify patients according to any existing taxonomies but to analyse the complaints in behavioural terms. At the time of the interview one must first obtain a clear description of each complaint as it occurs, at the same time trying to determine the stimulus situation which evokes the undesirable behaviour and the consequences which maintain it. Information is also sought to identify the mood states which affect the patient and any circumstances in the patient's environment that could advantageously be modified such as personal, social or financial relationships. Once the current status of complaints is defined and understood, in the broadest sense, one takes each complaint aetiologically to determine its onset in behavioural terms, relating it to traumatic experiences if any, or to more gradual ongoing stresses. In other words, each complaint is taken historically with special attention to possible stimulus–response connections and response generalization, including symbolic generalization. The treatment will eventually be based on this understanding. The analysis of the patient's complaint is supplemented by a full personal history including that of the family. This provides the background against which to evaluate the current complaints of the patient. For instance, it is of practical interest to know if the patient shows a marked personality disorder, i.e. a long-standing maladjustment in various areas of activities, or to see if the complaint is more circumscribed. It is also considered essential for the patient to be screened by a medically qualified colleague if the behaviour therapist is not medically qualified, to identify any possible organic pathology. During the interview, hypotheses are developed about current problems and by going back into the patient's childhood one may elicit information which would support or make the therapist abandon these hypotheses. Needless to say, confirmation of one's hypotheses is highly rewarding.

Some behaviour therapists would not engage in such time-consuming activities but would only look at the current complaint and its development. Whether the detailed analysis suggested is better remains to be seen. In our experience it has proved to be extremely useful because behaviour is complex and a complaint seldom appears in isolation. It is evident, on the other hand, that not all the information gathered in the interview is useful for making formulations and one may be left with the current complaint only. This should not disturb the behaviour therapist, since he can still attempt to modify the behaviour which he observes. One must also constantly watch for information that comes to light later during therapy and which may change the course of treatment.

Therapeutic Relationship

As the interview proceeds and the therapist makes formulations about his patient's behaviour, he must also plan his own behaviour so that it is an important variable in the treatment. The therapist aims to structure his behaviour as a potent social reinforcer. For the behaviour therapist, unlike other therapists, there is more than one type of relationship to be developed with the patient. For instance, some therapists are encouraged to remain ambiguous stimuli so that certain 'curative processes' have a better chance to develop. This is not so with the behaviour therapist, who must adjust his behaviour to meet the needs of his patients. If, for instance, the basic problem presented is fear of authority, then the therapist will behave in such a way as to make it easier for his patient to learn skills appropriate when dealing with people in authority. On the other hand, the therapist who treats an isolated phobia will attempt to inspire confidence and to make his patient relax in his presence. There are of course limitations to any therapist's flexibility and adaptability, but conceptualizing the patient's problems in learning terms acts as a guide to the behaviour therapist. A note of caution must be sounded in view of the considerable amount of evidence of verbal conditioning, particularly in the therapeutic or quasi-therapeutic situation. It has been demonstrated that not only are verbal statements changed by social reinforcers from the therapist but also that the client can change the the the therapist's behaviour (Conger, 1971). This is a greater danger for a therapist whose orientation requires him to deal with underlying conflicts which he must discover indirectly for himself. The behaviour therapist who deals with directly observable complaints has more opportunity for external validation, whatever his hypotheses.

Baselines

The detailed interview described above takes on average about four hours and will often suggest questions which need to be answered by some form of standardized investigation such as psychological tests or psychophysiological measures. The results of these tests are sometimes used as baselines which will enable both therapist and patient to assess changes during treatment. In any case baselines are always established before treatment is initiated. The types of baseline recorded depend entirely on the presenting complaint. Apart from standardized tests it may take the form of a crude subjective fear rating (0–100) when dealing with a phobia, a detailed daily record of verbal interaction between husband and wife who seek help for marital problems, or any other direct observations made in the natural setting of the patient.

Finally, whenever possible, spouses, near relatives or close friends of the patient are also interviewed by the therapist himself before the treatment is designed.

Techniques

One finds in the recommended literature on behaviour therapy a tendency for the books to be divided into sections either dealing with different techniques of behaviour therapy (for example, Bandura, 1969; Franks, 1969) or relating psychiatric diagnoses and the possible techniques applied to each diagnostic group (Yates, 1970). The authors who emphasize behaviour therapy as an approach rather than a technology are still in the minority (Kanfer and Phillips, 1970; Meyer and Chesser, 1970; Meyer, 1973). So, the overall impression given is that behaviour therapy consists of well-established techniques which the therapist aims to master. We shall attempt to summarize the techniques which have developed to assist in practising behaviour therapy but we emphasize throughout that they are adjuncts which the therapist will need to select carefully on the basis of the behavioural analysis. The techniques will be broadly classified under the learning principles which were initially thought to guide them: counterconditioning, extinction, classical and operant conditioning. This classification is at best crude, since in many instances more than one principle is likely to be operative while in others the principle originally

227

thought to be operative may turn out to be irrelevant. The type of research which has investigated therapeutic processes involved in various types of behaviour therapy has not yielded categorical answers and our classification must therefore remain tentative. It is impossible to make a comprehensive list of all our techniques since it would run to over a hundred. This reflects the fact that each patient must be approached as an individual and that in practice behaviour therapists must be flexible and must innovate.

Counterconditioning

Generally speaking, when one deals with a condition which is mediated (overtly or covertly) by anxiety, for example, a phobia, there is a tendency to treat it on the basis of counterconditioning principles, i.e. responses incompatible with anxiety are associated with the stimuli which evoke anxiety. This principle was put forward by Wolpe (1958; 1969) and his original desensitization technique has probably been the most widely applied and investigated. Some form of relaxation is usually chosen as the response incompatible with anxiety and this relaxation may be taught to the patient or achieved with the use of drugs or hypnosis. The stimuli to be desensitized are graded and then presented either in imagination or *in vivo* or by a combination of both methods. Examples of other techniques thought to be based on counterconditioning are modelling, including various forms of role-playing and assertive training; contact desensitization; anxiety relief; and anxiety management training (AMT). In modelling (Bandura, 1969) the phobic subject observes a 'brave' nonphobic subject interact with the phobic object without anxiety. Contact desensitization is a form of modelling (Ritter, 1968) in which the phobic subject makes the contact with a phobic object assisted by the model. In the method of aversion relief (Solyom and Miller, 1967) the subject is punished, usually by an electric shock, and the feared stimulus is associated with the end of punishment, hence with anxiety relief. During anxiety management training (Suin and Richardson, 1971) the subject is trained to relax and subsequently presented with fearful stimuli which are not associated with his phobia but which elicit anxiety, such as the more macabre work of Edgar Allan Poe recorded and presented to the subject until counterconditioning occurs. It is hoped that this training in self-control will generalize to the phobia and any other future anxiety-provoking situation.

Extinction

Another principle guiding attempts at eliminating anxiety is that of extinction. Various so-called flooding/implosion methods are used which involve evoking maximum anxiety in the patient and at the same time making it impossible for him to make avoidance responses. As with desensitization the anxiety may be evoked in imagination or *in vivo* or both. Marks (1972) and Morganstern (1973) have assessed this rapidly developing area. Probably also based on extinction is the 'apotrepic therapy' devised by Meyer (1966) and Levy and Meyer (1971) which has been applied to obsessionals who show ritualistic behaviour. This behaviour is continually prevented by various means until total extinction occurs. The negative practice of undesirable habits such as ticks, stammering and various other motor errors has also led to extinction. This was one of the earliest attempts systematically to change behaviour in the clinic (Dunlap, 1932).

Classical and Operant Conditioning

When dealing with behaviour habits which are rewarding to the subject but not acceptable to society, such as drug-taking, alcoholism or sexual deviations, aversion therapies are indicated. These are reviewed by Rachman and Teasdale (1969) and Barlow (1972). Aversion therapies can be designed in terms of classical or operant conditioning principles. Chemical or electrical aversive stimuli have been commonly used. More recently aversion therapy is given covertly—that is, punishment is presented in imagination alone (Cautela, 1971). This increase in the development of techniques based on self-control or self-management (anxiety management training previously mentioned was another example) considerably adds to the armamentarium of behaviour therapists in suggesting ways of dealing with relatively diffuse psychiatric conditions. Another considerable gain for the patient is heightened self-esteem.

When the problem is one of developing new, non-existent behaviour or strengthening desirable ones, one tends to employ operant procedures. A brief reference will be made to a technology which is developing to assist in obtaining self-control of autonomic and somatic functions through the use of biofeedbacks (Gannon and Sternbach, 1971; Budzynski et al., 1970). This expansion is usually attributed to the work of N. E. Miller and his associates on autonomic conditioning. Various psychosomatic conditions such as migraine, tension headaches and high blood pressure can now be ameliorated using learning principles. In these cases the monitoring of the relevant bodily function is conditioned, usually by shaping the required response. For instance, Budzinski et al. (1971) shaped the relaxation of their subjects' frontalis EMGs to a tone. As low EMGs were mastered, subjects suffered fewer tension headaches. This area, which by its nature is extremely specialized, in documented in Stoyva et al. (1972).

In conclusion, it will be obvious to experienced clinicians of all persuasions that there can be no simple relationship between technique and diagnosis. Isolated complaints are rarely found and very few patients show more than a moderate fit to their diagnosis. The reputation of behaviour therapy as a technology which the therapist applies rigidly has in part been earned by behaviour therapists themselves who have reinforced a limited range of referrals. Furthermore, a great deal of research has been carried out by non-clinicians testing the merit of various techniques on minor problems such as 'small animal phobias'—snakes, spiders, mice—and some social fears which are never likely to warrant psychiatric attention. The recent increase in this type of research by our current generation of graduates is a salutary indication that they seek to investigate what they view as 'relevant' problems. We do not mean to say that these minor phobias are not interesting in themselves, but that they are of very limited values as analogues for more severe complaints encountered in a psychiatric practice. This and other areas of research will be discussed after we have elaborated our own therapeutic procedure.

Treatment

Applicability

Originally, an ideal case for behaviour therapy was one which could easily be fitted into a stimulus–response model. This meant that early behaviour therapists were dealing mainly with phobias and other well-defined cases such as compulsive behaviour, stammering and ticks. The latter types of cases were considered acceptable because, even though the stimulus was not well determined, the response was obvious. It was less likely that diffuse conditions, i.e. free-floating anxiety, personality disorders, existential problems or depression, would be referred to behaviour therapists. In a sense one can understand why this happened. The simple and mechanistic formulation put forward by the behaviour therapists themselves meant that, in practice, they were given cases that fitted this simple model. The early behaviour therapists were reluctant to put forward formulations which would enable them to design treatment for the more complex problems. This is no longer the case, and it has been shown that it is possible for the behaviour therapist to analyse an increasing range of problems behaviouristically and on this basis to evolve a behaviouristic treatment. In theory at any rate, behaviour therapy should be able to help all psychiatric conditions. In practice evidence is gradually accumulating in the literature to confirm the applicability of the behaviour therapy approach to an ever-increasing range of problems.

Formulation of the Problem

When all the relevant evidence derived from the diagnostic interview or interviews is collected, the therapist makes a formulation which he gives to his patient in simple terms and without jargon. The therapist takes each complaint in turn and attempts to trace its aetiological development up to the present time. Patients are encouraged to add their comments and generally to discuss the therapist's formulation. In cases of marital problems when the problem involves interaction between two people, both are included in the discussion. In those cases where the therapist finds it impossible to offer a clear-cut formulation to account for the problems, this is admitted to the patient and the treatment starts on an experimental basis in the hope that in due course the patient's reaction will guide the the therapist.

On the basis of the formulation offered, the therapist suggests goals for treatment. However, this is never imposed on the patient and if the patient rejects the goal of treatment suggested by the therapist further discussion takes place until both patient and therapist can reach a compromise. The treatment can only start with a perfect understanding on both sides. It is also felt to be important that when the therapist treats a relationship problem the other partner must be made aware and accept by implication the changes which the therapist hopes to induce—for instance when a passive wife is trained to be more assertive.

Treatment Programme

When both therapist and patient are in agreement about the goals to be achieved through therapy, the therapist instructs the patient about a suitable programme of treatment. This is usually done by giving the patient information about the possible outcome expected when reports or results are available in the literature. This is considered to have considerable advantages, since studies such as that of Goldstein (1962) suggest that it is better if the patient has a realistic expectation as opposed to being too optimistic or too pessimistic. The rationale underlying the approach the therapist has planned and every step of the procedure are explained to the patient. It is hoped that this complete sharing of information with the patient will gain his confidence and put him in the right frame of mind and that in the long term the patient, whenever possible, will become his own therapist and take complete control over his treatment.

The behaviour therapist should be sensitive about the unfortunate public image which is often projected about his work. This image is exemplified in the popular 1972 film 'A Clockwork Orange'. There, the therapist changes the patient against both his will and his knowledge. More generally, even people who accept a degree of planning and control over economic and political affairs view any form of behaviour engineering with horror. Behaviour therapists hope, therefore, to minimize their ethical problems by giving the patient enough information for him to be able to reject or accept the treatment. Beyond making an informed choice, the patient is also expected to involve himself in his own treatment as much as it is feasible.

The procedure must be dictated by the presenting complaint. In certain cases, for instance when a patient is suffering from a phobia, a whole spectrum of treatments is presented (e.g. those listed under counterconditioning) and the patient is asked to choose one method. This approach is more likely to secure closer cooperation and since, as will be shown later, studies investigating the outcome of various methods suggest very little difference between their efficacy, the patient may as well choose the method most appealing to him. However, even when a well-established technique such as Wolpe's (1969) systematic desensitization is chosen, the behaviour therapist must be prepared to meet less than the ideal case and be able to adapt the treatment if, for instance, the patient cannot relax, or cannot imagine, or if there is no transfer from the therapeutic session to real life.

With more complex cases, very often innovation is the main aspect of treatment. It is the behavioural analysis of the problem, with a sound understanding of the patient's personal weaknesses and assets, as well as those of his social environment, which will determined the therapeutic approach. Behaviour therapy in this sense must remain an ongoing process where the therapist becomes a scientist in the tradition of experimental psychology. He collects observations which he interprets in terms of his model, testing the hypotheses which suggest themselves once he is engaged on a particular course.

During the actual treatment, two of the most difficult problems encountered by behaviour therapists are firstly, control over the disordered behaviour between treatment sessions and secondly, the planning of a treatment which ensures generalization outside the therapeutic situation. To achieve control over the undesirable behaviour, the therapist tries to manipulate the appropriate discriminate stimulus or tries to give the patient some way to control his behaviour. Various gadgets have been developed for this purpose (Schwitzgebel and Ackerland, 1972). Occasionally the therapist may be forced to admit the patient into hospital when control outside it is impossible, for example, in cases of agoraphobia and chronic obsessionals. One can envisage a welcomed and logical development of therapy to include the patient's natural environment as well as to engage the help of other professionals for this purpose. This trend was evident in a recent International Conference on Behaviour Therapy (Clark et al., 1971).

In our own work two considerable changes have taken place as our experience expanded, in terms of dealing with more varied cases. Firstly, we begun to include psychodynamic formulations using learning principles; and secondly, we involved ourselves in a social work along the lines indicated by Jehu (1972). Possibly the best way to characterize the general position of the behaviour therapist vis-à-vis his patient in the light of our therapeutic procedure is as one in which both therapist and patient become partners in achieving commonly set goals. We have also become aware over the years of the fact that marked response fluctuation is a cause for concern. We take it as a suggestion that the behavioural analysis may not have been adequate and that we may not be treating the right complaint.

To illustrate how the treatment programme evolves directly from the behavioural analysis and particularly how similar complaints have different aetiology, and therefore demand a different approach, three different types of examples are given.

Type 1

A mother comes to a child guidance clinic with her son complaining that he spends a considerable amount of time throwing temper tantrums. Observing them interact, it becomes apparent that the mother responds to her child in a positive way only when he behaves aggressively. When the boy behaves constructively he is ignored. Furthermore, it becomes apparent that the louder the noise, the quicker the mother responds to him, embracing him, giving him sweets or playing games with him. The temper tantrums started a year ago in the following circumstances. At that time the mother was in the habit of playing with her son for two to three hours a day. Subsequently the father lost his job and the mother had to go out to work. This meant that she could no longer have the same relationship with the child, who tried to regain her attention with no success until on one occasion he hurt himself and screamed. This made the mother respond in her former manner. Very quickly a learning situation developed and the child was quick to associate screaming with immediate attention. The mother, tired and pressurized by intolerant neighbours, could not tolerate the screaming. There were no other problems that could be elicited regarding the family. In this case the behavioural analysis indicates that the mother's behaviour should be changed with training (modelling) until the mother ignores the temper tantrums, which should disappear when no longer reinforced, and gives attention to the child when he is *not* having tantrums.

Type 2

Suppose that a patient complains of fear of going out. The behavioural analysis indicates that the stimulus which brings most anxiety is fast-moving cars. Again no other complaint. The history indicates that the patient had one accident with her husband driving the car. Unfortunately a second accident occurred soon after, while her husband was also driving. The patient began to feel anxiety when entering her husband's car after the first accident and after the second she ceased to go out on streets full of traffic. The history also indicates that the patient had made a good adjustment to life, leaving the phobia as a circumscribed problem. On the basis of this information the therapist is able to ask his patient to choose one of the well-established techniques used to treat phobias.

Let us contrast this case with that of another woman who is totally housebound, complaining of feeling anxious and depressed most of the time, though she shows few signs of a severe depression. Her interpersonal relationship are generally poor, including her relationship with her husband, and she is frigid. Behavioural analysis indicates that she finds home to be the only place of security and just to be outside it is incapacitating. If she experiences any psychological or physical restraints outside her home it brings on a great deal of anxiety which can only be relieved by running home. There is every reason to believe that the patient is continually afraid of doing something silly which would bring attention to herself, for example, fainting on the street would lead to criticism by other people. Her history indicates that she has been in the habit of avoiding all situations where she was likely to be judged, such as tests, entering arguments with other people and any other confrontations. Her parents were viewed as strict and as demanding standards which were impossible to meet. On the basis of this information one can develop a hypothesis that all her complaints can be subsumed under one heading of fear of criticism and failure in any sphere or else that they are the result of a tremendous discrepancy between her ideal self and reality. Her problems were exacerbated after the birth of her first child, when she was forced to take on more responsibility. Very often phobias appear for no apparent reason, that is, the life stresses noted at the time have no direct connection with the symptoms. The behaviourist explanation would probably be that anxiety is additive, especially in a person such as the patient described who appears to show some predisposition to anxiety. The therapist treating such a case would be well advised to begin by reducing her anxiety of failure, enhancing her self percept and reducing her level of aspiration by teaching her to take increasingly more responsibility which she should accept realistically. Attempts could probably be made to make her husband a more interesting stimulus. If the agoraphobic symptoms do not improve by this approach the therapist could always try to treat them directly. In this type of case, unlike the first agoraphobic mentioned above, the problem is so much more complex and generalized and it is unlikely that the patient would regain and maintain her mobility with a direct attack on her presenting complaints.

Type 3

In another hypothetical case, suppose a well-adjusted homosexual, one who accepts and enjoys his sexual activity and who is able to sustain prolonged relationships with males of his choice, is sent by the court for treatment after he was caught with a minor. He committed the offence under the influence of alcohol and didn't know what he was doing. He has no motivation whatsoever to be converted to heterosexuality. The behaviour therapist would not impose a goal of heterosexuality since it is not the wish of the patient. A therapist would probably try to help him control his drinking, if this was shown to be a problem, and also to teach him to discriminate between minors and socially acceptable partners.

Many homosexuals, on the other hand, cannot accept their homosexuality. They give convincing reasons why they want to change their sexual orientation, for example, to be in the majority, to form stable partnerships which will result in a home and family, to be promoted in their jobs, etc. In a case such as this, the behaviour therapist will attempt to help the subject develop heterosexual relationships. We do not believe that the application of a simple form of aversion therapy is likely to achieve this aim. It is true that aversion therapy can suppress homosexual behaviour, but it cannot be expected automatically to generate heterosexual behaviour. The therapist must understand first how the behaviour developed. He usually finds strong reinforcement of homosexual behaviour in adolescence (McGuire *et al.*, 1965). The subject may have tremendous anxiety about sexual intercourse and/or lack of social skills in relating to girls. Again, the problems which will be tackled depend on the behavioural analysis, but as a general guideline one should not expect that heterosexual behaviour will automatically appear when homosexual behaviour is reduced. The therapist should, for example, explore the subject's factual knowledge of heterosexual behaviour and attempt to correct any misconceptions before he tries to reduce any excessive anxiety about heterosexual behaviour.

The main point we are trying to make by including the above examples is that the most essential aspect of behaviour therapy is the detailed analysis of the problem. This analysis determines the goal for treatment and indicates the therapeutic procedure to obtain it. It is very unlikely that any two patients with the same 'symptom' or 'presenting problem', let alone the same diagnostic label, would require the same type of handling. In our view, it would not only have been ineffective to treat the two agoraphobics and the homosexuals in these examples in the same way because they were classified as either agoraphobic or homosexual. It might also have created considerable problems during treatment.

Research

Research into behaviour therapy has been tremendously impressive in terms of volume: no other therapeutic approach can claim such research attention. This is most likely because its formulations are relatively simple and based already on laboratory established data. Also, being a comparatively new therapy, its adherents were impatient to test and demonstrate its value by making comparisons with traditional methods. We have already mentioned its appeal as an applied and relevant topic for academic research. Therapists who use different frameworks will undoubtedly be surprised to learn that some people who do research on behaviour therapy have never treated actual psychiatric patients.

The research can roughly be divided into three areas: the studies investigating outcome; the studies investigating relevant components or processes and non-specific agents; the studies investigating theoretical issues. There is often considerable overlap between the first and second area. We have no space to make a comprehensive review of all the relevant research, particularly since the senior author has already discussed, in some detail, the impact of research on behaviour therapy (Meyer, 1973). We shall limit ourselves to abstracting some salient findings from the whole field.

Outcome Studies

In the area of outcome studies, one can say that if one selects phobic patients one can produce more improvement with systematic desensitization and in a shorter period of time than with certain types of psychotherapy, individual or group. However, the studies which support this conclusion are not very well controlled and one can always argue about the suitability of the criterion used to assess the outcome. Treatment of enuresis with the bell and pad method can produce considerable improvement in 80 per cent of those cases treated. Such results are better than if the subject receives no treatment or some type of psychotherapy. Finally, token economy projects for a variety of chronic schizophrenics appear to evoke desirable behaviour quicker than conventional types of treatment. The schizophrenics have shorter stays in hospital and they remain in employment outside the hospital longer. However, there is no evidence that readmission rate to hospital is reduced. The problem of generalization outside the hospital has proved in some instances insurmountable. The analogue studies which have been carried out mainly on students suffering from 'small animal phobias' are also shown to have a great number of flaws, making their results inapplicable to psychiatric patients (Bernstein and Paul, 1971). In fact if one takes into consideration Paul's criteria, it is very difficult to see how it is possible to conduct a convincing outcome study using present methodology (Paul, 1969). In some cases two behaviour therapy methods have been compared, for example, desensitization *versus* implosion. There are eight studies comparing the efficacy of desensitization and implosion—two only on psychiatric patients—and findings divide themselves into three categories: no difference, desensitization better than implosion, implosion better than desensitization!

Process Studies

As far as the components of treatment are concerned, there is no consistency in the research findings. For instance, in systematic desensitization, the most thoroughly investigated method, the components isolated depend on the theoretical orientation of the researcher. Directly related to this problem, there are 13 studies which investigate the relevance of therapeutic instructions to outcome. The same lack of consistency is apparent; half of the studies indicate that therapeutic instructions help, the other half that they make no difference to the outcome.

Theoretical Issues

Closely related to the studies above are those which are conducted to settle theoretical issues. Systematic desensitization has been said to operate on the following principles: counterconditioning, extinction, habituation, various cognitive factors, operant principles, Guthrian principles, feedback progress and self-instruction. Again, we find lack of consistency in this area. The evidence is carefully assessed by Wilson and Davison (1971) and Davison and Wilson (1973), who conclude that systematic desensitization must be a very complex procedure involving a great number of processes; no active ingredient has been isolated which would compel any procedural alteration of the basic techniques; as long as one exposes the patient to the phobic stimulus, preventing avoidance responses, he is most likely to improve.

Similarly with aversion therapy, the results of the research into its theoretical basis have been disappointing and inconclusive. For instance, recent attempts to isolate classical conditioning components when alcoholics were given aversion therapy have not been encouraging (Hallam *et al.*, 1972).

In general, it seems surprising that so much effort has been spent on the theoretical issues raised by the application of these techniques with so little progress. Perhaps one should remember that those undertaking pure research on learning have not yet been able to design crucial experiments to settle many of the basic issues using rats; behaviour therapists who cannot exert the same control on their patients should not expect miracles. Unfortunately, as things stand research has produced considerable confusion, but one hopes this is just a necessary developmental stage and that order will soon be restored as better methodology is evolved and research workers show more patience. At the moment clinicians profit most from pure research in various aspects of learning, for example, Azrin and Holt (1966) on punishment. They can extrapolate these 'hard findings' and procedures to clinical cases. Reports on individual cases can also give the clinician new ideas on how to conceptualize problems and consequently how to treat them. Another area of study which assists the clinician is detailed analysis of behaviour, for example, comparisons of alcoholics and social drinkers (Schaeffer *et al.*, 1971). Behaviour therapists are generally very interested in studies of the type carried out by Truax (1966) and Liberman (1971), who have shown how learning principles enter into other types of therapies. They hope to be able systematically to utilize this type of information.

Concluding Remarks

Basis of Behaviour Therapy and Training of Behaviour Therapists

If the basis of behaviour therapy is experimental psychology—particularly learning principles—it is important to question the validity of this source. We must accept the criticism that there is a noticeable lack of supporting parametric studies for some of our principles. This has been pointed out not only by cognitive therapists, but also by behaviour therapists themselves (Buchwald and Young, 1969). Recently Waters and McCallum (1973) answered the other criticism which is repeatedly made in some quarters that behaviour therapy is more mentalistic than behaviouristic. They state that many of the arguments are barren and based on irrelevant semantic differences; furthermore, that all types of therapies can be described equally well in either mentalistic or behaviouristic terms. Behaviour therapists do not deny the existence of mental phenomena though they describe them in different terms. They also accept that mental phenomena must be taken into consideration when making behavioural analyses and planning treatment programmes.

Behaviour therapists must content themselves with what Waters and McCallum term 'a loosely knit framework of principles', i.e. they use operationally defined learning principles. Trying to prove that they use a framework other than their own seems a futile exercise. For example, describing systematic desensitization as decreasing expectation of disastrous consequences or increasing objectivity may be merely labelling and will not help to solve its theoretical problems nor add to its therapeutic efficiency (Davison and Wilson, 1973).

Obviously, when the behaviour therapist administers his therapy it is impossible for him to refer continually to basic knowledge. Different types of interactions occur, verbal and non-verbal, that are not always consciously governed by learning principles; the therapist must behave spontaneously and use his clinical experience and commonsense. Apart from that, he must be alert to the possibility of using any other available knowledge to the benefit of his patient. The pure knowledge, i.e. learning principles, should only serve to guide the therapist's behaviour; the animal studies on which it is based are analogues for human behaviour and the therapist must use ingenuity to extrapolate the information to his own immediate problems.

It will be sobering to remember that whatever treatment is administered to psychiatric patients it is invariably associated with some degree of improvement for some cases. Unidentified processes must be common to all types of therapy and the model on which each therapeutic method is based cannot be the only relevant one. The behaviour therapist's whole approach to the selection of treatment goals and design of treatment will be based on learning principles and procedures derived from them. It is impossible to be completely rational when trying to explain why one favours one approach rather than another, especially in a field fraught with so much ambiguity and contradictions. It would be extremely difficult to understand any aspect of human behaviour without making prior assumptions. Consequently there is a tendency for a theoretical straightjacket to be imposed on patients.

Generally, it is felt that the training of behaviour therapists can be done by a combination of academic instruction and supervised clinical practice. Ideally, trainees should have a good knowledge of experimental psychology, particularly the field of learning, and considerable clinical experience. It is not essential for trainee therapists to have undergone treatment themselves.

General Issues

The relationship between the behaviour therapist and his patient is conceptualized in terms of learning principles from the start of the behavioural analysis. The patient's life style will give some idea of what type of behaviour the therapist must show to become a potent reinforcer. For the behaviour therapist there should be almost as many types of relationships as he sees patients. This adaptability is more important in cases of interpersonal problems than with isolated phobias. The behaviour therapist aims at something approaching an instructor/trainee relationship; he tries to avoid hiding behind a therapeutic veil. In the ideal situation he hopes that the patient will gradually become his own therapist and their interaction should reflect this.

It is important to the behaviour therapist that his patient does not see himself to be suffering from an 'illness', because in our view this induces passivity in the sense that the patient believes that some process in therapy will somehow eliminate the 'illness'. Rather, he should be encouraged to view his reasons for referral as problems in living for which he seeks guidance. Our approach stresses active participation in treatment and between treatment sessions. Because behaviour therapists do not accept the concept of mental illness nor the concept of ideal man, it follows that the concept of cure does not enter into the approach. The behaviour therapist attempts to adjust the patient to the existing norm of his milieu. However, when the therapist is trying to make this patient ajust to some social norm, he should be aware, as Kanfer and Phillips (1970) pointed out, that because there is so much technological and social change occurring in society it is difficult to adjust a patient to something stable. We must adjust ourselves and our patients to change.

Behaviour therapists also hope to overcome some of the ethical problems facing those in a position to manipulate human behaviour by keeping their patient informed during every step of treatment. This is viewed as safeguard against 'brainwashing'. It is also indicated by evidence in the literature that awareness of goals can facilitate or hinder conditioning (Bandura, 1969). In any case, it is essential to define what has to be modified as it helps to monitor the patient's behaviour, and indeed self-recording alone has often modified behaviour. The extent to which goals have been achieved or not may be assessed by the patient, significant people in his environment and the therapist. The patient will remain the final arbiter. The assessment of outcome is dependent on the establishment of good baselines at the beginning of treatment. It is obvious, on the other hand, that not every goal can be assessed objectively; it remains for the patient to decide whether he has improved or not.

We think that assessment of outcome of any psychotherapy can be 'scientific' provided that the concept of improvement is objectively specified. Outcome comparisons become impossible if the goals of therapy are different or specified loosely, for example, reorganization of personality, increased insight. The greatest problem in assessing the efficacy of behaviour therapy is that to maintain experimental rigour every patient must receive a standardized form of treatment without considering individual differences, and some patients will be mistreated. Once individual differences are taken into account, experimental rigour is sacrificed. Therefore a suitable methodology must be developed to overcome this problem.

We do not see behaviour therapy as something to be contrasted with psychotherapy, particularly 'dynamic psychotherapy'—the basic approach of behaviour therapy can be used by any therapist provided his aetiological formulations and his goals are specified as outlined here. Sometimes the behaviour therapist himself may conceptualize the patient's problem in 'Rogerian', 'Sullivanian' or 'social psychiatric' terms. His aetiological formulation and his goals of treatment may seem to be very close to these approaches. However, the way in which the behaviour therapist will go about achieving the set goals will be explicitly and systematically guided by learning principles.

In essence, we see behaviour therapy as emphasizing the continuous rather than discontinuous links between normal and abnormal behaviour; based on loosely knit principles rather than rigid theories; using sensitive innovation rather than mechanical reapplication; directed by clear-cut goals rather than diffuse ideals—in all, an approach rather than a technology.

References

Ayllon, T., and Azrin, N. H. (1968). *The Token Economy*, Appleton-Century-Crofts, New York.

Azrin, N. H., and Holt, W. C. (1966). 'Punishment', in W. K. Honig (Ed.), *Operant Behaviour*, Appleton-Century-Crofts, New York.

Bandura, A. (1969). *Principles of Behavior Modification*, Holt, Rinehart & Winston, New York.

Barlow, D. H. (1972). 'Aversive procedures', in W. S. Agras, *Behavior Modification: Principles and Clinical Applications*, Little, Brown, Boston.

Berkowtiz,B. P., and Granziano, A. M. (1972). 'Training, parents as behaviour therapists: A review, *Behav. Res. & Ther.*, **10**, 297.

Bernstein, D. A., and Paul, G. L. (1971). 'Some comments on therapy analogue research with small animal 'phobias', *J. Behav. Ther. & Exp. Psychiat.*, **2**, 225.

Buchwald, A. M., and Young, R. D. (1969). 'Some comments on the foundation of behavior therapy', in C. M. Franks (Ed.), *Behavior Therapy: Appraisal and Status*, McGraw-Hill, New York.

Budzynski, T., Stoyva, J., and Adler, C. (1970). 'Feedback-induced muscle relaxation—application to tension headache', *J. Behave. Ther. & Exp. Psychiat.*, **1**, 205.

Cautela, J. R. (1971). 'Covert conditioning', in A. Jacobs and L. B. Sachs (Eds.), *The Psychology of Private Events: Perspective on Covert Response Systems*, Academic Press, New York.

Clark, F. W., Evans, D. R. and Hamerlynck, L. A. (Eds.) (1971). *Implementing Behavioral Programs for Schools and Clinics*, Research Press, Illinois.

Conger, J. C. (1971). 'The modification of interview behavior by client use of social reinforcement', *Behav. Ther.*, **2**, 52.

Davison, G. C., and Wilson, G. T. (1973). 'Process of fear-reduction in systematic desensitization: cognitive and social reinforcement factors in humans', *Behav. Ther.*, **4**, 1.

Dunlap, K. (1932). *Habits: Their Making and Unmaking*, Liveright, New York.

Ernst, F. A. (1971). 'Behavior therapy and training in clinical psychology: A student's perspective', *J. Behav. Ther. & Exp. Psychiat.*, **2**, 75.

Franks, C. M. (1969). *Behavior Therapy: Appraisal and Status*, McGraw-Hill, New York.

Gannon, L., and Sternbach, R. A. (1971). 'Alpha enhancement as a treatment for pain: A case study', *J. Behav. Ther. & Exp. Psychiat.*, **2**, 209.

Goldstein, A. P. (1962). 'Therapist–patient expectancies in psychotherapy', Pergamon, New York.

Hallam, R., Rachman, S., and Falkowski, W. (1972). 'Subjective, attitudinal and physiological effects of electrical aversion therapy', *Behav. Res. & Ther.*, **10**, 1.

Jehu, D. (1972). *Behaviour Modification in Social Work*, Wiley–Interscience, New York.

Kanfer, F. H., and Phillips, J. S. (1970). *Learning Foundations of Behavior Therapy*, Wiley, New York.

Kanfer, F. H., and Saslow, G. (1969). 'Behavioral diagnosis', in C. M. Franks (Ed.), *Behavior Therapy: Appraisal and Status*, McGraw-Hill, New York.

Krasner, L. (1971). 'Behavior therapy', *Ann. Rev. Psychol.*, **22**, 483.

Levy, R., and Meyer, V. (1971). 'Ritual prevention in obsessional patients', *Proc. Roy. Soc. Med.*, **64**, 1115.

Liberman, R. P. (1971). 'Behavioral group therapy: A controlled clinical study', *Brit. J. Psychiat.*, **119**, 535.

McGuire, R., Carlisle, J. M., and Young, B. G. (1965). 'Sexual deviations as conditioned behaviour: A hypothesis', *Behav. Res. & Ther.*, **2**, 185.

Marks, I. M. (1972). 'Flooding (implosion) and allied treatments', in W. S. Agras (Ed.), *Learning Theory: Application of Principles and Procedures*, Little, Brown, New York.

Meyer, V. (1966). 'Modification of expectations in cases with obsessional rituals', *Behav. Res. & Ther.*, **4**, 273.

Meyer, V. (1973). 'The impact of research on the clinical application of behaviour therapy', in T. Thompson and W. D. Dockens III (Eds.), *Proceedings of the International Symposium on Behavior Modification*, Appleton-Century-Crofts, New York.

Meyer, V., and Chesser, E. S. (1970). *Behaviour Therapy in Clinical Psychiatry*, Penguin, Harmondsworth.

Morganstern, K. P. (1973). 'Implosive therapy and flooding, procedures: A critical review, *Psychol. Bull.*, **79**, 318.

Paul, G. L. (1969). 'Behavior modification research: design and tactics', in C. M. Franks (Ed.), *Behavior Therapy: Appraisal and Status*, McGraw-Hill, New York.

Rachman, S., and Teasdale, J. (1969). *Aversion Therapy and Behavior Disorders: An Analysis*, University of Miami Press, Miami.

Ritter, B. (1968). 'The group desensitization of children's snake phobias using vicarious and contact desensitization procedures', *Behav. Res. Ther.*, **6**, 1.

Schaeffer, H. H., Sobell, M. B., and Mills, K. D. (1971). 'Baseline drinking behaviors in alcoholics and social drinkers; kinds of drinks and sip magnitude', *Behav. Res. & Ther.*, **9**, 23.

Schwitzgebel, R. L., and Ackerland, V. (1972). *Psychotechnology Supplement: A Compilation of Techniques and Apparatus for Behavior Modification*, Psychotechnology Lab., 8857 Central Avenue, Montclair, CA 91763.

Solyom, L., and Miller, S. D. (1967). 'Reciprocal inhibition by aversion relief in the treatment of phobias', *Behav. Res. & Ther.*, **5**, 313.

Stoyva, J., Barker, T., DiCara, L., Kamiya, J., Miller, N. E., and Shapiro, D. (Eds.) (1972). *Biofeedback and Self Control: an Aldine Annual on Regulation of Bodily Processes and Consciousness*, Aldine-Atherton, Chicago.

Suin, R. M., and Richardson, F. (1971). 'Anxiety management training: A non specific behavior for anxiety control', *Behav. Ther.*, **2**, 498.

Truax, C. B. (1966). 'Reinforcement and non-reinforcement in Rogerian psychotherapy', *J. Abnorm. Psychol.*, **71**.

Waters, W. F., and McCallum, N. (1973). 'The basis of behavior therapy, mentalistic or behaviouristic? A reply to E. A. Locke, *Behav. Res. & Ther.*, **11**, 157.

Wilson, G. T., and Davison, G. C. (1971). 'Processes of fear reduction in systematic desensitization: Animal studies', *Psychol. Bull.*, **76**, 1.

Wolpe, J. (1958). *Psychotherapy by Reciprocal Inhibition*, Stanford University Press.

Wolpe, J. (1969). *The Practice of Behavior Therapy*, Pergamon, New York.

Yates, A. J. (1970). *Behavior Therapy*, Wiley, New York.

13

BEHAVIOUR MODIFICATION

Chris Kiernan

Introduction

This paper will have four main goals. First of all it will try to define the area denoted by the term behaviour modification—to try to distinguish this area from other areas of contemporary development of the application of behavioural principles. Secondly it will try to outline the basic principles of behaviour modification and to demonstrate the extent to which these principles can be elaborated. The third aim is to exemplify the usage of the behaviour modification approach in a number of therapeutic contexts. Many of the contexts in which behaviour modification is applied would not normally be called therapeutic. The normal school setting is probably the clearest example. As we shall see, the use of the term therapeutic tends to beg several critical questions concerned with the alternative service models available for the exploitation of behaviour modification principles. The final goal of this paper is to highlight problems and issues within the sphere of application of behaviour modification. The Editor asked that 'issues dying and issues rising' should be discussed. These issues will be raised in the course of discussion of usage of behaviour modification.

The paper will be organized in four sections. The first will deal with the definition of behaviour modification. The second with procedures and principles of behaviour modification. In the third section problems of organization and content of programmes will be considered. Finally the relation of applied to pure research in the area will be discussed.

There are a wide variety of settings in which behaviour modification programmes have been attempted or completed. For the psychiatrically normal deviant child or adult of normal intelligence programmes have been set up in the home, the work environment, in normal school, in schools for the delinquent and in prisons. Psychiatrically disturbed individuals have been programmed for in home, work, schools and recreational setting as well as extensively in institution. Programmes for the mentally retarded have been set up in the home and school, at work and in recreational settings both in and out of institutions. Throughout this variety of contexts the same basic questions of programming, procedures and outcome are raised.

Definition of Behaviour Modification

The term behaviour modification is used loosely and in a different way in different contexts. Early uses of the term by Watson (1962) and Krasner and Ullman (1966) emphasized the analysis of clinical situations which could be used effectively in therapy and in which there was an emphasis on learning. Included in these areas of consideration were structured interviews, hypnosis and a variety of other procedures which could be interpreted in behavioural terms, or according to Krasner and Ullman which could be shown to be effective in changing behaviour. Clearly this approach is highly inclusive. All the procedures usually subsumed under behaviour therapy and indeed many other therapies would be interpreted as behaviour modification procedures. This type of definition is in fact used, especially in the United States (cf Agras, 1972).

The problem of definition may be approached from a different angle. Conceptually there are three interrelated threads in behaviour modification. The first is the reliance on operant principles in the analysis of behaviour (Bijou and Baer, 1961; Skinner, 1938; 1953). This factor distinguishes the approach from the behaviour therapy tradition, which owes its conceptual roots more to Pavlov, Hull and latterly Eysenck.

The second thread is, as we shall see, critically related to the basic premises of operant analysis. This is the argument that in order to treat or change behaviour the environment of the individual must be changed. Put another way, the argument is that behaviour cannot optimally be modified by brief sessions in an environment isolated from the individual's life space. Optimal change occurs when the social and material environment is changed. This argument has particularly powerful implications for provision of services. If the social and physical environment is critical, then the day-to-day custodians, family, nurses or teachers, become the principal agents of change and therapy must include modification of their behaviour, and of the physical environment as it lays the basis for their behaviour, as well as that of the client.

The third thread in the behaviour modification approach is the assertion that the behaviour of normal and deviant groups, whether they be mentally handicapped, psychotic, criminal or neurotic, is subject to the same laws. In other words, it is assumed there is a continuity of normal and deviant behaviour.

These three features may be used to distinguish the approach from others. They also allow the definition of an area of literature at the lowest level by the extent to which the authors refer to Skinner, Bijou or to publications in the *Journal of Applied Behaviour Analysis*. However, there is a substantial artificiality about these distinctions since the underlying theory applies equally fruitfully to area of work normally seen as within the behaviour therapy sphere in the United Kingdom. In particular the operant analysis of phobic responses is rare. However, the work of Agras, Leitenberg and their colleagues indicates that valuable insights can be provided by this type of approach to what is traditionally a 'behaviour therapy' area (Agras *et al.*, 1968; Leitenberg *et al.*, 1968). In practice the bulk of behaviour therapists and behaviour modifiers use a mixture of techniques. Where differences are likely to occur is in the style of therapy. The behaviour therapy tradition might well favour emphasis on a medical treatment model involving greater reliance on the particular expertise of the therapist rather than an environmental modification approach with a greater reliance on modifying the behaviour of significant individuals in the individual's social environment.

The Basic Principles of Behaviour Modification

The fundamental assumption of behaviour modification is that the behaviour of the individual is the prime datum with which we should deal. Bijou argues that we should look at 'retarded behaviour' as opposed to 'retarded mentality'. Secondly it is assumed that the control and explanation of the behaviour of the individual can best be effected by a consideration of the environment which supports his behaviour. This assumption has several facets. It involves an emphasis on the analysis of stimulus conditions in the environment, and the behaviour, the actual responses of the individual.

Within the theory responses are classified as either operants, broadly speaking (and loosely speaking) voluntary skeletal responses, and respondents, classically conditioned responses which may be primarily emotional responses. Skinner's original statement of the theory argued that operants were controlled by their consequences, for example lever-pressing was maintained by delivering of grain to the pigeon, whereas respondents were elicited (Skinner, 1938). The model for the respondent was the classical Pavlovian conditioning setting. Aside from problems of distinguishing operants from respondents even in the salivary conditioning situation, recent demonstrations have shown that heart-rate, vasoconstriction and intestinal responses, all considered as respondents, can be brought under control of consequences. In other words they can behave as operants (Katkin and Murray, 1968). Behaviour modification work has tended to ignore respondents. The vast bulk of studies deal with behaviour as if it was purely operant. This point may be critical and we shall return later to its possible implications.

Stimuli are classified into three broad groups. They may elicit respondents, they may set the occasion for operants and they may reinforce responses. Some stimuli may operate in all three ways. Thus the presence of an adult in a ward may act as an eliciting stimulus for a profoundly retarded child to smile if the adult is associated with pleasant events. The same adult may set the occasion for operants like approaching, speaking or pulling his hand. Finally the presence of the adult may be rewarding both in the sense of eliciting positive respondents and through dispensing other rewards, for example, physical contact, as following approach by the child.

This example indicates the possible complexity of analysis offered by the operant approach. Several studies illustrate this complexity. Redd and Birnbrauer (1969) used a procedure in which mentally retarded children were rewarded by one adult for 'appropriate play' while a second adult rewarded the children regardless of their behaviour. The authors found that when the adult who rewarded appropriate play came into the room the children began to play appropriately. When the other adult

came in the behaviour of the children did not change. In this case the adult was functioning as a discriminative stimulus for behaviour. In a further study Redd (1969)
showed that as an adult sometimes rewarded contingently for appropriate
behaviour and sometimes non-contingently the behaviour he typically produced
was not modified overall. The children would behave appropriately with a 'contingent' adult but not with the 'mixed' adult. However, if the mixed adult withheld
reward for non-appropriate play the children began to play appropriately. In other
words the children had learned to discriminate the situation in which non-reward
occurred and had learned to switch to appropriate play given this contingency. In
overall terms the adult was functioning as a discriminative stimulus for appropriate
play only when the reinforcing stimulus was *not* being delivered following *inap*-
propriate play. Thus the reward–non-reward situation had in itself discriminative
properties.

The Redd studies illustrate some complexities of stimulus analysis and make the
point that rewards themselves can have crucial stimulus properties.

Within the theory several authors would distinguish a separate category of setting events within the discriminate stimulus category. A setting event is an event
which affects a whole set of succeeding events. For example, brain damage, disease,
infection, the action of some drugs, deprivation of food or social contact may all be
seen as setting events (Bijou and Baer, 1961). This concept allows more of the
biological and historical elements in behaviour to be assimilated into the theory.
However, it is a relatively poorly developed concept although it could be of great
use. For example, one of the major phenomena in the behaviour of some groups of
retarded or psychiatrically disturbed people is their mood swings. An operant
analysis of this phenomenon would be possible given the conceptual tools available
but has not been undertaken, at least to this author's knowledge. Similarly the
theory would suggest that different responses had differing probabilities given
varied settings. Despite the possible important nature of this proposition to
modification of behaviour, little significant attempt has been made to analyse
response probabilities in differing settings.

A final word should be added about the types of rewards and punishments normally used in behaviour modification projects. As already indicated, rewards and
punishments are defined empirically. In other words the reinforcers used must be
tailored to the needs of the individual. Rewards group themselves into two broad
categories. On the one hand there are edible and sensory rewards, food, the opportunity to experience simple sensations or to play with simple toys. This group of
rewards may be of prime value with the retarded, especially the profoundly
retarded, since they may be only rewards which reinforce their behaviour. However,
these rewards present problems for a number of reasons. The basic laws of acquisition suggest that the most rapid change in behaviour will come about if rewards or
punishments are delivered immediately following every response and if reward or
punishment is of high quality or magnitude. Edible or sensory rewards present
problems from all of these viewpoints. Their administration is often cumbersome
and they are often subject to rapid satiation effects. One solution to the satiation
problem with edibles has been to use the individual's normal meals as reinforcers.

Whilst this can be seen as justifiable under some circumstances, it makes for ethical problems which are not easy to resolve.

Partly as a consequence of these considerations, and partly in realization of the need to integrate the individual into a normal system of reinforcers, substantial emphasis has been placed on social rewards and conditions rewards such as tokens or points. The social reward, particularly verbal social rewards, are optimal from the viewpoint of learning economy. They can be delivered very rapidly following response, they can be graded in quality, the 'cost' little and satiation effects, although demonstrable, do not present the same problems as with edible rewards. Tokens or points are clearly more artificial. These rewards are normally used within token economy systems in which 'payment' is made for completion of jobs, appropriate behaviour or whatever is deemed necessary within the system. Many such systems have been developed in many settings (Ayllon and Azrin, 1968; O'Leary and O'Leary, 1972). From the reinforcement viewpoint one critical element in both social and token systems is the provision of a wide range of back-up reinforcers, rewards which follow positive social behaviour or which the individual can 'buy' with his points or tokens. Without these behaviour will not be maintained by conditioned rewards. Back-up reinforcers may include edible rewards, toys, activities such as visits to the cinema or special privileges. Critical to the success of the system of back-up rewards is that they should be of a sufficiently wide range to allow for individual differences in the group concerned. If a back-up system involves choice on the part of the individual, sampling from a menu, it partly copes with the satiation problem.

Punishments may be similarly grouped. They may be either direct, such as electroshock, or indirect, such as negative social reinforcement or loss of tokens or points within a token economy system. Problems concerned with the use of punishers will be taken up in the next section.

Learning Settings

The basic learning principle involved in the operant approach is that behaviour is controlled by its consequences. Thus positive consequences, rewards defined as events which the individual will approach, will lead to an increase in responding if they follow a response. Negative consequences on the other hand will lead to a decrease in response probability if they are made to follow a response. These two situations represent the simple reward training and punishment training situations. Two further simple training paradigms are possible. The first, time-out from positive reinforcement, involves the withdrawal of the individual from a rewarding situation following an undesired response. Examples of time-out are easy to come by. Effective control over unacceptable mealtime behaviour can be readily attained by removing food for a brief period of time following the undesired response (Barton et al., 1970) or alternatively by removing the individual from the table. Other simple examples include withdrawal of attention for inappropriate behaviour or exclusion from a television room or recreational setting for specified behaviours. The defining features of the time-out procedure are that the 'loss' of reward or exclusion from a reward setting occurs immediately following an unacceptable response. Secondly the exclusion is for a fixed period of time which may vary from seconds upwards but is normally less than 30 minutes, after which reward or a rewarding setting is reinstated—provided the undesirable behaviour has stopped. This last point could be important. There is little to be gained by ignoring for a fixed period of time an individual who is having a tantrum if he is to be then given attention again regardless of his behaviour. What may well happen in this case is that extended tantrums are rewarded.

The final procedure involves the withdrawal of punishment following appropriate behaviour. In order to implement this procedure the individual must be subjected to an unpleasant event from which he escapes only by behaving appropriately. The best everyday example of this procedure is the nagging situation in which the individual escapes from the aversive stimulus by doing what he is asked to do, at least in theory. This procedures, escape training, is very rare in behaviour modification work, for clear ethical reasons and also because of its relative inefficiency as a teaching procedure.

These four learning situations do not exhaust all possible paradigms although several common procedures can be seen as special cases of this classification. For example, extinction is a special case of either time-out from reward or escape training. These and other situations are all assumed to involve basic laws of learning which we mentioned in the last section. These were that learning will be more efficient if consequences follow immediately on behaviour, if they follow every time responses occur and if they are of high magnitude.

There are clear problems with some of the procedures. The most effective punishing stimuli will be intense, and will be delivered every time a response occurs immediately following the response or will continue until a response occurs in escape learning. For some aversive events, for example, the delivery of electric shock, this fact leads to substantial ethical problems, to say nothing of practical difficulties. Other aversive events, for example, loss of points in a token economy, may be easier to manage. However, on an overall basis it is clearly more congenial for staff or therapists, and more practical, to use procedures involving the presentation and withdrawal of reward as the prime means of modifying behaviour.

The empirical evidence on the relative effectiveness of procedures using positive and negative reinforcers appears fairly clear. Reward training on its own can be highly effective (Kiernan, 1974). On the other hand punishment training on its own is an uncertain procedure and time-out will be effective only under certain circumstances. The reasons lie in the fact that in order to be effective both time-out and punishment require the development of competing responses. Bostow and Bailey (1969) used time-out in an attempt to control loud abusive verbal behaviour in a hospitalized retarded woman. The woman, who was non-ambulatory, was removed from a chair, seated on the floor and ignored for two minutes for shouting. After the two minutes a 15-second interval of silence was required before she was put back in the chair. She then had to remain quiet for a further 10 minutes, at which time she was then given things which she liked. In addition she was given a treat, favoured object or attention at least once every 30 minutes if she refrained from the loud abusive behaviour. Bostow and Bailey were successful in bringing the behaviour under control. In a similar study Vukelich and Hake (1971) reduced dangerous aggressive behaviour in an institutionalized woman by systematic programming of time-out and initial massive positive social reinforcement for non-aggressive behaviour. Vukelich and Hake then phased out the additional social reinforcement but found that it was not possible to phase it out completely. In the end six minutes' attention per hour for non-aggressive behaviour was programmed. This level successfully controlled behaviour.

These studies lead to consideration of a critical issue in behaviour modification. Is it ever necessary to use procedures involving aversive events? In the examples quoted it would seem that the active element in modification was the development of competing behaviour through reward. One can argue that the individuals in both studies appeared to be living in severely deficient environments (an environment in which six minutes' attention per hour must be *programmed*) and that teaching the individual responses which could be rewarded or rewarding him for existing acceptable behaviour provided the essential element in changing behaviour.

The same general position holds with punishment training. Both basic laboratory studies and case studies suggest that rapid learning will occur if reward and punishment are used differentially in the same setting. But the use of punishment on its own appears to produce unstable results (Azrin and Holz, 1966). Corte *et al.* (1971) found it necessary also to punish self-injurious behaviour in several settings and in the presence of several individuals before generalization occurred, and also report recurrence of self-injurious behaviour in one of their four subjects. Again the development of competing responses which are positively reinforced appears necessary (Kiernan, 1974).

There are, however, instances where the use of punishment training appears necessary. These are situations in which the behaviour concerned is self-injurious, for example head-banging, eye-gouging or vomiting, and where as a consequence the behaviour must be eliminated as rapidly as possible. There are several demonstrations of the effectiveness of punishment procedures as a rapid way of eliminating such behaviours. For example, Lovaas and Simmons (1969) recorded up to 9,000 self-destructive responses (hitting self) in a retarded autistic child before the behaviour extinguished in one setting. The effect did not generalize to other settings. Twelve one-second electroshocks over 14 sessions eliminated hitting completely in a second setting, and without the development of other self-destructive behaviour. This study is fairly representative of published studies on punishment in showing rapid effects. One can conclude that if punishment training can be this effective with these difficult behaviours its use can be welcomed.

The second situation in which punishment may be felt necessary is that where the resources of the environment do not provide enough opportunity for positively reinforced activity. This may result from lack of personnel, from lack of facilities or from the unsuitability of the facilities provided for the population concerned. Under these circumstances the use of punishment training procedures would seem in general unacceptable. The problem shifts clearly to administrators and agencies providing funds and making decisions on salary levels and conditions of work.

Remarks on unacceptability apply more to work with the severely retarded and chronic schizophrenic populations, for whom punishment is likely to involve aversive events like electroshock. Since the early work of Weiner (1962) it has been clear that response-cost procedures, for example loss of points, can be highly aversive for individuals working in a token economy setting. For example, Kaufman and O'Leary (1972) showed that disruptive behaviour in a token economy classroom for pupils in a psychiatric hospital could be reduced by reward for appropriate behaviour or loss of points for inappropriate behaviour. No differences appeared between the conditions and there were no adverse side-effects in the form of increases in inattention, aggression, 'time-off task' or decreases in achievement or attendance. This and many other studies suggest that the response-cost form of punishment training may be of substantial value. However, the response-cost procedure makes the assumption that the individuals have something to lose, that the environment can and does provide adequate sources of reward which can be manipulated to achieve given ends.

We might summarize this argument by saying that under circumstances where the environment is highly deficient punishment training may be the only effective means of changing behaviour since it is the cheapest means of modification. This use of the procedure does not seem acceptable. Where the environment does provide facilities other procedures are possible, some of which may be formally equivalent to punishment training.

Overall the procedures of choice in changing behaviour are reward training and time-out from reward. Punishment, if used, must be coupled with reward training to be effective.

Organization and Content of Behaviour Modification Programmes

In this section we shall try to lay out some of the issues arising from the organization of behaviour modification programmes. These issues were implicit in the discussion in the last section. They will now be made explicit.

We can draw an initial distinction between the teaching and the maintenance or living environment of the individual. These environments have different requirements from a behaviour modification viewpoint and with many individuals will need to be different in practice.

A good learning environment, i.e. an environment in which rate of learning can be maximized, is one in which the reinforcers, whether they are positive or negative, can be delivered rapidly and if necessary in varying degrees and at various frequencies. Secondly the environment should be one in which the desired behaviour can be brought out at its highest initial natural rate. This may involve using particular discriminative stimuli, for example, talking or singing to an individual in order to encourage verbalization. In addition competing responses may be discouraged by removing stimuli which may lead to them occurring. So toys would be put out of sight and distracting sounds eliminated as far as possible. The ideal teaching environment is therefore likely to be highly simplified in order to allow a focus on the responses to be trained. It may end up as a small bare cubicle in which the therapist works with the individual. The precise requirements of the ideal teaching environment will be dictated by the particular task. The crucial features are that responses which may compete with the to-be-trained response are discouraged and reinforcers can be efficiently delivered at will.

The living or maintenance environment will similarly vary with the target behaviours and the target population. For adolescent delinquents in Achievement Place, a therapeutic home and school setting (Phillips, 1968), the ideal environment may represent one in which they are required to perform certain duties, to take certain decisions and to behave in agreed ways. In this environment they receive rewards in the form of points on agreed scales which can be traded for privileges. For profoundly retarded children the ideal environment may be one in which there is a rich supply of settings in which the individual can use his limited capacity to operate toys or do chores which may in themselves be rewarding or may lead to reward (Kiernan *et al.*, 1973).

From the behaviour modification viewpoint there are three elements in the ideal living environment. The first and most critical is that the individual should be able to respond appropriately to the environment in a way which produces reward. The second common element is that the environments should be coordinated with the natural environment as closely as possible if the final aim of the programme is entry or return to the natural environment (Baer and Wolf, 1970). The third common element concerns the way in which the first and second are to be coordinated. For both groups in our examples the living environment provides a means of generalizing and consolidating learned behaviours. For the profoundly retarded this may involve transfer from a specific learning situation. For the adolescent or the psychiatric patient the concern in the living environment may be with direct learning in that environment or with simply maintaining existing behaviour.

Returning to our first common element, the creation of an environment which provides an adequate range of response possibilities is partly a matter of imaginative planning and partly a financial matter. The need to provide such an environment is clear from the arguments of the previous section. Optimal space, privacy, recreational materials and social contact must be available in the direct living environment. In addition most individuals require special facilities which may be used as back-up reinforcers or simply to enrich experience. These may include work facilities, shops, cinemas, dance halls, swimming pools and holidays. One of the apparent problems with institutions is that they are frequently geographically isolated. Consequently, although substantial efforts may be made to provide direct and general facilities, the expense which this entails both in personnel and materials is too great and the result is inadequate provision as compared to that offered by the natural community. There is a clear advantage to facilities placed in the natural community in this respect as also in their ability to recruit and retain staff.

A final point should be made concerning the requirements of the direct living environment. We could clearly run the risk of producing an environment which is too 'educationally' oriented in the sense of being 'school-like'. The mentally retarded, psychiatrically disturbed, delinquent or normal school population must be seen as having the right to 'fun', to elective enjoyment which has no direct educational aim.

Provision of attractive clothes, records, games, pin-ball machines, comics, alcohol or girlie magazines may all be argued as reasonable if this point is accepted. Access to these provisions may still be programmed but their nature may be determined by the individuals involved.

The second common element in all programmes is the coordination of the programme with the natural environment. There are two aspects of this problem which require separation. On the one hand there is the need to specify the behaviour required by the natural environment. On the other there is the need to analyse and plan for the contingencies which operate in the natural environment, to find out how behaviour is normally reinforced.

Put another way, there is a need to specify the targets of the programme. In some cases these targets are easy to specify. For example, the achievement of independent toileting represents a relatively easy behaviour to specify, although even with this example problems concerned with programme planning can be substantial (Tierney, 1973). Similarly the elimination of problem behaviours may involve a fairly easily specified goal behaviour although again the route to achievement of the goal may be complex. For example, elimination of self-destructive behaviour may involve a substantial programme of training in competing behaviour (Callias et al., 1973).

Where the individual's behaviour is severely deficient, or deviant in several ways, if is often difficult to specify exactly what target behaviours would be required by the natural environment.

One substantial attempt to specify target behaviours was made by Lent et al. (1967). These workers established a token programme for 27 retarded girls (IQ 25–55) in an institution. They analysed the requirements for integration into the local community and then established programmes in relevant skills, for example, personal appearance, gait, sewing, ironing, leisure-time activities and town orientation. Transfer to the community setting was mediated by project staff accompanying the girls into work settings and identifying problems which they experienced. This allowed gradual shift of control to natural contingencies with problems isolated and eliminated in the process.

Rather more typically than in the Lent study, target behaviours are specified arbitrarily or rationally and appear to bear more relation to maintaining behaviour at an adequate level in the institution than an attempted discharge and personal development. Winkler (1970) rewarded psychiatric patients with tokens for getting up, attendance at morning exercises, bed-making and dressing; he removed tokens for noise-making and violence. Similarly Davidson, quoted by Ayllon and Roberts (1972), related his goals explicitly to his 'institution'. The project involved two battalions of army trainees (2,500 men). Target behaviours were specifically oriented to training and included physical fitness, marksmanship and performance on inspection.

The general point is that if the 'syllabus' for the programme is institution-oriented then all that may happen is that the programme will produce more effectively institutionalized individuals. A similar point is made by Winett and Winkler (1972). They argued that classroom applications of behaviour modification procedures have concentrated on elimination of disruptive behaviour, aggression and inattention rather than on positive aspects of classroom interaction. The children are being taught to 'be still, be quiet, be docile' and behaviour modifiers have been 'instruments of the *status quo*, unquestioning servants of a system which thrives on a petty reign of "law and order" to the apparent detriment of the educational process itself' (1972, p. 501).

These assertions are hotly denied by proponents of token economies. The general point made is that although token economies *could* be used in a repressive way there is nothing inherent in the system which forces them to be used in this way. Ayllon and Roberts (1972) point out that token economy systems must be subject to 'constant adjustment in order to maximize motivation, learning and growth', they must respond to the individual's needs. Similarly O'Leary (1972) in a reply to Winett and Winkler lists educational areas in which behaviour modification has been used successfully. These include academic achievement, including reading and other behaviour in disadvantaged children, and a substantial block of work on speech development and on the development of positive social responding in children. Ayllon and Roberts and O'Leary both emphasize that there is a distinction between the use of procedures and the goals of a programme. Behaviour modification represents an approach to the analysis of behaviour and a set of developing techniques. As yet the developing body of theory underlying behaviour modification is poorly developed. Therefore behaviour modification offers means of modifying behaviour but does not indicate exactly what behaviour should be modified or to what end. Once this point is realized it becomes clear that close attention must be paid to working out who should set goals for therapy, with what justification these goals are set and what they imply for the future overall adjustment of the individual to society. This is the fundamental ethical issue of behaviour modification as with all therapy. Because the nature of the populations usually dealt with by behaviour modifiers makes them particularly subject to coercive control and because the techniques are effective this problem is especially acute and requires clear definition and debate.

The third common element across all programmes concerns the way in which learning and living environments and the overall goals of a programme may be coordinated. In other words, how should programmes be set up and goals achieved? Two dominant considerations, one organizational, the other conceptual, need to be taken into account. The organizational component is the need for adequate planning. The conceptual component is the need to plan for appropriate generalization of learned behaviours. Both throw up several needs.

The first of these needs, to specify target behaviours, has already been discussed at some length at a general level. The specification of target behaviours involves a clear behavioural statement of the type 'When spoken to with his name the individual will turn, smile and say "Hello" whilst establishing eye contact with the speaker', or 'will assemble components putting faulty or inappropriate parts in a separate pile. If a run of 10 faulty or inappropriate parts occurs will call the supervisor'. In these statements individual terms may be additionally specified as they affect task requirements, for example, 'faulty part'. This procedure of specification of target behaviours is similar to that used in occupational areas (Davies, 1971). It has the virtues that it requires the teacher to specify clearly what he wants in the situation and can allow him any particular level of initiative which he may specify.

Having decided on target behaviours, the next step is to break down the behaviours into steps for training. How much of this procedure is necessary depends on the intellectual level of the individuals concerned. In general the mentally retarded will require a closer breakdown of skills than most other groups.

There is general agreement on the need to structure learning in the behaviour modification literature. In an operant programmed ward for profoundly retarded children Kiernan and Wright (1973) found it necessary to restructure the environment and to introduce timetables in order to allow staff to do individual training sessions. Similarly Ayllon and Azrin (1968), Panyan et al. (1970) and Thompson and Grabowski (1972) emphasize the need to plan and structure the activities of wards in order to allow programmes to be implemented.

These projects and others have used parents, teachers, nurses or hospital attendants as the main change agents. The reasons for this move stem from the fundamental proposition underlying behaviour modification—that the total social environment of the individual is critical rather than one specific individual, the therapist. There is now a substantial literature which shows that it is perfectly feasible to train non-professionals to use behaviour modification procedures effectively (e.g. Bijou and Ribes-Inesta, 1972). How effective these training programmes are overall is questionable. Gardner (1973) in a review of the literature points out that there is relatively little general evidence to demonstrate effectiveness and few well-specified programmes (Kiernan and Riddick, 1973; Riddick and Kiernan, 1973). What does exist is evidence that individual parents or teachers can be highly effective. For example, Hall et al. (1972) showed that parents could use behaviour modification techniques effectively in eliminating behaviour problems of diverse types in normal children. These included programmes relating to the use of an orthodontic device, performance of household tasks and other behaviours. Other workers have reported similar individual or group success with disturbed children (Johnson and Brown, 1969; Wahler and Erickson, 1969).

There is little doubt that individuals can be trained to various levels of competence in behaviour modification. Gardner (1973) distinguishes four levels of possible competence. These are the 'technician' level, the 'specialist', an individual who is highly specialized in one area, the 'generalist' who can work with a variety of problems and the 'consultant' who generally trains non-professionals in behaviour modification principles and techniques. One clear problem is what level the training of non-professionals should proceed to if effective behaviour modification is to occur. The question has obvious implications for service provision in planning requirements and training for psychologists or psychiatrists who might act as consultants and for the training of teachers and nurses who presumably may act as consultants, generalists or specialists.

Development in the use of non-professional therapists has been substantial but as yet inadequate. The depth of the problems presented by therapy with some groups is indicated by Kazdin and Bootzin (1972) in a review of work on token economies.

They point out that although success in development of these programmes has been reported those running the programmes have failed to generalize them to the natural environment. Whilst this is a clear defect in the implementation of programmes, the job of training extensive cohorts of non-professional individuals in and out of institutional settings is probably beyond the resources of most current researches. It is only when training has been extended that adequate tests of the generalizability of token procedures can be made. Even if the scope of a programme is restricted to a single environment the use of groups of individuals to operate as therapists clearly involves organizational problems. These vary from area to area. In the retardation field and in token economies the overall needs are for uniformity and consistency of approach to maximize rate of learning of clients and for provision of guidance for individuals working at the technician or specialist levels. This requires an organization which allows checks on what is being done with a particular individual and what his specific needs are. In many token economies the turnover of staff is high (e.g. Worters and Thorpe, 1973) and consequently the need for communication and organization is increased still further. The twin needs of structuring activity for therapists and communication are often met by drawing up specific programmes which detail steps in training and allow a recording to be made of trials completed or frequency of responding. For example, suggested steps in play and dressing were devised by Kiernan and his colleagues to guide the work of nurses with profoundly retarded children (Kiernan *et al.,* 1974). The programme was devised to give suggestions on steps and also to allow the nurse to see some structure or progression in work on the children's programmes. This aspect of reinforcement of staff by feedback from a programme or from generalists and consultants who can track the progress of training may be crucial in maintaining staff behaviour and morale.

This brings us back to the recurrent theme of goals and goal specification. In assigning priorities to goals there are clearly several possible influences. These include the priorities of the individual as he expresses them, the priorities expressed by parents or other relatives, the priorities expressed by prison officers, nurses and teachers and the priorities expressed by physiotherapists, speech therapists, psychologists, psychiatrists and medical personnel who may have contributions to programming. These several sets of priorities may conflict and some clear means whereby professional competence and human rights can be brought into harmony needs to be devised.

From the viewpoint of the educationalist or psychologist specification of programmes often requires assessment. In general, existing assessment instruments are of little help in programme planning (Jones and Kiernan, 1973). They have often been devised for administrative purposes, i.e. to assign rather than to diagnose, and even when diagnostic procedures have been to the forefront the data they yield, for example, a Rorschach protocol, is of doubtful behavioural significance. Several attempts have been made to develop approaches to programme planning which involve more precise specification of goals and steps. Bricker (1972) provides a detailed breakdown of the steps required in teaching language to the mentally retarded. This programme is described in the form of a lattice, a systematic layout of the steps required in training. Similar lattices have been developed by Budde and

Menolascino (1971) for diverse types of self-help and other skills. Jones and Kiernan (1973) developed an educationally oriented battery of tests for the profoundly retarded. An example of one of their lattices is given in Figure 1.

These lattices are of interest in several ways. They reflect the fact that there is a need to provide structure and direction to programmes by allowing progression. The also reflect the fact that when an attempt is made to specify exactly how an ability is attained, what steps are necessary, the situation emerges as one in which the steps are complex and our ignorance of correct sequencing massive. It is often pointed out that we do not know how complex behaviour is until we try to teach someone. This point is also brought home forcibly by the exercise of trying to specify steps in a teaching programme.

The idea behind specification of programmes is partly analytic and partly an aid to transmission of information. The question of what types of behaviour should be taught has a further aspect. Some types of behaviour, for example, language behaviour, appear to be more generally valuable than others. With language even a rudimentary knowledge or willingness to communicate can effectively mesh the individual into the discriminative and reinforcement structure of the natural environment. Other behaviours may be similarly valuable. For example, the tendency to imitate on cue models presented, generalized imitation, may be a very valuable ability for the non-verbal individual. Aside from being a possible precursor to language it appears to have value in itself as a tool to mediate learning. Kiernan and Saunders (1974) examined the transfer from one setting to another and from one individual to another of the tendency to imitate. Profoundly retarded children were tested in the training room and in the ward setting by the trainer, a nurse and a stranger on separate occasions. The average score over six subjects is shown in Figure 2. Generalization between settings was clearly almost complete. Generalization across individual testers was good and was maximized when the nurse and stranger rewarded appropriate imitative responses.

Both language and imitation can free the individual to an extent from the constraints of the immediate training situation. Other behaviours which have been taught.systematically also share this characteristic. Bandura (1965) and Kanfer (1970) have written extensively on the development and training of self-regulation of behaviour. Kanfer and Phillips (1966) used procedures in which individuals were trained to observe their own behaviour, evaluate and categorize it and then to reorganize their environment on the basis of learning principles and reward appropriate behaviour.

Miechenbaum taught impulsive children to talk to themselves as a means of self-control (Miechenbaum and Goodman, 1971). The procedure involved the therapist modelling the required task behaviour of talking himself through a task, after which the child repeated the task, first talking himself through it and subsequently whispering and then 'talking silently'. The modelled verbalizations involved questions and answers, self-instructions and self-reinforcement. The procedure was effective at the time of training and positive effects were shown in a one-month follow-up. Extensions of this work have been reviewed by Miechenbaum (1973).

These studies are of both theoretical and practical interest. They represent a

PERCEPTUAL PROBLEM SOLVING

Name _____

Date _____

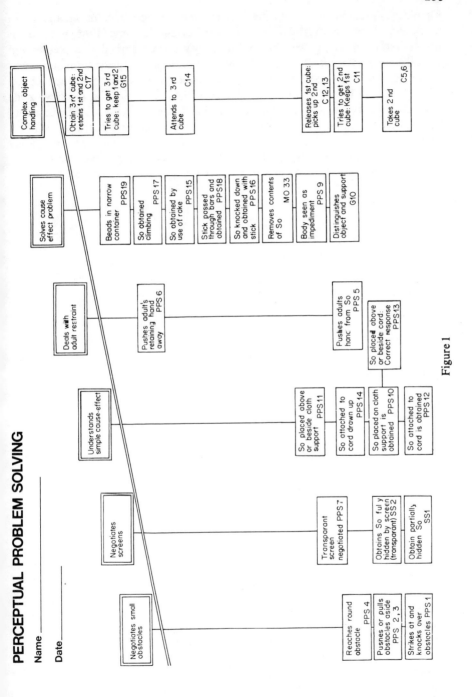

Figure 1

significant development in the behaviour modification approach in the attempt to teach and use internal verbal regulation of behaviour. Homme (1966) pointed out that 'coverants' may be amenable to control by the same general principles as hold for other operants. On the practical side the provision of programming of self-regulated cues and rewards has already been exploited in some types of application with obesity and drug dependence. The possibility clearly exists of allowing the mentally retarded and schizophrenic individual a greater degree of autonomy through teaching him how to regulate his own behaviour and the rules he should follow in this process. Coupled with careful programming of teaching the individual to make choices, this aspect of programme development offers a means whereby an individual may be allowed to break free from the need for custodial care.

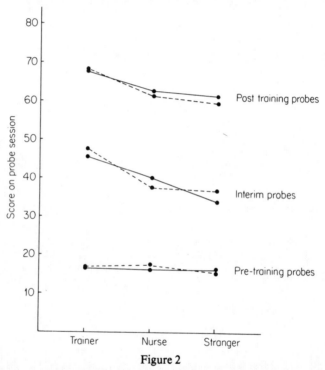

Figure 2

This raises the final crucial issue in any therapy. Does it allow the therapist to produce a cure? No substantive answer can be given to this question for behaviour modification. This is partly because of problems in the definition of 'cure' in a context where several variables are modified by 'treatment', and partly it is because the population dealt with through behaviour modification procedures have often been subject to such neglect that 'cures' could not reasonably be expected. Currently there are several projects aimed at early intervention with the mentally retarded in which the overall viability of the model in producing substantial and permanent change in behaviour can be evaluated (e.g. Bricker and Bricker, 1972). However, until such projects come to fruition the behaviour modification approach can claim substantial amelioration of a wide variety of problems despite the relative recentness of its development as a therapeutic procedure.

One feature of behaviour modification work which has militated against evaluation is the tendency for workers in this area to stick closely to operant methodology and to reject the concept of control group research. Many of their arguments are perfectly reasonable. They do not wish to substitute statistical for experimental control. They argue that techniques which are effective should be shown to be effective with all individuals rather than losing individual differences in the outer darkness of the error term of the analysis of variance. However, certain types of question cannot easily be answered without control group methodology. In particular, questions concerned with the overall effectiveness and cost efficiency of services require that comparisons are made at least between existing service and new service provision (Kiernan et al., 1973). There are, however, clear indications from published studies that these questions are being seriously considered. It is to be hoped that the integration of control group and operant methodologies will lead to more fruitful methodological procedures in which both individual and group considerations can be given full account.

Concluding Remarks

One final issue concerning behaviour modification needs to be covered. Despite its foundations in laboratory experimentation behaviour modification has surprisingly little contact with empirical research in other fields. Two levels of contribution to the applied behaviour modification field can be distinguished. Firstly there are possible contributions from operant studies in the laboratory setting. Secondly work in cognate applied fields could clearly be of value. Rather surprisingly, the latter contributions appear better assimilated. Examples have already been quoted from the child development and language fields and others are common as content for programmes.

It is from the first field, that of laboratory operant studies and conceptualization, that there is a relatively clear and unfortunate separation. This has several possible dangers which can be illustrated by an example. As noted in an earlier section, the division of responses into operants and respondents is one which concerns many workers in the pure field. On the one hand there is an attempt to elucidate and redefine the concepts (e.g. Catania, 1971). On the other much contemporary work is given over to the examination of aspects of the interrelation of operants and respondents traditionally defined (Gilbert and Millenson, 1972).

We noted earlier that there is the tendency for applied workers to treat virtually all responses as operants. Therefore responses such as self-destructive behaviour, disordered speech or aggression are treated as operants and extinguished or reinforced accordingly. The assumption is often made in these cases that a peculiar reinforcement history has led to the shaping and maintenance of these responses, but almost without exception these retrospective histories are untested and, by the very nature of retrospective histories, untestable.

If we examine these examples in the light of pure research in operant work it

258

becomes clear that examples like those quoted could be analagous to the schedule-induced emotional responses studied in rats in the laboratory. These responses include water, air and nitrogen drinking, wheel-running, copulation and eating (Segal, 1972). The responses can be *treated* as operants in that their probability can be affected by consequences. However, a proper understanding of the variables involved in induction of the response lies in recognizing their 'emotional' or 'mood' basis. If the responses of human beings which have this basis are treated as operants it may well be that they can be modified. However, the theory underpinning operant work as it is developing in the laboratory may well suggest more subtle and effective means of dealing with the behaviour. One would hope to see a trend in the future towards an increased recognition of the need for more complex analyses in applied work.

This point links with our final point. Perceptive readers, if they are still with us at all, will have noticed the avoidance of the term applied behaviour analysis in this paper. This alternative to behaviour modification as a term seems to imply that studies involve a close analysis of discriminative and reinforcing stimuli and a close analysis of response topographies prior to modification. In fact this approach is rare in the applied field; there are few good examples of full-scale analysis of behaviour (Gardner *et al.*, 1968). There are several reasons for this. Behaviour analysis or functional analysis is a procedure which requires observation, the formulation of hypotheses, intervention in order to check hypotheses and then subsequent reformulation in order to allow identification of relevant stimuli. This is a long-winded process often beyond the resources of the practitioner (Kiernan, 1973). Secondly it is often possible to override the effects of currently operating discriminative, setting and reinforcing stimuli with new clearer and more powerful ones. For example in the deficit environment of a hospital ward the introduction of clear communications and reinforcers will be quite likely to override the effects of vagueness of instructions and infrequent reinforcers which may have been operating before. If the behaviour of parents, teachers or nurses has been leading to disturbed behaviour, changing their behaviour may be adequate with a full-scale analysis being undertaken before changing it. The approach may be rough-and-ready, but if it is effective in deficit environments it seems justifiable. On the other hand it may be dangerous as a strategy in more complex environments. One would hope to see an increasing tendency on the part of behaviour modifiers to analyse behaviour before they attempt modification, and trust that this would lead to more efficient modification procedures.

References

Agras, W. S. (Ed.) (1972). *Behaviour Modification: Principles and Clinical Applications,* Little, Brown, Boston.
Agras, W. S., Leitenberg, H., and Barlow, D. H. (1968). 'Social reinforcement in the modification of agoraphobia', *Archieves of General Psychiatry,* **19,** 423.
Ayllon, T., and Azrin, M. (1968). *The Token Economy,* Appleton-Century-Crofts, New York.

Ayllon, T., and Roberts, M. D. (1972). 'The token economy: Now', in W. S. Agras (Ed.), *Behaviour Modification: Principles and Clinical Applications*, Little, Brown, Boston.

Azrin, N. H., and Holz, W. C. (1966). 'Punishment', in W. K. Honig, *Operant Behaviour: Areas of Research and Application*, Appleton-Century-Crofts, New York.

Baer, D. M., and Wolf, M. M. (1970). 'The entry into natural communities of reinforcement', in R. Ulrich, T. Stachnik and J. Mabry, *Control of Human Behaviour. Volume Two From Cure to Prevention*, Scott, Foresman, Glenview, Illinois.

Bandura, A. (1965). 'Vicarious processes: A case of no-trial learning', in L. Berkowitz (Ed.), *Advances in Experimental Social Psychology*, Academic Press, New York.

Barton, E. S., Guess, D., Garcia, E., and Baer, D. M. (1970). 'Improvement of retardates' mealtime behaviours by timeout procedures using multiple baseline techniques', *Journal of Applied Behaviour Analysis*, **3**, 77.

Bijou, S. W., and Baer, D. M. (1961). *Child Development 1: A Systematic and Empirical Theory*, Appleton-Century-Crofts, New York.

Bijou, S. W., and Ribes-Inesta, E. (1972). *Behaviour Modification: Issues and Extensions*, Academic Press, New York.

Bostow, D. E., and Bailey, J. B. (1969). 'Modification of severe disruptive and aggressive behaviour using brief time-out and reinforcement procedures', *Journal of Applied Behaviour Analysis*, **2**, 31.

Bricker, W. A. (1972). 'A systematic approach to language training', in R. L. Schiefelbusch (Ed), *The Language of the Mentally Retarded*, University Park Press, Baltimore, pp. 75–85.

Bricker, D. D., and Bricker, W. A. (1972). *Toddler Research and Intervention Project. Report Year 1, IMRID*, Peabody College, Nashville, Tennessee.

Budde, J. F., and Menolascino, F. J. (1971). 'Systems techology and retardation: Applications to vocational habilitation', *Mental Retardation*, **9** (2), 11.

Callias, M., Carr, J., Corbett, J., and Jenkins, J. (1973). 'Use of behaviour modification techniques in a community service for mentally handicapped children', *Proceedings of the Royal Society of Medicine*, **66**, 1140.

Catania, A. C. (1971). 'Elicitation, reinforcement and stimulus control', in R. Glaser (Ed.), *The Nature of Reinforcement*, Academic Press, New York.

Corete, H. E., Wolf, M. M., and Locke, B. J. (1971). 'A comparison of procedures for eliminating self-injurious behaviour of retarded adolescents', *Journal of Applied Behaviour Analysis*, **4**, 201.

Davies, I. K. (1971). *The Management of Learning*, McGraw-Hill, London.

Gardner, J. E., Pearson, D. T., Bercovici, A. N., and Bricker, D. E. (1968). 'Measurement, evaluation and modification of selected social interactions between a schizophrenic child, his parents and his therapists', *Journal of Consulting and Clinical Psychology*, **73**, 844.

Gardner, J. M. (1973). 'Training the trainers: A review of research on teaching behaviour modification', in R. D. Rubin, J. P. Brady and J. D. Henderson, *Advances in Behaviour Therapy*, Volume 4, Academic Press, New York.

Gilbert, R. M., and Millenson, J. R. (1972). *Reinforcement: Behavioural Analyses*, Academic Press, New York.

Hall, R. V., Axelrod, S., Tyler, L., Grief, E., Jones, F. C., and Robertson, R. (1972). 'Modification of behaviour problems in the home with the parent as observer and experimenter', *Journal of Applied Behaviour Analysis*, **5**, 53.

Homme, L. E. (1966). 'Perspectives in psychology—XXIV. Control of coverants, the operants of the mind', *Psychological Record*, **15**, 501.

Johnson, S. M., and Brown, R. A. (1969). 'Producing behaviour change in parents of disturbed children', *Journal of Child Psychology and Psychiatry*, **10**, 107.

Jones, M. C., and Kiernan, C. C. (1973). 'The development of a teaching oriented assessment battery for the profoundly retarded', Paper to the Third International Congress of IASSMD, The Hague, September, 1973.

Kanfer, F. H. (1970). 'Self-regulation: Research, issues and speculations', in C. Neuringer and J. L. Michael (Eds.), *Behaviour Modification in Clinical Psychology*, Appleton-Century-Crofts, New York.

Kanfer, F. H., and Phillips, J. S. (1966). 'Behaviour therapy: A panacea for all ills or a passing fancy', *Archives of General Psychiatry*, **15**, 114.

Katkin, E. S., and Murray, E. N. (1968). 'Instrumental conditioning of autonomically mediated behaviour', *Psychological Bulletin*, **70**, 52.

Kaufman, K. F., and O'Leary, K. D. (1972). 'Reward, cost and self-evaluation procedures for disruptive adolescents in a psychiatric hospital school', *Journal of Applied Behaviour Analysis*, **5**, 293.

Kazdin, A. E., and Bootzin, R. R. (1972). 'The token economy: an evaluative review', *Journal of Applied Behaviour Analysis*, **5**, 343.

Kiernan, C. C. (1973). 'Functional analysis', in P. Mittler (Ed.), *Learning in the Mentally Handicapped*, Churchill Livingstone, London; Williams and Wilkins, Baltimore, Md.

Kiernan, C. C. (1974). 'Behaviour modification', in A. M. Clarke and A. D. B. Clarke, *Mental Deficiency: The Changing Outlook*, 3rd edition, Methuen, London.

Kiernan, C. C., Harlow, S., Saunders, C., and Riddick, B. (1974). *Programme Materials 2*, University of London Institute of Education, Thomas Coram Research Unit, London.

Kiernan, C. C., and Riddick, B. (1973). *A Programme for Training in Operant Techniques, Vol. 1, Theoretical Units*, University of London Institute of Education, Thomas Coram Research Unit, London.

Kiernan, C. C., and Saunders, C. (1974). 'Generalized imitation, Final Report to the DHSS, Unpublished.

Kiernan, C. C., and Wright, E. C. (1973). 'The F6 Project—a preliminary Report', *Proceedings of the Royal Society of Medicine*, **66**, 1137.

Kiernan, C. C., Wright, E. C., and Hawks, G., (1973). 'The ward wide application of operant techniques', Paper to the Third International Congress of IASSMD, The Hague, September, 1973.

Krasner, L., and Ullman, L. P. (1966). *Research in Behaviour Modification*, Holt, Rinehart & Winston, New York.

Leitenberg, H., Agras, W. S., Thomson, L. E., and Wright, D. E. (1968). 'Feedback in behaviour modification: An experimental analysis in two phobic cases', *Journal of Applied Behaviour Analysis*, **1**, 131.

Lent, J. R., LeBlanc, J., and Spradlin, J. E. (1967). 'Designing rehabilitative culture for moderately retarded, adolescent girls', in R. Ulrich, T. Stachnik and J. Mabry, *Control of Human Behaviour. Vol. Two, From Cue to Prevention*, Scott, Foresman, Glenview, Illinois.

Lovaas, O. I., and Simmons, J. Q. (1969). 'Manipulation of self-destructive behaviour in three retarded children', *Journal of Applied Behaviour Analysis*, **2**, 143.

Miechenbaum, D. H. (1973). 'Cognitive factors in behaviour modification: modifying what clients say to themselves', in R. D. Rubin, J. P. Brady and J. D. Henderson (Eds.), *Advances in Behaviour Therapy*, Vol. 4, Academic Press, New York.

Miechenbaum, D. H., and Goodman, J. (1971). 'Training impulsive children to talk to themselves. A means of developing self-control', *Journal of Abnormal Psychology*, **77**, 115.

O'Leary, K. D. (1972). 'Behaviour modification in the classroom: a rejoinder to Winett and Winkler', *Journal of Applied Behaviour Analysis*, **5**, 505.

O'Leary, K. D., and O'Leary, S. G. (1972). *Classroom Management: The Successful Use of Behaviour Modification*, Pergamon, New York.

Panyan, M., Boozer, H., and Morris, N. (1970). 'Feedback to attendants as a reinforcer for applying operant techniques', *Journal of Applied Behaviour Analysis*, **3**, 1.

Phillips, E. L. (1968). 'Achievement Place: token reinforcement procedures in a home-style rehabilitation setting for predelinquent boys', *Journal of Applied Behaviour Analysis*, **1**, 213.

Redd, W. H. (1969). 'Effects of mixed reinforcement contingencies on adults' control of children's behaviour', *Journal of Applied Behaviour Analysis*, **2**, 249.

Redd, W. H., and Birnbrauer, J. S. (1969). 'Adults as discriminative stimuli for different reinforcement contingencies with retarded children', *Journal of Experimental Child Psychology*, **7**, 440.

Riddick, B., and Kiernan, C. C. (1973). *A Programme for Training in Operant Techniques. Vol. 2, Practicals*, University of London Institute of Education, Thomas Coram Research Unit, London.

Segal, E. F. (1972). 'Induction and the provenance of operants', in R. M. Gilbert and J. R. Millenson, *Reinforcement: Behavioural Analyses*, Academic Press, New York.

Skinner, B. F. (1938). *The Behaviour of Organisms*, Appleton-Century-Crofts, New York.

Skinner, B. F. (1953). *Science and Human Behaviour*, Macmillan, New York.

Thompson, T., and Grabowski, J. (1972). *Behaviour Modification of the Mentally Retarded*, Oxford University Press, London.

Tierney, A. J. (1973). 'Toilet training', *Nursing Times*, **1973**, 1740.

Vukelich, R., and Hake, D. F. (1971). 'Reduction of dangerously aggressive behaviour in a severely retarded resident through a combination of positive reinforcement procedures', *Journal of Applied Behaviour Analysis*, **4**, 215.

Wahler, R. G., and Erickson, M. (1969). 'Child behaviour therapy: A community programme in Appalachia', *Behaviour Research and Therapy*, **7**, 71.

Watson, R. I. (1962). 'The experimental tradition and clinical psychology', in A. J. Bachrach, *Experimental Foundations of Clinical Psychology*, Basic Books, New York.

Weiner, H., (1962). 'Some effects of response cost on human operant behaviour', *Journal of the Experimental Analysis of Behaviour*, **5**, 201.

Winett, R. A., and Winkler, R. C. (1972). 'Current behaviour modification in the classroom: be still, be quiet, be docile', *Journal of Applied Behaviour Analysis*, **5**, 499.

Winkler, R. C. (1970). 'Management of chronic psychiatric patients by a token reinforcement system', *Journal of Applied Behaviour Analysis*, **3**, 47.

Worters, A. R., and Thorpe, W. H. (1973). 'The Phoenix Ward', Paper to a symposium of the Institute of Mental Subnormality, Lea Hospital, Bromsgrove, Worcestershire, Unpublished.

14

WHAT IS BEHAVIOURAL PSYCHOTHERAPY?

P. T. Brown

The term 'behavioural psychotherapy', recently coined for political ends, has been rapidly enshrined in a British Association. That such an event neither stirred antagonism nor was heralded by any charter statement of intent and purpose should not be surprising, for it marks the apotheosis of eclecticism; that is, by dignification, a resounding non-event. Rarely can a scientific/therapeutic grouping have been formed which has so little clarity of purpose other than to provide an umbrella obfuscating all (professionals) beneath. Picture an increasingly crowded small area (as professionals, especially those under real or assumed threat, find joining irresistible) in which those with something to shout about seek to outdo each other with increasing stridency while those hoping to learn hear only the shouts of those nearest in a background of unfiltered noise. Then tremble for the future of therapeutic skills clearly established and knowingly defined.

This is not to deny or impute the honest purpose of those setting up the British Association of Behavioural Psychotherapy. But it is to question their wisdom. No psychologist, psychiatrist or social worker can be unaware of the guarded acceptance which his or her expert status receives within the community at large. To increase the role confusion that there is at present, thereby more confounding, serves no ends except those of self-preservation by protectionist professionals. The converse is needed—role definition based upon functional differences, in which the community can distinguish who does and offers what and professionals themselves can encompass a body of professional knowledge and experience which is recognized by other professionals as being their especial contribution to whatever help mankind needs. The rediscovery of human nature by 'the public' (*vide Time* 2.4.73) may be an assertion of autonomy with which the experts are quite unequipped to cope. Deterministic culture of, say, 1940s and 1950s films,* apparently resolving once and for all the question of responsibility by denying its existence, looks simple-minded in retrospect. But at least the point of view is clear. The eclecticism of 'behavioural psychotherapy' which by neglect states nothing is no alternative.

If the term 'behavioural psychotherapy' is to have any value, the confusion implicit in the first *Newsletter* of the British Association of Behavioural Psychotherapy (1972) requires overt recognition before it gets out of hand, and before it is too widely and uncritically adopted. By way of an approach, in the following passage the second two paragraphs of the first editorial are reprinted essentially as they appear, but broken up into what appear to be the key statements and numbered (1), etc., while the commentary in brackets is my own.

(1) The first Executive Comittee of the BABP consists of different professions, psychiatry, psychology and social work, but represent a common philosophy which we hope will benefit clients at a time of rapid change in therapeutic approaches. (The Association is interdisciplinary. Rapid change and consequent anxieties force us to herd together, and we hope something comes out of it.)

(2) The reorganization of the NHS in 1974 and the Foster Report with its discussion of the possible registration of psychotherapists are two issues which will, and should, have profound effects on the personal and health services of everbody in Britain. (Is all the world confusion? The registration of psychotherapists will in fact affect no one but psychotherapists.)

(3) It is important that professional differences are not allowed to interfere with the advancement of behavioural approaches. (Let's get everyone together to make sure that nobody pre-empts what anybody else would wish to be doing in the registration scramble.)

(4) We welcome correspondence, news, requests for information, or short reports on research, from anyone in 'behavioural psychotherapy'. (As we don't know what behavioural psychoth⌣apy is, we have to put it in quotes right away.)

(5) This title may seem strange to those not at the inaugural meeting, but it was obvious very quickly to those present that they could argue *ad infinitum* over the choice of the perfect word. (There was in fact no real choice to be made, as no one knew what it was all about except the protection of professional interests. The title seemed strange to those who *were* at the meeting.)

(6) What we see as important at this stage in the history of psychological approaches to human problems, whether they be behaviour therapy, behaviour modification or behavioural intervention, is the reliance on the principles of scientific psychology. (What's happened to the psychotherapy bit? In desperation we can wave the banner of scientific psychology.)

* As it is impossible to offer the reader a quick appropriate film at this point, the following 'psychiatric folk song' will capture the spirit of the above statement in words:

At three I had a feeling of
Ambivalence towards my brothers,
And so it follows naturally
I poisoned all my lovers.
But now I'm happy; I have learned
The lesson this has taught;
That everything i Do that's wrong
Is someone else's fault—O.H.MOWER (1960)

(7) We are pleased to include in the first issue the thoughts of our Chairman. . . .(For binding in red covers and waving?) He says:

(8) '. . . I do believe that the case for the formulation of the British Assiciation for Behavioural Psychotherapy is an overwhelming one. The approach to psychological treatment, *originally known as behaviour therapy,* has a relatively short history . . .'. (Italics mine. Doesn't 'psychotherapy' get a look in anywhere?)

(9) . . . its conceptual framework has become greatly extended and its principles are as relevant to ward, classroom and community programme as to individual therapy. . . . moreover, its practice, unlike that of dynamic psychotherapy, does not have a metropolitan focus but is spread evenly throughout the country. (With psychotherapy relegated to the dynamic metropolis, what relevance does it have to behavioural? Would 'psychotherapeutic behaviourism' be as acceptable? Why does behaviour therapy have to sneak around in disguise these days?)

No further demonstration of confusion is necessary. Yet what might an editorial actually have said that would have been helpful to our present condition—by which I mean the recognition of human dis-ease but a relative incapacity to provide a reliable remedy?

There might at least have been a recognition of the fundamental difference between behaviour modification and psychotherapy—the difference that is not simply solved by transliteration of the phenomona of one into the language of the other or the juxtaposition of terms. This difference lies in the approach of each to the understanding of another human being. The application of learning theory is just that: application. It looks suspiciously as if the BABP is simply offering another brand, indistinguishable from the real thing by taste but with better spreading characteristics. Such a simple-minded marketing will not do.

In the form in which it is typically understood, the function of the behaviour therapist is to conceive of one human being as a person subject to lawful processes for whom, by the exercise of expertise, the lawful processes will be made manifest. Or at least if not manifest, then operative; and so the individual is essentially re-educated or adjusted. No attention is in any way paid to the 'meaning' of an individual's life, or the complexity of strife and striving within which any particular 'maladaptive' behaviour appears. The phenomonology of existence at a philosophical and experiential level passes the behaviour therapist by. His formal language cannot admit it. This is not to deny that under some circumstances of limitation, such as severe subnormality, the principles of learning theory and their application may be the best therapeutic contribution that can be made. We should be hasty, however, if we assumed that in all other conditions they are either sufficient or best. It may be that the most useful outcome of the application of learning theory under the severe conditions of long-term hospitalization will be a development of our understanding that it is the limited conceptions of those who set themselves up as therapeutic agents which limit the development of those we seek to help—an observation which is not new but whose lesson is hard to accept. It is more comforting to assume the efficacy of learning theory than accept any understanding of therapist limitation.

A further aspect of the practice of behaviour modification which might have stimulated the editors into a consideration of the similarities between behaviour therapy and psychotherapy instead of consigning the latter to oblivion should not go unnoticed, and that is the therapist effect. It is recognized in a simplistic fashion in Wolpe's formulation of the efficacy of the therapist as an anxiety reducer (Wolpe, 1958). What behaviour therapist, however, is taught to consider, let alone taught to value, the effect of feelings of hope, longing for comfort, need for reassurance which, by their presence in an anxious person, make him (the therapist) effective? Or conversely, the feelings of hostility, social dissonance and despair which make him ineffective. Is it the therapist who is effective or the receptive perceptions of the person seeking aid which endow him with whatever efficacy he has? The behaviour therapist seeks to define away, in classical or operant terms, those life-based qualities of humanity which his presence as a helping agent paradoxically demonstrates. This is not to deny the contribution of individuals such as Friedman (1972) who, pragmatically, has responded to the felt human need embodied in marital and family tension. But it is well to observe that it is not learning theory which gives him his starting point, but his response as a human being to felt human need.

The single most trenchant objection to the ethos of behaviour modification, for whose development within his own development this author shares the blame, is that it dehumanizes.* To classify any behaviour as 'maladaptive' implies value judgements similar to those of 'illness', and any therapist who starts from such an assumption puts himself in a position of moral rectitude which limits his therapeutic sharing in the life-striving of the individual with whom he is intimately concerned. It is a fundamental tenet of this author's approach to therapeutic participation in the life of any other person that, at any point in time, each individual is providing himself with the best possible *adaptive* solutions that he can. The only authority that I as an individual have to share in another's life-striving derives from the other person's wish to involve me, in the explicit knowledge that I offer to him a fundamental belief in his worth and value as a human being as I assign these characteristics to myself; and that the search for help is not a recognition of inadequacy but part of the process of developing adequacy. A 'patient' uses a 'therapist' in the same way that a 'therapist' might consult an accountant—as a person who can make available resources not immediately or easily available from any other source. In my interaction with an accountant I feel in no way diminished, but were I to be offered five minutes of grudging time once every three weeks by an accountant who frequently changed his manifestation by nationality and/or interest, as would be the case if I were attending an NHS out-patient accountancy clinic, the effect upon me would undoubtedly be altogether different.

Unlike behaviour therapy, the process of psychotherapy conceives of an individual in whom the affective component is of paramount importance. In practice, the central focus of interest has varied, from the formality of the analytic couch and the unconscious of the analysed (e.g. Fromm-Reichmann, 1949), through the exploratory concerns of daseinsanalysis (e.g. Condran and Boss, 1968) which ad-

---

* At a summer school on measurement techniques in 1969, Dr J. M. M. Mair first faced me with the real dilemma of classification by psychometric investigation—that is, its dehumanizing assumptions about the individual. The provocative collection of papers by Sahakian (1970) left me with input that could no longer be ignored.

mits behaviour as an exploratory rather than cathartic act, to the central concern of common language and facility of communication as exemplified by Berne (1961) and the transactional school. Concern for the affective state of the individual is not limited to the analysand but also includes that of the analyst, and so psychotherapy operates within a set of assumptions which, within the theoretical model, admits of the interactive emotional forces of human beings. Thus, for instance, White (1964) lists five basic processes 'which pretty well cover the action that goes on in psychotherapy' as:

(1) the therapeutic relationships;
(2) expression of feelings;
(3) pointing out feelings;
(4) transference;
(5) new behaviour.

It is only with the latter that the behaviour therapist is theoretically and practically equipped to cope, though undoubtedly the variables of personal interaction establish therapist effects, observed in variable outcome rates from therapists applying similar conditioning treatments (e.g. Schmidt *et al.*, 1965).

It is in this that the non-sense of the term 'behavioural psychotherapy' lies, for the behaviour therapist excludes from deliberate concern those variables which the psychotherapist seeks to use therapeutically, but which are present *de facto* in that behavioural situation.

Yet perhaps a recognition of the meaningless juxtaposition of terms will permit a meaningful exploration of what possibilites might really be inherent in this composite term that is now coming into use. For it is my judgement that therapeutically exciting possibilities are contained within a concept of behavioural psychotherapy once the muddled uncertainty of the present state of confusion is removed.

The position I espouse, and from which the management of the case described below has both evolved and simultaneously contributed to the evolution of my own ideas, is anti-model and experiential. It does not ignore theory or knowledge but incorporates whatever is available within formal systems that is within my comprehension. Thus it is not *limited* by theory or model, except insofar as the limitations of my own experience and of my own knowledge and capacity to respond emphathetically to others in a therapeutic context impose boundaries beyond which my conceptual system can conceive only of the (personally) incomprehensible.

This approach imposes upon the therapist—the behavioural psychotherapist—a unique position of which he needs to be aware, because it carries obligations that are inescapable. In the first place, he assumes within society the professional responsibility for acting and interacting as a full human being, developing for the benefit of those with whom he interacts professionally the full capacity of their joint humanity. In the second place, he makes explicit to himself and to anyone with whom he interacts professionally the nature of his own perception about what being a human being is about—in the campus jargon, where he's at. That is to say he exposes to another human being his own conception of humanity so that the other human being can decide *whether* or *not* to involve his existence in the existence of the therapist, for while the therapist can in no way carry the responsibility *for* the other person's life, he carries a considerable burden of neglect if he fails to explain his own ground rules. If he does fail to make them explicit, he dehumanizes the individual by offering him no real choices, for he has not used the other person's human capacities to make his own choices upon the basis of information freely sought and received. Hence his therapeutic efforts are *ulta vires*. In the third place, he makes himself as competent in knowledge as his own limitations permit. In the fourth place, he makes himself as open and receptive to understanding the world of the other person as he can be, both by encounter as a human being and by the formal procedures of psychological enquiry. And in the fifth place, he recognizes the limits of his own conceptual boundaries—what I call above an awareness of the (personally) incomprehensible. Herein lies safety, for the therapist accepts the obligation both to proceed into the unknown yet not without caution or unknowingly; and hence he knows when he is incompetent or ill-prepared to proceed.

We have then started out with some exploration of the state of being a therapist, and the therapist is one of three resources which come to a therapeutic situation. The second is the other human being, the he or she client, patient, colleague or whatever. The therapeutic task is to offer to this person an extended awareness of life possibilities. On the assumption that the individual who seeks out the therapist does so as part of his continuing life statement of a search for self-fulfilment, self-actualization or development of his own potential, he comes not as an 'ill' person or 'neurotic' person or a person with 'personality disorder', but as a human being making the best statement of his life that he possibly can at that point in time in the explicit understanding that he is still searching. Thus the therapeutic task is to help the individual acquire more of the expertness of being a human being. (He or she may, of course, be more expert than the therapist; or may be an individual not really seeking change but with an overburdened expectation of life failure using the therapist as a further confirmation of that expectation, driving the therapist who is overcommitted to changing people and getting them 'better' to heroic therapeutic endeavour. But that is no one's fault but the therapist's, who failed to understand and who thereby left himself no option to refuse to be involved to the other person's life statement, which he, the therapist, has a perfect right to do.)

The third resource is time. It is a gross presumption to imply that my time as a therapist is any way intrinsically more valuable than another person's. It is equally an offence to his humanity to let it be assumed that his life experience, which is time-based, can be conveniently fitted into my time demands. I may as a therapist be unable, for all kinds of practical reasons, to meet his time demands (both in amount or interval), but that is a limitation of mine, not a matter to be subverted under the phrase of 'neurotic demand' or some such. In a goal-orientated, high-achieving Western civilization, shared time becomes such a precious commodity that individuals will spend inordinate amounts of private time in order to have a fraction of another person's time (think of an out-patient department), when both people sharing the time know that what they give to each other is inadequate for their actual needs and both feel frustrated in consequence. As psychologists involved in the experience of another person, it is the other person's time-base of which we need a critical understanding.

Given the involvement of two human beings and the availability of time, for what purpose does the therapeutic situation exist? As already implied, it arises from the needs of one and the availability (and often the needs) of the other. It exists for the client to conduct a further exploration of the possibilities of life. Maslow's (1967) statement contains the kernel of my own belief, which is the basis of my own explicit interaction with clients.

All the evidence that we have (mostly clinical evidence, but already some other kinds of research evidence) indicates that it is reasonable to assume in practically every human being and certainly in almost every new born baby that there is an active will toward health, an impulse toward growth, or toward the actualization of human potentialities. But at once we are confronted with the very saddening realization that so few people make it. Only a small proportion of the human population gets to the point of identity, or of selfhood, full humanness, self actualization, etc., even in a society like ours which is relatively one of the most fortunate on the face of the earth. This is our great paradox. We all have the impulse toward the development of humanness. Then why is it that it does not happen more often? What blocks it? One consequence of the usage of 'full humanness' rather than 'psychological help' is the corresponding or parallel use of 'human diminution' instead of 'neurosis' which is a totally obsolete word anyway. Here the key concept is the loss or not-yet-actualization of human capacities and possibilities, and obviously this is also a matter of degree and quantity. Furthermore, it is closer to being externally observable, i.e. behavioural, which of course makes it easier to investigate than, for example, anxiety or compulsiveness or repression. Also it places on the same continuum all the standard psychiatric categories, all the stuntings, cripplings and inhibitions that come from poverty, exploitation, maleducation, enslavement, etc., and so also the newer value pathologies, existential disorders, character disorders that come to the economically privileged. It handles very nicely the diminutions that result from drug addiction, psychopathy, authoritarianism, criminality, and other categories that cannot be called 'illness' in the same medical sense as, for example, 'brain tumour'.

It is therefore upon this sort of basis that I would propose a definition of the term behavioural psychotherapy: it is that form of therapeutic concern which seeks to explore by whatever appropriate and practical means possible the development of the individual's life statement of his own humanity. In such terms 'behavioural psychotherapy' is not a matter for professional defensiveness, but a strong (though still incomplete) statement about deliberate intervention in the problem of growth as a human being.

The report below presents the essential detail of a year's therapeutic involvement with a person whose life solution has, as part of its content, established her as a welcomed friend. The circumstances of my therapeutic involvement with her (what in earlier terms I would have referred to as 'the management of this interesting case') were both germane to my own development as a person and a therapist and I have every reason to believe beneficial to her.

Mrs N.D., married lady of 31, was referred by a psychiatrist colleague with a diagnosis of lesbianism for assessment with a view to aversion therapy. The referral arose from a depressed suicidal episode two weeks earlier and a subsequent understanding by the visiting psychiatrist of a five-year history of falling in love with women.

Life circumstances were as follows. Born as an illegitimate child to working-class parents who subsequently married and in marriage had a son four years younger than N.D., she had married, at the age of 20, a man 35 years her senior. Her mother had acted as his domestic help, he being employed in an executive management capacity in the woollen manufacturing industry. Five years prior to his marriage he had experienced a heavily publicized divorce, there being three children of the previous marriage with whom he had no contact following the divorce. At the time of referral the present marriage was of 11 years' duration, with one child of seven. The husband's Roman Catholic family had rejected his new wife on religious and social-class grounds from the outset.

N.D. herself, on first meeting, was a meticulously groomed and expensively dressed lady, slim and attractive in behaviour and appearance, and evidenced the acquisition of a wide range of social skills commensurate with the social position of a high-achieving industrialist.

My feeling reaction to her was that she was a brittle person. By the conclusion of history-taking over two hours it became an increasingly strong feeling that the response suppression technique of aversion therapy would be a damaging experience for her, which she would in any event probably (and quite rightly) reject. Casting around within a behavioural framework it appeared possible that a response substitution procedure might be worth trying, the intention being to use hypnotic relaxation as a means of helping her to maintain a level of emotional contact with women whom she found attractive in the absence of sexual feelings. N.D. stipulated that, whatever else, she wished to remain friends with the woman to whom she felt sexual feelings at present.

General enquiry established the fact that throughout her childhood and her teenage years her family—parent and younger brother—had lived next door to a woman referred to by the courtesy title of aunt, with whom N.D.'s father conducted an extra-marital relationship and who was a frequent visitor to N.D.'s house. N.D. had been put to bed early most evenings well into her teens while father went next door, mother having gone out each evening to work as a cleaner. The aunt's visits to N.D.'s home were almost always marked by critical attack upon N.D.'s mother for various minor domestic lapses. Father did not protect his wife from these attacks, nor did mother defend herself. N.D.'s communicating relationship with aunt ended at age 15 when, on a combined holiday, she slapped the aunt on the face in public as a consequence of yet more critical remarks directed against her mother. She herself was physically ill-treated by father in consequence. Throughout her teenage years N.D. objected strongly within herself to being left in charge of her brother each evening, whom she also felt was spoilt by her parents.

Throughout her life experience there had been three strong emotional bonds with women. The first, with a person of similar years five years prior to referral, had resulted in a brief physical encounter. This N.D. described as resulting in the best loving feelings she had ever had. Her friend on this occasion expressed strong anxiety subsequent to the single occasion of physical contact and left the area soon afterwards without making further contact. The second relationship, three years later, had been with a woman some 25 years older and had had no overt physical accompaniment. There was, nevertheless, a good deal of sexual fantasy on N.D.'s part, and the relationship ended suddenly with the unexpected death of her friend. A current relationship was with a person of similar age to the recently deceased friend, with whom N.D. adopted an adoring daughter/fantasy lover relationship as in the immediately previous relationship, the experience being very similar by description to those of teenage girl crushes on older girls, but classified and feared by N.D. as homosexual and lesbian.

Prior to marriage N.D. had had no sexual intercourse, and had had one foreign boyfriend whose parents objected to his friendship with N.D. and had taken him away. Within her present marriage sexual experience was tolerated, never resulting in climatic release, and limited by husband's prostatectomy resulting two years prior to referral. Sex was generally construed within an avoidance/fear system which, however, her one homosexual physical contact denied, consequently reinforcing the assumption within herself that she was basically lesbian.

The one boyfriend relationship, terminated by his parents, had led to a suicidal gesture. In the 11 years of her marriage there had been two admissions to different psychiatric hospitals, both of which she had left on impulse, and a six-month period of psychoanalysis which had terminated without benefit. Psychiatric notes referred to hysteria, immature personality, psychopathic personality, reactive depression and poor prognosis.

The first two months of treatment sessions, at weekly intervals, were devoted to discussion of the week's events in terms of stimuli situations and her response, and continued training in relaxation and its application. At the end of that time N.D. spontaneously confided in her friend (who for the sake of clarity I will call A) the sexual nature of her feelings for her, which were received in an accepting and trusting manner, without reproach. This resulted in a considerable feeling of well-being, but after two further weeks there was a strong resurgence of sexual feelings and N.D. felt isolated and rejected in not being able to express them. Masturbation was unacceptable to her. Within four months of the start of treatment a picture of depression, anxiety and guilt left her helpless at home, and admission to a nursing home was arranged.

Up to this point in time a behavioural procedure had followed its normal course, but apart from its generalized aspects of 'support' had appeared to make no real impact on N.D.'s life difficulties. The admission to nursing home marked the turning point in my own therapeutic understanding and attempts. For a period of 12 days it was made explicit to N.D., the nursing home staff, the general practitioner involved and N.D.'s husband that I would, within the limits of my commitments, be continuously available to her for whatever help I could be, day or night, at N.D.'s demand. Anti-depressant and tranquillizing medication which had been variably available throughout the previous four months was kept at a minimum. Throughout the 12 days there was a dramatic development of well-being, and I began to understand the central dilemma in N.D.'s life, which was the lack of a reliable, loving friendship and parental origins to which she could no longer return and which had, in any event, been of limited comfort to her.

N.D.'s marriage had been a series of invalidations. Moved from her own social background she had been required to fulfil her husband's social demands, and he had groomed her for the role in a punishing, Eliza Doolittle model. They had lived in isolated commuter country, without near neighbours, and N.D. recalled vividly her continuous feeling that she would in no way match up to her husband's expectations of her. Yet, as observed initially, she did manage to establish the behavioural components of her role very effectively. At an affective level, however, she felt a fraud. N.D. represented in some way a 'safe' marriage for her husband—he could make her into the sort of woman he wanted and so avoid the hurt and trauma of his previous marriage. He compared N.D.'s inability to meet his demands with an idealized view of chorus girls who successfully married dukes.

Discharge from the nursing home resulted in a reduction of from often twice daily meetings to once weekly, but the change in well-being was maintained for six weeks, a period ended by a visit to a theatre with A in the company of other social acquaintances. An incident there triggered off feelings of social gaucherie which produced strong reminiscences of her early marriage days and, moreover, the play was about illegitimacy and contained not infrequently the term 'bastard', which she could never bring herself to use. Her husband was abroad at the time, and she eventually returned home tearful, upset and anxious with even her son, aged seven, away for the night. At 2.30 am I was called by A, who had spent the previous two hours with N.D. after a phone call to her, N.D. having consumed a good deal of spirits.

No immediate sources of help were available. The inebriated individual is likely to receive short commons from any agency in the early hours of the morning, and in any event emergency admission to a hospital would itself have damaging personal consequences. It was uncertain how much medication there was in the house, and a search would have been a violation. A felt unable to cope. The house was isolated. It being a growing principle within me that the first and most important resource an individual brings to any treatment encounter is himself, the situation required whatever humanity was available. A willingly returned to her home. I sat by N.D.'s bedside, holding her hand in a reassuring fashion, acutely aware of ever 'professional' injunction forbidding my presence but observing the calming effect. N.D. slept.

The following morning arrangements were made for friends to look in, and 24 hours later N.D. was well and happy. Her conversation centred on the topics of caring, the bounds of clinical and personal commitment and a strong verbal expression of love for me followed by the surprise observation 'that I don't feel like that about men'. We left it there, laughing and bemused, I to cope with professional anxieties of every kind. My summary notes at the time say: 'despite her longstanding H/S feelings N. is now expressing strong hetero.s. feelings in the context of (yet another) unattainable relationship/transference. At least she can:
(1) realistically express her feelings under control,
(2) risk rejection,
(3) test out the limits of clinical involvement.
In the context of her development it is possible that if she can maintain a working relationship with me, and then not have to reject me at my lack of personal response beyond an understanding of caring, then she may (hopefully) reduce the level of H/S

involvement which she has felt and internalize her own evidence for lack of H/S role. She is, however, still very vulnerable. She needs strong, consistent, mutually involved relationships, but at present seeks them from sources which cannot reciprocate'.

The following day there was a tremendous anxiety expressed following our sharing of the day before about her sexual feelings. She had imagined that upon my departure I had gone to inform the general practitioner that I was terminating contact. More discussion ensued on the fact of her heterosexual feelings.

Ten days later, after intervening appointments, an evening call from a 'phone-box announced that she had been driving aimlessly by herself, had rung her husband for help who had asked the police to find her, and she was now being taken to a police station. Some hours of discussion there left her able to go home, with I myself oscillating strongly between clinical anger about psychopathic, hysterical, controlling, demanding patients who had to be kept under control and my awareness of her well-being in a relationship which had explicit boundaries and which she needed, quite realistically, to test. Four days later she took 20 codeine tablets and was admitted to a general hospital medical ward, and from there to a psychiatric hospital, and after a further five weeks to a nursing home for eight weeks.

This period of time, maintained, so far as possible, within the previous framework was characterized by restlessness, uncertainty and testing out, in a situation of my continuous availability, by presence or telephone, with N.D. continuously aware of my daily timetable. 'So far as possible' refers to the psychiatric hospital admission, at which institutional constraints prevented any real continuation of a personal relationship and in which the attempt to maintain such a relationship aroused staff and other person hostilities to an extent that the interactions crucial to the experience of a relationship were stifled. The decision to transfer to the nursing home was in order to facilitate interaction. Moreover, the casual/intense nature of hospital contacts, with both other patients and staff, were outside N.D.'s range of skills in her search for 'friends', and the uncertainty of trends in brief relationships confused and depressed her.

The transfer to the nursing home marked the end of nine months' involvement, in which the first three months had been formal behaviour modification and the subsequent six months had increasingly become, as a gradual response to my own perception of the requirements of the situation, an attempt to supply at least one viable heterosexual friendship in the life experience of N.D.

The admission to the nursing home resulted in a further daily series of extended visits and frequent contact by telephone, usually to pursue some aspect of an earlier discussion which had caused doubt and uncertainty. The opportunity to monitor her present state with a grid analysis was discussed with her, and the actual feedback of that increased her confidence that it was possible to achieve at least some kinds of understanding of oneself. Using the procedures described by Makhlouf-Norris and Norris (1972) and Makhlouf-Norris and Jones (1971), plots of conceptual structure and self-identity as shown in Figure 1 were obtained.

The self-identity plot (Figure 1(b)) arises from elements (people) in 16 triadic comparisons of 20 personalized roles, in which No. 3 (myself as I am) is an element

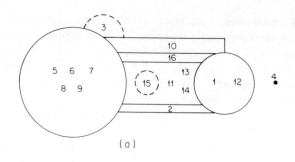

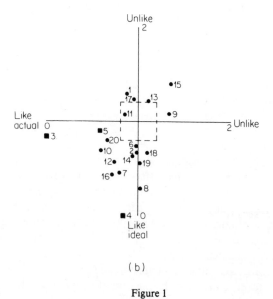

Figure 1

in every triad. The roles to which individual names were assigned were as follows:

1. Mother
2. Father
3. Myself as I am
4. Myself as I would like to be
5. Myself as seen by others
6. Brother
7. Sister
8. Old friend of the same sex
9. Partner
10. Liked teacher
11. Disliked teacher
12. Liked boss
13. Disliked boss
14. Liked person
15. Disliked person
16. Successful person
17. Unsuccessful person
18. Religious person
19. Ethical person
20. Doctor

and 16 bipolar constructs were elicited as follows:

1. Don't creep   Ingratiating

2. Knows when to keep quiet	Can't keep quiet
3. Stand by what they believe in even if wrong	Will back down
4. A bit theatrical to cover up unease	Go quiet when they feel uneasy
5. Sympathetic and soft	Hard
6. Can make people feel small and anxious	Doesn't make people feel small and anxious
7. Petty	Fair
8. Warm	Cold
9. Demonstrative	Undemonstrative
10. Wonder what people think about them	Unconcerned what people think about them
11. Honest—will deal with reality of the situation	Willing to compromise—avoids issue
12. Dominated by other people	Independent
13. Emotions under control	Emotions not under control
14. Consistent as a person	Inconsistent—too many faces
15. Unadaptable—for one reason or another	Adaptable—chameleon-like
16. Shy underneath	Self-confident

The self-identity plot demonstrates at this stage a lack of isolation or alienation. In other words, N.D. sees herself as a person in a community of people about whom she can make realistic judgements in relation to her actual and ideal self, and she does not feel markedly separated from that community—i.e. she has some sense of belonging. The less she had such a sense (i.e. the more the element points clustered into the right upper quadrant) the more would there have been concern about her self-destructive impulses.

On the conceptual structure display (Figure 1(a)), however, there is a marked lack of cohesion in the linkage structure, with the main clusters of this fragmented articulated system containing relatively few constructs. The primary left-hand grouping describes a person who is sympathetic and soft, doesn't make people feel anxious and small, is fair, warm and demonstrative, all of which are statements about her actual and ideal self, as are the constructs in the right-hand grouping of not creeping and being independent, though the ideal self is seen as possessing more of these characteristics than the actual self. In the centre, however, is a linkage of constructs all bearing very little relationship to each other, though each uniting the two primary groupings, weak though each of those are. Thus N.D. has the capacity to be a diverse number of people or, conversely, she finds it extremely difficult to act consistently because of the poor integration of her conceptual system and the relative lack of dominance of any one group of constructs. Thus at any point in time her behaviour is likely, to an observer, to be unpredictable, and is similarly so to herself.

This nursing-home period marked a final stage of 'testing out'—such as a phone call late evening from the depths of the countryside, whence N.D. had driven (being, of course, able to have a car available to her as part of an intention *not* to reduce her responsibility for herself) and had taken some considerable quantity of spirits. A journey to collect her resulted in subsequent attempts to throw herself out of a moving car and sufficient anger in myself to strike her smartly in the face at the second attempt, which had both the immediate shock effect of communicating through the alcohol-induced distress and subsequent discussion about the continued nature of caring. It became an expressed agreement between us that N.D. was free to go off and drink if she wished, but that for the anxiety it caused me, and the concern of the nursing home, I would not conduct further rescue forays. And because everything else we had agreed together had predictably been followed through, there were no further drinking episodes.

The two months of nursing-home care concentrated upon exercises in structuring the day. Without conceptual certainty as to which kind of a person at any time she might be, N.D. felt she should do nothing in order to be safe, but in consequence had the experience of being an inactive non-person. With guidance she began to organize her day around deliberate and sometimes trivial events, so that at the end of each day she felt increasingly that she had been in charge of the day's experience. A continued to visit, and N.D. found her homosexual feelings increasingly diminished. She continued to explore her feelings for me and mine for her verbally, and despite an impetus towards sexual intercourse at one stage gradually accepted the requirements of external choice and constraints. Discharged from the nursing home, she asked herself to be readmitted 10 days later after feeling that she could not cope with her husband's hostility, but after a further week discharged herself again saying that she was ready to try again and felt more able to explore difficulties with her husband after the exploration of her own feelings with me and mine with her without a loss of relationship. Three weeks after leaving the nursing home she volunteered the fact that drinking excessively or driving aimlessly or both were no longer any use to her. She reduced her frequency of telephone contact, and tolerated a forthcoming absence of myself for a month with equanimity with the promise that she would write, which she did—it having been the case throughout her marriage, based on early disparaging remarks from her husband about her poorly formed handwriting, that she would not write to anyone; yet she did it without difficulty, and has done so subsequently.

A repeat examination of the self-identity plot and conceptual structure at this stage produced the results shown in Figure 2.

It can be seen in Figure 2(b) in comparison with Figure 1(b), that there is slightly less distance between actual and ideal self (3 and 4) and movement of her community of people closer to her actual self, along the horizontal axis.

The displayed conceptual structure (Figure 2(a)) shows considerable resolution of the previously fractured structure, and provides the basis of improved construct certainty and hence less self-uncertainty.

In the year subsequent to this, the conclusion of formal therapeutic involvement, N.D. has had one brief hospital admission, at her request, in which I was a friend who visited, not a formal therapeutic agent. The conclusion of formal treatment, 13 months after its inception, was assured understanding that a natural friendship was established and the normal behaviours of friendship could properly extend from that.

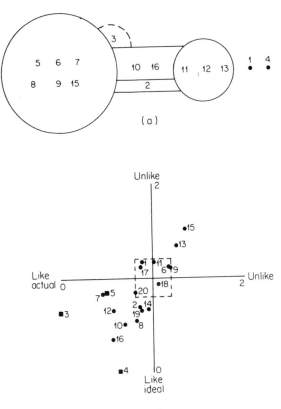

Figure 2

In the period of 13 months, therapeutic involvement, 110 specific occasions of meeting were recorded by arrangement, request or crisis. The time involved was not recorded, but might have averaged out at three hours per week, based entirely upon N.D.'s perceived or explicit needs after the first three months. She now has the experience of a relationship which, under privileged conditions, we both worked at developing. Some evidence of benefit lies in the diagrams above, but more in the certainty of her own daily feelings of development and strength, which are their own internal best evidences.

References

Berne, E. (1961). *Transactional Analysis in Psychotherapy,* Grove Press, New York.
British Association for Behavioural Psychotherapy (1972). *Newsletter,* December 1972, Vol. 1, No. 1.

Condran, G., and Boss, M. (1968). 'Existential analysis', in J. G. Howells (Ed.). *Modern Perspectives in World Psychiatry*, Oliver & Boyd, Edinburgh and London, pp. 488–518.

Friedman, P. H. (1972). 'Personalistic, family and marital therapy', in A. A. Lazarus (Ed.), *Clinical Behaviour Therapy*, Brunner/Mazel, New York; Butterworths, London, pp. 116–54.

Fromm-Reichmann, Frieda (1949). 'Recent advances in psychoanalysis', *J. Amer. med. women's Assoc.*, **4**, 320.

Makhlouf-Norris, Fawzeya, and Jones, H. G. (1971). 'Conceptual distance indices as measures of alienation in obsessional neurosis', *Psychol. med.*, **1**, 381.

Makhlouf-Norris, Fawzeya, and Norris, H. (1972). 'The obsessive compulsive syndrome as a neurotic device for the reduction of self-uncertainty', *B. J. psychiat.*, **121**, 277.

Maslow, A. H. (1967). 'Neurosis as a failure of personal growth', *Humanitas*, 1967, **3**, 153, in W. S. Sahakian (1970), *Psychopathology To-Day: Experimentation, Theory and Research*, Peacock, Illinois, pp. 122–30.

Mowrer, O. H. (1960). '"Sin", the lesser of two evils', *Amer. psychol.*, **15**, 301.

Sahakian, W. S. (1970). *Psychopathology To-Day: Experimentation, Theory and Research*, Peacock, Illinois.

Schmidt, Elsa, Castell, D., and Brown, P. T. (1965). 'A retrospective study of 42 cases of behaviour therapy', *Behav. Res. Ther.*, **3**, 9.

White, R. W. (1964). *The Abnormal Personality*, 3rd edition, Ronald Press, New York.

Wolpe, J. (1958). *Psychotherapy by Reciprocal Inhibition*, Stanford University Press.

AUTHOR INDEX

279

SUBJECT INDEX